The Voice of the Phoenix:

Metaphors of Death and Rebirth
in Classics of the Iberian Renaissance

To John Mariani with all friendship and fond memories of our meeting in Highlands, NC at the "Root Bound" festival in February 2018,

Bryant

Medieval and Renaissance Texts and Studies

Volume 272

The Voice of the Phoenix:

Metaphors of Death and Rebirth
in Classics of the Iberian Renaissance

by
Bryant Creel

Arizona Center for Medieval and Renaissance Studies
Tempe, Arizona
2004

The publication of this volume has been greatly assisted by a grant from the Program for Cultural Cooperation between Spain's Ministry of Culture and United States Universities.

© Copyright 2004
Arizona Board of Regents for Arizona State University

Library of Congress Cataloguing-in-Publication Data
Creel, Bryant L.
    The voice of the Phoenix : metaphors of death and rebirth in classics of the Iberian Renaissance / by Bryant Creel.
       p. cm. — (Medieval and Renaissance texts and studies ; v. 272)
    Includes bibliographical references and index.
    ISBN 0-86698-315-5 (alk. paper)
    1. Spanish literature — Classical period, 1500–1700 — History and criticism. 2. Spanish literature — Classical period, 1500–1700 — Psychological aspects. 3. Love in literature. I. Title. II. Medieval & Renaissance Texts & Studies (Series) ; v. 272.

PQ6066.C74 2004
860.9'354—dc22
                                                2004053116

∞
This book is made to last.
It is set in Classic Garamond
smythe-sewn and printed on acid-free paper
to library specifications.

Printed in the United States of America

To James Creel and George Creel, *in memoriam*, and to my mother, Josephine Creel

Contents

Acknowledgements		ix
Introduction		xi
1.	Entombed in Love: Fateful Passion and Prison Imagery in Fifteenth-Century *Cancionero* and Popular Lyric	1
2.	Subjection to Fate or Passionate Willing? Reassessing Love in Garcilaso in the Light of Value Theory	27
3.	Obsequious Love as the Ego's Release from Frustration through Mortification of Self: Interpreting "Masochistic" Rescue Fantasies in Elegiac Love Lyric	53
4.	The Death of Love's Hopes: Garcilaso's Sonnet 22 Considered in the Light of Phenomenological Ethics of Values	95
5.	Ambivalent Love and the Birth Pangs of Individuation in Garcilaso, Fray Luis de León, Fairbairn, and Jung	119

6.	The Despondence of Orphaned Humanity: Love's Protest against Sovereignty in Fray Luis de León's "En la Ascensión" and in Garcilaso	155
7.	Moral Disfranchisement as Ironic Rebirth in *Lazarillo de Tormes*	175
8.	The Agony and Apotheosis of Innocent Love: Bernardim Ribeiro's *Book of Sorrowful Longing*	195
9.	Chaste Love as Metaphorical Death: Montemayor's "Nicodemist" Vindication of Human Passion in the *Diana*	220
10.	Finite Reality's Rebirth as Poetic Imagery: Theoretical Implications in Don Quijote's Idea of Enchantment	252

Conclusions	277
Works Cited	283
Index of Names	306
Subject Index	321

Acknowledgements

This book was slow in materializing because of my progressive discovery of the complexity of the materials I was analyzing, as I felt the need to evolve approaches that did not match the existing trends of critical methodology. In those circumstances the encouragement that I received from friends, colleagues and relatives was invaluable to me. My thanks go to Oscar Rivera Rodas; Francisco Márquez Villanueva; Antonio Carreño; Joseph Ricapito; Samuel Armistead; Stanislav Zimic; my son, James Creel, who tragically died of a brain tumor in 1994; my daughter, Celeste Creel, a recent graduate in theater arts; my mother, author Josephine Shields Creel, who lives in Australia; and to my wife, Johnnie Larguier Creel, and my stepchildren, Burton Cooper and Sarah Cooper, for their having patiently endured the demands of my developing and committing to writing many of the ideas presented in this book. I am deeply grateful to my father, George William Creel, Professor of English, and my former advisor, Antonio Sánchez Romeralo, both of whom contributed so much to my love of literature before they passed away in 1998; John Romeiser, who in 1996 granted me the only one-semester research leave that I have had in my twenty-four years of full-time teaching; Gustavo Bodelón Velasco; my brother Stephen Creel, psychiatrist and author; my sister, Alison Creel Shields de Bodelón; her husband, Eduardo Bodelón Velasco; my brother Evan Creel; my sister Jennifer Creel; Jay Hanan; Bernardo Fernández; Fred Frey; Jon LaCure; John Crispin; David Quinn; Javier Mariño; Jack Nissen; Larry Dorety; Dee McKinnon; and María Pilar Manero

Sorolla. Jack Barlow referred me to new readings in psychoanalytic theory. My other dear friends and colleagues and those who, like some mentioned above, generously wrote letters of reference for me — they all know who know who they are — kept me going mentally, emotionally, and professionally. I wish to acknowledge the noble souls who staff the academic institutions and library facilities where I have worked and who are not in it for the money, as well as my patient students, especially those who have disagreed with me and said so. Shane Vande Brake especially made me feel encouraged when it could not have mattered more. By no means least, I wish to express my deep appreciation to the anonymous readers who diligently scrutinized the typescript of this book and made suggestions for revision, and to the incomparable Leslie S. B. MacCoull: thank you for your intelligence, erudition, truthfulness, and patience. I am grateful also to Robert Bjork for having initially considered my manuscript for publication with MRTS, to Roy Rukkila for patiently seeing this book through the various editorial stages; to Karen Lemiski, for her talent, kindness, and enthusiastic assistance in work on the indexes; and to Deb Stevenson, for her contributions to the cover. I can never begin to thank you all enough. Also, for help in preparing the indexes, I received from the University of Tennessee a Professional Development Grant and an EPPE grant, as well as support from MARCO (Medieval and Renaissance Curriculum and Outreach).

An earlier version of chapter 4 was published as "Garcilaso's Sonnet XXII: A Re-Examination in the Light of Phenomenological Ethics of Values," *Calíope* 3 (1997): 51–70; an earlier version of chapter 6 was published as "Love's Protest against Sovereignty: Anguish and Reproach in Fray Luis de León's 'En la Ascensión' and in Garcilaso," *Journal of Hispanic Philology* 12 (1987 [1988]): 37–50; much of chapter 8 was published in "Bernardim Ribeiro and the Tradition of Renaissance Pastoral," in *Renaissance and Golden Age Essays in Honor of D. W. McPheeters*, ed. Bruno Damiani (Potomac, MD: Scripta Humanistica, 1989), 27–48; an earlier version of chapter 9 was published as "Aesthetics of Change in a Renaissance Pastoral: New Ideals of Moral Culture in Montemayor's *Diana*," *Hispanófila* 99 (1990): 1–27; and the better part of chapter 10 was published as "Theoretical Implications of Don Quijote's Idea of Enchantment," *Cervantes* 12 (1992): 19–44. I thank the editors of those publications for their permission to republish, in revised form, some of the materials presented in this volume.

Knoxville, Tennessee
August 2004

Introduction

This book studies literary works created in a past age primarily from a psychological point of view. Operating from particular premises about the early modern period (listed below), and working in a fashion different from that of most historicist criticism, I emphasize value theory, psychoanalytic insight, and the power of metaphor in discussing these works as they were read at the time and as they may be read today. And I contend that from the interaction of the writer's state of mind when writing and the reader's state of mind when receiving the work, a deepening of our interpretive grasp can result.

Naive humanity is relatively defenseless against life's harsh realities. Lacking experience and one-sided in its own subjective tendency, its vulnerability is such that outward affliction and untimely death are its constant bedfellows. Yet the innocence of the pure in mind is sacred, for by constituting a living example of implicit trust and kind concern for others — the quality of "goodness," of the loving disposition — it exercises a regenerative, redemptive influence on all who behold it. Without struggling to maintain their purity, human beings would be inferior to animals, which are pure in that they hardly have freedom to choose and so are without guilt. The works examined in the present volume all represent, in one way or another, the plight of naive innocence, that "death" (either painful loss or actual destruction) to which innocence is inevitably subjected by its contact with the real world. Those works are also eloquent testimonies to the high esteem in which goodness was held in the period when they were written and is today, when we continue to foster literary culture. That testimony is specifically given in the great strength with which affliction to kindness and devotion is countered, either in the tenacity with which such affliction is combated or in the degree of pain with which it must be endured. Through the triumph represented by that moral strength's mere existence and the spectacle of struggling innocence as an end in itself, the ideal of naive humanity commemorated in works such as those analyzed here is "reborn," its power regenerated in the spirits of the personas/protagonists, the reader, and society at large. In that way literature functions as what Northrop Frye termed a "secular scripture." It is because the works I examine present variants on the pattern of loss and regeneration that I speak of them, on the most fundamental level, as "metaphors of death and rebirth"; and since their style is never doctrinaire or moralistic, those metaphors remain subtle, implicit, and "modern" elements of an ideological, axiological infrastructure (the term "axiological" referring to the philosophical study of values).

My broad use of the term "metaphor," as in the title of this book, is, in principle, not intended to be esoteric. At times I see in an entire work an analogy to a pattern involving death and rebirth or to the ironic inversion of that pattern or to an experience of either death or rebirth. In that case, "metaphor" can be interpreted to mean "allegory," not in the sense of (to apply Frye's distinction in *Anatomy of Criticism*, 54–55, 89–91) "actual" or "genuine" allegory[1] but in the sense of thematically significant imagery that lends itself to allegorical interpretation. Frye considers the basis of poetry to be metaphor and the basis of allegory to be mixed metaphor (*Anatomy*, 91). The idea that an entire work can be seen as a metaphor is important to Leslie Levin's *Metaphors of Conversion in Seventeenth-Century Spanish Drama*. Levin writes, "An entire dramatic work can be a metaphor for the triumph of Christianity..." (124). It is this meaning of metaphor that Maxim Gorky must have had in mind when, in letters to Chekhov, he describes Chekhov's stories as "elegant, cut-glass flasks filled with all the perfumes of life" and observes, "*Uncle Vanya* and *The Seagull* are a new type of dramatic art, in which realism is elevated to an inspired and profound symbol" (*Letters*, 22–23, 17). Wilbur Urban has noted that "the essential character of every symbol is that it is a metaphor "because it must be interpreted in the context in which it is

---

[1] It is in this sense that the term "allegory" is used by C. S. Lewis in *The Allegory of Love*.

Introduction   xiii

used" (*Language and Reality*, 433). In other instances in the chapters to follow, I see metaphors of death and/or regeneration as being implicitly evident not so much in an entire work as in one of its prominent thematic dimensions. Thus, I myself sometimes apply the concept of death and/or rebirth metaphorically, as a way of interpreting the meaning of central images in a work.

Although chapters 1, 2, and 3 have a polemical dimension, an important goal in them, as in chapters 4 and 5, is to suggest new, less traditional and limiting, approaches to interpreting the poetry of Garcilaso de la Vega. Chapter 1 begins with an overview of fifteenth-century *cancionero* scholarship that relates to the motif Rafael Lapesa has characterized as "amor por destino" [love by destiny], the presentation of passionate love as a surrender to fate. Lapesa saw "amor por destino" as a theme in Garcilaso de la Vega's early verse, before his development of a full "Renaissance" maturity. The perspectives of critics such as Van Beysterveldt, Aguirre, Whinnom, Macpherson, Lida de Malkiel, Boase, and Luhmann are considered in an effort to determine the extent to which "love by destiny" as Lapesa understood it is present in that lyric and to address problems that arise when the motif of "amor por destino" is understood literally, as it is by Lapesa and others. I then address the extent to which the influence of Christianity can account for the emergence of the motif of fateful passion, the possibility that the use of that motif in lyric was motivated rhetorically, and the implications of seeing it as erotic innuendo. There follows a discussion of love–anguish in examples of the type of popular lyric that drew the attention of *cancionero* poets in the fifteenth century, and speculation on possible explanations for certain differences between popular and *cancionero* lyric. The subtle complexity of popular lyric is explored in more detail by concentrating specifically on the different possible meanings of the "prison/bonds of love/loving" theme in popular and learned traditions (as in the romance with that title by Diego de San Pedro) and the relation of that motif to Max Scheler's theory of tragic, guiltless guilt and the tragic hero's confined sphere of choice. After possible relations are considered between popular and *cancionero* lyric, I propose a new interpretation of the motif of fateful love in *cancionero* lyric, one that recognizes the influence of Christianity, takes into account the persona's rhetorical intent and his sensual motives, and views that motif as a subtle, revolutionary metaphor that combines the depiction of a predicament of "medieval" subjection with an advancement of values that were completely consistent with a fully developed Renaissance humanism.

Chapter 2 further considers issues introduced in chapter 1. In relation to value theory, I interpret Garcilaso's famous Sonnet 1 and a passage from a poem by the *cancionero* poet Hernán Mexía and call into question the assumption that seems to have originated with Hayward Kenniston but that received its strongest impetus from Rafael Lapesa, that a body of Garcilaso's "early poems" represents love as a fate that the will has no power to resist. The central focus is on whether Lapesa is correct in asserting that the poet–persona does not actually mean it when he says that he has consciously chosen to be condemned or to perish for his love. The conclusion reached is that rather than being contrary to the will, the reference to love as an inevitable fate is a metaphor for love's passionate willing. On the basis of that premise, I then question the validity of Lapesa's basing a chronology of Garcilaso's poetry partly on what he purports to be the presence in some of them of a traditionalistic, "un-Renaissance" submission to fate. The presentation of values of the individual as the highest values complements the ethos of Renaissance humanism. I further propose that, in addition to its metaphorical meaning, the motif of fateful love has the aesthetic function of presenting the poet as possessing the courage to bear the consequences of great emotions. Beneath an ostensible attitude of being morbidly prostrate before an irresistible force, Garcilaso is celebrating the passionate will to live.

A subordinate element in chapter 3 is that it calls into question the tradition of viewing Garcilaso's poems as being autobiographical in character (a tradition promoted above all by Lapesa) instead of interpreting them as broad metaphor. Instances of maintaining that Garcilaso's poems are autobiographical are the assumption that the figure of the beloved lady in them is a real person known to the poet and the view that the persona's morbid suffering in love can be understood clinically, as "masochistic" behavior. Garcilaso's Sonnet 2 and *Canción* 1 (primarily its flamboyant opening stanza) are considered in detail, and it is argued that even if one postulates personas who have all the psychological and clinical complexity of real persons, in order for the persona's "masochistic" behavior traits to be contemplated as having an artistic function, they must be interpreted metaphorically. Attention is concentrated on the following two issues: (a) what general problems and characteristics of past Garcilaso criticism have prevented approaching that poet's love lyric as broad metaphor?; (b) what possible broad metaphorical or allegorical interpretations of Sonnet 2 and *Canción* 1 give meaning to the elements in those poems that correspond either to the motifs of masochistic submission to bondage/captivity or to the ordeals necessary for

Introduction   xv

achieving release from that state? It is proposed that elements of an allegorical reading of masochistic rescue fantasies in those poems are suggested by first identifying psychodynamic theories that interpret the type of situation presented in such fantasies and then adapting those theories so that they conform to the characteristics of literary genre (tragedy and pathetic satire) and of the historical context in which such a literature of anguish was written. Thus, for example, submission to the lady who cruelly persecutes the poet or requires ritualistic self-sacrifice of him can be seen as corresponding to the "captivity" or torments of an unsatisfied longing for love, for feelings of security and worthiness as a person. Likewise, masochistic rescue fantasies in those poems can be interpreted as a metaphor for overcoming the ego loss that is a result of the aggressive reaction to feelings of insecurity and unworthiness (of "lovelessness" in a brutal world) and as movement forward to embrace the future, as a ritual prelude to individuation and freedom (which are considered in chapter 5).

Chapter 4 proposes a new interpretation of one of Garcilaso's most elusive and complex poems, Sonnet 22. The many paradoxes in the language of that poem are explored in detail and in the light of previous critical analyses. The central issues examined are the ethical implications of the lady's defensive response to the poet's attention and the possible relation of Garcilaso's interest in that subject to the cultural–historical developments in his day. The idea that I ultimately propose is that when in that poem the poet–persona's hopes are shattered by the lady's conventional attitude of modesty, he is led to feel that she does not regard him as a person. Such an inordinate emphasis on the sensual as threatening deprives sensual experience of its rightful place in life, one that Garcilaso, as a Renaissance humanist, sought to restore. The poet–persona in Sonnet 22 can thus be seen as representing a humanity that strives to overcome bondage in the natural order and fulfill its spiritual, human destiny.

In chapter 5 Jungian analytic psychology is combined with, primarily, the object-relations theory of the Scottish psychoanalyst Ronald Fairbairn for purposes of interpreting the imagery of Garcilaso's Sonnet 38 and Fray Luis de León's Sonnet 2 and explaining the traumatic dilemmas depicted in those poems. Particular attention is focused on interpreting the paradox of the poet–persona's seeing the lady as both a threat and a source of hope, on the morbid dimension of the persona's anxiety, and on the thematic meaning of the alternatives of progressive and regressive movement. When the emotionalistic helplessness depicted in works like the two considered are related to Fairbairn's views on how the ego reacts to unmet needs for good object relations (for love) and to Jung's theories on individuation, those poems can be interpreted as treatments of the phenomenon referred to by psychoanalysis as the struggle to overcome the regressive pattern of an attitude of infantile identification with a mother figure, who is actually the representative of the poet–persona's own regressive tendency. The poems in question can then be interpreted in broad terms as metaphors for the painful emergence of human individuality, the struggle to exercise autonomy and self-determination and fulfill the claims of personality. In that light, the interest in the complexity of inner conflicts displayed by Garcilaso and Fray Luis makes them both precursors of modern psychological analysis.

The subject of chapter 6 is Fray Luis de León's famous ode on the Ascension, in which the disciples express their anguish at feeling abandoned by Christ as he rises to heaven on a cloud after his resurrection. After examining in detail former interpretations of that poem, this study offers a reading that correlates with my sense of Fray Luis the man who was in conflict with authoritarian elements in the Church and that also correlates with the skeptical attitude towards society that he expresses in other of his poems. A comparison is developed between the anxieties of the disdained persona–lover in a number of Garcilaso's poems and the anguish of the disciples when they feel that the affinity implied in the personal love they shared with Christ is jeopardized by the superiority resulting from their teacher's transmutation, which to their perception separates him from common humanity. Psychoanalytic models are applied in order to understand the broader metaphorical implications of the poem on the basis of separation anxiety expressed by the disciples. The courtly-love paradigm of the lover experiencing frustrations in the context of an unequal relationship based on infantile dependence can be read as a metaphor for the conflict between disinterested devotion and the goal of self-assertion and superiority, between love and the will to power. Christ's transformation into a visibly divine being shakes the disciples' attitude of identification with him, with the result that they reveal the same attitudes of regressive dependence and ambivalence toward a loved one that can be found in Fray Luis's Sonnet 2 and Garcilaso's Sonnet 38. The chagrin expressed by the disciples suggests an attitude of resentful regression, an attitude that Fray Luis may well have considered the "human condition" and seen as representing humanity's perennial failure to forfeit its "symbiotic" dependence on higher powers.

Chapter 7 concerns a central problem faced by readers of the earliest and most famous picaresque novel, *Lazarillo de Tormes*. Is the satiric vision of life and

Introduction   xvii

morality presented in the *Lazarillo* given specifically in the point of view of the protagonist–narrator, or does the novel place the protagonist–narrator himself (both as a youth and as an adult) in a critical perspective as well? Adverse judgements of the *Lazarillo* are considered and their validity weighed, and it is noted both that certain characteristics of the protagonist make it difficult to classify him as a rogue and that certain characteristics of the novel make it difficult to classify it as "picaresque." Whether readers both in the sixteenth century and in the present age view the protagonist of the *Lazarillo* in sympathetic or in satirical terms depends not just on qualities in the book itself but on the ideological premises of the reader. From the point of view of philosophical currents that were viable in the sixteenth century, an attitude of general impatience or strong ambivalence toward the protagonist–narrator can be seen to represent the innatist, "Platonist" view of the human mind (that the natural human propensity for right action is failed or betrayed by base behavior). In contrast, a generally approving attitude toward the protagonist–narrator (the perspective of most of the great *Lazarillo* critics) represents the empiricist, "Aristotelian" view of the mind as a *tabula rasa* (that an individual's character is determined by the influence of his environment). Attention is focused on the blame that can be said to fall to the adult Lázaro in the situation at the end of the novel, and it is proposed that the *Lazarillo* presents a starkly deterministic view of the protagonist, with the effect of prompting an idealistic, innatist impatience toward him on the part of the reader. Thus, the work ultimately affirms the perspective, also consistent with Aristotelian ethics, that the presumption of innate character constitutes a basis for moral accountability, even though what Aristotle called "excusing factors," such as a deprived upbringing, must be weighed as well. After further consideration of the shocking realities of Lazarillo's lot in life, I maintain that this story of a character's rise in society is actually an ironic chronicle of progressive moral disfranchisement, a portrait that challenges conventional standards of social respectability as well as the modern state's responsibility toward its citizens.

   In chapter 8 the originality and many perplexing characteristics of Bernardim Ribeiro's *Menina e Moça* (otherwise known as *Livro das Saudades* [Book of Sorrowful Longing]) are described and discussed in an effort to understand the significance and appeal of that work in the context of a period when the repressive authoritarianism of the counterreformist Church was at its height. The reasons for Inquisitorial censorship of that book are also considered, and its mannerist style and symbolism are interpreted in relation to the work's thematic dimensions.

Menina e Moça is seen to encourage a culture of sentiment that militates against the brutal inhumanity and cold fanaticism that divided Europe during the Reformation–Counterreformation struggle. By advancing both the absolute value of an almost morbidly self-abnegating, innocent love-idealism and a secular gaiety subtly disguised as brutal affliction, Bernardim Ribeiro contributed with, paradoxically, astute candor to the transvaluation of values that cleared the way for modern attitudes, and his book probably seemed offensive to Inquisitorial authorities in various ways. *Menina e Moça*'s mannerism was intended to detract from the entertaining surface of the plot and prevent it from drawing attention away from the work's deeper thematic implications.

Jorge de Montemayor's *Los siete libros de la Diana* is discussed in chapter 9. Departing from the premise that Montemayor cloaked his frenzied celebration of the love of the sexes with a melancholy tone and an exaggerated emphasis on chastity, my chapter explores the different ways in which Montemayor's pastoral romance ran counter to the ideological underpinnings of the conservative culture of his day. An effort is made to account for the fundamental reasons for the *Diana*'s enormous success in Europe in the sixteenth century and for the hostility that it seems to have provoked among conservative elements of the clergy. The *Diana* posits the naive innocence of the passionate love of the sexes in order to combat the traditionalistic principle that human sexual passion, as the original sin, is an adverse fate; but it does so in a way that, when viewed superficially, seemed compatible with the same depreciation of human love it was combating. In a wide variety of ways, the *Diana* is consistent with the humanistic opposition to tenets of the official culture: the doctrine of Original Sin, the asceto-monastic depreciation of human sensuous nature, submission to authoritarianism, and the heroic capacity for aggressive violence. Instead, it offers the alternatives of sexual desire that is consistent with innocence, the affirmation of human physical nature, the autonomy of the self-dependent individual, innocent love-idealism, and languishing ingenuousness. Like Ribeiro's *Menina e Moça*, the spirit of the *Diana* and the values in which that spirit is rooted constitute a secular, humanistic offensive against patriarchal and authoritarian asceto-monastic tyranny.

Chapter 10 concentrates on the metaphorical implications of the theme of "enchantment," the most frequent subject of conversation in *Don Quijote*. This chapter explores the theoretical origins and the epistemological and symbolic implications of the way Don Quijote holds that empirical reality should be viewed with suspicion, as an illusion created by "enchanters." Attention is also directed toward parallels to Don Quijote's idea of enchantment and intellectual currents in the present day. When analyzed in relation to epistemological theories current in Cervantes's day, the theme of enchantment in *Don Quijote* can be seen as a means that was used to articulate the theoretical basis of Cervantes's affirmation of aesthetic and moral idealism. The Renaissance tension between the idea that intelligible reality is a creation of the mind's conceptual activity and the idea that sense impressions are an adequate basis for knowledge has a parallel today in the polemic between structuralists and their opponents. Cervantes conceives enchantment as a metaphor for epistemological realism, and Don Quijote's tragicomic Platonist effort to free himself from the spells of enchantment is both a metaphor for the dissident creative imagination's struggle to remake reality artistically and a possible analogy for the heroic quest of Cervantine romanticism.

§

Some comments may be in order concerning the general approach used in the preparation of these chapters. One concern was to concentrate primarily on making careful and penetrating readings of individual works and to avoid broad generalities that are separated from the examination of literary texts. More important, however, is the primacy I have assigned to the semantic dimension of those texts. That emphasis is a response to my having felt, for a number of years, that because critical interpretation of early modern literature has tended to be too conservative in the ways it addresses thematic issues, it has not adequately suggested the greatness and broad human relevance of individual masterpieces. The requirement that scholarship be academically rigorous accounts in part for that conservatism: assertions as to what a work implies must be supported by some sort of evidence, and that evidence generally assumes the form of references to knowledge that has already been established. The authority upon which that knowledge is based is generally either the identity of an observer or author from the period in which the work was written, or of a critic who has written since that time. Critics make too little use of scholarship that is indirectly related to a literary work but that would support a free interpretation of a work's possible meanings. Much is lost by this state of affairs, since the practice of critical interpretation is such that it is quite rare that one is able to provide hard evidence to support a given reading; and very often the "authority" of others that critics invoke is ultimately only someone else's opinion. When we recall that there is never empirical proof for "solutions" to metaphysical problems — hence there are no definitive solutions to such problems — and that artists themselves work in a way that is largely intuitive and thus have only a certain degree of conscious awareness of much of what their works imply, the conclusion naturally suggested is that in order for the critical interpretation of literature to be as rich and interesting as it could be, critics must recognize and accept the fact that a large part of the meaning they attribute to a work is, more than anything that can be established objectively, what they themselves see in it. The exercise of a considerable degree of free association in the interpretation of literature is not only inevitable but represents a challenge that should be embraced willingly and deliberately. Mario Vargas Llosa once observed that the best critics are those who not only explain an author's views but offer ideas of their own. Perhaps this opinion was based on the premise that it is ultimately impossible for anyone to claim authoritative knowledge of a literary work's "meaning" — especially of modern works, which typically avoid didacticism. Beyond a reasonable attempt at clarifying a work's semantic nucleus that corresponds to what seems to constitute its unique essence, the quality of literary criticism is primarily a function of the imagination, insight, knowledge and personality of individual critics, who inevitably become a part of the subject of their own analysis. There would seem to be some basis for the view that theory is autobiographical.

The tendency of relatively free and imaginative critical interpretation to become subjective and impressionistic is, at the same time, a pitfall that must be scrupulously avoided. Even if a critic suggests interpretations that definitely seem not to have been articulated theoretically in the period when a work was written, those angles of vision must be substantiated as approximately as possible in terms of the culture of that period and advances in our own day. In the chapters that follow, the authority of major thinkers or scholars is invoked so that the serious, academic character of the arguments advanced is made evident. No single approach is used exclusively in the interpretation of a work; instead, a number of approaches have been combined freely to befit the individual case. For that reason, the areas of learning represented cover a relatively wide range. They include ethics, aesthetics, analytic psychology, sociology, art history, mythology, symbology, critical theory, religion, theology, historiography, epistemology, and the elusive yet crucial study of what has been referred to as "the history of sensibility." It is hoped that the reader will indulge that eclecticism, which was necessary for achieving the ultimate goal of linking the intellectual culture of the Renaissance with that of our own day and discovering a common ground between them, whether that common ground concerns practical interests, cognitive issues, aesthetic culture, or historical realities. Perhaps the most boldly innovative feature of the approach I have employed is my having done "contemporary readings" of works written centuries ago. Yet I also draw heavily on the intellectual culture of the period in which the authors lived, and I try to correlate contemporary perspectives and the cultural–historical environment from which the works originally emerged. Also, even when I apply esoteric contemporary thought in elucidating a text, my justification for doing so is that the principal phenomena at issue in that work are of such central human importance that in some form its authors must have been aware of them, even if they were not discussed with specialized terminologies such as those used today. Certainly the greatness of a Shakespeare, for example, resides in what we refer to as his "universality," that is, in the fact that, apart from his formal skill, the depth, acuity, and complexity of his vision are such that it is not only at least as rich and relevant as our own but is even modern like ours. He wrote at the beginning of our own age and in a world that, like our own, was controlled by international banking organizations and was gripped by materialism and national wars, circumstances whose culturally retrograde effects were resisted creatively by many artists and writers as they are today. The authors of the works studied in the following chapters were approximately contemporary to Shakespeare and, like him, exercised a lasting effect on culture.

In addition to my interest in psychology, which must naturally be recognized as having relevance to the literature of all ages (but especially in modern literature), I place considerable emphasis on the examination of values as they are revealed in the works studied. The phenomenological theories that are applied (primarily those of Max Scheler and Nicolai Hartmann) are particularly useful precisely because, as phenomenology, they analyze the content of ethical phenomena without the relativism that can be incurred by relying on references to cultural–historical contexts. Yet Hartmann, for example, is aware that everything human is relative and situational and that "autonomous values" evolve with history. For that reason, he divides his analysis of moral values in Volume 2 of his *Ethics* into the broad groups of "ancient," "Christian," and "other." Hartmann's work has been indispensable in my effort to overcome the primary obstacle to making "contemporary readings," namely, the historically specific character of Renaissance culture and art. Far from my having misgivings about emphasizing axiology (study of the nature, types, and criteria of values) or drawing on psychodynamic theory, I believe that both of those disciplines have been applied to the analysis of literature far less than they deserve to be. Interest in psychoanalytic theory has unfortunately diminished as a result of issues that are extraneous to its cognitive value, and many of its greatest advancements have never been applied to literature, especially to the analysis of Renaissance lyrical poetry. As for the importance of the study of values in exploring the thematic dimensions of literature, the case is made by René Wellek and Austin Warren in their statement, "We cannot comprehend and analyze any work without reference to values" (*Theory of Literature*, 156). Admittedly, however, there were moments when my efforts to comprehend a work's aesthetic value by applying insights drawn from tangentially related disciplines resulted in difficulty – for example, when a clinical interest in a character simply fails to describe that character's significance in the overall context of a work. In those cases the problems encountered have been explored as a subject of interest in its own right.

In more technical terms, I could characterize my general approach to the metaphorical interpretation of literature as follows. I anticipate that a criterion I will use to judge my success will be whether or not I identify in a work the elements that make it both "Renaissance" and modern. After establishing consistency of meaning of a text or an element of a text in the terms of the text itself, or simultaneously with doing so, I approach the broader interpretation of an early modern work that I find to be highly suggestive with certain substantive premises concerning the cultural–historical and social–political context in which it was written, always bearing in mind the dynamic, contradictory, and evolving nature of that context. Such premises are, for example:

1. The early modern period is a period of crisis.

2. The Renaissance is a self-conscious culture of anti-dogmatism, anti-misogynism, cosmopolitanism, synthesis, humaneness and humanism, secularism, a revolution of sentiment, healthy skepticism, rationalism, incipient democracy, and subtle sophistication of artistic form.

3. In Spain the early modern period is characterized by contradiction, complexity, and conflict, and retrograde traditionalism occurs side by side with progressivism and new threats to social culture (such as Machiavellianism), so that the innovative and retrograde often take on the appearance of each other.

4. In early modern Spain the dominant high secular culture was traditional, aristocratic, and spiritual (emphasizing the morally noble, courage, etc.), and it combined with a traditional urban-democratic spirit, a popular tradition, and with monumental "middle-class," "urban," "Renaissance" attainments in acute critical observation and artistic form, thus reflecting the increasing power of a new rationalism.

5. The Renaissance is the period of the revolutionary, large-scale emergence in Europe of individual human identity, individual goals, and interest in the individual.[2]

6. The early modern period is both a period of religious revolution and of a revival of medieval traditionalism.

7. Early modern society was autocratic, theocratic, authoritarian, and elitist.

8. Humanism (even in secular form) was much influenced by Christian moral idealism.

9. In the early-modern period the development of courtly love along tragic and philosophical lines was a vehicle of progressive change in the realms of ideology and sentiment (which were interrelated, as they were in the religious arena).

10. The humanist movement was a revival of interest in Greco–Roman classicism and pagan skepticism.

And so on. Important in this regard (and to my subject in general) is Konrad Burdach's view that humanism and the Renaissance cannot be explained merely in terms of scholarly discovery and intellectual effort but were born of the passionately anxious expectation and striving of an aging epoch that was eager for a new youth (*Riforma, Rinascimento, Umanesimo*, 108). Referring to Burdach's views, Bakhtin writes, "the word *renaissance* did not mean a revival of the ancient arts and sciences. It was an immensely important and significant word, rooted in the very depths of the ritualistic, ideological, and visual imagery of mankind" (*Rabelais and His World*, 57). Arnold Hauser sees the Renaissance as contributing

---

[2] Cf. William J. Bouwsma, "The Liberation of the Self," in idem, *The Waning of the Renaissance 1550–1640* (New Haven: Yale University Press, 2000), 20–34.

to the social dynamism that changed the face of Western Europe at the end of the medieval period and as being rooted in the rationalism that came to dominate the intellectual life of the time, thus deepening the late medieval striving towards the capitalist economic and social system: calculation and control are reflected in art as the principles of unity and of the harmonious exclusion of discord and the irrational (*Social History of Art*, 2: 17).

Such premises on my part are not dogmatic preconceptions but a realistic concession to the principle (noted by Mark Johnson, *The Body in the Mind*, 181) that "all meaning is context-dependent." Raymond Gibbs also emphasizes the constraining influence of context on our interpretation of figurative language (*The Poetics of Mind*, 83–119). To use Antonio Damasio's terminology (*Descartes' Error*, 198), I would characterize such premises as being terms of working memory rather than automated biasing mechanisms. By referring not only to the fictional context of the work but also to the world inhabited by the reader, I apply a reader-response approach. But observing and inferring the interplay between a work's images and the changing world in which it was written and has been read makes it possible to observe how in the Renaissance and also today metaphor has had, in Lakoff's and Johnson's words, the power "to create a reality rather than simply to give us a way of conceptualizing a preexisting reality" (*Metaphors We Live By*, 144). I must acknowledge my debt to Paul Ricoeur's perspective on metaphor for the view that deciphering metaphor is a source of *new* predicative meaning ("The Metaphorical Process," 144). I also develop a "Marxist" analogy between Ricoeur's concept of semantic innovation resulting from establishing a new congruence (a reader's interpretation and experience of a text) and literature's historical influence of suggesting ways of re-shaping people and society. Both reading and social evolution require imagination. Imagination, as Mark Johnson defines it, is "our capacity to organize mental representations . . . into meaningful, coherent unities. It thus includes our ability to generate novel order" (*The Body in the Mind*, 140).

Seeking what Ricoeur names "coherence" and what Mark Johnson (*The Body in the Mind*, 148) refers to as the synthesizing or unifying activity of imagination seems to me to be the principal challenge of critical interpretation. My own preference has been to emphasize the power that metaphor has to shape readers' values, which explains the prominence of value theory and psychology in this book. I thus see metaphor both in terms that are consistent with Lakoff's and Johnson's experientialist (as opposed to an objectivist or a subjectivist) perspective

(Lakoff and Johnson, *Metaphors We Live By*, 185–94) as well as with Gibbs's views on the communicative and social functions of metaphor. Gibbs notes the usefulness of metaphor in making it possible to express that which would otherwise be difficult to express clearly, in providing a compact and vivid means of communication, in reinforcing intimacy between speakers, in avoiding the direct statement of one's true beliefs, in serving to signal membership in a subgroup or "in" crowd, and in enhancing a speaker's status (*The Poetics of Mind*, 124–40). Such communicative and social functions of metaphor are also highly effective means of defining, reinforcing, and modifying values and social attitudes in what Stanley Fish terms an "interpretive community." Thus, whereas "death and rebirth" is a mere schema, a recurrent pattern or structure for organizing experience, it becomes propositional and metaphorical not just by being seen in context but by being embodied in rich, concrete images or mental pictures (Johnson, *The Body in the Mind*, 23, 29). Such a rich metaphor thus becomes what Wilbur Urban (with Dunbar) refers to as an "insight symbol," one that "does not merely describe and make concrete, through images drawn from the data of sense, an object otherwise known (conceptually) — as does the merely descriptive symbol [based on a "rule reflection," such as a lion symbolizing courage] — but is given importance as a gateway into something beyond" (*Language and Reality*, 416). Damasio's views on the neural basis of consciousness suggest that the process whereby readers are affected and changed by metaphor in literature is one whereby the brain reacts to an image corresponding to a newly perceived entity by generating an image of the organism being perturbed by that image and by building a dispositional representation of the self in the process of changing as the organism responds to the object imaged (*Descartes' Error*, 240–43). Most likely it is on such interconnections of the literary work as object and self imaged in relation to an author's historical context that I subconsciously rely as I work as a critic, recording, both in terms relevant in the early modern period and in terms relevant now, the event of a work's changing me and my insights in a way that I imagine it changed readers in its day. The process of interpretation in the chapters to follow thus involves exploring the range of implications that certain such metaphorical images afford and attempting to match implications with significant elements of a historiographically conceived, broadly based cultural–social panorama.

1
Entombed in Love:
Fateful Passion and Prison Imagery in Fifteenth-Century Cancionero *and Popular Lyric*

Over fifty years have elapsed since the publication of Rafael Lapesa's *La trayectoria poética de Garcilaso*,[1] a work the influence of which on Hispanic studies would be difficult to overstate. Few books are likely to have had as much bearing on how a major poet is read and understood, yet that same powerful influence makes it all the more important for Lapesa's work to be read with circumspection. The present chapter and the one to follow are concerned, in part, with whether certain key elements of Lapesa's critical perspective on the works of Spain's great classic lyrical poet, Garcilaso de la Vega (1499?–1536), might now be reconsidered. As is well known to Hispanists, Lapesa's reading of Garcilaso is based on his theory of a chronology of Garcilaso's works that develops in three stages. First there is an earlier period, when the poet was influenced strongly by fifteenth-century *cancionero* poetry and Ausias March. Here, Garcilaso's poetry is relatively abstruse, austere, and impersonal, representing with

---

[1] Originally published 1948, now in idem, *Garcilaso: Estudios completos* (Madrid: ITSMO, 1985), 7–210.

passion but verbal complexity the poet's submission to love conceived as an irresistible fate and evoking only minimally the outside world and intimate feelings of the poet himself. There follows a brief period of personal and stylistic crisis in which the poet is much influenced by Petrarch and, still, Ausias March. In this period Garcilaso is resigned to the devastations of irrational passion and writes with a style of nervous and tormented vehemence. Garcilaso then arrives at his "period of plenitude," when he lived in Naples and achieved his stylistic maturity — his "fórmula definitiva" (Lapesa, *Estudios*, 65) — through a full assimilation of the influence of Italian Renaissance culture. Here, Lapesa sees Garcilaso as displaying strong Italian and classical influences and as cultivating an exquisite, mature style characterized by sweet melancholy, the poet's presentation of his own intimate feelings, and the evocation of the beauty both of nature and of the beloved lady. Lapesa presents a schematic chronology of Garcilaso's works in his introduction (explaining it in Appendix I) and then, in the study itself, argues for the accuracy of that chronology and develops it further by attributing to Garcilaso's works stylistic features of successive stages in his development as a poet. Such an order of presentation is not without its dangers. Since the author commits himself from the outset to many of the conclusions at which he arrives, he has a tendency to see matters in a way that suits his stated purpose.

The term "amor por destino" [love by destiny] was coined by Lapesa in his *Trayectoria poética de Garcilaso* to refer to what he regarded as a typical feature of fifteenth-century Castilian lyric, the emergence of, in his words, "un clima poético afín al petrarquista: entra la idea del amor por destino, impuesto a pesar del albedrío humano" (["a poetic climate similar to that of Petrarchism: the idea enters of love as a fate, imposed in spite of human will"]; Lapesa, *Estudios*, 216).[2] Elsewhere (*Estudios*, 22) he writes, "Como en Petrarca, penetra la idea del amor ineludible, impuesto por una fuerza superior que sojuzga el albedrío humano: admitida así la intervención del destino, las protestas de firmeza sentimental toman carácter estoico" ["as in Petrarch, the idea is introduced of ineluctable love, imposed by a superior force that subjugates human will: once such an intervention of fate is accepted, protests of firmness [assertions of resolution] take on a Stoic character"]. Critics such as Alan Deyermond, Otis Green, and Amadeu Solé-Leris follow Lapesa in characterizing *cancionero* or "medieval" courtly-love literature as fatalistic.[3] To the extent that the phenomenon of

---

[2] All translations in this chapter are mine.

[3] Deyermond, describing the characteristics of courtly love, writes, "El amor cortés (quinto distintivo) es un amor frustrado, sea por la imposibilidad de la consumación ...,

love–anguish in the Petrarchan tradition, in authors like Garcilaso and Montemayor, is addressed at all in scholarship on Golden Age literature, it is interpreted either in the terms used by Lapesa or is accounted for simply as a manifestation of "courtly love." In chapter 2, I analyze Garcilaso's Sonnet 1 and a portion of a poem by Hernán Mexía in order to question the view that the representation of love as unrelieved suffering should be interpreted literally. I suggest that Lapesa's advancing that view may have been a result of a desire on his part to support his aforementioned theory of the stages of Garcilaso's stylistic development, the theory upon which he partly bases his chronology of Garcilaso's works. I argue that fateful passion in Garcilaso and *cancionero* poets such as Mexía should be interpreted rhetorically and metaphorically, that rather than being evidence of medieval fatalism, the representation of love as a surrender to adverse fate is, among other things, a tragic and heroic and thoroughly Renaissance representation of the reckless intensity of passionate willing. In the present chapter, I propose to explore the issue of whether "amor por destino" in the *cancionero* lyric that influenced Garcilaso ought necessarily to be interpreted as Lapesa and others have interpreted it and to analyze similar motifs in the tradition of popular lyric that attracted much attention in the fifteenth century, as it still does. I will address critical

---

sea porque el desastre sigue inmediatamente a la consumación. En sexto lugar, el amor cortés es trágico y no cómico, a causa de *ese sino fatal* y también de la teorías médicas que están en boga": *Historia de la literatura española: La Edad Media*, trans. Luis Alonso López, 15th ed. (Barcelona: Ariel, 1992), 42. The English of this would be "courtly love (fifth characteristic) is a frustrated love, either because of the impossibility of consumption . . . , or because of the disaster that immediately follows consummation. In the sixth place, courtly love is tragic and not comic, because of *that fateful destiny* and also the medical theories that are in vogue" [my emphasis, although the same reference to fate is not present in the original, English version of his book]. Green writes, in relation to Garcilaso, "The theme of love by destiny is thoroughly familiar to us from our study of the courtly tradition in Spanish love poetry: the lover is predestined to love a certain lady. Garcilaso, exactly like Amadís, suffers such a destiny, determined by his star. . . .": *Spain and the Western Tradition*, 4 vols. (Madison, WI: University of Wisconsin Press, 1964), 2: 325. Green then goes on to quote lines 167–169 of Égloga 2, spoken by Albanio, as though they could be assumed to express the attitude of Garcilaso himself. Solé-Leris has stated, in relation to Montemayor's *Diana*, that Montemayor's "fatalistic acceptance of the power of love, seen as not amenable to the exercise of reason or free will," is a hallmark of "the characteristic conception of medieval courtly love": *The Spanish Pastoral Novel* (Boston: Twayne, 1980), 38.

opinion on some of these issues and consider certain possible relations between the popular and the *cancionero* lyric.

To give my discussion of so-called "love by destiny" a concrete focus, I will cite a stanza from Juan del Encina (copied from Pedro de Cartagena) that articulates that principle:

> Es amor ...
> Una poderosa fuerza
> Del forzado consentida ...
>   Es un compuesto de males
> Hecho para el corazón
> De solo tres materiales:
> Cuidado, fe y afición,
> Cuyas propiedades son
> Quitar con su poderío
> Libertad al albedrío
> Y el poder á la razón.[4]

[Love is a powerful force consented to by the one it compels ... It is a composite of ills made for the heart of only three materials: anguish, faith, and fondness, [and] whose properties are to take by its might freedom from will and power from reason.]

There is so much empirical truth in these observations (couched as they are in terms — "materials," "properties" — that satirize the lingo of scholastic learning) that it is not difficult to understand how they might be taken quite seriously. The question, however, is whether lines such as these, in any given context, can be thought of as literally representing what the poet or even the persona really thinks or whether the spirit in which they are uttered requires that they be seen as a display of artistry calculated to impress with a style based on bold, hyperbolic rhetoric and a conventional formalism that curbs sentimentality. For example, the following two stanzas, numbers seven and eight of a twenty-one stanza poem by Diego del Castillo in the

---

[4] Ed. A. Van Beysterveldt, *La poesía amatoria del siglo XV y el teatro profano de Juan del Encina* (Madrid: Ínsula, 1972), 50.

Cancionero de Estúñiga (24, lines 61–80), are a typical example of how the principle of "love by destiny" emerges in the *cancionero* lyric:

> El que bien es fortunado
> al nasçer es libertado,
> el que nasçe syn themor
> de la conquista de amor
> llamen bienauenturado;
> que yo, triste, por nasçer,
> se partió de mí placer,
> do dieron fin a mi gloria,
> y de mi fuerça, uitoria
> a quien non quiere ualer.
>
> En mi afflicta concepción
> fue criada perdición,
> en mis días abatidos
> fueron males repartidos
> syn auer contradición;
> e perdí yo por mi fado
> el poder preuillejado
> de mi franca libertad,
> por seruir con lealtad
> do soy mal galardonado.[5]

[He who is fortunate is, upon being born, liberated; he who is born free of having to fear love's conquest should be called blessed; sad me, because of being born pleasure took its leave of me, and the end of my glory and my strength gave the victory to one who will not surrender. Upon my afflicted conception, perdition was created, in my downcast days grief was allotted with no opposition; and it was my fate to lose the privileged power of my full freedom because of serving with loyalty where I am poorly rewarded.]

---

[5] Ed. M. and E. Alvar, *Cancionero de Estúñiga* (Zaragoza: Institución Fernando el Católico, 1981), 124–25.

Certainly the "idea" of love as a fate that subjugates human will is present here, and in the stanzas leading up to those cited and the two following them the poem continues in the same vein, giving strenuous testimony to the persona's agony. But this work is not an autobiographical confession: it is a poem in the courtly-love tradition. In stanzas eleven and twelve the persona begins to direct his complaints specifically against the lady to whom the poem is addressed. He says that his reason cannot defend him against her, and his weariness in contending with her pitiless combativeness has left him without the opportunity to express his grief. At this point the persona's rhetorical intent becomes clear: he wants to elicit compassion and respect in order to lessen the lady's resistance. Thus, the "idea" or attitude presented in the two stanzas cited above — that in loving, the persona is surrendering to his fate — can now be seen as serving the persona's purpose of presenting himself as an innocent victim of insensitivity who deserves to have his patience and loyalty rewarded. He also wants his courage to be seen as meritorious. Anthony Van Beysterveldt (*La poesía amatoria*, 199) has observed that in the *cancionero* love lyric depictions of the lover as victim are always combined with elements that also represent the lover as heroic. An example is the following poem by Soria, which will add to giving the present study a more specific focus:

> De grado porque es razón,
> de fuerça, porque es forçado,
> os tengo, señora, dado
> mi alma y mi coraçón.
>   De tal suerte me prendí,
> viendo vuestro merescer,
> que no guardé para mí
> sino solo el padescer:
> si no me aueys compassión,
> pues vos me aveys penado,
> contadme por sepultado
> con los muertos de passión.
>   (ed. Van Beysterveldt, *La poesía amatoria*, 198–99)

[Willingly because it is right, by force because it is compulsory, I have given you, Madam, my soul and my heart. In such a way was I taken prisoner, seeing your merit, that I saved for myself only my suffering; if you have no compassion for me, since you have punished me, count me as entombed with those who died of passion.]

In lines such as these the heroic quality being celebrated is the persona's fortitude in suffering. Does this poem have a moralistic, didactic dimension as well? If the persona's surrender to his passion is taken at face value, one could conclude that it reveals an idea held by Soria, that passionate love is an irresistible fate of "imprisonment" in the anxieties of frustrated desire — "irresistible" even if the lover, as a good courtier, willingly surrenders to the devastations of such passion instead of renouncing it. From that point of view, a poem representing the afflictions of fateful love has, at least in vestigial form, the purpose of warning against the dangers of sexual love. I believe that on one level such poetry "allows itself" to be interpreted in those terms. Yet, I repeat, another matter is whether that reading captures the essential character of a work's totality or passes over important issues. Two such issues are particularly important: the use of the rhetorical language of praise and seduction and the socio-historical implications of elegiac courtly-love lyric's radical individualism.

In some studies that concentrate specifically on fifteenth-century lyric, fateful love is interpreted quite literally (as it is by Lapesa), and the use of images of painful subjection to depict the lover's frustration is seen as reflecting the influence of Christian asceticism. Van Beysterveldt, for example, in *La poesía amatoria del siglo XV*, interprets the representation of love as unrelieved suffering as evidence of Spanish courtly love's inability to overcome the Christian prejudice that the love of the sexes is the depravity of sensual appetite and subjection of the rational will (198–203). Van Beysterveldt does not see the *cancionero* poet–persona's willingness to suffer in love as an expression of recklessly heroic idealism, for he interprets in literal, sensual (Christian–ascetic) terms evocations of the lover's being compelled to love. In his view, even if the lover assumes an attitude of heroic resignation to death from the pains of love, he does so ultimately with the attitude that he is being punished for his concupiscence. José María Aguirre presents his own perspective on these issues in "Reflexiones para la construcción de un modelo de la poesía castellana del amor cortés," *Romanische Forschungen* 93 (1981): 55–81. Aguirre ("Reflexiones," 72–73) considers his approach to be supported by that of Van Beysterveldt. Van Beysterveldt sees Christianity as having kept courtly love in Spain from transcending a traditionalistic, ascetic depreciation of the love of the sexes, thus rendering a lyric that is dualistic and problematic (and even "pathological" [185], not to say schizoid). In a similar manner, Aguirre, along with P. J. Pidal, believes that in Spain Christianity kept courtly love from assuming the "heretical" (sexually licentious and adulterous) proportions that it assumed elsewhere: although passion dominates reason to the extent of preventing the lover from losing hope of fulfilling his desire, reason restrains passion by teaching him to adapt to the unattainability of the object. What Van Beysterveldt sees as the emergence in the fifteenth century of an unresolved tension between accepting love's power and rejecting it (*La poesía amatoria*, 202–3) is regarded by Aguirre as an emotional and intellectual paradox that is fundamentally Christian in that it is both romantic and classical: while the lover holds passion to be superior to reason and submits to its power, he also submits to the power of reason, the result being that he does not completely surrender to either ("Reflexiones," 68, 67, 58–59). Reason restrains the lover's seeking the satisfaction of his desire, but it does not check his desiring, his ardent hope (a Christian virtue); hence, the lover is a martyr who never despairs (72–75). Aguirre does not emphasize the anguish and helplessness that Van Beysterveldt (*La poesía amatoria*, 200, 150, 183) sees as characteristics of *cancionero* love poetry. Instead, he underscores its romantic elements of ideal devotion, denial of self, and genuineness of emotion. Yet because Aguirre sees those attitudes as having the doctrinal function of exalting the glory of loving, he does not consider them in the tragic-heroic terms of a rebellious individuaism.

Keith Whinnom expresses impatience with criticism's having paid too much attention to literal meaning in *cancionero* poetry, a phenomenon he attributes to the influence of the "idealistic" interpretation of courtly love.[6] The critical perspective proposed in that work, when applied to, for example, Soria's pleas for "compassion" in the poem cited above, would suggest an interpretation that recognizes different levels of meaning: beneath the sentiments expressing innocent and self-effacing devotion there lies the dimension of a spicily ambiguous, veiled eroticism and the persona's hint that the only way the pain that is killing him can be alleviated is if the lady grants him sexual clemency (37, 88). Although the *cancionero* poetry of erotic innuendo is not the subject of the present chapter, Whinnom's perspective is valuable for an understanding of the issues under discussion. Whereas Van Beysterveldt and Aguirre hold that idealism in *cancionero* love lyric cannot be compatible with sensuality, Whinnom takes the view that it can if sensual references remain on the level of innuendo (87–88). Of course, the idealism to which Van Beysterveldt and Aguirre refer is Christian spirituality and not courtliness; also, erotic innuendo is always present in matters concerning the love of the sexes. Nevertheless, Whinnom's theory represents an important advance in that it renders more visible the dialectical complexity with which *cancionero* poetry manages to unify elements that were held by the Church to be incompatible —

---

[6] Keith Whinnom, *La poesía amatoria en la época de los Reyes Católicos* (Durham: University of Durham Press, 1981), 33.

virtue and sexuality. But there is an element of Van Beysterveldt's and Aguirre's theories that Whinnom does not give its full due, namely the genuine emotion and elevated tone of much of the *cancionero* lyric. The fact that word-play and conventional hyperbolic rhetoric are used to prevent the tone from becoming overly sentimental does not appreciably lessen the earnestness of the emotions it expresses. The formal refinement of *cancionero* lyric bespeaks a seriousness of purpose that can include but ultimately goes beyond advocating personal sexual goals of a persona. Ian Macpherson follows Whinnom in recognizing different levels of meaning in *cancionero* poetry. In his study on secret language in the *cancioneros*, he does not hesitate to acknowledge an idealistic, courtly level of meaning that exists side-by-side with an erotic level and a religious level.[7] Although the issues considered by Whinnom and Macpherson are somewhat different from my subject of fateful passion, it is significant that neither of these critics assumes that suffering in love must imply a passion that is primarily sensual or is viewed by the poet with ambivalence.

I developed my impressions of *cancionero* poetry by studying influences on Garcilaso de la Vega. I was initially prompted to examine the subject of fateful passion more closely by my disagreement with Lapesa's view that those of Garcilaso's poems that show a strong influence of the *cancionero* tradition are his less mature works (poems such as Sonnets 1, 6, and 26 and *Canciones* 1, 2, and 4). I suspected that those poems were not necessarily less "Renaissance" than the ones that are attributed to Garcilaso's later period. In the above-cited poem by Soria I recognize the anguish and the ethical idealism that are expressed on a literal level. The persona tells the lady that his enthusiasm for her fine qualities is such that out of devotion to her he has freely surrendered both his spiritual life (his heart and his soul) and his well-being, and that he hopes she will not allow him to succumb completely by refusing to recognize his worthiness to be loved as well. But I believe that the *cancionero* poet–lover's presenting himself as surrendering to the devastations of love–anguish has the function of serving, either consciously or unconsciously, a cultural–historical agenda, that of thinly masking a central bliss of individual moral freedom the "fateful" (inevitable) consequences of which he heroically and tragically wills to accept. The influence of such tragic art — in this case, of an elegiac love lyric that is akin to Petrarchan lyricism — contributed much to what I see as the important process of individuation (the emer-

---

[7] Ian Macpherson, "Secret Language in the *Cancioneros*: Some Courtly Codes," *Bulletin of Hispanic Studies* 62 (1985): 51–63, here 53, 54, 62.

gence of individual human identity) and cultural renovation in the early modern period. One may transcend a literal reading of elegiac love lyric by seeing conventional courtly-love motifs as implicitly advancing the heterodox humanist doctrine that the passionate love of the sexes (representing value-directed individual volition) is a noble value that can determine absolutely and, hence, can be a basis for moral greatness.[8] Recognition of *cancionero* love poetry's romantic character is a perspective that I share with Aguirre, but I see the *cancionero* poet–lover more as a tragic hero than as a martyr, which is why I would oppose interpreting literally the lover's "Christian" resignation to frustration, self-denial, and suffering. Both the martyr and the hero are great and constant sufferers whose inspired vision gives them the courage of noble emotions and unbounded devotion. Also, the hero can become a martyr. Yet martyrdom proper involves a passive submission to power in the historical present in order to affirm one's own convictions as a matter of conscience. The martyr, who, in history or legend bears witness to his faith through suffering or death, influences history indirectly, through his example and the splendor and radiance of his own person. In contrast, the hero proper serves as an exemplar of vital values and energy by incurring suffering and death by actively advancing purposes of willing that meet resistance in the world. The hero has the capacity for abandoning the present and losing himself in striving for the Idea, for that which is future and uncertain but is consistent with the value the hero thinks should be preferred.[9] It is partly because I interpret elegiac love-passion in early lyric as a metaphor for struggle for the attainment of higher values that I see it as heroic. Also, such poetry's presentation of love as a reflection of the moral greatness of the lover seems to justify such an interpretation, and the *cancionero* lyric has even more of a heroic cast than Petrarchism.

---

[8] Whereas the moral greatness to which I refer is secular in character, Charles Williams has developed along Christian lines a perspective similar to the one suggested here. His concept of "romantic theology" is "the identification of love with Jesus Christ, and of marriage with His life" (*Outlines of Romantic Theology*, 14).

[9] My observations here on the martyr, as a subtype of the saint, and the hero were informed by passages in Max Scheler, *Person and Self-Value* (Dordrecht: Nijhoff, 1987), 149, 192–93; Alfons Deeken, *Process and Permanence in Ethics: Max Scheler's Moral Philosophy* (New York: Paulist Press, 1974), 207; and Nicolai Hartmann, *Ethics*, trans. S. Coit (London: Unwin, 1932), 202, 314 (on the value of the morally noble and on the Platonic Eros as an element of the value of the love of the remote respectively). See also Peter Brown, *The Cult of the Saints*, 5–6 on the close intimacy with God and the role of intercessor that distinguish the martyr from the hero.

Rather than elaborate on my own ideas, I want to consider further the interesting views of critics who are better versed than I in the subject of fifteenth-century Spanish lyric. Some of their views lend credence to my own. María Rosa Lida de Malkiel, in her *Juan de Mena, autor del prerrenacimiento español* (México: Colegio de México, 1984), notes that critics who are not Spaniards are often surprised by the intimate and unsuspecting coexistence of religious and secular elements in the literature of Spain, where that phenomenon is especially accentuated. She says that the religious element in fifteeth-century Spanish love lyric resulted in a "sacro-profane hyperbole" that borders on heretical religious parody. It is Lida de Malkiel's view that religious references and religious elation served to counteract confusion, pessimism, and cultural degeneration in a painful period of historical transition, and that they also had the valuable rhetorical function of deepening and spiritualizing the subject of human love (*Juan de Mena*, 92–94, 98–99). Although she is referring more to the bitter melancholy expressed in poems by Juan de Mena than to what she refers to as the "frivolidad galante" of *cancionero* poetry, I believe that her observation can be extended to include some of the latter type of poetry as well. In any case, Lida de Malkiel suggests that the influence of Christianity indirectly contributed to the emergence of a love poetry that is elevated and heroic, in contrast to Whinnom's emphasis on the sensual, since, one may note, mastery of erotic instincts is an attribute of the hero.[10] Yet she also sees the fundamental idealism of that poetry as being free both of the moralistic asceticism that Van Beysterveldt sees and of the Christian optimism implied in Aguirre's view.

Roger Boase, in an article on Ximénez de Urrea, has observed, "Late mediaeval poets frequently had recourse to war and prison imagery in their attempts to reconcile their experience of compulsion in love with their conviction that love is compatible with reason and free-will."[11] Judging from the context in the article in which Boase makes his observation, he would seem to be referring to the metaphor of the lover as one who is taken by irresistible force and confined in a state of torment, the cruel subjection of his will representing the pain and injustice of his love's not being reciprocated. I will return to the subject of prison imagery below. Here, I wish to emphasize Boase's view that late medieval poets believed that love was compatible with

---

[10] Scheler, *Person and Self-Value*, 193.
[11] Roger Boase, "Imagery of Love, Death, and Fortune in the Poetry of Manuel Ximénez de Urrea (1486–1530), *Bulletin of Hispanic Studies* 57 (1980): 17–32, here 26.

free will and to consider how his view compares with those of others. Lapesa, Van Beystervoldt, and Aguirre all conflict with Boase on this point. Lapesa holds that when *cancionero* poets claim that they have willingly caused their own suffering, it is a means of cloaking their attitude that their will is powerless before an irresistible fate.[12] Van Beystervoldt considers the *cancionero* poet–lover to be asserting an inspired free will only to the extent that he voluntarily submits to love's painful captivity (*La poesía amatoria,* 150, 198). Aguirre ("Reflexiones," 58) believes that the *cancionero* poet's anguish is incompatible with his reason, but that his anguish does not compromise his free will; however, by holding that the poet–lover sees himself as having no choice but to suffer, Aguirre ultimately assumes the same position as Lapesa and Van Beystervoldt. Aguirre sees the courtly lover's reason and his freedom as being usurped by passion and desire, even if reason also convinces him that the lady is unattainable (67). My own view is that the lover's voluntary submission to anguished suffering as a "captive of love" is both a strategy of conquest and a subtle, highly innovative metaphor that serves implicitly to assert the individual's right to absolute self-determination through preferred values, which are represented as having as much legitimate power to compel as collective moral law. I believe with Whinnom and Macpherson that love in the *cancionero* lyric is not primarily a function of sensual desire. I also agree with them that the conventional meaning of the persona's representing himself as being willing to forego possession of the lady is that he is asserting, in the courtly-love tradition, that his love is not self-seeking but a noble value that is an end in itself. In any case, it is unfortunate that Boase does not explain his paradoxical view that fifteenth-century poet–lovers represented with prison imagery a love that they saw as being compatible with free will; but his position is consistent with my own, as I shall explain below.

I recently found a source that presents a point of view that directly complements the one at which I had arrived independently and will refer to below. In his book *Love as Passion: The Codification of Intimacy* (Cambridge: Polity, 1986), Niklas Luhmann observes (58–75) that when the concept of passion had its original meaning of a mental state in which one suffered passively instead of actively doing something, actions could be thought of as originating in passion yet not as being free of guilt. But as the meaning of passion began to shift and the inability to control passion came to be seen as evi-

---

[12] Lapesa writes, "la aceptación de la suerte adversa reviste el mismo carácter de resolución voluntaria que hemos visto en los cancioneros . . ." ["the acceptance of adverse fate is cloaked by the same character of voluntary resolution that we have seen in the cancioneros"] (*Estudios,* 50).

dence of love's strength, there emerged the expectation that one submit to passion when entering into a love relationship. As passion came to be seen as a self-exonerating motive of passionate action, it freed conduct in affairs of the heart from social and moral responsibility.

> In this case the semantics of passion was used to shield institutionalized freedoms, i.e. to protect and at the same time mask them. Passion thus became freedom of action and neither it nor its consequences needed to be justified; activity became disguised as passivity, freedom as compulsion. (*Love as Passion*, 60)

The time when this change in the concept of passion occurred is situated by Luhmann somewhat vaguely in the early modern period. He sees it as having been completed by the seventeenth century, but Jane Yvonne Tillier suggests that in Spain that change was well under way in the fifteenth century.[13]

§

In the lyric of the popular tradition, I was surprised that I was able to discover few poems if any that express the torments of love as tragic–heroic, passionate willing, poems in which the persona states, in so many words, "I will bring about my own ruin because my passion gives me no choice." Upon further reflection I decided that the relative absence of fateful love laments in the popular tradition may be explained by the fact that the individualism that such laments express would not have been cultivated by the common people as much as it was by courtier–poets who were increasingly exposed to the influences of Renaissance humanism. Also, in court lyric the fashionable means of representing love–passion as grandiose tragic sentiment was to emphasize the lover's reckless and even defiant courage. As Nicolai Hartmann observes, in the early war-waging period of a nation's history, courage, or "manliness," is held to be synonymous with all virtue (*Ethics*, 2: 245). Unlike the aristocracy, which was a military class, the presumed originators of the popular lyric probably did not see courage as the central virtue. Hence, the relative lack of heroic love sentiment in the

---

[13] Jane Yvonne Tillier, "Passion Poetry in the *Cancioneros*," *Bulletin of Hispanic Studies* 62 (1985): 65–78, here 73.

popular lyric may be explained by the probability that the popular masses did not share the nobility's taste for imagery representing violent enmity. The elaborate discourse of romantic love was essentially a court convention. The fact that the self-conscious cultivation of one's image as a lover was mainly a characteristic of the nobility is reflected in the following poem from the popular tradition:

> Labradorcico amigo,
> que los amores has,
> amando morirás.
>
> Nunca vi labrador
> de tales maneras:
> deja su labranza
> y vase a las doncellas:
> quítate de entre ellas,
> que te perderás;
> amando morirás.
>
> Nunca vi labrador
> de tal ejercicio,
> que a los del palacio
> quitase el oficio:
> quítate ese vicio,
> que te perderás;
> que amando morirás.
>
> (M. Frenk Alatorre, *Lírica española de tipo popular*
> [Madrid: Cátedra, 1989], 163–64)

[Little farm-hand friend, you who are in love, you will die of love. I have never seen a farm-hand behave like that: he leaves his farming and he goes to the maids: get away from them, you will cause your ruin, you will die of love. I have never seen a farm-hand given to such practices, to taking the job of the men in the palace away from them: get rid of that vice, you will cause your ruin.]

Entombed in Love: Fateful Passion and Prison Imagery

As compared with courtly circles, the need to love with stylish, reckless abandon was probably felt little among the common people. Perhaps another explanation for my not finding examples of fateful passion in the popular lyric was that much of the heroic perseverance expressed in tragic love sentiment was probably related to such obstacles to love as the formalism at court and the ubiquitous presence of conservative religious authorities, obstacles that were either absent or relatively absent among the rural masses. In the popular lyric, it seems that one at most finds a poem such as,

> Yo bien puedo ser casada,
> mas de amores moriré. (Frenk, *Lírica española*, 145)

[I may well be married, but I will die of love.]

Such brief *villancicos* present their own problems of interpretation because they do not provide details that would suggest an orienting context. Which interpretation one makes of them depends upon how one construes that context. One interpretation that can be made of this poem is that the persona is committed to an unhappy marriage in which her love is not reciprocated by her husband. Perhaps a more plausible explanation for the element of the anguish of unrequited love in this poem is that the persona loves someone whom she is prevented from reaching, and the pain that is "killing" her is a result of the fact that there is no outlet for her passion. It is in terms similar to these that Jane Tillier interprets the image of the prison of love: "the lover is bound by his emotions, but these chains are ones which he is ready to accept. . . . The reality of the *prisión* is that there is no outlet for the *pasión*" ("Passion Poetry," 73). The idea that marriage is a situation of forced confinement for the individual seems to be suggested in the following poem:

> Casadita, dímelo,
> dímelo tú que lo entiendes:
> la cadena del amor,
> ¿cuántos eslabones tiene?
>   (E. M. Torner, *Lírica hispánica* [Madrid: Castaila, 1966], 391)

[Little married woman, tell me, tell me, you who understand: the chain of love, how many links does it have?]

Yet here the question as to the number of links that are in the chain of love can also be a subtle query as to the extent to which the married woman is able or willing to take extramarital liberties. Whether one views metaphorical imprisonment as being a result of psychological or social constraints, the reference is still to emotional bondage, to the lover's state of mind. But another way of interpreting both the image of the prison of love and the poem "Yo bien puedo ser casada, / mas de amores moriré" is that the persona's reference to being constrained implies that she feels trapped and subjected in her marriage, which she yearns to escape because she perceives it as an obstacle to love.

Of course, the way one interprets any instance of the image of the prison or bonds of love will be influenced by the specific context in which it occurs. Among critics of fifteenth-century court literature — be it the *cancionero* lyric or the sentimental romance by Diego de San Pedro — there seems to be a predisposition to interpret such images in terms of submission instead of as rebellion.[14] Yet consider a *villancico* such as the following:

> ¡Ay, cadenas de amar,
> cuán malas sois de quebrar! (Frenk, *Lírica española*, 165)
>
> [Oh, chains of loving, how hard you are to break!]

Since it would not seem possible to understand the persona here to be resigned to confinement, it would be unlikely that these lines would be interpreted to imply an attitude of surrender before an irresistible fate, as Van Beysterveldt interprets the poem by Soria I cited above. Yet the only way the Soria poem can be interpreted to represent an attitude of "voluntary captivity" (Van Beysterveldt, *La poesía amatoria*, 198) would be if the lines "si no me aueys compassión / ... / contadme por sepultado / con los muertos de passión" ["if you have no compassion for me ... count me as entombed

---

[14] In relation to the *cancionero* lyric, see the views of Lapesa referred to at the beginning of this study and the opinions of critics in note 3. For *Cárcel de amor*, apart from Tillier's view mentioned above, n. 10, Whinnom, in the introduction to his edition of Diego de San Pedro's romance, interprets the image of the prison of love in as referring to "el amor aprisionador" [imprisoning love] and a "prisión emocional" [emotional prison] (51–52); and Boase refers to Diego de San Pedro's image of the prison of love as "a metaphor for the lover's state of mind" ("Imagery of Love, Death, and Fortune," 24), which seems to mean that the lover feels imprisoned.

with those who died of passion"] were interpreted literally and their rhetorical intent of eliciting pity were ignored. Otherwise, there is nothing in the Soria poem that would justify seeing it as expressing less of an attitude of resistance to confinement than the *villancico* just referred to, unless one assumes that Soria was writing in a repressive court setting. But the *villancico* could also be interpreted to mean "I must yield to the claims of my passion." In fact, this *villancico* and the poem by Soria as well can be interpreted both on a literal level, as expressing submission to fate, and on a rhetorical level, as expressing a desire to be "free" in an ambiguous combination of the negative sense of "freedom from" restraints on love that inhibit it by making it dangerous or painful and the positive sense of "freedom to" flee the torments of passion. The following *villancico* presents a similar situation:

> No puedo apartarme
> de los amores, madre,
> no puedo apartarme.
> (Margit Frenk Alatorre, *Estudios sobre la lírica antigua*
> [Madrid: Castalia, 1978], 197)

> [I can't get away from love, mother, I can't get away.]

This poem, apart from evoking simple emotional disruption, can be seen to represent an attitude of resignation to the pain of unfulfilled longing. Yet there are other possibilities as well. It can be seen to evoke the innocence of the persona, who, instead of wanting fulfillment in love, wants to flee her own emotions; yet the persona's "not being able to" flee love can also mean "not wanting to," "willing" (passionate volition) thus being seen as the essence of love. This element of haunting ambiguity and, hence, complexity is a quality that the popular lyric and the *cancionero* lyric have in common. In the case of the *villancico*, that rich multi-dimensionality of meaning complements conciseness and the intense emotion with such compositions were undoubtedly sung.

The three *villancicos* I have cited above are as deeply anguished as any love lament that I have found in the early popular Spanish lyric, and they do not express the recklessly self-destructive type of "fateful" attitude that is fairly common in the *cancionero* lyric. It might seem that one would be justified in deducing from that circumstance that the popular lyric does not represent love as being noble and courageous (tragic–heroic) or that it does not assert values of the individual. In order to address these impressions, as well as to examine further the subtle complexity and deeper suggestions of meaning in the popular lyric, I will concentrate attention specifically on metaphorical implications of the image of the chains of loving as it appears in the *villancico* "¡Ay, cadenas de amar, / cuán malas sois de quebrar!" referred to above. Most of what can be said about that image also applies to the image of the prison of love.

The chain can be a symbol of bonds, communication, matrimony,[15] and punishment. As "bonds" it can refer to restraint, constraint/confinement, imprisonment, captivity, burden/affliction (of pain, insomnia, or unfulfillment), intransigence/ commitment (relating to the toughness of its material), permanence of union, and solidarity. As a literary symbol, the chain's significance is ultimately spiritual (aesthetic and cognitive), but the situation to which it implicitly refers can be psychic, social, or a combination of the two. Of the fourteen examples of poems selected by Torner in *Lírica hispánica* that contain the motif of the chains of love, seven refer to commitment, four refer to affliction, two refer to permanence of union, and one refers to confinement. Such a grouping, however, is not necessarily representative of the most frequent metaphorical significance of that motif, since Torner's purpose is to identify parallels between the popular and learned elements.

I have made what I believe to be ten valid interpretations of the *villancico*, "¡Ay, cadenas de amar, /¡cuán malas sois de quebrar!" Four of them place a cautionary, "medieval" emphasis on the unhappiness caused by love. They are as follows:

1. Love is a prison in which the lover is trapped and from which he wants to escape: he or she wants to pull away from love's powerful grip.

2. The "chains of loving" imply willing and courageous resignation to the sufferings of frustrated love contemplated as a fate. The attitude on the part of the persona that they express is, "I have no more choice but to act as I do and follow the dictates of my passion than I would if I were in prison, so I will endure the fate of my defeat nobly."

3. The repressive force of public morality, combined with the official anthropological pessimism represented in the church's dogma of Original Sin, caused there to be a natural tendency to interpret the torments of unrestrained passion as punishment for sins, which would explain the frequent references to love's "prison" or "chains" understood specifically as the torments of frustrated sensual desire.

---

[15] J. E. Cirlot, *A Dictionary of Symbols*, trans. Jack Sage (London: Routledge, 1967), 41.

Entombed in Love: Fateful Passion and Prison Imagery   19

4. Feeling restrained, restricted, and cut off from success, as well as doing things that are dangerous and that give feelings of insecurity a real basis, can be excuses for *not* acting, for avoiding decisions.[16] Hence, chains of loving can "tie one" to an unhappy, unreciprocated love that one chooses not to renounce (as in the above-cited poem uttered by the married woman).

Two possible interpretations place a "Renaissance" emphasis on love as a source of central joy and on the idealism of the persona's attitude of absolute surrender:

5. Being in the chains of loving means having surrendered absolutely to the ennobling bliss of love because of "not being able to help it," that is, because of passionately willing to do so.

6. Instead of love's being represented metaphorically as chains or a prison (the enchainment that loving is), love itself is seen as being "chained" or "imprisoned" (loving's chains in the sense of loving's being chained, restrained), which is a figure for the lover's being in that state. Like the image of "love that is imprisoned," reference to "chains" in the sense of "restraint" presupposes a desire to be free of restraint, so imagery that suggests love's straining against chains serves to evoke the intensity of a yearning to overcome whatever hinders love, be it external or internal.

In the next two interpretations of the poem, love is regarded ambivalently as a source of both peripheral unhappiness and central happiness:

7. To the extent that loving or being loved is like living in a paradise of appreciation and security, seeing oneself as "chained" to such a dimension can imply a regressive urge to seek refuge from the responsibilities and challenges of the real world.

8. In loving, the will's preference is not really subjected by any external force or circumstance, but the persona's *sense* of a subjection of the will, that love has assumed a "fateful" and potentially tragic character, is a result of the fact that a preference for one value conflicts with the fulfillment of other values of similar

---

[16] Alfred Adler, *The Neurotic Constitution*, 1926, trans. Bernard Glueck and John E. Lind (North Stratford, NH: Ayer, 1998), 60.

grade (the value of that which would have to be sacrificed for one's love is comparable to the value of one's love).

In the ninth interpretation, the central bliss caused by love outweighs the suffering it causes and becomes a stimulus to action:

9. Reference to wanting to "break the chains of loving" but not being able to do so expresses recognition of one's having capitulated to a reluctance to act on one's feelings, but such recognition is a prelude to overcoming that reluctance.

The final interpretation of the *villancico* "¡Ay, cadenas de amar, / icuán malas sois de quebrar!" presents a fully Renaissance tragic–heroic view of the ambivalence and complexity of the experience of passionate love, which is nevertheless viewed as being ultimately positive because the central bliss that it provides outweighs the considerable peripheral suffering that it entails. This interpretation emphasizes the romantic character of the lover's idealism:

10. If the persona is contemplated as the archetypal "true lover" and the image of the chains of loving is interpreted to refer to the persecution of the persona by those who love falsely or do not love at all, the persona's dilemma of whether to submit to the chains/prison of loving or to struggle to free herself from them is the dilemma of whether to continue to suffer the noble torments (the "passion") of rebelling against an order of arrogance and apathy or to escape into the drab security of the known, conventional, and average. That is, the persona *prefers* to stay in the noble but agonizing chains of loving and is inhibited from doing otherwise by a lack of inclination.[17]

Now, if it is indeed true that "¡Ay, cadenas de amar, / cuán malas sois de quebrar!" can be given not only the conservative interpretations at the beginning of my list but also the ones at the end, especially the last one; and if I am right in claiming that a fateful love lament in the court tradition such as the one by Soria can also be inter-

---

[17] See Hartmann, *Ethics* 2: 197 for a discussion of nobility's (the morally noble's) characteristic trait of going beyond common standards in the choice of values and basing such choice on "preference," on a preferred direction in the realm of values.

preted in idealistic, tragic–heroic terms, then two conclusions are possible. First, there is a strain, even if it is not a typical strain, of lyric in the popular tradition that shares a fundamental thematic trait with the heroically elegiac *cancionero* love lyric. That trait is the element of a noble rebellion of the morally autonomous individual against that which would negate values of the individual. The second conclusion is that the upsurge of interest in popular lyric that took place in the fifteenth century may have resulted partly from the fact that its characteristic exaltation of innocently passionate value-feelings of the individual complemented the ideological agenda of the humanistic *cancionero* love poets. Both the *cancionero* love lyric and the renewed interest in the popular love lyric can be seen as representing pre-Renaissance, pagan traditions that reflect the high value that was increasingly being placed on the will and aspirations of the individual.[18]

---

[18] Early modern love lyricism's relation to individual willing and its impact on cultural evolution are prominent subjects in the present volume. That lyricism contributed to bringing about the emphasis on human subjectivity that is one of the central features of the modern culture. As a secular *religio amoris*, its subjective orientation complemented that of individual, affective Reform spirituality's emphasis on divine love (grace). The process of superceding the traditional, theological emphasis on objective, supernatural forces (a perspective based on the principle of foreordination and on medieval transcendentalism) was further advanced by influences noted by Arnold Hauser (*The Social History of Art* [New York: Vintage Books, 1957], 180–82), namely, nominalism, the Copernican theory, the world-view of divine immanence, pantheism, and the conception of natural law as a power that works from within. If it seems that in the period under discussion in the present chapter Spain was too isolated or backward to have been contributing to modernizing trends, it should be remembered that, as Antonio Domínguez Ortiz points out in "El Renacimiento español" (in *El Renacimiento*, ed. Domínguez Ortiz et al. [Madrid: Ministerio de Cultura, 1978], 5–27, here 12), under the Catholic kings Spain's political orientation became increasingly international, and by 1492 it is possible to speak of a Spanish empire and of Spain as a great European power. Scheler's view that tragic suffering is not an effect of moral guilt is corroborated in part both by Northrop Frye's comments on moral reductions of tragedy (*Anatomy of Criticism*, 210–12) and by George Steiner's perspective emphasizing the opposition of tragedy and justice (*The Death of Tragedy*, 4–5). The difference between these authors and Scheler on this point is that Scheler goes on to address the complexity of the reality that actual circumstances can trap a subjectively guiltless person, who aims to do right, in a position of guilt that is "objective" in that it conflicts with universal moral principle, with values as categories in the ideal (vs. the individual, actional) ethical sphere.

If one considers the metaphorical implications of the image of the chains of loving in relation to certain characteristics of tragic literature, not only does the possibility of interpreting that image in humanistic and Renaissance terms become increasingly plausible, but it would also help explain the powerful influence exercised by Diego de San Pedro's *Cárcel de amor* throughout Spain's Golden Age. In his study entitled "On the Tragic," Max Scheler rejects what he refers to as "the schoolmasters' theory that a moral guiltiness is to be sought in tragedies" and argues that the tragic hero retains his purity of will because he acts in error in completing the duty of the noble.[19] Scheler distinguishes between moral or "guilty guilt" and tragic or "guiltless guilt." The difference between the two is that whereas in moral guilt the sphere of choice of possible actions contains guiltless possibilities, in tragic or guiltless guilt the sphere of choice contains no objectively guiltless possibilities, so the tragic hero's act of choice is actually free of guilt — even if it is not so from the point of view of the ruling morality. Hence, the tragic hero "falls into guilt" while remaining guiltless, and for him death is deliverance from guilt, not punishment ("On the Tragic," 27–29): he is imperfect, unfortunate, and accountable but not guilty. I believe that the restricted sphere represented by the chains or the prison of love can be seen as being analogous to Scheler's confined sphere of choice in which there are no guiltless possibilities. The persona–lover in a poem such as "Ay, cadenas de amar" will incur guilt whether he (or she) acquiesces to constraints on love or strains against such constraints; he inevitably violates either personality's legitimate claim to self-fulfillment or the forces that oppose passion. The rhetorical value of using the image of "chains of loving" is that by presenting the lover as submitting to a power from which there is no escape, he is represented as suffering passively and through no fault of his own, not as actively doing something that could be blameworthy. Thus, actions originating in passion become implicitly exonerated, and passion becomes a way of masking while at the same time affirming what is actually a new, revolutionary emphasis on individual freedom of action.[20]

---

[19] Max Scheler, "On the Tragic" in *Tragedy, Vision and Form*, ed. Robert Corrigan (New York: Harper & Row, 1981), 17–29, here 29.

[20] William Bouwsma has noted that thought in the Renaissance was increasingly characterized by a vision of human existence as incessant movement and a dynamic conception of the self as a mysterious and undifferentiated unity (referred to as "the heart"). That vision had the effect of dethroning reason, which was traditionally conceived of as the sovereign ruler in a properly ordered personality. "Will, no longer guided toward virtue either by reason or toward wickedness by passion, was increasingly seen as autonomous" ("The Liberation of the Self," 26).

I mentioned earlier that the *cancionero* poet–lover's presenting himself as surrendering to the devastations of love–anguish can be seen as a rhetorical means of thinly concealing a central bliss of moral freedom. Religious elements of language in love lyric can be seen to serve the same purpose. Because that technique was cultivated in Spain more than it was elsewhere, its use is a characteristic trait of the early Spanish love lyric, and its emergence can probably be attributed to the powerful influence of ascetic Christianity in Spain but in a way that Van Beysterveldt and Aguirre do not mention. It draws attention away from the implicitly heterodox, humanistic celebration of the passionate love of the sexes and from the exaltation of that love as a lofty virtue. Is there a comparable trait in lyric of the popular tradition? It was Margit Frenk who noted that a characteristic of the Castilian *villancico* is that alongside the pathos in those works there exists a lightness of tone, an unaffected elegance ("una ligereza, una gracia" [*Estudios sobre la lírica antigua*, 33]). Although I have found that the element of a grandiose, fateful passion is not typical of the popular lyric, a feature that is characteristic of both the *cancionero* lyric of fateful love and the popular lyric of pathos is the contrast between an innocent outward appearance and a serious inward intent. It may be that it was this element that the *cancionero* poets drew from the popular lyric and that they were able to apply in such a way as rhetorically to "mask" as surrender to a power beyond their will their joyous and festive celebration of a new order of secular and individualistic revolt against asceto-Christian traditionalism. The extent to which this eclecticism was conscious and deliberate or was an evolutionary adaptation to the cultural environment is hard to know, which is one of the reasons for its being so effective. It is this perspective that Luhmann's views would seem to support.

Further to synthesize and sum up, my primary point in this analysis concerns the theme of love in *cancionero* and popular lyric. To assume that the presentation in such literature of love as an adverse fate that the will is powerless to resist can be explained as an attitude that was really held by its authors is to mistake semblance for essence, to stereotype that literature as late-Gothic, and to ignore the richness of semantic implication that is characteristic of both traditions. There is a thematically atypical but formally typical strain in the popular tradition of primitive Spanish lyric that shares with the *cancionero* poetry of fateful passion the presentation of love as tragic, "guiltless guilt" that is heroically and freely willed. In general, both popular and *cancionero* love lyric depart from an official asceto-monastic ideology based on the dogma of the inherent sinfulness of human nature in that they reveal a spirit that is essentially consistent with the new Renaissance exaltation of the ennobling innocence of human love. That same shift is exemplified in changes in the meaning of the word "passion," as is observed by Luhmann and Tillier. In relation to the influence of ascetic Christianity on the early love lyric, Luhmann advances a perspective that is different from that of Van Beysterveldt and Aguirre but one that is also questionable. Whereas Van Beysterveldt and Aguirre consider ascetic Christianity to have prevented romantic love from fully emerging in Spain in the fifteenth century, Luhmann holds that, in general, romantic love *presupposes* asceticism in the sense of the postponement of satisfaction (*Love as Passion*, 152). Van Beysterveldt and Aguirre seem to share with Lapesa the tendency to interpret the rhetorical element in *cancionero* lyric too literally, to overlook its rhetorical character and mistake its metaphors for themes. I believe that it is also inaccurate to see, as Van Beysterveldt and Aguirre do, the passionate celebration of the love of the sexes as directly reflecting the Christian celebration of love. The personal love of the sexes is too distinct from the Christian love of neighbor or even the mystical love of God to be related to these as more than an analogy, which is the way it is used in the poetry of San Juan de la Cruz. Certainly the element of altruism is common to them both, but in Christianity that moral value is not as much an end in itself as it is connected to a primary, *religious* emphasis on other-worldliness, on the attainment of glory in the afterlife or union with God. As regards Luhmann's idea that romantic love presupposes asceticism, I would take exception to viewing the postponement of pleasure as a condition for the emergence of sexual love, at least insofar as such "virtuous" postponement implies a Christian-ascetic *depreciation* of sexual passion and of individual willing in general. It would seem difficult to support the argument that the personal love of the sexes is a result of the negation of the value of the individual person. I believe that the love of the sexes is, rather, a result of the enhancement of that value, that it is primarily a vital and psychological (a "sexual") event that has a definite but secondary sensual component. For thinkers in the twenty-first century to contemplate the love of the sexes as being primarily sensual, even on an assumption such as that the supposedly tradition-bound, fifteenth-century poets understood it in that way, is simplicistic and unacceptable from an academic point of view, since it ignores modern contributions to our understanding of love, such as those of philosophy and psychology (not to mention evolutionary neuroscience).

In both the *cancionero* poems of fateful passion and the popular lyric of love–pathos, it is the value of the individual person that is asserted and celebrated rhetorically, ironically, and strategically in the guise of lamentation at cruel subjection. Also, in both types of poetry, far from referring to subjection in the literal sense, the lover's subjection to bondage serves simply to represent the phenomenon to which Alfred Adler refers as the mutual subjection and adaptation of our will that is characteristic of love in general.[21] Complexity of language notwithstanding, that poetry's use of prison or bondage imagery in relation to fateful love serves to present in eclectic terms a human situation of great complexity. On the one hand, it evokes the "conservative" and "medieval" circumstance both of the persona–lover's experience of being trapped in an order of values that will stifle any rebellion against its limitations and of his anticipation of being isolated and punished. Yet on the other hand, it evokes the experience of courageously bearing the consequences of a particular course of action that is indicated by a prospective value discerned by the persona–lover and him/her alone (hence the frequent personification of the "eyes" and the role, in the Neoplatonic tradition, of "seeing" the lady's virtues). The latter, "progressive" and "Renaissance" perspective in this poetry is represented as the persona's willing subjection to his/her highest value. The strongest argument in favor of such an interpretation is this poetry's emphasis on the self-effacing altruism and the nobility of disposition of the person who loves (a nobility of central willing that is often associated with the metaphor of the "heart"). The primary impact on us as readers of the tragic-heroic synthesis that is present in both the *cancionero* and the popular lyric and is represented by the examples cited here is, beyond its edifying and inspiring us with the protagonist's fortitude in suffering, that it emphasizes and clarifies an essential feature of human experience. It allows us to witness either the prelude or the actual event of an extremely uneven conflict between the isolated and innocent will to live (the yearnings of the human heart) and subjection to the inhumane rigidity of a closed and impersonal, immovable external order (represented as chains or a prison), a conflict that presents no guiltless possibilities. The explanation, then, for the paradox of Boase's idea of compulsion that is compatible with free will is that voluntary captivity in the "prison" of fateful passion is not surrender to fate but confinement in the claims of passionately preferred values.

---

[21] Alfred Adler, *The Neurotic Constitution* (North Stratford, NH: Ayer, 1998), 392–93.

2
Subjection to Fate or Passionate Willing? Reassessing Love in Garcilaso in the Light of Value Theory

I began chapter 1 by presenting a broad overview of Rafael Lapesa's theory of Garcilaso's stylistic evolution and its relation to the chronology of Garcilaso's works upon which Lapesa bases his historico-biographical approach to Garcilaso criticism. An important component of Lapesa's claim that Garcilaso evolved from an early style when he was influenced by *cancionero* lyric to a later, mature style that was fully Renaissance is Lapesa's concept of "amor por destino" [love by destiny], love experienced as a force that the will has no power to resist. Lapesa regards "amor por destino" as a characteristic of *cancionero* lyric, and he implicitly maintains that it can be contrasted to "Renaissance" attitudes. Lapesa believes that "amor por destino," is an element of Petrarch's poetry and that it emerges in Castilian *cancionero* lyric in the fifteenth century, approximately the same time Petrarch's influence had begun to be felt in Spain. Whether such a concept of love evolved spontaneously or originated elsewhere, Lapesa explains, "se formó en la lírica de Castilla un clima poético afín al petrarquista: entra la idea del amor por destino, impuesto a pesar del albedrío humano" (["there developed in Castilian lyric a poetic climate akin to the Petrarchist: the idea appears of love as a fate, imposed in spite of human will"]; *Estudios*, 216). In the present chapter I will argue that it ought by no means to be a foregone conclusion that in the poems Lapesa cites as examples of works expressing an attitude of "love by destiny" the poet–persona sees himself as submitting to fate; and I hold that it is even less clear that the persona's insistence that he consciously wills to succumb to his own reckless passion is, as Lapesa also maintains, a means by which the persona cloaks such a submission to fate. My polemical point is that such views are based on the fallacy of mistaking for theme in a poem elements of rich metaphorical language that are understood more or less literally.[1] My ultimate intention is to suggest the broader range of possibilities to which interpretations of Garcilaso's poetry can lend themselves.

The issue of whether the poet–persona is really submitting to an irresistible force or is exercising his will as he says he is may appear unimportant: but Lapesa's claim that fateful love in Petrarch, certain *cancionero* poets, and Garcilaso is a force that is contrary to the will clearly serves as an implicit basis for arguing that poems representing passion as fateful are less fully "Renaissance" than poems that do not. For Lapesa, "amor por destino" implicitly means a medieval depreciation of human freedom, one that is contrary to the humanistic ideals of the Renaissance. Largely on that basis he seeks to lend credence to a chronology in which Garcilaso's poems treating the subject of fateful passion are seen as having been written prior to the poet's period of maturity. The biographical considerations upon which that chronology is based are presented in Appendix I of *La trayectoria poética de Garcilaso*. Actually, many of those considerations are purely speculative in nature, and certain of those poems that Lapesa regards as products of an early, less mature stage in Garcilaso's evolution as an artist — for example, Sonnets 1, 6, 26, 38 and *Canciones* 1, 2, and 4 — are, in my opinion, among Garcilaso's most powerful and interesting. The works that Lapesa identifies as representative of Garcilaso's period of plenitude (for example, Sonnets 11, 12, 22, and 29) are indeed less introspective and anguished; however, they are more "Renaissance" only in what has come to be regarded as a somewhat cliché, Romantic sense of that term, a result of placing emphasis on High Renaissance harmony and idealizing Renaissance culture by overlooking the economic, social, and political conditions of the period. The claim that fateful passion is incompatible with a full Renaissance point of

---

[1] An earlier and much shorter version of ideas developed in this chapter has been published as B. L. Creel, "Garcilaso y el mito de la sumisión al amor-hado en la tradición cancioneril," in *Actas del XIII Congreso de la Asociacioón Internacional de Hispanistas, 1998*, ed. F. Sevilla and C. Alvar (Madrid: Castalia, 2000), 309–17.

Subjection to Fate or Passionate Willing? 29

view would be comparable to asserting that Shakespeare's "dark" poems and plays are more traditional, "medieval," and immature than his more romantic works. In our day there is a greater social-historical awareness of the Renaissance as a period of crisis and skepticism, characteristics that are reflected in mannerist style and the revival of tragic art. Lapesa's views on the meaning of fateful passion in *cancionero* poetry and Garcilaso seem to have influenced criticism in other genres as well: for example, Solé-Léris has stated, in relation to Montemayor's *Diana*, that Montemayor's "fatalistic acceptance of the power of love, seen as not amenable to the exercise of reason or free will," is a hallmark of "the characteristic conception of medieval courtly love" (*Spanish Pastoral Novel* 38, as quoted above).[2]

I wish to reiterate that in disagreeing with Lapesa on certain points I by no means presume to minimize the richness of his contributions to the appreciation of Garcilaso in many other areas, not to mention his many other fine achievements as a scholar. In fact, the view that Garcilaso's poetry expresses a submission to love conceived as a fate did not originate with Lapesa. It first appeared in Hayward Kenniston's book *Garcilaso de la Vega: A Critical Study of His Life and Works* (New York: Hispanic Society of America, 1921), where one reads, in relation to Canción 4, "But there are moments of real feeling, and of especial interest in [sic] his confession of acquiescence in his fate" (196). That passage was cited by Lapesa in his *La trayectoria poética* (*Estudios*, 76; 1948 ed., 71).

In order not to be reflecting in a vacuum, let us focus our analysis upon an examination of Garcilaso's famous Sonnet 1, a work that Lapesa sees as belonging to Garcilaso's early period and as exemplifying the theme of love as subjection to fate. It is as follows:

> Quando me paro a contemplar mi 'stado
> y a ver los passos por dó m'han traýdo,
> hallo, según por dó anduve perdido,
> que a mayor mal pudiera haver llegado;
>   mas cuando del camino 'stó olvidado
> a tanto mal no sé por dó é venido;
> sé que me acabo, y más he yo sentido
> ver acabar comigo mi cuydado.

---

[2] I address problems in that view of the *Diana* below in chapter nine.

> Yo acabaré, que me entregué sin arte
> a quien sabrá perderme y acabarme
> si quisiere, y aún sabrá querello;
> que pues mi voluntad puede matarme,
> la suya, que no es tanto de mi parte,
> pudiendo, ¿qué hará sino hazello?[3]

[When I stop to contemplate my state and to look at where my footsteps have led me, I find, considering where I wandered lost, that I might have come to greater harm. But when I forget the road, I know not how I came to so much harm; I know I am approaching my end, and I have regretted more seeing my love–anguish die with me. I will end, for I have surrendered artlessly to one who will find a way to ruin me and destroy me if that person so wished, and so it shall be; for since my will can kill me, that person's, which has less regard for me, being able to, what will it do but do it?]

(my translation)

Let us also consider another work that Lapesa adduces as an example of love being represented as a fate: it is a portion of a poem by Hernán Mexía from the *Cancionero General*:

> Yo ya me quiero perder
> por las señas que me diste,
> pues no me dexas poder
> para poderme valer,
> según lo que me dexiste;
> y si fuere condenado
> porque quise yo perderme,
> no yré muy desesperado,
> que la causa del pecado
> tiene poder de assolverme. (In Lapesa, *Estudios*, 29)

---

[3] For Sonnet 2 have used *Garcilaso de la Vega: Obras completas con comentario*, ed. Elias Rivers (Columbus: Ohio State University Press, 1974), 68–69.

[I now want to bring about my destruction because of the signs you gave me, since you leave me no power with which I can save myself, according to what you told me; and if I am condemned because I sought to destroy myself, I will not go very despairingly, for the cause of my sin has the power to absolve me.] (my translation)

Both poems present a situation involving the love of a persona, a man implicitly identified with the poet, for a woman in terms of a dialectical opposition between reason and love–passion. But whereas in Garcilaso's poem the poet speaks in the first person, Mexía's poem has the form of a debate between personifications of "pensamiento," or "thought" in the sense of obsessive preoccupation (i.e., love) and "sesso," or "brain" (i.e., practical sense), the latter capitulating in the stanza quoted above. In both poems the personas characterize their passion as resulting from a despotic power associated with the lady: Mexía writes, "no me dexas poder / para poderme valer" [you leave me no power with which I can save myself], and Garcilaso writes, "la [voluntad] suya, ... ¿qué hará sino hacello [matarme]?" [that person's [will], being able to, what will it do but do it [kill me]?].

Since the personas anticipate the effects of the lady's power as being devastating, Lapesa's conclusion that love is a fate to which the poet–lover submits seems justified: love appears to be a destructive force that the persona is unable to resist. As we shall see, however, closer examination reveals that love in these poems is actually represented as being only a *potentially* destructive force that the persona *could resist but wills not to*. For the sake of clarity, I will summarize the crux of my argument from the outset. Lapesa maintains that when the persona says he wants to bring about his own ruin and thus be sacrificed to his passion, beneath that superior attitude of reckless willing ("noble altivez" [noble pride], "abandono y voluntarismo" [abandon and voluntarism]) (*Estudios*, 82, 28), he actually regards his love as an inevitable destructive fate. The perspective I wish to propose is that the persona does not see his love as inevitable fate at all, nor is his claim that he chooses to love and to suffer mere outward display. Whereas he does submit to the dictates of his passion (and of the lady's beauty), he wills to do so. He responds to the preferential character of his love, which is "fateful" only in the metaphorical sense that the single-mindedness and moral power implicit in the strength of that emotion oblige him to love with unbounded devotion and selfless abandon — truly, courageously, and "fatefully" in that he gives free rein to the bold, "Renaissance" greatness of his own individual moral spirit. I would further suggest that Lapesa's perspective is made to appear to be more grounded in reality by a certain ambiguity in his discussion of the Petrarchan origins of fifteenth-century Castilian lyric. What he starts out by referring to as an "idea" in the sense of a conventional rhetorical stance adopted by "the poet" as persona ("Como en Petrarca, penetra la idea del amor ineludible, impuesto por una fuerza superior que sojuzga el albedrío humano" (["As in Petrarch, there pervades the idea of ineluctable love, imposed by a superior force that subjects the human will"]; *Estudios*, 22) is shortly afterwards referred to in terms that can also be understood to mean an attitude held by "the poet" in the sense of the author as a real person ("en Petrarca, la entrega del enamorado al dolor es conformidad con la atracción irresistible . . .: así corre el poeta hacia su desdicha" (["in Petrarch the surrender of the lover is conformity to irresistible attraction: thus the poet runs toward his unhappiness"]; *Estudios*, 28). Once it is implied that the conventional identification of the author and the persona (referred to as "the poet" or "poets") is accepted as fact by the critic, the assumption is established that the attitude of the first-person speaker in a poem is less a rhetorical stance that is subject to metaphorical interpretation than it represents literally the outlook of the poet himself ("los cuatrocentistas castellanos . . . gustan de presentar como autodeterminación . . . la aceptación de lo inevitable . . ." (["fifteenth-century Castilians are fond of presenting as self-determination the acceptance of the inevitable. . . ."]; *Estudios*, 28). In that way, Lapesa implies that the ultimate issue and object of analysis is not a symbolic fictional construct but is rather the author's biography. For my part, I will regard the poet–persona as a fictional character whose attitudes must be interpreted metaphorically.[4]

An element in the poems I have cited that seems to contradict Lapesa's claim that in them love is a power the will cannot resist is the circumstance that the poet-personas in those works assert that they are determined by their own will. In the case of Mexía, the persona says, "Yo ya me quiero perder" ["I now want to bring about my destruction"] and "quise yo perderme" ["I sought to destroy myself"], and Garcilaso says, "pues mi voluntad puede matarme" ["since my will can kill me"]. As we saw, Lapesa

---

[4] This position on my part is consistent not only with the censure of biographical approaches implied in Wimsatt's and Beardsley's concept of the "intentional fallacy" but also with C. S. Lewis's opposition to what he terms "the personal heresy" — the belief that poetry expresses the poet's personality and that "all poetry is *about* the poet's state of mind" (*The Personal Heresy*, 2). In the debate between Lewis and E. M. W. Tillyard, Lewis emphasizes the character of poetry as a new mode of consciousness that transcends the personal because it communicates the experience of humanity; however, he does not discuss metaphorical language, which I consider to be the basis of poetry's super-personal character.

holds that such expressions constitute mere outward display intended to give the poems greater dramatic effect. His theory is that, like Petrarch, fifteenth-century Castilians represented in their poetry the idea that love is subjection to fate, but whereas Petrarch presents himself as painfully conforming to a superior force with an attitude of submissive acceptance of the inevitable, the Castilians were given to cloaking their submission to fate by claiming that they willingly chose the afflictions to which their passion gave rise (*Estudios*, 28). A characteristic of Castilian poetry in the *cancionero* tradition, Lapesa explains, is that the poet adopts an attitude of "grandioso orgullo" [grandiose pride], of "noble altivez frente a la adversidad" ([noble haughtiness in the face of adversity]; *Estudios* 8, 82) by defending his autonomy and transforming "en viril resolución el abrazo con el destino adverso" (["the brush with adverse fate into virile resolution"]; *Estudios*, 65). He argues, I repeat, that poets writing in the *cancionero* tradition (the mainly fifteenth-century tradition of collections of lyric), such as Garcilaso, like to represent their surrender to the irresistible fate of love as an experience that was willed by them, even though at bottom they themselves know that such is not the case. They are, that is, disguising their acceptance of the inevitable with the attitude that they actually will what is happening to them, with "el presentar como elegida por ellos la suma de males acarreada por su pasión" (["presenting as chosen by them the sum of evils brought down by their passion"]; R. Lapesa, *Poetas y prosistas de ayer y hoy* [Madrid: Gredos, 1977], 174). Referring to the above-cited stanza from Mexía, Lapesa writes, "los cuatrocentistas castellanos sustituyen por enérgicas manifestaciones de resolución consciente este abandonarse a una asunción plácidamente aniquiladora; gustan de presentar como autodeterminación, como voluntad de perdimiento, la aceptación de lo inevitable, y por eso enfatizan las expresiones volitivas" (["fifteenth-century Castilians substitute for that self-abandonment to a placidly self-annihilating acceptance manifestations of conscious resolution; they are fond of presenting as self-determination, as a wish for one's own destruction, the acceptance of the inevitable, and for that reason they emphasize expressions of will"]; *Estudios*, 28). Thus Lapesa claims that poets in the *cancionero* tradition present as self-determined actions what was in fact a coercion of their will. In relation to the line in Garcilaso's Sonnet 1, "que pues mi voluntad puede matarme . . ." ["for since my will can kill me . . ."], Lapesa writes, "la aceptación de la suerte adversa reviste el mismo carácter de resolución voluntaria que hemos visto en los cancioneros . . ." (["the acceptance of adverse fate is cloaked by the same character of voluntary resolution that we have seen in the *cancioneros*"]; *Estudios*, 50).

The misconception that anguished, passionate love in *cancionero* or "medieval" courtly-love literature posits a fatalistic negation of human will appears in the writings of other critics besides Lapesa, although Lapesa may have been the originator of that view. Examples referred to in the previous chapter are Deyermond, Solé-Leris, and Green, who, like Lapesa, extend that observation to Garcilaso.[5]

Lapesa's view that in poems such as the two I have cited passionate love is represented as acting contrary to the poet's (the persona's) will would seem to have its most likely basis in the circumstance that in those poems love is presented as occasioning suffering or death: in any case, there is no element in the poems or in Lapesa's explanations of his views to suggest that the source of his point of view lies elsewhere. It may seem logical that one who loves passionately and either suffers or stands to suffer greatly as a consequence would choose *not* to love if he could, if his will were not subjected by passion; but in the works we are considering the poet–lover clearly states that he does not choose to act differently even though he could. Are we to assume that he cannot be responsible for what he says because his passion is speaking for him? There is no basis in the text for that assumption; for, actually, what may appear in these poems to be the subjection of the persona's will is an emotional state to which the lover has, as he says, boldly consented,[6] a commitment to the beloved that is so violently passionate and recklessly self-sacrificing as to require being represented — probably metaphorically — as his being placed in grave danger. Daniel Heiple has observed that a salient stylistic feature of Spanish Petrarchism is "extreme postures of suffering and depression,"[7] yet such a reaction (apart from its role and thematic implications in the tragic as a genre) can also be seen as having a possible factual basis, for the feelings of unworthiness following rejection can result in morbid depression (aggression against the self) and severe loss of libido: "melancholia."[8] Instead of necessarily being a mere "posture" or one that conceals a capitulation of the will, it might well be that such defiantly morbid tenacity *is* the very commitment of the will — or, more accurately, the will that we see as being "the poet's" (the persona's) at the

---

[5] See chapter 1, note 3.

[6] For a discussion of consent as an act that completes willing by one's making necessity one's own, see Paul Ricoeur, *Freedom and Nature*, trans. E. V. Kohák (Evanston, IL: Northwestern University Press, 1966), 343–47.

[7] Daniel Heiple, *Garcilaso de la Vega and the Italian Renaissance* (University Park, PA: Pennsylvania State Univertsity Press, 1994), 148.

[8] For an overview of the importance assigned to the subject of melancholy by thinkers and writers in the Renaissance, see Teresa Scott Soufas, *Melancholy and the Secular Mind in Spanish Golden Age Literature* (Columbia, MO: University of Missouri Press, 1990), esp. 64–100.

moment of utterance is the passionate will of his love. There are indications in both poems cited above that the poet–lover (the persona) wishes to emphasize that he has *consciously chosen* to surrender to the "despotic" influence of the lady (who personifies his love) and to perish in a gesture of total devotion. In the poem by Mexía the persona indicates that he feels he would be absolved of his act of willful self-destruction by the inspired nature of his passion, and in Garcilaso's sonnet the persona states that by placing himself in the lady's hands he has willed his own death. Neither persona suggests that the behavior to which he is spurred by his passion — destructive though it may be — is contrary to his will. Just the opposite: the persona's assertion that he is incapable of defending himself against the lady's despotic power constitutes a vivid, wittily metaphorical evocation of the degree to which all of the forces of his will have been incited by the extraordinary value of which he sees his lady as the bearer. It would not seem accurate to regard poems such as the ones I have mentioned as presenting what is in essence an attitude of helpless submission to fate, partly because the lack of any active commitment in such submission is incompatible with their tone of reckless courage.

Characterizing Garcilaso's poetry, Lapesa has referred to "una actitud reiteradamente atestiguada en su poesía y en la de no pocos trovadores castellanos del siglo XV, la 'voluntad de perderse' " (["an attitude repeatedly evidenced in his poetry and that of not a few Castilian troubadours of the fifteenth century, the 'will to bring about one's own destruction' "]; *Poetas y prosistas de ayer y hoy*, 174), which "enfatiza como afirmación de la voluntad personal el sometimiento al destino" (["emphasizes as an affirmation of will of the person the submission to fate"]; *Estudios*, 218). In order to examine the validity of Lapesa's perspective, let us consider the phenomenon to which he refers, the "voluntad de perdimiento" ["will to bring about one's own ruin"], as it appears in the poems I have quoted. The first instance is in lines 7 and 8 of Garcilaso's Sonnet 1: "sé que me acabo, y más he yo sentido / ver acabar conmigo mi cuidado" ["I know I'm approaching my end, and I have regretted more seeing my love–anguish die with me"]. First, however, I will interpret the entire poem in order not to take those lines out of context. In the first stanza of Sonnet 1, the poet–persona states that when he contemplates life as a journey and a process of change,[9] his present state of affliction

---

[9] See Cirlot, *Dictionary of Symbols*, 157 on how thinking (study, inquiry, seeking discovery) is symbolically represented by the "journey" — hence the contemplative persona in Garcilaso's Sonnet 1 is a traveler. For a discussion of the metaphor of life as a journey, see Steven Hutchinson, *Cervantine Journeys* (Madison, WI: University of Wisconsin Press,

appears as just one point in his life, for he recognizes that on other occasions in the past he experienced adversity as well.[10] In stanza two the persona goes on to note that when he "forgets the road," i.e., ceases to see life as a process that constantly presents new possibilities and experiences and in which nothing stays the same for very long, his obsession with circumstances in the present makes it seem to him that he could not be in more dire straits than those in which he finds himself, when he is dying from an anguished love–passion that he values more highly than he does his own life. The persona's present predicament is the subject of the poem, and the contrasting perspectives presented in the first and second stanzas suggest interesting possibilities for the interpretation of that predicament. In the first stanza he sees himself retrospectively as a reckless youth who wandered blindly in the labyrinth of immediate experience ("por do anduve perdido"). In stanza two the persona can be understood to see part of the hopelessness of his present situation in the ironic fact that in the present, at a stage of greater maturity, he has allowed himself to become even more jeopardized than he did in the past. The persona seems to recognize the irony that in the present, as he ventures in the ethical fullness of life, fully able to assume responsibility for his own actions, he is consciously placing himself in just as much peril as he did when, as a youth, he "wandered lost," i.e., when he was too inexperienced to make conscious decisions and acted on account of what Aristotle referred to as "non-culpable ignorance."[11] Stanzas three and four state in part that the painful emotional state described in stanza two, as opposed to the more rational point of view to which he referred in stanza one, corresponds to the situation in which he finds himself at the moment of

---

1992), 72–80 and Northrop Frye, *Myth and Metaphor* (Charlottesville, VA: University Press of Virginia, 1990), 212–26; and for an analysis of the image schema of "paths" see Mark Johnson, *The Body in the Mind* (Chicago: University of Chicago Press, 1987), 113–17. The metaphor of life as a journey is also a patristic topos.

[10] This reading is based on my interpreting the words "a mayor mal pudiera haber llegado" ["I might have come to greater harm"] to mean "I could have come to greater harm in the past than that which I am facing now," as opposed to Rivers's interpretation (in Garcilaso, *Obras completas*, 66), which would seem to be "my present situation could be worse than it is." I believe that the former reading is more consistent with the development in the first two stanzas of a contrast between the past and the present and the persona's ironic view his own predicament.

[11] Richard Sorabji, *Necessity, Cause, and Blame: Perspectives on Aristotle's Theory* (Ithaca, NY: Cornell University Press, 1980), 236.

utterance. Those two stanzas also offer certain specifics concerning the source and nature of that situation: the poet–persona's anguish is a result of the fact that he surrendered himself totally, unreservedly ("sin arte" can mean "sin cautela," "sin reserva"), that is, he committed himself absolutely, to one whose disposition ("will," i.e., intention) is likely to be no more given to taking the persona's interest into account than he himself is. In a final note of bitter anguish transparently cloaked with a modern note of almost bemused detachment, the persona ironically observes that his own self-effacing devotion is indeed shared by his beloved, insofar as his willingness to die of love for her is matched by her willingness to have him do so.

In any case, in lines 7 and 8, the persona says that he sees himself faced with death yet regrets more that his passion will die with him. Does he speak with an attitude of defeat or of persistent tenacity? Is the persona surrendering to the negation of will, or is he defying the threat of his own destruction with an attitude of unyielding persistence, saying that his giving his life for his passion causes him no regrets and that he would do it again? The former represents a paradox of "willing submission" and an attitude of surrender to adverse fate, whereas the latter alternative discloses the ethical idealist's ability to make sacrifices. That Lapesa's interpretation corresponds to the former is evidenced in his observation on lines 7 and 8: "surge, dominadora, la certeza de la propia perdición, aceptada resueltamente: sólo se duele el poeta de que su pasión no pueda sobrevivirle inmortalizada" (["there emerges, dominant, the certainty of one's own perdition, resolutely *accepted*: the poet regrets only that his passion cannot survive him immortalized"]; *Estudios*, 77). For Lapesa, Sonnet 1 displays "conformidad estoica con el hado" (["stoic conformity to fate"]; *Estudios* 109). But I believe that conformity to fate is not a theme in Sonnet 1. The persona does indeed "resolutely accept his own destruction"; however, he does so in the sense that he is irrevocably committed to his own highest value, not in the sense that he regards his love as an irresistible fate to which he nevertheless conforms. The central idea of Sonnet 1, as I proposed above (and will discuss more fully below), is the poet–persona's recognition of the irony that in the present, when he is sufficiently experienced to assume responsibility for his own actions, his love has caused him consciously to place himself in as much peril as in the past, when he wandered blindly in the labyrinth of immediate experience. So it is that in the words in line 12, "mi voluntad puede matarme" ["my will can kill me"], the persona is not acknowledging his own death wish but is expressing his will to suffer for the ideal that inspires him. Those words seem to express less an attitude of "aceptación de la suerte adversa" ["acceptance of adverse fate"] with "resolución voluntaria" (["voluntary resolution"]; *Estudios*, 50) (an instance of grandiose Spanish pride, an expression of vain pretense) than a courageous individualism — a value of the subject that is realized in the subject's disposition itself.

The attitude expressed in Sonnet 1 is not fatalistic[12] in the sense of regarding affliction as inevitable. The persona is, rather, a "fatalist" in the sense that he is prepared for self-sacrifice if it is the inevitable condition for freely striving to realize his hope and ardent desire: sustained by his deep and mighty faith in a higher order, he is prepared to risk all on a single issue. In the classical ethical conception of the communal being, the collective unity is the carrier of greater aims and values, in comparison with which values of individuals must take second place (Hartmann, *Ethics* 2: 106–8). Personal love, which is a value of the individual, was not regarded as a special moral value in classical culture. Although in Romance cultures the passionate love of the sexes came to be regarded as an instance of courageous individual striving, it was not identified with the attainment of any tangible end. The strivings of the individual in themselves are thus represented as having the highest value.[13] In them the persona "fatalistically" gives himself through abandoning himself and being transported beyond himself. By venturing alone into an uncertain future for an ideal that only he envisions, he actualizes the higher values in himself and attains fulfillment as a personality.

The second instance I will consider of Lapesa's concept of the "voluntad de perderse" ["will to bring about one's own destruction"] is in Mexía's words "yo ya me quiero perder" ["I now want to bring about my destruction"]. The latter is understood by Lapesa to mean that although the poet–persona surrenders to a destructive passion that he cannot resist, he does so with rhetorical bravado, by proclaiming that he has

---

[12] See D. Brumble, *Classical Myths and Legends in the Middle Ages and Renaissance* (Westport, CT: Greenwood Press, 1998), 119–21 and 123–26 s.v. "The Fates" and "Fortune" on the Christian-Platonic conceptions of these forces in the Renaissance, when Fate was typically regarded as "the working out *in time* of the plan of Providence" (120).

[13] Unlike my own view that the unattainable nature of the object of desire is the basis of the moral value of a commitment to its attainment, Anthony Cascardi, in "Instinct and Object: Subjectivity and Speech-Act in Garcilaso de la Vega," *Journal of Interdisciplinary Literary Studies* 6 (1999): 219–43, regards the occasion for subjectivity that is a consequence of love's being unfulfillable as serving the poet's purpose of creating his own self-consciousness by enlisting the power of poetic discourse. Although there is a similarity between these two perspectives, I would argue that a limitation in Cascardi's is that it implicitly contradicts the possibility of the fundamental altruism and hence authenticity of the persona's love — its character as a moral disposition, a preoccupation with that which is beyond the self.

acted willingly. While I agree with Lapesa that the expression "yo ya me quiero perder" is rhetorical, I believe that one can question his interpretation of its meaning, the view that such words camouflage ("reviste," cloaks: *Estudios*, 50), the persona's attitude that his will is powerless before an irresistible fate. That view seems to be based on the assumption that a renunciation of self-interest is inconsistent with willing, that no one would seriously will his own affliction: hence, "the will to bring about one's own destruction" ["la voluntad de perderse"] must be rhetorical posturing. Rhetorical it is, but to what extent is it mere posturing? It is logical to assume that if the persona could submit to the dictates of his passion without being ruined by it, he would prefer to do so. On that basis, one can conclude that even though he is risking perdition, he does not actually wish for his actions to have that effect; so his saying that he does wish perdition must be regarded as rhetorical. But I believe that it is not the case that by claiming to be acceding to love's dictates willingly the persona must be seen as cloaking his inability to resist those dictates. More likely would seem to be that the rhetorical sense of his saying he wants to bring about his own ruin is that he is completely prepared to do so if it is the necessary condition for being true to his real feelings and to the fulfillment of his life's meaning that his love promises. He says he is risking himself willingly because he actually wills to risk himself. Any person who has a will and acts consciously acts in relation to his will's tendency. Even if he acts "against his will," his will must consent to his doing so; otherwise he could not act. Every action involves a "decision of the will" in the sense of a preference for one of its inclinations over others.

The concept of fate in the sense of an irresistible force before which the individual is powerless does indeed appear in Garcilaso's poetry — for example, in Sonnets 6 and 25 — but it does not refer to passionate love. In general usage, the word "fate" refers to an incomprehensible fixed order beyond human control. It is blind necessity, indifferent to ends. If the poet–persona's love were really like fate in that sense, he would be compelled to follow the dictates of that love whether he liked it or not: his volition would be as Lapesa sees it, a hollow pretense. True, the persona is driven "fatefully" by a necessity, but it is not the aimless, external necessity of fate. The necessity that drives the persona is internal, and it is actually "necessity" only in the figurative sense that it is *felt* by the persona to be a necessity, or in the sense that he responds to it by submitting to it absolutely, as though it were a necessity. That interpretation of the persona's internal situation is plausible by the standards of sixteenth-century thought in that it is consistent with the Aristotelian view that human actions that are up to us or are of internal origin are voluntary and, hence, incompatible with determinism, even though the individual's disposition may be influenced by natural constitution, instruction, or habituation. Aristotle considered virtuous action to be especially voluntary since it must be based on deliberation — although he considered wicked action to be voluntary as well.[14] Did the authors of the poems we are considering regard the love that prompts the persona to act and that he sees himself as being threatened by to be a virtue or a vice, a (positive) value or a disvalue? Certainly Lapesa's concept of love-passion as an involuntary force by which one is fatefully driven to destruction has overtones of a reference to the Catholic doctrine that the inherited evil of human moral frailty is revealed by experiences of sexual drives that escape the control of the will.[15] In my view, it is preferable to avoid facile explanations of the theme of love in Renaissance literature, as is borne out by my studies in this volume concerning ambivalent love in Garcilaso and Fray Luis de León and by my analysis of Montemayor's *Diana*. Suffice it to say in the context of the present chapter that in the poems I have been considering, there is no reason to assume that the persona's "love" is not genuine (mere sensual desire); furthermore, this love is given a heroic cast by being represented as a value for which the persona wills to risk himself. It is also consistent with what Alexander Denomy terms the "heresy" of courtly love: "From the point of view of the troubadours, ... love, illicit and adulterous at least in aspiration though it may be, is the source of all good and of all virtue, even of chastity."[16] The "fateful" love that is the subject of the poems discussed here is both an aesthetic value and a moral value, a virtue — a character-value. It is the felt, internal necessity of nobility of character, of being guided by the creative power that is fostered by being drawn toward perceived values. Nor is such a necessity a result of deliberate reflection and choice: its elevated quality is such that it can be said to derive from "a clairvoyant discernment, a conscious emotional rapport with the transcendent powers of the genuine self-subsisting ideal" (Hartmann, *Ethics*, 2: 199).[17]

---

[14] Sorabji, *Necessity, Cause, and Blame*, 233–37, 266–67.

[15] On Augustine's views concerning Original Sin as a loss of the primal harmony of body and soul evidenced, in part, in sexual sensations that escape the control of the conscious will, see P. Brown, *The Body and Society*, 416–17.

[16] Alexander J. Denomy, *The Heresy of Courtly Love* (Gloucester, MA: Peter Smith, 1965), 27.

[17] Basing himself on Enrique Moreno Báez's distinction between, on the one hand, love in the fifteenth-century sentimental romance and in, on the other, pastoral works by Montemayor, Gil Polo, and Lope de Vega and Cervantes, David Darst has posited a distinction between love conceived in "Aristotelian" terms and love conceived in "Platonic"

As the lines from Mexía's poem make clear, what drives the persona is the moral quality of his intention coupled with his belief in his own native nobility of character:

---

terms. Aristotelian love, which is represented by Petrarchism in the *cancionero* tradition of Spanish poetry, is concupiscent love that dominates will, obfuscates reason, and is a source of affliction. In the Platonic type, which reflects the subsequent full influence of Renaissance Platonism, love is conceived as good, consistent with reason, and the source of spiritual fulfillment. See David Darst, *Juan Boscán* (Boston: Twayne, 1978), 56–57, 67–68, 116–18. The influence of Lapesa's views is evident in Darst's scheme; however, Lapesa does not refer to love that subjects human will as "Aristotelian"; nor does Moreno Baez. Anne Cruz (*Imitación y transformación: El petrarquismo en la poesía de Boscán y garcilaso de la Vega* [Amsterdam: Jan Benjamins, 1988], 48–51) disagrees — rightly, I believe — with what she considers to be Darst's overly schematic distinctions on the grounds that there was a full interpenetration of Platonist and Aristotelian influences both in Boscán's poetry and in Spain in the fifteenth century. It could be argued further that the tradition of regarding love as a source of suffering and hence as evil is less Aristotelian than scholastic. As an ancient Greek, Aristotle "looked on the physical attraction of sex for sex ["Eros"] as a biological phenomenon, which did not admit of moralization any more than hunger or thirst" (see *The Ethics of Aristotle: The Nicomachean Ethics*, trans. J. A. K. Thompson [London: George Allen & Unwin, 1953], 202). Although the view that medieval courtly love is less Platonist and more sensual than is generally thought is supported by Whinnom and others (Keith Whinnom, *Medieval and Renaissance Spanish Literature*, ed. A. Deyermond et al. [Exeter: University of Exeter Press, 1994], 123–24, and Cruz, *Imitación y transformación*, 137–38, n. 34), Aristotle himself only refers to Eros in critical terms to the extent that it assumes the form of incontinence and, hence, conflicts with reason (see, e.g., sections *De Anima* 433 a 8: ". . . the reasoning faculty makes no assertion about what is to be avoided or pursued . . .: on the contrary, action is determined by desire; in the case, for instance, of the incontinent man. The continent, though they feel desire, that is appetite, do not act as their desires prompt, but on the contrary obey reason.":) trans. R. D. Hicks [New York: Arno, 1976], 149. As for "love that dominates will" as it is conceived by Lapesa and Darst, in Aristotle it corresponds not to a profound emotion or elevated vital passion that would be commemorated in poetry but merely to "concupiscible appetite," sensual desire. Even if the Greeks did not conceive Eros as a component of Philia (friendship) or discuss personal love between men and women, it seems rather odd to attribute those same attitudes to fifteenth-century Europeans, after centuries of social evolution and of Marianist worship of woman. That perspective is born out by the feminist character of the fifteenth-century Spanish sentimental romance. In any case, it is interesting to note in relation to Cruz's reservations toward Darst's reading of Boscán that without referring specifically to the issue of "love by destiny" or to Lapesa's reading of Garcilaso, Cruz arrives at conclusions (*Imitación y transformación*, 50–51) in relation to Boscán that roughly coincide with the views I advance in the present study in relation to Garcilaso.

>   y si fuere condenado
>   porque quise yo perderme,
>   no yré muy desesperado,
>   que la causa del pecado
>   tiene poder de assolverme.

> [and if I am condemned because I sought my own destruction, I will not go very despairingly, for the cause of my sin has the power to absolve me.]

Not only does the persona reveal a free, unbound, and uncompromising devotion to that for which he feels genuine enthusiasm, Mexía's poem attributes the quality of an audacious courage to those same feelings — his feelings toward his own personality: the courage of great emotions. His love is indeed comparable to an adverse fate insofar as he is driven by it and threatened by it, but the analogy could have further validity only if what is referred to by the persona as his own volition is regarded not as a consciousness that seeks and turns towards values (even if without explicit deliberation) but rather as an arbitrary impulse or a desire of the moment. Yet there is no evidence either in Mexía's poem or Garcilaso's that such is the case. On the contrary: the personas in these poems take moral pride in the passion that drives them and to which they are yielding, even though they are threatened by it — Mexía by the consequences of defying communal command, and Garcilaso (Sonnet 1) by the disappointment of non-reciprocity or an analogous non-specific "death" that suggests either psychic castration, physical death (morbid self-neglect), divine punishment, or all of these. In general, volition can be diverted from the direct pursuit of what one ideally "Ought to Do" (from the principle or moral law) not just downward by a lower value; it can also be diverted upward toward higher values by the ideal Ought-to-Be of the individual, the values of personality — "by their whole generic nature the values of personality are the higher values" (Hartmann, *Ethics*, 3: 188). Guilt for having violated the principle is incurred in either case. In a situation involving the love of the sexes, a strong interest in the instinctive egoism of sensual motives will always be suspected unless there is convincing evidence to the contrary. The poems in question lead us to understand that the persona has been willing to offend against a lower, universal moral principle as the "fateful" price for affirming a value of the individual, what for him is a higher moral value. That value is the self-sacrificing idealism of his love. In the case of Mexía's poem, if the persona's passion were not noble, it is unlikely that he would consciously and proudly choose to be ruined for it. In the case of Garcilaso, the same point is made even more eloquently: how could the poet–lover be motivated by trivial or egoistic ends if he is willing to sacrifice his life for his love?

Certainly there are ways in which love–passion in the poems discussed here appears to be as Lapesa characterizes it, a force that is separate from human willing and even runs counter to it. But in its essence love here is the reverse of such a force. In order to describe the paradoxical phenomenon whereby fateful love is able to compel at the same time that it is an intense form of willing, it may be useful to characterize it as an instance of what Hartmann calls "the aporia of free necessity," while his idea of "real necessity" could describe what is referred to by the term "fate." The latter, i.e., "real" or "ontological necessity," emerges when an object of the real world is possible, that is, when all the conditions for its coming into being exist, for at that point the object is also necessary: a closed chain of conditions turns into an irresistible compulsion, and the object can no longer fail to appear. Yet such compulsion is without any goal; it simply has to be and cannot turn out differently. That process seems quite comparable to the unpredictable though not arbitrary workings of "fate." In contrast, "free necessity" posits as "necessary" that which perhaps ought to be but is not actually necessary, for instead of being the necessity of something real on the basis of a real possibility, it is the necessity for something ideal on the basis of an ideal value, of an essential and ideal possibility. Free necessity can become an actual determinant in the real world only through the agency of a will that decides in favor of its claims.[18] The concept of "free necessity" aptly characterizes love's demands on the loved one, without whose reciprocation love remains an unfulfilled possibility. But it also describes love's power over the one who loves insofar as its compelling force acts through the will of the subject who experiences it as a "passion," as an absolute claim that his individual ethos or characteristic disposition places upon him (the "Ought-to-Be" in the values of personality). That state of affairs remains the same when the situation is one involving an unrequited love, such as in the examples of elegiac lyric that I have cited. For while the emotions of love arise spontaneously (naturally, in a manner marked by freedom from constraint) and are not typically subject to control of the will, loving is not contrary to willing because love has a will of its own, a will that can be

---

[18] See Hartmann, *Ontología*, trans. J. Gaos (México: Fondo de Cultura Económica, 1986), 4: 305–12; *Ethics*, 1: 305–6; W. H. Werkmeister, *Nicolai Hartmann's New Onthology* (Tallahassee: Florida State University Press, 1990), 81–82.

very powerful. The strivings to serve the beloved in absolute devotion and to fulfil the ethos beheld in the beloved can engage the entire volitional energy of the lover, and a love that is deep and strong can endure even when it is not reciprocated — its pain and suffering can even be happy (Hartmann, *Ethics*, 2: 372–77). In any case, it can thus be seen that love's "free necessity," what it deems ideally ought to be, instead of being an ineluctable force, stands free from the conditions of real necessity and becomes able to predetermine the real only through the intervention of a real will. The assertion that love — however "fateful" the experience of it may seem — could ever be actually contrary to will is untenable. It may appear that what I am objecting to is not Lapesa's holding that the poems in question express the *feeling* that love is a fate contrary to will but only to his elaborating a chronology of poems whereby works in which love is experienced as a fate are designated as being less Renaissance in spirit — his implying that such an impression on the part of the poet–persona corresponds to factual reality. Actually, I am objecting to the claim that such a feeling is expressed in the poems as well, for in them, the personas proclaim quite unequivocally that they believe their actions are determined by their own will.

Perhaps Lapesa's reason for not believing the claim that the personas in these poems will their own affliction is that those assertions seem to him to be empty rhetoric in the courtly-love tradition. Garcilaso's persona says that his willingness to suffer pain and anguish is causing his death, and Mexía's persona says he is anxious for the guilt that will cause him to be condemned. It is true that human beings want what is contrary to value only for the sake of another, positive value; and it is true that the moral value of any action depends upon the positive or negative value of the purpose it is intended to accomplish (Hartmann, *Ethics*, 2: 177). Yet for those very reasons there indeed exist both a will to suffer and a will to guilt. As Hartmann points out, it is not unusual for a person to want to suffer for the sake of a high goal, and to suffer for a person whom one loves brings with it a depth of communion with that person to which there is no equal (*Ethics*, 2: 141). As for guilt, it is the inevitable condition for moral freedom. The person whose actions are dictated by moral law is "good" and untroubled; but in submitting to the external power of principle he relinquishes his moral freedom just as much as if he allowed himself to be absolutely determined by natural law. So it is that an animal, given the great extent to which it is determined by natural processes, cannot be guilty but is also not morally free. Only those who are not free are guiltless and untroubled, and only the free can be morally culpable; for as soon as one is faced with a conflict of values, especially values of similar grade, and is required to make a choice between them, guilt becomes inevitable, simply because fulfilling one of the values requires violating the other. Of course, the will can bring about its own, internal determination through the principle, through a decision to conform to it: a "good will" can be a free will just as much as a "bad will" can. From the point of view of freedom, the important thing is that one's decision be one's own and that it not be dictated by an Ought, even an Ought of personality. In any case, responsibility and guilt, which fall upon the free person, are part of the ethical fullness of life.

Mexía's unconventional will to guilt is not inconsistent with goodness if goodness is defined as favoring the highest value. The poet–persona in his poem justifies his moral freedom by stating that he has decided in favor of the value that he deems to be higher, even if in doing so he has offended against a universal value, i.e., one that stipulates what persons in general ought to do. Mexía, like Garcilaso, consciously defies a lower norm and accepts the consequences, for just as there is no freedom without moral conflict, there is no freedom without guilt (Hartmann, *Ethics*, 2: 145). When the personas in the works I have cited indicate that they "want" their own affliction, their specific rhetorical intent must be scrupulously considered. They do not want suffering or guilt for their own sake; they "want" them (only) insofar as their passion is a striving for their own highest value and is impossible without them. The willingness to accept physical, psychic, and even moral affliction in order to affirm the ideal value of the beloved object is direct testimony of how strong and passionate their love's will is. Again, love here is shown to be not contrary to the will but rather its very fulfillment. In weighing the validity of the supposition that such sentiment is of a "medieval" cast, it would be well to take notice of the implicit secularism of such a will to guilt. By imposing the moral commandments of God, religion offers deliverance from guilt, but by thus negating moral pride in self-determination it also takes freedom from human beings. In the *religio amoris*'s secular inversion of traditional religiosity — a trend that culminates in the elegiac love lyric of the Renaissance — the universal, unconditional compliance with moral principle was rivaled by an equally unconditional requirement of compliance with values of the individual. The voluntaristic gaiety of this new, freely-inspired, individual morality based on the love of the sexes was concealed by an aura of "fateful" necessity and even stoic martyrdom. In its extremism, the new literary exaltation of the Platonic eros, of personal love conceived as a noble love of the remote, celebrated a type of striving that is individual yet that leaves behind all preoccupation with the self, even a personal interest in guiltlessness. Instead, it often represented individual guilt as being a higher value than what was generally regarded as virtuous, even if the claims of universal values required representing such guilt as being painfully expiated.

By arguing that love in these poems is subjection to fate, Lapesa creates the logical necessity of maintaining as well that the persona's claim of responsibility for his own demise is a mere rhetorical pose. For since moral culpability presupposes the possibility of acting differently, if the lover's acceptance of responsibility for his actions is understood as being expressed in earnest and he is seen to be acting consciously and to be exercising his will, it would not have been inevitable that he follow the dictates of his passion. Actually, requirements of authenticity notwithstanding, there is a way in which it can be seen as peculiar for a critic or reader to be speculating on whether the events referred to in a poem are represented rhetorically or correspond to fact. As what Wimsatt terms a "verbal icon," a poem is primarily intended to elicit a response in the reader, and authors seek to accomplish that end by whatever means they deem necessary. The issue of whether or not the events referred to in a work correspond to empirical fact naturally gives way to the suspension of disbelief because it is conventionally taken for granted that those events are fictional. As Northrop Frye has noted, "literary meaning may best be described ... as hypothetical, and a hypothetical or assumed relation to the external world is part of what is usually meant by the word 'imaginative'."[19] The issue is not whether the persona's words are rhetorical or spoken in earnest: we assume they are rhetorical because poetic expression is based on "an associative rhetorical process" (Frye, *Anatomy of Criticism*, 271). The issue is: given the persona's words, to what can they be seen as referring and what are their thematic, moral–philosophical implications? Those who maintain that it is implausible that the persona would intentionally incur the guilt and invite his own perdition could base themselves on the argument that beyond a certain point suffering and guilt become disvalues that degrade the person. If the course of action that the persona has chosen is causing his perdition, he would act differently. That objection, however, overlooks the fact that the *moral* issue of freedom and guilt is not a psychological issue but one that concerns objective ethical phenomena. From the point of view of the moral issue and whether or not an individual intentionally incurred guilt, what is important is not whether or not the factors necessary to move a specific individual to act in a specific way existed at a particular time; what is important is simply whether when he acted as he did alternatives to his conduct existed (Hartmann, *Ethics*, 3: 22–25). If he had options *at all*, he made a decision and is responsible for the result. Conversely, when-

---

[19] Northrop Frye, *Anatomy of Criticism* (Princeton: Princeton University Press, 1957), 74.

ever a person can be said to be responsible for his actions, it is implied that he could have acted differently. He would not have been able to act differently only if he were determined by a strict causality, if, rather than possessing the propensity for being axiologically self-determined, he were either a machine or were determined only ontologically and from without, as by natural law. If persons confronting a choice between intense passion and conformity to the claims of universal values choose the former, it is not because they could not have done otherwise. Perhaps it could be argued that the poet–persona yields to his passion because his personality has prompted him to: one does not choose one's personality, and the claims of one's ideal ethos of personality can be an element of unfreedom for the actual, empirical person. Yet while the persona may not have been able to control his feelings or their intention,[20] he would still have had the capacity to control his own actions. Some free capacity in him, "he" as actual person — a determining power that is distinct from the claims of the value of the individual in the person, from his values of personality, or from "him" as ideal ethos of personality — made him exercise his initiative and by initiative decide in favor of one of the opposing values. Values, including values of personality, are mere ideal forms. Beyond their power to convince, they depend for their effectiveness upon the intervention of human will. In contrast, moral freedom is an actual power in the living person (Hartmann, *Ethics*, 2: 177). The persona as actual person is the "he" that in principle could have acted differently and could have chosen a more secure alternative by conforming to moral principle or to natural law (e.g., his instinct of self-preservation). He did not do so, but it was not because he had no choice. Even if he was determined by the absolute Ought-to-Be of the personal individual, he was still self-determined. No matter how much one's "Ought-to-Be" is defined by his individual ideal ethos of personality and is bound to the validity of its claims, as actual person he remains autonomous. "Of themselves, values have no power to move what actually exists. Such a power can issue only from ... an actual person and in so far as he commits himself to them" (Hartmann, *Ethics*, 3: 211). If there were a compulsion, an inevitability that emanated from values, one might very well speak of a "fate" by which the persona has been determined. In fact, however, his decision is his own positive self-determination. It is only with the performance of the poet–persona's act of willing that

---

[20] On Scheler's concept of intentional feelings and love as a dynamic act of discovering value-preferences, see Alfons Deeken, *Process and Permanence in Ethics: Max Scheler's Moral Philosophy* (New York: Paulist Press, 1974), 30–33, 181–87.

issued in a decision of the will that it begins to be possible to say, in the loose sense, that he "could not have acted differently." That decision of the will is what Alexander Pfänder refers to as the "intent as proposed, or the *voluntarium*": "By the performance of a genuine act of willing, the ego is charged with a certain intent. To this extent the act of willing is, therefore, also an act of self-charging . . .; the ego charges itself with an intent."[21] Thus charged, the ego is not only made responsible for performing a particular action but, in cases of intense willing, also becomes comparable to a potent stream of energy moving in a certain direction. Yet there is still a possibility of acting differently: no matter how difficult doing so may be, that decision may in principle be reversed or changed: otherwise, it would have no ethical value and, hence, no aesthetic value.[22]

In sum, if the term *"albedrío"* ["will"] is understood to mean the faculty or capacity to decide, favorable disposition, consent, or determination in the sense of striving (conation), it would seem that by taking the view that Castilian poets considered passionate love to be contrary to will, Lapesa could have been referring to "will" only in the sense of the faculty of deciding, not in the other senses. But even that position would have to be based on the fallacy of supposing that a conscious decision is necessarily one that is made with explicit deliberation.

Consciousness is clearly important in making decisions, since an awareness of alternatives and their implications is essential in deciding. However, a deliberate weigh-

---

[21] Alexander Pfänder, *Phenomenology of Willing and Motivation and Other Phenomenologica*, trans. Herbert Spielberg (Evanston, IL: Northwestern University Press, 1967), 23.

[22] The possibility of acting differently, which exists in principle, is a crucial condition for moral freedom in spite of the fact that for a person of high moral standing a particular course of action will often be experienced as involuntary (Max Scheler, *Formalism In Ethics* [Evanston, IL: Northwestern University Press, 1973], 43). Hartmann points out that one's state of freedom does not consist in a consciousness of it, but is independent of such consciousness. "And his moral value is so much the higher, the less he is in need of making a special decision and the more stable his basic attitude is. But the fundamental disposition itself, which is the carrier of his moral value, is based upon freedom: the disposition in itself could have been different" (*Ethics*, 3: 25). The latter idea was expressed by Aristotle in his *Nicomachean Ethics* (see Sorabji, *Necessity, Cause, and Blame*, 236). Of course in order to carry responsibility, "disposition" must understood to be an attribute of consciousness in the sense of "consciousness proper": not an inward beholding that is closed in the depth of the ego but an evaluating tendency and attitude of mind that springs out of such a world of the emotions. For observations defining "disposition" along such lines, see Hartmann, *Ethics*, 2: 134.

ing of the desirability of prospective ends is not the only form of consciousness on which a choice between alternatives may be based. That criterion would only apply to values of ends — the communal moral virtues, which refer to what in general persons ought to do. There is another criterion for deciding between alternative courses of action. It is the criterion of actional values, values of acts, of the individual. In spite of referring to the individual, these values do not imply an egoistic individualism in the negative or "anti-social" sense, since they are compatible with self-sacrifice and concern not the empirical, self-serving ego but the supra-empirical ideal essence of the person, the ideal ego. Here the standard is not the height of the thing striven for but the greatness of mental attitude or commitment of the subject. Values of the individual transcend in axiological height those of the commonality, and "human greatness is never with the crowd but is always and necessarily an affair of individuals" (Hartmann, *Ethics*, 2: 110, 112). Fateful love is not a fate: it is a value of the individual, of the morally courageous individual. A decision in favor of values of the individual will be made on the basis not of practical considerations, a deliberate selection of ends, but rather on the basis of a felt value-preference, and such intentional feelings are fully a form of consciousness. It is this type of value-preference that underlies love's strivings, which are typically stronger, more spontaneous, and more courageously "fateful" the more fully the values directing those strivings are felt. For the goals of such value-directed striving "are experienced *in* conation, not prior to it."[23] Such a perspective makes understandable Charles Renouvier's observation that "presque tous les grands hommes, les hommes de volonté mêmes, ont été des fatalistes" (["almost all great men, men of will, have been fatalists"]; my translation).[24] As Scheler notes,

> among persons of very powerful will, and especially among energetic groups in history, the very consciousness of the departure of willing from the "ego" ... was developed least. They experienced the effectiveness of their will as "grace" (e.g., the energetic English Puritans, like Cromwell and his circle), or they felt themselves to be completely tools of God (e.g., Calvin, as God's "instrument"), or they experienced the stages in their life-development as "*fate*" (e.g.,

---

[23] Max Scheler, *Formalism in Ethics*, trans. M. S. Frings and R. L. Funk (Evanston, IL: Northwestern University Press, 1973), 39.

[24] Charles Renouvier, *Essais de Critique Générale* (Paris: Armand Colin, 1919), 2: 91.

the energetic Arabs and Turks, Wallenstein, and Napoleon). ...
(*Formalism*, 61–62, my emphasis)

Far from surrendering to an inevitable circumstance and merely "claiming" to be doing so by choice, the poet–personas in works such as those by Mexía and Garcilaso cited above *will* the actions to which they are moved and do so with such passionate intensity as to risk spending themselves on the object. That is the danger, the "fate," with which they are faced:

> [Every intense act of willing] is always characterized by its *drawing us beyond* the ideas of the reactions it evokes in our states, especially in our sensible states. For instance, we do not notice that we hurt ourselves during a dangerous kind of work, or that feelings of tiredness and even pain protest against it. All passionate willing, especially its highest forms, leaves simultaneously sensible feeling-states, or those to be expected, completely outside the sphere of givenness. (Scheler, *Formalism*, 61)

It is characteristic of passionate willing that its acts do not *seem* to result from conscious choice. So it is that the individual's "subjection to love" is a metaphor that serves to emphasize the passionate nature of that love. León Hebreo, for example, writes in his *Diálogos de amor*: "las sujeciones corporales únicamente dejan libre la voluntad, pero la atadura del amor encadena primero la voluntad del amante y después toda su persona a la vez" ["corporal subjections only leave the will free, but the bondage of love enchains first the lover's will and afterwards his entire person at the same time"].[25] The second part of this sentence, instead of reading "but the bondage of love enchains first the lover's will and afterwards his entire person," without its metaphorical imagery, could read "but the claims of love exercise a powerful influence first over the lover's will and then over his entire person." In the poems I have considered, the persona's passionate will *is* his love. There is a long tradition of philosophers who have identified love directly with "will" in the sense of value-directed volition. They include Plato, St. Augustine, St. Thomas, Duns Scotus, Ockham, and Ficino.[26]

---

[25] León Hebreo, *Diálogos de amor* (1535), trans. Carlos Mazo del Castillo, 2nd ed. (Barcelona: PPU, 1993), 157; my translation.

[26] For a discussion of a number of philosophers, including those mentioned here ex-

The view that tragic love in Garcilaso's poetry is the negative opposite of active striving, ethical inertia in the face of a force that is contrary to human will, is a mythical invention of literary scholarship. In fact, passionate willing in Garcilaso's poetry, the celebration of the courage to bear the consequences of great emotions, is a direct reflection of the relatively new, Renaissance emphasis on the value of human will. Elements of *cancionero* style such as word play and a focus on internal struggle are not a sufficient basis for regarding as early productions poems in which Garcilaso treats the subject of fateful love. Tragic art is introverted by nature yet ultimately festive nonetheless, and from the fifteenth through the seventeenth centuries, *conceptista* verbal complexity had, in part, the purpose of dissipating a potentially maudlin sentimentality. In any case, I do not deny that a poem such as Garcilaso's Sonnet 1 *could* have been written early in the poet's career, but rather that it is less mature or more "un-Renaissance" than works such as Sonnets 11, 13, 23, and 29, which, because of their pagan elements and plasticity, Lapesa sees as being later productions. The mind-spun verbal complexity of *cancionero* poetry is felt by many to be affected and overly conventional. Whereas such a criterion of taste may be legitimate, the preference for the aestheticist paganism of Italian forms over native tradition can also be seen as a concession to a certain artificiality of fashionable taste. Oskar Hagen suggests that such a concession was made not just in poetry but in painting and religion as well.[27] It is a fallacy to equate the first signs of "modernity" in Spain with the cosmopolitan acceptance of Italian influences. If my argument is sound, Sonnet 1 and poems like it that incorporated elements of *cancionero* style could be among Garcilaso's mature productions as well. By presenting values of the individual as the highest values, values that determine absolutely and even tragically, poems such as the two I have considered here reflect as much influence of Renaissance attitudes as works that describe natural settings or the physical features of the beloved. Poems such as Sonnets 1, 6, 26, and 38, and *Canciones* 1, 2, and 4 (in spite of *Canción* 4's references to a conflict between

---

cept for Ficino, and their theories of will in which love is seen as the central or distinctive function of volition, see J. Bourke, *Will in Western Thought* (New York: Sheed, 1964), 129–47. For Ficino see Paul O. Kristeller, *The Philosophy of Marsilio Ficino* (Gloucester, MA: Peter Smith, 1964), 256–88.

[27] Oskar Hagen, *Patterns and Principles of Spanish Art* (Madison, WI: University of Wisconsin Press, 1948), 137–38.

reason and appetite,[28] since for Ficino "appetite" was synonymous with the cosmic force of love) could have been written at any point in Garcilaso's brief writing career (which could not have lasted for more than some seventeen years). In those works, instead of the persona, in Lapesa's words, emphasizing "submission to fate as an assertion of personal will" (*Estudios*, 218), submission to fate is used as a metaphor for the persona's persistence in his own passionate willing. The "fate" of unhappy love in Garcilaso is not an instance of late-Gothic surrender to a power beyond human control; it is an assertion of the will to live.

---

[28] For my view that this conflict does not have the traditionalistic and moralistic implications that are generally attributed to it, see below, chapter 4.

3

Obsequious Love as the Egos' Release from Frustration through Mortification of Self: Interpreting "Masochistic" Rescue Fantasies in Elegaic Love Lyric

A perennial problem in Garcilaso scholarship concerns the figure of the beloved lady. Is this lady a real, living person, or is she more often a stock motif in a period that placed high value on the imitation of traditional forms? The issue obviously would not apply to types of love poetry that are definitely allegorical, such as Dante's *Divina Commedia* or *Vita Nuova* or the poetry of Lorenzo de' Medici;[1] it concerns elegiac

---

[1] In addition to existing in herself, Dante's Beatrice "is an image of nobility, of virtue, of the Redeemed Life, and in some sense of Almighty God himself" (Charles Williams, *The Figure of Beatrice* [New York: Noonday, 1961], 8). On allegorical meaning in the poetry of Lorenzo de' Medici (1449–1492) see the still profound study by Angelo Lipari, *The Dolce Stil Novo According to Lorenzo de Medici* (New Haven: Yale University Press, 1936). Lorenzo's "lady" is a personification of the qualities of beauty and human *gentilesse*. Her death is the mystical death whereby those qualities have achieved perfection by the extraction of their pure form from the material object incarnating them; and the poet's grief at that event is the occasion for his own mystical death, his learning to distinguish between inward and outward form, and the commencement of his *nuova vita*, i.e., his spiritual

works, which are so intimately individual that interpreting them in broad, allegorical terms becomes difficult. Of that variety is poetry in the Petrarchist tradition. If the lady in Petrarchan lyricism is seen as a stock motif, a metaphor, we again find ourselves in the realm of allegory, but "allegory" of a more subtle and elusive, less conventional, variety. We know that in the case of Petrarch himself the identity or meaning of the lady ("Laura") was a complex matter.[2] And among poets in Spain? The tradition of seeing Garcilaso de la Vega's works as reflecting the personal experiences of the poet was challenged in the late 1970s by a group of critics who rejected as inaccurate and "mythological" the biographical claims upon which such interpretations are based. Critics such as Manuel Sito Alba, Frank Goodwyn, David Darst, and Pamela Waley[3] questioned whether there really exists even a circumstantial basis for the assumption that Garcilaso's poems refer to the women with whom he is thought to have had relationships. The skepticism of those critics is similar to that which is expressed by Don Quijote when, in discussing Dulcinea, he tells Sancho that the women who poets claim inspired their compositions do not exist in reality but are fictions that serve to provide a poetic subject and make poets be seen as "enamorados y . . . hombres que tienen valor para serlo" (["enamoured and . . . men who have the courage to be so"]; 1.25). Elsewhere (2.1), Don Quijote speaks of poets as being disdained by their "feigned ladies" ["damas fingidas"]. Cervantes would thus seem to suggest that a literature in which the poet represents himself as being in love is a conventional vehicle of sentiment, and that the role of the lady is simply to provide an occasion for cultivating or celebrating feelings of courageous devotion to an ideal. In the final analysis, however, we must recognize on the basis of common sense that to assert categorically

---

elevation and his realization of the philosophical concept and artistic ideal personified by his lady. Hence, the *"gentilesse"* of death (108–9, 156–57, 308–9).

[2] See Marjorie O'Rourke Boyle, *Petrarch's Genius* (Berkeley: University of California Press, 1991), 126–27; Maude F. Jerrold, *Francesco Petrarca* (Port Washington, NY: Kennikat, 1970), 42, 153; and Umberto Bosco, *Francesco Petrarca* (Bari: Laterza, 1961), 15–23.

[3] Manuel Sito Alba, "¿Un tiento de Garcilaso en poetas portuguesas? (Notas a la lectura de la Égloga III)," *Boletín de la Real Academia Española* 56 (1976): 439–50; Frank Goodwyn, "New Light on the Historical Setting of Garcilaso's Poetry," *Hispanic Review* 46 (1978): 1–22; David H. Darst, "Garcilaso's Isabel and Elena: The Growth of a Myth," *Journal of Hispanic Philology* 3 (1979): 261–68; and Pamela Waley, "Garcilaso's Isabel, and Elena: The Growth of a Legend," *Bulletin of Hispanic Studies* 56 (1979): 11–15. Lapesa discusses the ideas of Sito Alba and Waley in *Estudios*, 200–5.

that Renaissance love poetry never concerns a real lady would be just as naive as to assume that it always does. Neither alternative brings us closer to a better appreciation of the lady's complex and often perplexing significance in the great Spanish classics of elegiac love lyric.

One feature of the new, 1985 edition of Rafael Lapesa's *La trayectoria poética de Garcilaso de la Vega* (original 1948), published with materials added and under the new title *Garcilaso: Estudios completos*, is that it serves to orient a counterattack against those who would question the validity of Lapesa's essentially biographical approach to the reading of Garcilaso.[4] Citing a historiographic study by Enrique Martínez López, which brings to light new particulars concerning Alfonso de Fonseca, the husband of the woman Garcilaso is presumed to have loved,[5] Lapesa seeks to take issue with those who reject the claim that many of Garcilaso's greatest poems are, above all, testimonials of his passion for the Portuguese beauty, Isabel Freire. But proponents of the biographical interpretation of Garcilaso (the most notable of whom is Lapesa himself) have neither refuted nor seriously addressed the broader implications of the argument that speculations concerning Garcilaso's love life cannot contribute significantly to an appreciation of his poetry. The biographical approach to the interpretation of his works first emerged in a fully developed form in Hayward Kenniston, *Garcilaso de la Vega*, published as long ago as 1922. Certainly a criticism grounded in what can ultimately be only hypothetical connections between an author's poems and known or possible events in his life is a relic of an age when literary criticism as we know it today was in its infancy and the principle known as the "the intentional fallacy" did not exist. That principle is valuable but over-limiting. Its claim that it is an error to look outside the text for the intentions of its author has validity insofar as it discourages trivializing a text by attempting to explain it as being motivated by particular experiences in the author's life, but to ignore the broad relations between an author or text and the world beyond them would be to deprive the thematic dimension of a text of many of its rich implications. As Gerald Graff has observed of critical interpretation in general, determining the relevant context of a work (and hence the kind of utterance it is) is as dependent upon inference as any other part of the interpretive process and is therefore just as open to dispute. According to Graff, a fundamental problem faced by criticism

---

[4] Lapesa, *Estudios*, 199–210. Heiple discusses elements of that polemic in *Garcilaso de la Vega and the Italian Renaissance*, 12–14.

[5] Lapesa, *Garcilaso: Estudios*, 209–10.

is that of distinguishing between relatively more and less defensible competing guesses as to which of a work's contexts is the more relevant.[6]

Why would the claim that the women loved by the persona in Garcilaso's poems were known by the poet himself have been considered to be a relevant context in the first place? Part of the answer undoubtedly concerns our natural interest in the life of the figure who is considered to represent the quintessential Spanish Renaissance man (poet–courtier and warrior), who died in war at a young age, and who — because he is among the most, perhaps is the most, anguished of voices in all of Spanish lyric — seems to be a Renaissance author of fully modern sensibility. But literary criticism is ultimately a way to discuss a work of art, a way that is well informed at the same time that it is as interesting; and, unfortunately, biographical readings of Garcilaso are relatively uninteresting and lead one to suspect that the tenacity of biographical readings of Garcilaso's poems may well be testimony to criticism's relative failure to solve the problem of deriving alternative, convincing relevant contexts for interpreting and allegorizing above all his sonnets and *canciones*, the works that have been the most neglected by imaginative criticism. On the other hand, the difficulty of solving that problem in the case of any important artist, and hence the continued challenge represented by his or her work, is an unmistakable sign of that artist's greatness. I do not wish to suggest that all critics read Garcilaso with as much emphasis on the strictly biographical as Lapesa does, or that Lapesa does not contribute in other areas to an understanding of Garcilaso's works. However, the vast majority of Garcilaso critics follow Lapesa and so limit their consideration of the contents of those poems, either by confining them to an antecedent tradition or by situating them in a chronology that correlates a "trajectory" of Garcilaso's life or experiences in love and his formal evolution as a poet, even if doing so assumes (as in the case of Kenniston and Lapesa) the inconspicuous form of postulating a chronology of his stylistic development. On the basis of one hypothetical chronology or another, the critics note isolated details concerning resources of language, thematic motif, and intertextuality, continuing tacitly to suggest that the major thematic dimensions of Garcilaso's poetry have been accounted for.[7] Yet Lapesa's having developed and maintained a following is understand-

---

[6] Gerald Graff, "Determinacy/Indeterminacy," in *Critical Terms for Literary Study*, ed. Frank Lentricchia et al. (Chicago: University of Chicago Press, 1990), 163–76, here 166, 167, 169.

[7] Examples are Cruz, *Imitación y transformación*; Antonio Gargano, *Fonti, miti, topoi: Cinque saggi su Garcilaso* (Naples: Liguori, 1988); and Ignacio Navarrete, *Orphans*

able, for he presents his perspective with such patient diligence and commanding language that it is easy to overlook the many arbitrary speculations upon which that perspective is based. Besides, those who question the validity of the biographical approach to Garcilaso's poetry have yet to advance an alternative that is the equal to that approach in the extent to which it postulates a real, vital, human basis for most of the poems.

This issue is as important as it is problematic, and it is worth pausing a moment to consider some of general the implications that it has for literary scholarship. I will briefly concentrate on a specific instance so as to give my observations concrete relevance. Probably the most sensitive and valuable comments that have been written to date on Garcilaso's Sonnet 2 are in Daniel Heiple, *Garcilaso de la Vega and the Italian Renaissance*. Heiple sees Sonnet 2 as, together with Sonnets 9 and 3, belonging to a group of three poems that he believes Lapesa correctly situated in Garcilaso's early period (143). The contents of Sonnets 9 and 3 are quite conventional and accessible, and Heiple interprets them capably, concentrating mainly on stylistic characteristics. He introduces Sonnet 2 by recognizing it as one of the most intense and violent of Garcilaso's works. Since I will consider Sonnet 2 in the present study, I will transcribe it at this point.

> En fin a vuestras manos é venido
> do sé que é de morir tan apretado
> que aun aliviar con quexas mi cuidado
> como remedio m'es ya deffendido:
> mi vida no sé en qué s'ha sostenido
> si no es en aver sido yo guardado
> para que sólo en mí fuesse provado
> quánto corta una 'spada en un rendido.
> Mis lágrimas an sido derramadas
> donde la sequedad y el aspereza
> dieron mal fruto dellas, y mi suerte:

---

of Petrarch: Poetry and Theory in the Spanish Renaissance (Berkeley: University of California Press, 1994).

ibasten las que por vos tengo lloradas;
no os venguéys más de mí con mi flaqueza;
allá os vengad, señora, con mi muerte!

[Finally I have come into your hands, where I know I will die gripped so tightly that even the remedy of relieving my anguish with complaints is forbidden to me: I know not on what my life has sustained itself if it is not on my having been kept so that on me alone it might be proven how much a sword will cut in one who has surrendered. My tears have been shed where dryness and harshness bore poor fruit of them, and my fate: may those that I have already wept for you suffice; avenge yourself on me no more with my frailty; avenge yourself, Madam, with my death!][8]

After interpreting the poem's content on a literal level, as a surrender of the poet–lover to a cruel mistress, Heiple observes that in the case of this work it is difficult to understand what the surrender means on a literal amorous level because lines 9 and 10 suggest that the poet–lover has already made his suffering known to the lady, and the poem states that he will surrender begging for death because he has reached the end of his ability to suffer. Before concluding with some rather recondite details of language, Heiple observes that the obscurity of what specific instance of surrender the poem refers to can be discounted if the poem is not seen as describing a real event but is seen as an elaboration of the traditional Petrarchan metaphor of love as war, the realistic horror of its images standing for the extremity of the poet's commitment and passion (150–51). As can be seen, Heiple first situates the poem in the stage in Garcilaso's career when it was written, considers the extent to which it can be seen as referring to a specific event in what he terms "the trajectory of the love affair" (apparently meaning equivocally either a love affair of Garcilaso's or the archetypal love affair), and then concludes that an interpretation of the poem must be based on seeing it as an extension of literary tradition, as "literature made out of literature" (149). But certain important paradoxes in this poem have not been addressed by that literal and intertextual perspective. For example, if Sonnet 2 is a love poem, what is its purpose?

---

[8] The Spanish versions of the poems by Garcilaso de la Vega are from the edition by Elias Rivers. English translations are mine.

Is that purpose praise and seduction? Is the poem a personal lament? Why is the beloved lady represented as being not only violent (which can be explained as a rhetorical expression of the passion she provokes in the poet–persona) but inhumanly sadistic and brutal? Is the poet not attributing qualities to her that are so repugnant that she would find them repugnant? Is his doing so a function of his melancholia? How could he feel love for a woman whom he is able to describe in such terms, even figuratively, much less expect her to reciprocate his love? Does he hate her? Does he ambivalently both love and hate her? Does he hate himself for continuing to desire her and so projects his self-hatred onto her? Has the poet–persona's frustration or disillusionment provoked in him an aggressive anger that he now seeks to deny by attributing it to the lady, for how could the lady whose beauty has presumably moved him to desire her so intensely be anything but the complete opposite of the lady he describes? And what is the persona's "death?" Is it a stock motif, referring metaphorically and hyperbolically to the culmination of his unrequited passion,[9] or is it possible that, instead of being a reworking of a clichéd metaphor that has no reference to real life, the poem is indeed an elaboration of a traditional metaphor but a metaphor that has reference to such typical, universal experiences in real life as extreme disillusionment in love, depressive anxiety, and the morbid self-affliction that can result from the frustration of an aggressive libido? What can we infer from the poem as to the persona's psychological state and the nature of his predicament? And the lady, if she is neither someone we can identify in Garcilaso's life nor a lady from real life, does that circumstance mean that "she" has no reality as a threatening presence in the persona's tormented mind? Is she a real, inaccessible beloved lady at all, or is she the sinister personification of a tendency within the persona's own psyche, as he struggles furiously with uncontrollable desires and morbid fears? To what extent is this poem tragic (elegiac) and to what extent is it satirical? That is, ought we to feel the pathos of the devoted poet–lover's "masochistic" attitude of helpless submission and overlook the bizarre reversal of roles whereby the poet has become like the passive, weak, small female while the lady is imaged as a tyrannical and domineering male, or should we see all these elements of the poem as representing an ironic, quasi-humorous, urbane, and sophisticated wit that is playing on the courtly-love model it is calculated to query? As Northrop Frye has noted in relation to forced conceits in poems of paradox, "the

---

[9] See Whinnom, *La poesía amatoria*, 122–23, for a list of the different ways that the association of love in the *cancionero* tradition can have meaning.

paradox is among other things often a paradox of feeling as well, so that we are sometimes in doubt whether to 'take' the poem seriously or humorously" (*Anatomy of Criticism*, 299). In sum, although Sonnet 2 is an elaboration of an established metaphor, can it not also have far-reaching and important implications that are relevant to real life, implications that explain why the poem and that metaphor have remained a subject of interest until the present day?

I have no wish to minimize the learned contributions of previous Garcilaso scholars. After all, since interpretation is largely subjective, there are no provable answers to the above questions. From that point of view, such questions can even be considered impertinent. It may well be that if the poem afforded answers to such questions, it would lose its emotional power. Regarding the subject of dreams, Adler observed, "it occurred to me one day that perhaps the real significance of a dream is that it not be understood; that perhaps there is a dynamism of the mind working to baffle us; and that ... the purpose of a dream is achieved by the use of emotion and mood rather than reason and judgement."[10] Is a poem necessarily different in a fundamental way from a dream? If it is not, perhaps critics like Heiple who avoid "impertinent questions" are commendably respectful of the emotional dimension of a poem, wisely refraining from cluttering the experience of a work with myriad semantic possibilities. It is *my* approach to works like Sonnet 2, not Heiple's, for example, that deviates from the norm and must be regarded as tentative and experimental, as its imperfect results will undoubtedly bear out. On the other hand, the answers to the questions I have raised about Sonnet 2 rely on interpreting the poem freely and contemporarily as metaphor and not just as metaphor enlisted in the service of conventional rhetoric. Paul Ricoeur cites Jean Coen in referring to metaphor itself as "a semantic impertinence, meaning by that the violation of the code of pertinence or relevance which rules the ascription of predicates in ordinary use" (*Freedom and Nature*, 144). The element of riddle in the language of poetry is based on associations, on prompting such associations in the process of what Frye refers to as thematic criticism's "allegorization" of literature (*Anatomy of Criticism*, 280, cf. 53). In this regard, I can justify my attempt at a new approach to interpreting Garcilaso by coinciding with Urban:

> To be aesthetic the object must be enjoyed for its own sake and not
> for its practical, cognitive, or existential implications. But *the impli-*

---

[10] Alfred Adler, *Individual Psychology* (New York: Basic, 1956), 360.

cations are still there. Without these implications there would be no meaning, for meaning is always reference. Without these implications the object would not be enjoyed — even for its own sake.[11]

As Frye points out, in lyric the primary interest is in *dianoia* — the meaning, idea, poetic thought, or theme (*Anatomy of Criticism*, 52). What I ultimately propose accomplishing in my discussion of Garcilaso is to go beyond *dianoia* in the sense of literal and descriptive meaning in order to address the dimensions of *dianoia* concerned with what Frye refers to as a work's thematic or formal meaning (its relation as a form of imagery to a potential commentary), archetypal meaning (its significance as a literary convention or genre, in this case as tragedy and satire), and anagogic meaning (its allegorical and ritual spiritual significance) (*Anatomy of Criticism*, 365).[12] Stated in another way, instead of being content with perceiving gnoseologically (in terms of what is known) that a given poem is as it is, I will attempt to accomplish the higher and far more complex task of understanding ontologically *why* a poem is as it is.[13]

In any case, while Lapesa's biographical chronology was directly questioned in the studies I have mentioned above,[14] both Goodwyn ("New Light") and Nadine Ly ("Garcilaso: Une autre trajectoire poétique," *Bulletin hispanique* 83 [1981]: 263–329) proposed different bases for similar chronologies (political and stylistic respectively); Antonio Prieto embraced Lapesa's perspective with such fervor as to verge on turning critical readings of Garcilaso into a sentimental romance, yet he also makes valuable points of his own; and Bernard Gicovate, though he summarily dismissed Lapesa's chronology of Garcilaso's works, continued to follow him in interpreting those works biographically.[15] Today the predominantly biographically-oriented stylistic or chronological approach to a content reading of Garcilaso's poetry remains essentially unsuperseded, even if the present tendency is to concentrate on intertextual issues.

---

[11] W. M. Urban, *Language and Reality: The Philosophy of Language and the Principles of Symbolism* (London: Unwin, 1951), 460 (emphasis in original).

[12] Frye defines "anagogic" in terms that establish a modern parallel to its proper sense, which I have attempted to represent with my own definition.

[13] For a discussion of ontology as addressing the being of objects as opposed to gnoseology as addressing only the knowledge of objects, see Hartmann, *Ethics*, 1: 305–7.

[14] See note 3.

[15] See Antonio Prieto, *Garcilaso de la Vega* (Madrid: S.G.E.L., 1975), *passim*, and Bernard Gicovate, *Garcilaso de la Vega* (Boston: Twayne, 1975), 51.

Heiple, for example, objects to Lapesa's biographical chronology of Garcilaso's poems only insofar as it postulates expressions of sincere emotion on the part of Garcilaso himself seen as a real person, as opposed to seeing the poetry's sincerity as rhetorical language on the part of the poetic persona (*Garcilaso*, 8, 14, 20, 72). Hence the biographically-oriented and chronological approach to reading Garcilaso continues to be used, but it is a "bad fit," which is why critical studies such as the present one attempt to pass beyond the current erudition that emphasizes that poetry's intertextuality, analyzes its elegance of form, and situates it in relation to a profile of the world of litterateurs and formal literary trends in which Garcilaso moved,[16] and to turn instead to an effort to find meaningful ways further to fathom the sophistication of expressive resources, the uncanny power, and the human depth of some of Garcilaso's more intriguing individual works. In Navarrete's words, "Freed up of the trajectory, post-Lapesan Garcilaso criticism can open up new issues in both source scholarship and interpretation" (*Orphans of Petrarch*, 93).

The present study relies more on the view that the lady is a conventional metaphor than on speculations concerning the influence of a real lady on Garcilaso's creative activity. On the other hand, to identify her merely as the ideal, archetypal beloved lady (the stereotyped love-object of a stereotyped persona who is a displacement of the real poet himself) would be a truism as well as an oversimplification that would have little value for understanding what makes poetry great. If, as the Scottish psychoanalyst Ronald Fairbairn holds, the libidinal need for good love-objects is the primary life-drive,[17] a poem that treats an individual's arduous quest for love can be seen in broad, metaphorical terms as representing on a microcosmic scale "man's," i.e., humankind's, struggle for spiritual rebirth, for the fulfilment of human identity or human destiny. Hence, in an effort to transcend a reading based on a concern for finite individual experience, my general premise will be that elegiac love lyric in the Renaissance displays the anxiety that authors such as Nikolaus Pevsner, Arnold Hauser, Wylie Sypher, Jacques Bousquet, Frederick Artz, Roy Daniells, and Daniel Rowland have seen as

---

[16] Recent major contributions of this type are Heiple, *Garcilaso*; Navarrete, *Orphans of Petrarch*; and Cruz, *Imitación y transformación*. Using perspectives of intertextuality, they all reconstruct with an impressive command of factual information the literary environment in which Garcilaso moved.

[17] Harry Guntrip, *Personality, Structure, and Human Interaction* (New York: International Universities Press, 1977), 290.

characteristic of Western culture in the early modern period,[18] and that it displays that anxiety in much the way Wilhelm Reich saw masochistic character formations: as an unusual proneness to anxiety rooted in an unfulfillable need for love.[19] Seen in that light, elegiac love lyric can be considered in terms that are consistent with Jacques Bousquet's observation that the atrocious cruelty of the sixteenth century is evidenced in artistic depictions of sadism.[20] To that extent my perspective coincides with Elias Rivers's view that Garcilaso's *Canción* 1 depicts sadism on the part of the lady and masochism on the part of the poet. The first stanza of *Canción* 1, which I will consider in more detail below, is as follows:

> Si a la región desierta, inhabitable
> por el hervor del sol demasïado
> y sequedad d'aquella arena ardiente,
> o a la que por el yelo congelado
> y rigurosa nieve es intractable,
> del todo inhabitada de la gente,
>   por algún accidente
> o caso de fortuna desastrada
>   me fuéssedes llevada,
> y supiesse que allá vuestra dureza
>   estava en su crüeza,
> allá os yría a buscar como perdido,
> hasta morir a vuestros pies tendido. . . .

[If to the desert region, uninhabitable because of seething excess of sun and dryness of burning sand, or to that which because of freezing cold and harsh snow is unyielding, completely uninhabited by people, by some accident, or occurrence of miserable fortune, you

---

[18] For a summary of the views of those authors see James V. Mirollo, *Mannerism and Renaissance Poetry* (New Haven: Yale University Press, 1984), 31–35, 40–43 and "The Mannered and the Mannerist in Late Renaissance Literature," in *The Meaning of Mannerism* ed. F. W. Robinson et al. (Hanover, NH: University Press of New England, 1972), 7–24, here 13.

[19] Shirley Panken, *The Joy of Suffering* (New York: Aronson, 1973), 38–39.

[20] Jacques Bousquet, *Mannerism* (New York: Brazillier, 1964), 205–14.

Ire taken from me, and I knew that your harshness were there in all its cruelty, I would go look for you there like one lost, until dying outstretched at your feet.]

Later lines in the poem are "yo estoy aquí tendido, / mostrándos de mi muerte las señales, / y vos viviendo sólo de mis males" ["I am here outstretched, / displaying to you the signs of my death, / and you living only on my suffering"]. Elias Rivers, speaking of the poem as a whole, observes that ... the poet ... pleads for mercy. ... But at present the lady's sadism exceeds his masochism. ... It may seem anachronistic to apply to this poem such modern terms as sadism and masochism, but this is precisely the vicious circle of self-destruction which the poetry evokes (*Garcilaso de la Vega: Poems,* 38–39). The present analysis of poems by Garcilaso queries and finally coincides with Rivers's observation, yet it seeks to elaborate explanations of the masochism in question in more specific terms and to advance consideration of that subject to dimensions of the cultural–historical, the literary–symbolic, the psycho-dynamic, and the axiological. The justification for postulating a relationship between the phenomenon of masochism and, for example, the historical period of the author is that doing so opens up the possibility of interpreting that phenomenon in broader terms, terms that transcend concern for an isolated individual. Alfred Adler has referred to the masochistic transformation of aggressive drives as "a simile, a symbol."[21] If Adler "read" masochistic behavior patterns symbolically in the interest of understanding the adaptive mechanisms of individuals in the real world, it should be even more natural for masochism to be interpreted in broadly figurative terms in the formal-descriptive and interpretive exegesis of poetry. The alternative to interpreting masochism metaphorically — i.e., the practice of considering a poem's strong emphasis on masochistic behavior in a strictly clinical light — is a continuation or an extension of the biographically oriented approach, which tacitly identifies the poetic persona with the author himself in order to justify emphasizing speculation on issues such as when a poem was written or the real identity of the lady to whom it refers. Yet seeing poetry as expressing masochistic *fantasies* that are subject to allegorical interpretation does not necessarily imply that the underlying pain and suffering have no real basis. Art is a

---

[21] Alfred Adler, *The Neurotic Constitution* (1926) (North Stratford, NH: Ayer, 1988), 368, n. 2; Alfred Adler, *The Individual Psychology of Alfred Adler*, ed. H. L. Ansbacher (New York: Basic, 1926), 426.

sublimation of reality; for this reason Arnold Hauser, for example, is able to view the manneristic art of the sixteenth century, which he considers the precursor of modern art, to be rooted in the widespread alienation experienced during the period of acute cultural crisis known as the High Renaissance.[22] In analyzing the connection between elements of Garcilaso's poetry and attitudes that correspond to the modern concept "masochism," I will begin by discussing the previously cited first stanza of *Canción* 1 and to Sonnet 2. I will then refer to allegorical poems by San Juan de la Cruz and Santa Teresa de Jesús.

§

Psychoanalysts have associated such a wide range of phenomena with the term "masochism" that it is hard to give a unitary definition of it or to characterize its essential features. What seems to emerge consistently in behavior referred to as "masochistic" was observed by Freud, who defined masochism as "sadism turned round upon the subject's own ego," i.e., the gratification of self or satisfaction of some psychic need as a result of experiencing the aggression that one has provoked in another.[23] If one considers aggressive impulses to be associated with the libido, as Freud does, masochism will be seen as largely erotogenic and as being related to auto-eroticism; however, the masochist is not driven by a craving for erotic pleasure. As Ludwig Eidelberg points out, individuals can be referred to as a masochist only if they are interested in aims that are unpleasant to them, even if they enjoy the power that they have to provoke their own punishment at the hands of another.[24]

---

[22] Arnold Hauser, *Mannerism* (London: Routledge, 1965), 1: 111, 355–58.

[23] "Instincts and Their Vicissitudes," in *Complete Works, Standard Edition* 14 (London: Hogarth Press, 1957), 109–40, here 127.

[24] Quoted s.v. "Masochism," in *Encyclopedia of Psychoanalysis*, 233. And Freud writes, "... of course, it is not the pain itself which is enjoyed, but the accompanying sexual excitation. ...": "Instincts and their Vicissitudes," in *Complete Works, Standard Edition* 14: 109–14, here 129. So it is that Arnold Cooper states, "Masochistic suffering is a condition for pleasure, not a source of pleasure. That is, masochists do not enjoy the suffering per se; rather they willingly endure the pain as an unavoidable guilty ransom for access to forbidden or undeserved pleasures": "The Narcissistic-Masochistic Character," in *Masochism: Current Psychoanalytic Perspectives*, ed. R. A. Glick et al. (Hillsdale, NJ: Analytic Press, 1988), 117–38, here 120.

In considering the subjective psychological basis of the relationship between masochistic fantasy and poetry's depiction of the beloved lady as a cruel tormentor, one must also consider a possible social basis as well, that is, the role of masochism in the self's relationship with others. As we shall see, when interpreted as a function of masochism, the figure of the cruel lady assumes the character of a personified projection of the poet's own aggression, of his will to domination or mastery. Such self-identification with another is a characteristic feature of sexual love. Thus Hegel observed, "We see only ourselves in the beloved, whom we in turn, nevertheless, see as not ourselves — a wonder which I cannot comprehend"[25]; and Scheler noted, "Eros is the ultimate source of all identification and always remains so."[26] Garcilaso represents that experience of identifying with the beloved in the following lines from Sonnet 4:

> ... mi alma os ha cortado a su medida;
> por hábito del alma misma os quiero;
> cuanto tengo confieso yo deberos;
> por vos nací, por vos tengo la vida, ...

[my soul has cut you to its size; by/to be a habit of my very soul I love/want you; everything I have I confess I owe you; I was born because of/for you, because of/for you I have life].

What gives the phenomenon of masochism its complexity is that it has both an aggressive and a submissive meaning. In Renaissance lyric, the submissive meaning predominates on the surface, the primary focus being on the poet's jeopardy; but the lady's cruel aggression is referred to as the fictional explanation for that same jeopardy. Actually, as I have mentioned, analytic psychology would tend to regard "her" aggression as a projection of his own, which would mean that he fantasizes his own submission as hers. A different issue, and one that I will address below, is the metaphorical significance of such sadomasochistic elements.

---

[25] Merold Westphal, *History and Truth in Hegel's Phenomenology* (Atlantic Highlands, NJ: Humanities Press, 1979), 131.

[26] Max Scheler, *The Nature of Sympathy*, trans. P. Heath (London: Routledge, 1954), 92.

When current analyses of masochism are freely adapted to the relationship between the poet–persona and his disdainful lover, the images of the persona's own submission can be seen to have the following possible explanations, beyond the above-mentioned desire to compensate for feeling a lack of mastery by provoking an aggressive reaction in another:[27]

a. The poet–persona's submission is a means of mollifying his beloved in order to win her. (from C. Brenner, describing one general approach to sadomasochistic theory: Panken, *Joy of Suffering*, 1)

b. The persona's frustrations at being rejected have occasioned his experiencing unconscious fantasies of humiliating and triumphing over another, and he identifies with the figure of the lady in his fantasies. (from C. Brenner, describing another general approach to sadomasochistic theory: Panken, *Joy of Suffering*, 2)

c. Because of ambivalent behavior on the part of an idealized figure to whom the persona had related in an attitude of pleasurable obedience, the persona has introjected that figure as a quasi-demon or a witch. (from S. Ferenczi: Panken, *Joy of Suffering*, 2)

d. The persona defends against the dangers and anxieties associated with identity diffusion through the self-definition and self boundaries afforded by the self-

---

[27] The method I have used in elaborating the following list has primarily been to follow the survey of theories of masochism as they appear in Panken, *The Joy of Suffering*. This adaptation corresponds more closely to the character of Renaissance love lyric and presents those theories more intelligibly. As they are recast, the theories are not intended to reflect more than approximately the precise terms of the theories articulated by the authors in a different connection (not in relation to literature) and whose names I give in parentheses, followed by a colon and the references to the pages where they have been cited by Panken. I have generally not included in the list (a) explanations that conceive pain as a source of erotic pleasure or sexual excitement/stimulation (as opposed to a source of "sexual arousal" or "awakening," which imply a less profound shift from quiescence into activity, or a source of the intensification of sexual stimulation) or (b) explanations developed in terms of infantile sexuality and childhood trauma (explanations such as a need for punishment concerning unconscious incestuous guilt, a compulsive clinging to illness, and castration anxiety) simply because they seem to me to be relatively implausible, especially when applied to the poetry in question, and because they deviate too much from classical literature's tendency to avoid highly idiosyncratic portraiture.

inflicted pain that he experiences as a result of his preference for an antagonistic relationship. (from N. Fischer: Panken, *Joy of Suffering*, 3)

e. The persona's extreme aggression prompts a fantasy by which he relishes triumph in the power of self-destructiveness. (from O. Kernberg: Panken, *Joy of Suffering*, 5–6)

f. Prolonged association of lustful thought of the extremely vain beloved lady with the idea of being tyrannized has led to the lustful emotion's finally being transferred to the tyranny itself. (from R. Krafft-Ebing: Panken, *Joy of Suffering*, 13)

g. The persona's fantasy is a means of fomenting in himself feelings of aggression in order to compensate for actual or threatened general traumatic helplessness. (from L. Stone: Panken, *Joy of Suffering*, 34)

h. The persona's masochistic fantasies are manifestations of a submissive attitude that has ensued as a result of his having had to repress his aggressiveness. (from Freud on "feminine masochism": Panken, *Joy of Suffering*, 34)

i. The persona is an intimidated individual who seeks to cope with life and its dangers by gaining safety through ecstatic abandonment to misery and self-degradation. (from K. Horney: Panken, *Joy of Suffering*, 34)

j. The poet–persona's love is perversion to the extent that his sexual gratification depends on the feeling of his own insignificance as compared to the magnificence of his partner. Such love is a transitional stage to masochism. (from O. Fenichel: Panken, *Joy of Suffering*, 35–36)

k. Instead of the sadistic lady being a projection of the persona's own aggression, she is a real person and her aggression is real: it has been deliberately provoked by the aggressive persona seeking revenge on the lady for her having refused or failed to gratify him. The persona's masochism is due to guilt that he experiences as a result of his provocation's being directed toward those who are loved and from whom love is demanded. (from W. Reich: Panken, *Joy of Suffering*, 39)

l. The masochistic poet–persona seeks to parade his harmless ineptness, loving generosity, and suffering with the aim of concealing his aggressive, ambitious, revengeful, defiant impulses, which are revealed in the sadistic fantasies in his poetry. Also, by disgracing and humiliating himself, he takes the role of authority and chastises himself, thereby suspending punishment for his own aggressive self-aggrandizement. (from T. Reik: Panken, *Joy of Suffering*, 40) I. Bieber (50) also

Interpreting "Masochistic" Rescue Fantasies 69

considers the masochistic response to constitute a typical defense against anticipation of injury for self-enhancing behavior.

m. The masochistic persona subconsciously knows that, since love cannot be commanded, attempting to force others to give him love will have the opposite effect and be self-defeating. Not only does "Look how miserable I am" mean "Look how miserable you made me," but it also reveals an ambivalence toward the unavailable loved one, an ambivalence consisting in a simultaneous desire to use submissive behavior for purposes of blackmailing and a desire to torture sadistically and ultimately destroy the frustrating object. Also, the obsessive self-torture experienced as a result of alienating the loved one is a substitute for her warming proximity. (from O. Fenichel: Panken, *Joy of Suffering*, 41)

n. The persona's sadistic fantasies in which he envisions himself as victim are essentially defensive in that they are motivated by righteous indignation at retaliative refusal and rebuff that he unconsciously provoked due to previous experiences of wounds to his narcissistic megalomania. Because of his feeling victimized and self-pitying, his previous narcissism is to some degree restored. (from E. Bergler: Panken, *Joy of Suffering*, 50–51)

Some psychoanalytic explanations that may be applied to the imagery of a poet–persona's submission to a tyrannical lady seem particularly well-suited to a perspective emphasizing the increase in authoritarianism that characterizes the sixteenth century and the important role of the relationship between the poet as subject and his king or sovereign, i.e., emphasizing the power of the latter, who is displaced by the figure of the lady:[28]

o. The persona's fantasies of his own suffering and humiliation are motivated by a phobia of being tortured or punished in an uncontrollable way: his narcissistic mortification (extreme self-deprecation), in which he himself imaginatively creates

---

[28] See, for example, José Antonio Maravall, *Poder, honor y élites en el siglo XVII* (Madrid: siglo XXI, 1979), and Lawrence Stone, "The Rise of the Nuclear Family in early Modern England: The Patriarchal Stage," in *The Family in History*, ed. C. Z. Rosenberg (Philadelphia: University of Pennsylvania Press, 1975), 13–57 for discussion of the reinforcement of patriarchy and the trend toward authoritarianism in the sixteenth century.

scenes of his own punishment, both alleviate his apprehensions and appease a strong and powerful parent/sovereign whose affection/protection can be purchased only at the price of abject surrender. (from L. Eidelberg: Panken, *Joy of Suffering*, 52–53)

p. The persona's images of his own self-destruction have the unconscious aim of serving as self-preparation for fantasies of being incorporated, in the sense of achieving "a secure and physically gratifying union with an omnipotent figure." (from A. Blumstein: Panken, *Joy of Suffering*, 53)

q. Loss of a narcissistic and depriving parental figure/sovereign occurred as a result of the narcissism of that same figure and led to anxiety and to introjection of the object through a merging of self-image and ambivalent object. The contempt that the parental figure displayed with regard to the devalued child/subject and the hatred that the latter feels toward the parent/sovereign as a result are experienced as the sadistic hatred that the idealized self of the child/subject feels toward his own devalued ego. Thus also, the parent–child/subject–sovereign relationship is regressively restored. (from I. Bernstein: Panken, *Joy of Suffering*, 54)

Since the concern of the present study is amatory lyric, explanations that take into account the libidinization of suffering will be particularly relevant. Probably because masochism was initially viewed (by Krafft-Ebing and in Freud's early views) solely in terms of sexual perversion, the view that masochism is somehow related to sexual experience continues to enjoy considerable prestige. So it is that Arnold Cooper writes:

> While many definitions of masochism have been attempted, Brenner's (1959) definition has remained authoritative. He defined masochism as "the seeking of unpleasure, by which is meant physical or mental pain, discomfort or wretchedness, for the sake of *sexual* pleasure, with the qualification that either the seeking or the pleasure or both may often be unconscious rather than conscious." ("The Narcissistic-Masochistic Character," 121)

There is one explanation for masochistic character formations that has the advantage of combining the subject–sovereign relationship with libidinization of suffering:

r. The persona displaces his identification with an offended parent/sovereign by his fantasized identification with a beloved yet aloof lady, thus agreeing to the humiliation of his own punishment while, at the same time, sexual arousal affords him relief from the shame that he feels as a result of his offenses. (from H. B. Lewis: Panken, *Joy of Suffering*, 38–39)

In relation to the poems considered in the present chapter, a particularly suggestive approach to the specific phenomenon of eroticized sadomasochism is found in the gratification that the sadomasochistic pair experience in relation to bondage and release from bondage.[29] In commenting on feminine masochism, Annie Reich views the humiliations to which the submissive lover acquiesces as part of a love ritual, a scenario in which what is at first destroyed is later restored: one must first be castrated and destroyed in order to be loved afterward (Panken, *Joy of Suffering*, 35). S. Olinick and Stuart Asch have seen rescue fantasies as being rooted in the masochistic personality's having developed at childhood a compulsive need to repair the injured narcissism of a psychologically or physically dependent parental figure, such as a depressed mother (S. Asch, "The Analytic Concepts of Masochism," in *Masochism*, ed. Glick et al., 93–115, here 109). Stanley Coen believes that in sadomasochistic object relations, where hostile aggression is mixed with seductive fantasy, projective identification serves to allow the individual to disown temporarily negative aspects of the self: "The other is made the 'bad one,' who then must seek absolution and loving forgiveness from oneself. Phases of sexualized reunion are a means of making each partner feel forgiven, no longer bad, because badness is made not to count" ("Sadomasochistic Excitement," in *Masochism*, ed. Glick et al., 43–59, here 47).

Poetic imagery likewise makes use of rescue fantasies. In broad terms, instances of works expressing hope for salvation from unredeemed suffering abound in Romance literature in the Renaissance, both religious and secular. Obvious examples are the many secular works that develop the general theme of a longing for deliverance from agony leading to union with the beloved or with an equivalent idealized sphere — works such as the many poetic adaptations of Psalm 137 (136), "Super flumina Baby-

---

[29] For a survey of instances of the plot motif of bondage in seventeenth-century Spanish narrative, see George Camamis, *Estudios sobre el cautiverio en el Siglo de Oro* (Madrid: Gredos, 1977).

lonis" (the principal Peninsular versions being those of Camões and Montemayor),[30] elegiac pastoral romances such as Montemayor's *Diana* and Bernardim Ribeiro's *Menina e Moça (O Livro das Saudades)*,[31] Fray Luis de León's "Noche serena" and his "En la Ascensión,"[32] and poems that I shall consider by San Juan and Santa Teresa. Fantasies concerning release from the tyranny of unfulfilment and suffering are central to all these works. One could even venture to apply Annie Reich's observations concerning feminine masochism and speculate that in the literature in question "the greater the unhappiness over abuse or separation, the greater the joy of reunion" (Panken, *Joy of Suffering*, 35). A poetry in which relations between the poet–persona and the lady are contemplated as being sharply antagonistic and the lady is contemplated as being cruelly malevolent can be seen as representing a ritualized pattern of sexual arousal, an elaborate prelude to sexual seduction/reconciliation. Such a prelude can also be seen as serving the purpose of repairing the injured narcissism of both partners: the persona's insofar as the "injury" consists in his love's not having been reciprocated; the lady's insofar as the intrusive poet is an Actaeon archetype and the modest lady is a Diana archetype.[33] The theme of painful ordeal as a ritual prelude to rebirth/regeneration and sexual gratification was wittily developed as an ironic parody of the *pastourelle* by Juan Ruiz, in the *serrana* episodes of the *Libro de buen amor*, as well as by Góngora, in his well-known sonnet concerning a sick, lost traveler who is given refuge that will cost his life:

> Descaminado, enfermo, peregrino,
> en tenebrosa noche, con pie incierto
> la confusión pisando del desierto,
> voces en vano dio, pasos sin tino. . . .

---

[30] For a survey of poetic adaptations of Psalm 137 (136) both in and outside of Spain see Bryant L. Creel, *The Religious Poetry of Jorge de Montemayor* (London: Tamesis, 1981), 132–65.

[31] See chapters 8 and 9 below for moral-psychological and cultural-historical analyses of *Menina e Moça* and the *Diana* respectively.

[32] A review of scholarship on "En la Ascensión" and a new and broader interpretation of that poem are given below in chapter 6.

[33] In the myth, Actaeon is the hunter who surprised the goddess Diana disrobed on the bank of a pool where she was bathing. She transformed him into a stag and when he tried to run away his own hunting dogs tracked him down and killed him. See Brumble, *Classical Myths and Legends*, 5–6.

[Off the road, sick, pilgrim, in gloomy night, with uncertain foot, treading the confusion of the desert, called out in vain, stepped aimlessly . . .]³⁴

In the works by Juan Ruiz and Góngora, the poet's rescue leads to his "sexual bondage" (a term advanced by Krafft-Ebing), and he is able to "commute his punishment" and purchase his release only by affording sexual satisfaction to his captor.

To disclose an instance of truly masochistic libidinization of suffering, it is necessary to cite a more intense and transporting, even ecstatic, experience of love–anguish, one that is so powerful as to be analogous both to death and to sexual climax, even if the pain itself is not identified with sexual stimulation. Examples of sadomasochistic rescue fantasies containing the requisite voluptuous intensity of suffering are the first stanza of Garcilaso's *Canción* 1, referred to above, and his Sonnet 2. In the beginning stanza of *Canción* 1, cited toward the beginning of my chapter, the poet projects his own plight and the fantasy of his rescue as being those of his beloved, just as in Sonnet 2 his own aggressive libido is projected as the lady's. In attempting to apply psycho-dynamics to a reading of poems such as *Canción* 1, it is important not to lose sight of the rhetorical dimension. The poet–persona's expression of a willingness to "masochistically" endure with limitless patience any hardship, pain, humiliation, or sadistic behavior directed at himself makes him appear self-sacrificing and undemanding. What is meant by his compulsion to appease, by his sparing no effort to prove that he wants nothing for himself, is that his interest in the lady is devoid of self-serving impulses, that his aggressive (self-asserting) libido is completely subordinated to a desire to place himself at the service of the lady. His willingness to spend himself in that service is evidence of his high moral rank and his worthiness to be loved. Furthermore, in his attitude of self-effacement and benign docility, he imagines the lady to "step on him" and thus to occasion his innocent suffering and yet remain callous. In that way he justifies feeling unfairly neglected if the affection he seeks is not forthcoming, and by appearing as a victim of ingratitude, he can hope — along lines that are consistent with and even enlist Christian morality's emphasis on compassion — that the pity he arouses will prevail over the lady's modesty as well as prompt her to reveal her own need for love as well.

---

³⁴ Quotations from Góngora are from Rivers, ed. *Poesía lírica del Siglo de Oro*; translations are mine.

The remainder of *Canción* 1 develops the idea that, given the identification with another that is basic to love, the persona's gesture of protesting the cruelty he is suffering at the lady's hands is a way that he hopes will spare him the pain of co-experiencing her future agony of remorse for her disdainful treatment of him. The implication is that, far from regarding the lady as an antagonist, as appears to be the case on the literal level, the poet wants to rescue her from the future consequences of the suffering she will cause him. If we do not take such a poem "at face value" and interpret it in biographical or pseudo-biographical terms, the cruel lady can be seen as a personification of the poet–persona's own "tyrannically" obstinate will. Likewise, if she is represented as being in a position of jeopardy, that jeopardy can be seen as a projection of the persona's own unfulfillment and suffering. The first stanza of *Canción* 1 is a metaphor for finding oneself in the grip of a consuming, fateful passion the pain of which is as cruel as if it were being inflicted by an enemy whose unrelenting malevolence is comparable to the inhospitable settings described. Therefore, the fantasized rescue of the lady has the significance of the lady's rescuing the poet from his mortal despair at her disaffection. The subtle elegance of heartfelt flattery implicit in such a formula is certainly the essence of this poem's greatness. Again, the poem ends with the poet despairing of a redeeming impulse of compassion on the part of the beautifully sovereign lady, and he contents himself with death as he contemplates a final act of devout self-sacrifice. Is such a stance on the part of the poet ultimately no more than a thinly veiled, semi-ironic rhetorical disguise for a sophisticated rhetoric of seduction? It would be an oversimplification to assume that the persona's love can be reduced to self-seeking egoism. For an understanding of the elevation, universality, and enduring greatness of Garcilaso and the poets who wrote in his tradition, it is important to take into account, for example, Scheler's observation that love belongs to death in that love establishes the necessary conditions of sacrifice, of the loss of substance and the loss of power in procreation for the whole (*Centennial Essays*, ed. M. Frings [The Hague: Nijoff, 1974], 132).

In Sonnet 2, where, instead of the lady, the persona represents himself as the afflicted party — as a captive military enemy of the lady — the theme of the persona's rescue fantasy can be seen more clearly. The persona despairs of being released from bondage while he is still alive; instead, given the extreme sadistic cruelty of his beloved captor, he contemplates rescue by death as the only release that remains available to him. Hyperbolic rhetoric notwithstanding, the persona's reference to his having been brought to tears makes the evocations of his pain increase in authenticity, so that his unhappiness seems to be genuine despair and not mere self-indulgence in pain, and even less does it appear a cover for the crude egoism of the instincts. Yet one cannot underestimate the unpredictable character of such an aggressive intensity of passion. His having fantasized a situation in which a person who refuses to satisfy his need for love and intimacy has made him the object of her hatred and aggression naturally leads us to suspect that his attributing negative qualities to her is a result of his own resentment at frustration. And since a feeling of security is an important component of the satisfaction whenever a person receives love,[35] the poet–persona's representation of himself as being in a position of extreme jeopardy can be interpreted as his having translated her failure to gratify him into fantasies of his being threatened by persecution and violent death. From this point of view, the event of the persona's having transformed the real lady into a sinister fantasy, a bad internal object, is a result of her remaining exciting to him at the same time that she is frustrating, and the poet's reproaches against this introjected object can be seen as self-reproaches, a sort of masochistic self-loathing — either because of his embarrassment at feeling dependent on the being who rejects him or because the loss of that person has brought with it the loss of the part of his ego that identified with her and caused him to feel devalued and worthless. Likewise, his statement that he is willing to die before he renounces his love could be interpreted as a threat of self-punishment. But such painful effects of the subjection of one's will in love are not inconsistent with the courage that was referred to by Don Quijote and that I mentioned earlier.

I have suggested that the persona's acceptance of self-affliction in poems such as those discussed so far need not be seen as masochism in the clinical sense, but can rather be interpreted as a broad metaphor that expresses and represents the situation of the individual in the historical period when the poems were written. If the motif of submissiveness is interpreted in that way, the poetic utterance would not be seen as a means of providing compensatory ego-gratification or the gratification of a need. Yet if the utterance is not interpreted as serving the ego, as being primarily an attempt to have the beloved show the poet more kindness, the poet's willing subjection of his will would appear to be genuinely representing a desire to place himself at the service of the beloved. From that point of view, the exaggerated images of suffering and cruelty have the rhetorical purpose of evoking in poignant, vivid terms the degree of the persona's self-effacing devotion, as well as of protesting the lady's painful obliviousness where he is concerned. But how can it be known that what would might be called a

---

[35] Melanie Klein, *Love, Hate and Reparation* (London: Hogarth Press, 1967), 307.

"discourse of idealism" is not, like masochism, itself a form of self-serving manipulation, only now disguised with a greater degree of subtlety? One is tempted to respond to that question with observations such as that a great work of literature confronts readers with their own values in such a way that it tells them as much about themselves as it does about the work, that reality is what we make of it, and that for extreme skeptics all ideals are the cloak of a hidden egoism, whereas to the idealists — though their lives entail more risks and disappointments — there belongs the glory of having striven unselfishly for an ideal and sometimes even of having attained it.[36] The issue is ultimately whether psychoanalysis can be of any value for interpreting elegiac love lyric. In a sense lyric and psychoanalysis are natural bedfellows insofar as they both use metaphor to represent and analyze individual experience. It could rightly be said that modern literature is as concerned with psychological phenomena as psychoanalysis is poetic.[37] On the other hand, the aims of each, what they identify as the relevant con-

---

[36] That perspective, in a much more elaborated form, is developed in another treatment that I have given to the theme of the present study in B. L. Creel, "Canción I y Soneto II de Garcilaso y el problema del masoquismo en la lírica amatoria renacentista" in *Studia Aurea: Actas del III Congreso de la Asociación Internacional Siglo de Oro* (Toulouse–Pamplona: GRISO-LEMSO, 1996), 1: 299–307.

[37] See Suzanne R. Kirschner, *The Religious and Romantic Origins of Psychoanalysis* (New York: Cambridge University Press, 1996), 8–23 on the ways in which psychological knowledge is "literalized metaphor." Also see below, chapter 10, note 25 for Freud's observations on his own metapsychology and Einstein's physics. Incidentally, the validity of Kirschner's general thesis — that psychoanalysis is in its essence non-rationalistic — must be weighed in relation to the value of its subjectivist, Heideggerian concept of rationalism (see her definition of "objectivism" [7] together with Werkmeister, *Hartmann's New Ontology*, 5–11). Actually (the metaphorical nature of all language notwithstanding), psychoanalysis is a form of speculative rationalism concerned with metaphysical realities, and although its arguments are not subject to empirical proof, it is not, for that reason, any less objective or reliable than any other form of knowledge of non-material being. For the criterion of truth, see Werkmeister, *Hartmann's New Ontology*, 28–31. Skeptics have always tried to prove the relative nature of reason. In Garcilaso's day, the leading subjectivist and relativist movement was nominalism. For similarities between nominalism and, for example, structuralism, see below, 271 and chapter 10, n. 21. On the primarily metaphoric nature not just of language but of human cognition in general, see George Lakoff and Mark Johnson, *Metaphors We Live By* (Chicago: University of Chicago Press, 1980), and R. W. J. Gibbs, *The Poetics of Mind* (New York: Cambridge University Press, 1994). See also Antonio Damasio's observation that even words and arbitrary symbols organized in our consciousness exist as auditory symbols or visual images — topographically organized

Interpreting "Masochistic" Rescue Fantasies 77

texts of individual experience, are different. Like all tragic or tragi-comic art, the aim of elegiac love lyric is the stimulation of ethical and aesthetic emotions and of a sense of the complexity of life. What is "aesthetic" varies from age to age, but in Renaissance literature much emphasis was placed on celebrating exemplary character values such as devotion in love, a virile courage to suffer (in both men and women), and vital intensity of amorous passion. The aim of psychoanalysis is only covertly axiological, since its standard of "normality" is successful adaptation to the real world. Its emphasis is on the pathological, primary emotions and drives, basic adaptive mechanisms, and, in general, practical reality. Within the sphere of higher, "spiritual" values, psychoanalysis is limited to the cognitive values, whereas literature combines the latter with attention to the aesthetic and ethical values.

In the light of those distinctions, can the explanations for masochistic character formations listed above be applied to these poems? A number of the elements of those theories are suggestive indeed. However, for my specific purposes, their usefulness presents difficulties: they either represent the lover/"masochist" as being ultimately self-serving and manipulative, even if he acts unconsciously and is also manipulating himself, or they represent him as an innocent victim of circumstances beyond his control. The representation of him as manipulative necessitates attributing a satirical dimension to the poetry,[38] a dimension that would have to be seen as co-existing with

---

representations: *Descartes' Error: Emotion, Reason, and the Human Brain* (New York: Avon, 1994), 106.

[38] Note that in Panken's general comments concerning the theories of masochism, a healthy idealism on the part of the "masochist" would have no place: "In examining the literature on masochism, one notes two distinct tendencies. Some view the masochist predominantly as an intensely suffering person, victimized by the cruelties of his environment. Others see him as blackmailing, coercive, or paranoid, as someone who, through suffering, is excused from taking part in life and usually manipulates others into taking care of him" (*Joy of Suffering*, 125). There is an element of self-aggrandizement in the consciousness of the value of idealism that is implied in the tenacity with which the poet clings to that same idealism, an element that is more consistent with sadism than with either of the masochistic personality's two basic tendencies: the passive acquiescence of the victim and the manipulative coercion of the complainer. "The masochistic character, unlike the sadist, is, for the most part, completely unaware of his provocativeness. The sadistic personality possesses a weak, impotent, or crippled sense of self but is intent on self-aggrandizement and the acquisition of force" (Panken, *Joy of Suffering*, 125). Given Freud's definition of masochism as sadism directed against the self and the idea that sadism and masochism are phases of each other, it should not surprise us that the masochist has certain

its elevated tone (a surprising phenomenon that I will discuss shortly). That tone is derived from the ultimately enriching character of the love that is depicted, as commemorated by Hegel in the following passage:

> Only in love are we one with the object, neither dominating it nor dominated by it. . . . [Love is] a reciprocal giving and taking, [and] the lover who takes is not thereby made richer than the other. He is enriched indeed, but only so much as the other is. So too the giver does not make himself poorer. By giving to the other he has to the same extent enhanced his own treasure.[39]

The elevation of tone is also derived from the character of disinterested love as a high virtue and from the lover's willingness to sacrifice himself to that value, the quality that is recognized in the aforementioned observation by Don Quijote in his reference to the lover's "courage." The second perspective, that the masochist is a victim of circumstances, when applied to the poetry in question, has the drawback that it relies too heavily on a perspective that Wilhelm Dilthey perceptively held to be incompatible with Renaissance tragic art, namely, that the individual (the tragic hero in particular) is seen as a historical being who is shaped, conditioned, by social circumstances.[40] In

---

traits of the sadist. On the other hand, that circumstance could also be interpreted to indicate the limitations inherent in a conceptual framework based on a distinction between "sadism" and "masochism." So it is that, rather than attempting to suggest that the concept of masochism can provide a means of exhaustively analyzing the poetry in question, I regard that concept to be useful only for understanding certain of its elements. It does not account for the poet's idealism, any more than the poet who portrays himself as a victim can be seen as a sadist (even though a sadist might be seen as a victim).

[39] Quoted by M. Westphal, *History and Truth in Hegel's Phenomenology* (Atlantic Highlands, NJ: Humanities Press, 1979), 131.

[40] "Shakespeare no conoce aún al hombre histórico, la condicionalidad de la vida no parece existir para él" ["Shakespeare is still not acquainted with historical man, the conditionality of life does not seem to exist for him"]: W. Dilthey, "Shakespeare y sus contemporáneos," in idem, *Literatura y fantasía* (1959), in *Obras completas*, trans. E. Urgana and C. Gerhard (México: Fondo de Cultura Económica, 1963), 9: 54–102; my translation. Dilthey also wrote: "Never at any time did he [man] show his formative and creative power so forcibly as when he shed his medieval chains and moved forward to the enjoyment of unlimited freedom — hot-bloodedly, passionately and with his imagination released. What happened then was not determined by previous circumstances, nor could it be explained

his literary representations, Renaissance man gloried in seeing himself as self-determined and accountable for his own actions. Works of literature are to a large extent determined by literary tradition and convention,[41] and in the heroic literature of the sixteenth century much romantic emphasis was placed on ideal values and on the individual's refusal to be determined from without or be hindered by any obstacle in the attainment of those values, much like Hegel's characterization of the tragic hero as a being who "in the face of the forces that crush him to death ... maintains untouched the freedom and the strength of his own will."[42] On the basis of the tradition of literary conventions in which Garcilaso's poems participate, the ideal value being affirmed can be understood to be not just static physical beauty but the goodness, humanity, and moral beauty represented in the ideal ethos of individual personality of the beloved — an ideal the devotion to which is deliberately evoked as being even more laudable because it remains undaunted by the radical resistance presented by the beloved lady's actual, empirical personality.[43] The lady's ideal beauty is subtly made known through a sophisticated use of what may perhaps be termed wittily ironic "metaphorical inversion," whereby the poet suggests what he wants to communicate by veiling it with images that represent the opposite. Her delicate humanity is presented as her brutal inhumanity because of the agonizing passion that it inspires. Thus, in addition to being metaphorical (as I shall discuss further below), such language has the advantage of being highly evocative: the unbearable torture of unfulfilled longing is evoked by representing the courageous recklessness of the persona's nobly passionate devotion as a morbid, "masochistic" disorder, and his anguish at finding the lady to be

---

by the social conditions. These only precipitate great historical actualities as the rays of the sun make flowers grow. ... The works of that time reveal an understanding of man as an individual which, so far, leaves any scientific analysis behind and, in a sense, will always do so. These works reveal that life and the emergence of individuals is unfathomable: "The Great Poetry of the Imagination," in *Selected Writings*, trans. H. P. Rickman (Cambridge University Press, 1976), 79–84, here 84.

[41] René Wellek and Austin Warren, *Theory of Literature*, 3rd ed. (New York: Harcourt, 1977), 78.

[42] A. C. Bradley, *Hegel's Theory of Tragedy*, ed. A. and H. Paolucci (New York: Harper & Row, 1962), 367–88, here 376.

[43] For a discussion of the distinction between the empirical personality and the ideal ethos of personality, partly in the context of personal love, see Hartmann, *Ethics* 2: 342–46, 354–55, 371.

beyond his reach is evoked by representing his experience of her irresistible femininity as an encounter with sadistic malevolence.

It hardly seems necessary to interpret the characterological "masochism" represented in these poems literally, as a psychoneurotic disorder. Indeed, masochism is considered by some to be a "normal" phenomenon, normal in the sense that certain of its elements are not inconsistent with "normal" psychology, i.e., they are pervasive in both normal and neurotic individuals. In Panken's words (*Joy of Suffering*, 45):

> In all ages man has "denied and abused" himself, and this type of behavior has been greatly esteemed particularly when it has been ritualized in various religious practices (Salzman, 1959). Mortification, for example, has been considered a highly efficacious and moral activity auguring great rewards and frequently leading to sainthood. By emphasizing bodily injury or neglect, mortification negates mere bodily processes and exalts spiritual values. . . . Masochism is a "universal technique employed by man through the ages to deal with such problems of existence as guilt, helplessness and powerlessness." (Salzman, 1959)[44]

It is not difficult to understand an emphasis on the value of physical self-abnegation and detachment from the material world in the context of Christian spiritual fervor, any more than it is difficult to understand the repudiation of sensual desire in the context of representing disinterested feelings of love. And when the tradition of courtly love sheds its elegiac character and comes together with Christian spirituality, as in, for example, San Juan de la Cruz's "Llama de amor viva," the fulfilment of love–passion in a fantasy of rescue assumes a form that is not inconsistent with feminine masochism's characteristic "ecstatic abandonment to misery and self-degradation" (Horney in Panken, *Joy of Suffering*, 34). Such a state is one of "mystic dissolution of the person which has its climax in death during orgasm" (Annie Reich in Panken, *Joy of Suffering*, 35), a condition in which "one lives only through the partner, views oneself as nothing, the partner as everything" (Fenichel in Panken, *Joy of Suffering*, 35–36). The following stanza is from San Juan's "Llama de amor viva" [Living flame of love]:

---

[44] Panken's references in the passage cited are to L. Salzman, "Masochism: A Review of Theory and Therapy," in *Individual and Family Dynamics*, ed. Jules Masserman (New York: Grune & Stratton, 1959).

Interpreting "Masochistic" Rescue Fantasies

> ¡Oh cautiverio suave!
> ¡Oh regalada llaga!
> ¡Oh mano blanda! ¡Oh toque delicado!,
> que a vida eterna sabe
> y toda deuda paga;
> matando, muerte en vida la has trocado.

[Oh sweet captivity! Oh generous wound! Oh soft hand! Oh delicate touch that savors of eternal life and pays all debts; killing, you have changed death into life.][45]

In these lines the metaphorical aggressive action of the other has been incorporated as a blessing, and the degree of aggressive mastery that is exercised by the other is testimony of the victim's power to provoke or "merit" such mastery, which consists in the triumphant obliteration of the bondage/death of impure, temporal human being. In this connection one naturally thinks of Santa Teresa's religious adaptation of the secular love song "Vivo sin vivir en mí" and the stanza,

> Sácame de esta muerte,
> mi Dios, y dame la vida;
> no me tengas impedida
> en este lazo fuerte;
> mira que muero por verte,
> y vivir sin ti no puedo,
> *que muero porque no muero.*

[Remove me from this death, my God, and give me life; do not hold me fast in these strong bonds; look how I die to see you, and cannot live without you, *for I am dying because I am not dying.*][46]

---

[45] From San Juan de la Cruz, *Obras completas*, ed. Lucino of Ruano de la Iglesia (Madrid: Biblioteca de Autores Cristianos, 1982), 744; my translation.

[46] From B. W. Wardropper, ed., *The Spanish Poetry of the Golden Age* (New York: Irvington, 1971), 302–4; my translation, emphasis in the original.

or a stanza from another of Santa Teresa's versions of the poem:

> ¡Ay, qué larga es esta vida!
> ¡Qué duros estos destierros!
> Esta cárcel, estos hierros
> En que el alma está metida!
> Sólo esperar la salida
> Me causa dolor tan fiero,
> *Que muero porque no muero.*

> [Oh, how long is this life! How hard this exile! This prison, these chains in which my soul is placed! Only to await release causes me such fierce pain, *that I am dying because I am not dying.*][47]

Here, bondage and the agony of torture ("contino morir") are identified with temporal existence, the condition preventing union with God. The triumphant consummation of that union must, for the present, assume the surrogate form of utter surrender in anticipation. The existence of certain points of contact between Christianity and secular love lyric in the Renaissance is well known (both in works such as those quoted here and in religious adaptations of amatory lyric by authors such as Sebastián de Córdoba), even if one does not posit the influence of the secular Neoplatonist writings of that period and their emphasis on the ennobling effects of love. The religious, allegorical poems I have quoted here are relatively easy to interpret, since their doctrinal meaning is fairly definite. In this regard they are quite different from secular works. However, my consideration of similarities between religious and secular works is valuable in helping us to notice unsuspected dimensions of the secular tradition. Particularly significant is the unusual formula of a liberating spiritual triumph contemplated as being achieved in ritual death through surrender to the dominating power of the ideal. Like Christian spirituality, the elevated secular literary culture of elegiac courtly love can be related to a process observed by H. Hartmann: cultivation of an ideal of individual self-abnegation helps to neutralize the temporal, aggressive drive directed toward immediate objects and transform it into a more generalized aptitude

---

[47] From Santa Teresa de Jesús, *Obras*, ed. Silverio de Santa Teresa (Burgos: El Monte Carmelo, 1954), 1063–64; my translation, emphasis in the original.

for assertion, work, or mastery of the environment (Panken, *Joy of Suffering*, 33). A feature that the Christian idea of individual salvation and romantic love have in common is that the psychological value of both is rooted in the possibility of achieving fulfilment of the desiring self, or libido, which is thus delivered, rescued, from the anxieties of reality.[48] From this point of view, the state of ritual bondage implied in romantic love's component of willing submission to a loved one is *par excellence* the secular, modern counterpart of a spiritual exercise directed toward the individual's triumph over an attachment, a bondage, to non-spiritual goods,[49] a circumstance that leads us to think that if Ignatius of Loyola had written lyrical poetry, he would have a natural place in our study of masochistic fantasy. In the secularized, modern world,

---

[48] "Translated into dream terms, the quest-romance is the search of the libido or desiring self for a fulfillment that will deliver it from the anxieties of reality but will still contain that reality": Frye, *Anatomy of Criticism*, 193. Hegel has observed essential similarities shared by romantic love and the Christian ideal of individual salvation: he sees them both as expressing the "modern" (post-Greco-Roman) emphasis on subjective satisfaction of the individual (*Philosophy of Right*, trans. T. M. Knox [London: Oxford University Press, 1967] 124 [83–84]).

[49] In spite of such arguments as those advanced by, for example, Denomy, *The Heresy of Courtly Love*, the sensual component of courtly love has never seemed to me to outweigh its non-subversive elements or account for courtly love's being considered "heretical" by ecclesiastical authorities; indeed, according to Maurice Valency, it never officially was, not even during the Albigensian Crusade in the thirteenth century. Of course what members of the clergy may have felt was immoral or what happened unofficially or without explanation is another matter: "Although there is no evidence that the Inquisition ever persecuted the troubadours as such, these poets ceased to ply their profession in the Midi soon after its establishment" (M. Valency, *In Praise of Love* [New York: Octagon Books, 1975], 79). This phenomenon raises the interesting question of the possible existence of a "heterodoxy of spirit" or temperament (akin to the *gai science*) that is a secular counterpart of the heterodox Reformist spirituality of confident joy (see Creel, *Religious Poetry of Jorge de Montemayor*, 217–38). The evidence would suggest that, like the troubadours, Renaissance authors of both religious and secular literature were keenly aware of the revolutionary possibilities of activity in the arena of sentiment and of the moral–psychological, or "political," implications of counteracting what Heine referred to as "the traditionally dismal, languishing Catholicism." On the other hand, the solemn secular and worldly spirituality of the *religio amoris* that was developed along elegiac lines encountered opposition among the ultra-orthodox clergy. An example is the censorship of Montemayor's *Diana* by the Portuguese Inquisition (below, 250–51).

the ritual experience of love–passion broke away more and more from the religious realm, but it has remained a cultural necessity.

Yet the self-sacrificing character of romantic love is not enough to make it possible to see that character as being "masochistic," unless "masochism" is given the questionable definition of suffering or self-affliction by which the sufferer intends, either consciously or unconsciously, to derive some benefit for himself as an individual, even healthy benefit. Masochism has no monopoly on self-sacrifice, and genuine self-sacrifice can hardly be motivated by a desire for gratification of the self. The tendency to regard self-sacrifice as a means to self-gratification was denounced as pernicious and empty dogmatism by Hegel in his *Philosophy of Right*.[50] The very fact that suffering is, in fact, painful and undesirable is, paradoxically, what gives it its character as the value recognized by N. Hartmann:

> ... one who has a capacity for suffering is strengthened by it. His power of endurance, his humanity, his moral Being, grows under it. ... Suffering is the energy-test of a moral being, the load-test of his elasticity. ... [It leads to] an awakening of a deeper moral power. Whoever has been tested in suffering is tempered steel — for him nothing is too difficult; ... he is like a steel spring which returns to its original strength. ... If with his suffering a man purchases the highest values, the thought of a will to suffer has nothing absurd about it. There is such a will. ... It is nothing unusual for a man to want to suffer for the sake of a high goal, of an idea, for the sake of the communal life. But the will to suffer for love's sake ... is deeper still. ... In suffering for a person there is a puzzling and yet unmis-

---

[50] "Since the subjective satisfaction of the individual himself (including the recognition which he receives by way of honour and fame) is also part and parcel of the achievement of ends of absolute worth, it follows that the demand that such an end alone shall appear as willed and attained, like the view that, in willing, objective and subjective ends are mutually exclusive, is an empty dogmatism of the Understanding. And this dogmatism is more than empty, it is pernicious if it passes into the assertion that because subjective satisfaction is present, as it always is when any task is brought to completion, it is what the agent intended in essence to secure and that the objective end was in his eyes only a means to that": Hegel, *Philosophy of Right*, trans. Knox, 124 (83).

takable depth of participation, a communion with him, which for inward depth has no equal. (*Ethics*, 2: 139–41)

To recognize the experience of suffering as a value is not to point out its character as masochism, for what we have seen to be referred to as so-called "normal" masochism, i.e., the capacity to accept necessary suffering and holding such acceptance to be a value, is not masochism proper. Is masochism ever "masochism proper" in the sense of having suffering as a goal? Adler speaks of "pseudomasochism" almost as a synonym of "masochism." In his view, appearing weak and submissive and accepting pain and humiliation are neurotic expedients for gaining security or dominance and safeguarding feelings of superiority: " 'Feminine' final goals just as 'masochistic' ones are quite untenable assumptions, are only excuses; they are 'feminine' methods for the 'masculine' protest"[51] (the terms "feminine" and "masculine" in this context can both apply to either males or females and mean "deriving from feelings of being unmanly and inferior" and "deriving from feelings of being manly and superior" respectively, and "masculine protest" is one's aggressive striving for superiority and dominance as a reaction, a protest, against one's feelings of littleness and weakness). Adler notes that a motive neurotics can have in withdrawing and isolating themselves through an attitude of passive submission to domination from without is to *rescue their personalities* from colliding with reality.

Perhaps a general definition of "masochism" that is applicable for our purposes is Adler's use of the term as meaning "the wish to gratify ... unlimited desires by the most complete kind of submission" (*Practice and Theory of Individual Psychology*, 20). That definition captures both the rhetorically inverted situation of the poet's "erotic siege" of the lady and the compulsive character of the persona's radical submission that Rivers perceived. In addition, it has the advantage of emphasizing the highly individualistic mentality of the masochist, and individualism is so fundamental in the early modern period that the Renaissance has been seen as being, in its essence, a triumph of individualism.[52] What does the masochist desire? Adler holds that what the maso-

---

[51] Adler, *Neurotic Constitution*, 368, and *The Practice and Theory of Individual Psychology*, 97.

[52] I am aware that it would be an oversimplification to posit an antithetical contrast between a "medieval period" in which an appreciation for the worth of the individual was lacking and a "Renaissance" period in which the human greatness made possible by such an appreciation was finally able to emerge. In this regard, clarification as to some specific

chist desires above all is to satisfy a compensatory need to enhance and heighten his own ego-consciousness through feelings of superiority: hence, masochists *may* wish to rescue their personalities from the disappointments of failure; but deliberate, though unconsciously arranged, failure may be found to be the most useful expedient whereby the masochist avoids the ever-present *threat* of feeling worthless. Thus, for all his professions of love-idealism, Alonso Quijano (who imagines himself to be Don Quijote), for example, may be seen not only as a compulsive personality who unceasingly strives for success at the same time that he purposely fails (Adler, *Practice and Theory of Individual Psychology*, 21) but as an "ingenious" (as is stated in the title *El ingenioso hidalgo don Quijote de la Mancha*) form of the neurotic who, with predictable results, "masochistically" seeks to advance in the real world by championing high ideals and who, at the same time, safeguards his delusional feelings of superiority towards others

---

characteristics of the Renaissance emphasis on individuality can be provided by contrasting views of Arnold Hauser with others by Huizinga, the latter of whom, in the words of Wallace K. Ferguson (*The Renaissance in Historical Thought* [New York: Houghton, 1948], 373), "did admit the existence of a Renaissance, though he had grave doubts about it. He considered the historical tool implied in that term ... a dangerous and unreliable yet somehow indispensable tool for the use of historians." Huizinga writes as follows:

> This universal tracing back to the general is a quality that, under the label "typism," Lamprecht singled out as the very special characteristic feature of the medieval mind. But this feature is a mental consequence, a need, that arises from deeply rooted idealism. It is not so much an inability to see things in their own individuality as much as it is the deliberate desire to indicate the relationship of things to the highest point of reference, to their ethical ideality and their general significance. It was precisely the impersonal element that was sought out in everything; the value of anything was taken to be its value as a normal and model case. This lack of interest in a thing's individuality and uniqueness, to a certain degree intentional, is a universalizing habit of thought characteristic of a low degree of intellectual development. (*The Autumn of the Middle Ages* [1929], trans. R. J. Payton and U. Mammitzsch [Chicago: University of Chicago Press, 1996], 250–51)

Arnold Hauser sees as features of Renaissance culture the new recognition of the value, dignity, and freedom of man; the new unrestrained attachment to the values and experiences of earthliness; the new freely-ranging, secular and speculative rationalism; the new aesthetic appreciation of the world, of nature, and of the human body; and the new awareness of the revolutionary implications of emphasizing the values of personality: *Social History of Art*, trans. S. Godman, 4 vols. (New York: Vintage, 1957), 2: 1–7, 15.

by directing his efforts towards imaginary or unsuitable objects so as to avoid the pain of failing in the real world. Even the cultivation of virtues can serve the needs of an internal agenda on the part of the subject: Adler speaks of "courage" along with envy, pride, greed, cruelty, and revengefulness as means by which the neurotic negates his sense of inferiority (*Neurotic Constitution*, 61). One occasionally develops the sense in Garcilaso's poems as well, where the persona's attitude of solicitude borders on self-degradation, that the poet is addressing the problem not just of a love-idealism that is not appreciated but of love-idealism that is misguided — that by representing his persona as aggressively making extravagant sacrificial offerings of himself to a lady who regards him with "cruel indifference," Garcilaso could be raising the question of whether a lover's genuinely self-effacing and fervent devotion might not be a compensatory strategy and a vain delusion. Yet even if the poems are interpreted to be read as expressing satirical detachment from both the insensitivity of the other and the folly of the poet–persona, they still are able to be seen as retaining the element of sublimity. From this point of view, Garcilaso's more tortured poetic expressions of love–anguish might have the character of a lyrical and amatory form of what Schiller termed "pathetic satire," which, he observes, must "always derive from a temperament that is vigorously permeated by the ideal. Only a predominant impulse toward harmony can and may produce that profound sense of moral contradiction and that burning indignation against moral perversity which becomes the inspiration of a Juvenal, a Swift, a Rousseau, Haller, and others."[53] Thus, if one perceives a satirical element in Garcilaso, that element does not necessarily diminish the romantic element, the elevation of tone that I discussed earlier, any more than it does in *Don Quijote*: "there is genuine and invaluable moral strength inherent in the ethos of immature ideals. It must be retained in later life" (Hartmann, *Ethics*, 2: 324).

When works such as Garcilaso's *Canción* 1 and Sonnet 2 are interpreted as representing the masochistic tendencies of "the poet" without there being carried out any significant degree of further thematic and metaphorical interpretation, it is implied that the poem is essentially biographical or autobiographical, that is, that the poet–persona is Garcilaso himself and that the lady in question is a real, living lady known to Garcilaso. That type of reading tacitly favors the hypothesis of a chronology of Garcilaso's works based on the existence of such a lady. In addition, such a reading is based on the

---

[53] Friedrich von Schiller, *Naive and Sentimental Poetry and On the Sublime: Two Essays*, trans. J. Elias (New York: Unger, 1966), 83–190, here 119.

assumption that since the persona is *not* a poetic fiction and the "masochism" evidenced in the poem is *not* part of the poetic fiction as well, a critical interpretation that allegorizes the poem's imagery is unnecessary if not inappropriate. The biographical reading also implicitly or explicitly denies that the lady is a fiction. However, from the point of view of the object-relations psychology of Melanie Klein, masochism is aggression towards a bad object as that aggression is internally aimed as a result of the object's being internalized as a fantasy (Guntrip, *Personality, Structure, and Human Interaction*, 204) ("object relations" being relationships with other persons who, after their good qualities have been split off from their bad, "frustrating" ones, have been turned into fictions that reside in one's psyche). On those grounds it could be argued that any suppositions as to sadomasochistic relations between Garcilaso the man and a real lady whom he actually knew is itself a product of conventional thought, since masochistic character formations are always developed in relation to a fictional other, whether the fiction is poetic or not. Not only are there strong grounds for arguing that the poems in question, as works of art, are not autobiographical the way letters, a diary, or memoirs would be,[54] but the language they employ is subtle and elusive because it is highly rhetorical and figurative. Given the conventions of language in the courtly-love tradition,[55] complaints at the beloved's "cruelty" are most likely either a rhetorical means of referring to her coyness or are a hyperbolic metaphor intended to evoke the irresistible power of the beloved's beauty. Likewise, the beloved's "tyranny" is most likely the poet–persona's experience of absolute devotion to a being whose modesty or some other circumstance makes that being inaccessible: such can be seen more clearly to be the situation in the above-mentioned poems by San Juan and Santa Teresa. Yet since in the present chapter I have attempted to pass beyond "face value" in relation to the phenomenon of masochism, I ought also to do so in relation to rhetoric. Whereas it might be possible to claim that in secular love lyric professions of suffering conform to a rhetorical strategy of praise and seduction, it is more difficult to do so in the case of religious lyric. What does the mystic desire? Again, we encounter a conflict in criteria: the clinical and the artistic. From a clinical point of view the mystic's desires are unlimited indeed, for their fantasy of love relations with God

---

[54] In addition to views of C. S. Lewis, *Personal Heresy*, referred to above in chapter 2, note 4, see Wellek and Warren, *Theory of Literature*, 75–80, on the limitations of the biographical approach to interpreting literary art.

[55] Sandra Resnick Alfonsi, *Masculine Submission in the Troubadour Lyric* (New York: P. Lang, 1986), 112, 123, 255, 369.

himself could be regarded as expressing an infantile megalomania that reveals an attitude of superiority towards an environment which he or she regards as hostile (Adler, *Neurotic Constitution*, 422). Yet from an artistic and metaphorical point of view, mystic aspirations allegorically symbolize a morally noble self-effacement that is motivated by a desire to realize the highest propensities in the self.

§

I have suggested the possibility of doing a metaphorical reading of Garcilaso's poetry that is socio-historical and is related to the crisis of the age. While such a reading does not assume that the poetry is autobiographical, it is not inconsistent with the view that literature is ultimately and indirectly grounded in some form of experience on the part of an author. Even if the poet–persona is not directly identifiable with the author, as fictional characters he and the lady are given life in the work and, therefore, have psychological characteristics that can be analyzed. On the other hand, metaphorical imagery may be wholly psychological (Wellek and Warren, *Theory of Literature*, 188). There is no drawback in recognizing the correlation of historical experience and literary fiction if the scope of interpretation is not thereby inhibited. Let us attempt, then, for the sake of exercise, the rather novel challenge of applying both psychoanalytic, "empirical" insights and metaphorical and allegorical, i.e., "literary" principles to interpreting the broad features of the elements of "masochism" in Garcilaso's poems.

The basic phenomenon that I have concluded to be at issue in the apparent "masochism" in Garcilaso's poems is the poet–persona's state of complete willing submission and passive subjection to the will of another in anticipation of enhancing feelings of security, worthiness, or superiority. One could venture a theory along the lines of those listed above in an effort to attempt to explain the origins of the type of masochistic character formation that I feel is evidenced in the poetry under consideration and that characterizes the historical situation of humanist-intellectual poets in the High Renaissance. I do not, however, assert that such a theory would apply to the persona in these poems or constitutes an explanation of Garcilaso's poems as poetry any more than do the other theories I have listed. The theory I will suggest incorporates some elements of explanations referred to above (especially Reich in Panken, *Joy of Suffering*, 38–39, and Freud's definition of masochism), and it adds additional elements to these. Since it is just one more theory in a list, I will continue the use of alphabetical order:

s. Insecurity accompanying the general crisis of the age with its increase in authoritarian cruelty and rigidity gave rise to an unusual proneness to anxiety and an exaggerated, unfulfillable need for love. When that demand was not met, it resulted in an impotent and hence powerfully increased aggressiveness on the part of the poet (often a would-be warrior turned courtier), whose personality is representative of his age. Because that aggression has no immediate or identifiable object, it threatens to turn round upon the self and become destructive by avenging itself upon its bearer just because it exists. In order to neutralize that negative emotion and spare himself, the poet construes an elevated mythology (actually, participates in, cultivates, the existing courtly-love tradition) in which he assigns himself the role of a person who is benign and loving. Thus, his aggressive frustration is not repressed but is recast, redefined, and sublimated as he now unconsciously explains it to himself as the result of his being infinitely solicitous and benevolent.

Apart from the overly general and speculative nature of such a theory, its greatest limitations are that it addresses neither the rhetorical subtlety of language in, for example, Sonnet 2 nor the way language is used in the interest of evocation. I have mentioned those elements of Garcilaso's poetry above; here, I wish to concentrate on another limitation of the above theory and supply what it lacks, namely, a metaphorical interpretation of the "masochistic" motifs under discussion. In order to focus my analysis, I will apply it specifically to Garcilaso's Sonnet 2. Such an interpretation applied to that work would be as follows:

The abyss of radical deprivation experienced by the poet–persona at the hands of the rejective lady, his "bondage" in the "brutal" intensity of unsatisfied longing, can be seen in relatively elementary terms as being directly represented by the "cruelly" rejective lady, so that the poetic utterance addressed to the lady — words that express an attitude of both protest and appeasing submission — is seen as being addressed to the state of captivity from which he seeks to be released. This process would be described by psychoanalysis as an instance of "projective identification" whereby the persona's ego rids itself of its frustrated and hence unwanted (libidinal) aggression by identifying it with an external other in whom the ego now feels that part of it is imprisoned.[56] Under these circumstances the persona's unrequited love becomes a

---

[56] R. D. Hinshelwood, *A Dictionary of Kleinian Thought* (London: Free Association Books, 1989), 179, 187.

yearning for release from an oppressively harsh environment where the love he longs for is absent. It may not be a coincidence that the anguished pleadings for kindness so characteristic of Garcilaso's poems were written as the author pursued the career of a soldier, a soldier who has also been characterized as an ardent pacifist.[57]

But how can one explain the poet's masochistic behavior and the phenomenon of role reversal whereby the persona has assumed the identity of the submissive female while the lady is represented as the domineering male? An answer to these question requires addressing the issue of the lady's role and symbolic meaning in more specific terms. When the persona's intense need of her as a love-object became frustrated, he developed feelings of angry aggression toward her, yet his ambivalence toward her as an object for which he still feels a need is a source of intense anxiety that he fears and must suppress. He accomplishes that suppression by concentrating his libido's ruthlessly aggressive tendencies in that part of his ego that must suppress his libidinal needs, his "anti-libidinal ego." Thus, the lady is the image of the persona's anti-libidinal ego, and she is fantasied as crushing and suppressing the poet, who is the image of his own libido, of his "libidinal ego." "He can now be only passively dependent, helpless, inhibited, clinging, suffering — *the dependent masochist* — because of the terror he experiences over being in feeling and phantasy *the dependent sadist*" (Guntrip, *Personality, Structure, and Human Interaction*, 387, cf. 329).[58] The persona's agonized complaint, then, is a result of the fact that under these circumstances of repression his ego still needs and cathects the rejecting object; that is, since direct, oral incorporative desire of the lady is not permitted, the persona is forced to have recourse to identification, which is the only other way in which he is able to relate to that rejecting object. More specifically, his is what in modern, psychoanalytic terms would be described as the undifferentiated state of "secondary identification," of regressive agoraphobic withdrawal into the safe submission of infantile dependence on the lady as dominant and protective mother — "a flight into the womb and a fear of being reborn" (Guntrip, *Personality, Structure, and Human Interaction*, 314) that has led to the swallowing up of his personality in that of the other (the lady). But since the abyss (of the lady's oblivion), which is a place of darkness and misery from which there is no

---

[57] See Dámaso Alonso, *Obras completas*, 8 vols. (Madrid: Gredos, 1972), 2: 536 ("Un guerrero pacifista").

[58] Adler refers to the sadist as the "triumphant vanquished" and to the masochist as the "beaten victor." See *The Individual Psychology of Alfred Adler*, 426.

escape and for that reason is represented as bondage or captivity in such a place, is, symbolically, "the site of metamorphoses, transitions from death to life, and germination,"[59] the abyss of the poet's captivity also indicates, in addition to the vertical lines of descent, the lines of unlimited ascent. Thus, as for the mystic, the persona's state of bondage in love–anguish is a prelude to joy, light, unification and marriage: it is the indeterminacy, repression, and frustration of childhood that is followed by the liberating self-differentiation and fulfillment of adulthood.

Recognizing (as in "s" above) that at any particular time in history there is more than ever a concrete basis for the experience of the masochistic type of suffering that is represented in poetry can help to understand how such a literature originally emerged. It is another matter to assert that poems such as those I have mentioned here are direct evidence of such historical developments or that their artistic qualities can be explained in terms of those developments. What we can really observe with certainty in those works is a desperate hope for the prospect of achieving release from frustration of the ego through a radical negation of selfhood. To draw again from Hegel, "The lack that each self is, needing the other's love simply in order to be himself, makes of each self a primordial emptiness" (Westphal, *History and Truth in Hegel's Phenomenology*, 134). A typical pattern whereby the individual can be seen to rise above paralysis of the will is to experience a fantasized, psycho-dramatic repudiation of a weak, small, and dangerously dependent self and to construe that imaginary, fictional, poetic experience in terms that, while they arouse an aversion towards one's limitations, do honor to one's tenacious moral strength and humanity. If the ego is able to survive the experience of being thus mortified and purged of the "primordial emptiness" of its vulnerability and weakness, it can only move in an upward direction. It is at that point that meekness and humanity must draw on a reckless courage and even on pride in the fiction of one's superior strength if the individual is to move forward and struggle to fulfill his or her own destiny. Again in Dilthey's words, "never at any time did he [man] show his formative and creative power so forcibly as when he shed his medieval chains and moved forward to the enjoyment of unlimited freedom — hot-bloodedly, passionately and with his imagination released" ("The Great Poetry of the Imagination," 84). It was Maxim Gorky who saw in the instinct of self-preservation "a pagan instinct which created the Renaissance and has always served as

---

[59] J. Chevalier and A. Gheerbrant, *A Dictionary of Symbols* (London: Penguin, 1969, repr. 1996), 492.

a stimulus to the rebellion of man against his own, human conception of the invincibility of fate."[60] From a broad, historical point of view, the poems I have discussed represent a process that corresponds to the event of "individuation," a subject I will address in chapter 5 in relation to other poems by Garcilaso.

It is no accident that in 2. 25, when Don Quijote encounters the fugitive Ginés de Pasamonte disguised as a puppeteer named "Maese Pedro" who tells fortunes with a "divining ape," Don Quijote is not prompted by his obsessed interest in Dulcinea to ask a question about her, but rather it is his squire who asks a question about his wife Teresa Panza. Sancho is forced to inquire as to Teresa's activities at that very moment because Maese Pedro has made it clear that his ape can explain the past and the present but has no knowledge of the future. Perhaps the reason that Don Quijote does not ask about his beloved Dulcinea is that she has no existence in the fictionally empirical realm, which is surely what explains her never appearing in the novel. For Don Quijote she *is* the future, as it is shaped by the inspiring power of prospective ideal being as such. It is with such ideal being that Don Quijote identifies himself, the force that, he explains, "takes my arm as an instrument of her deeds. She combats in me and conquers in me, and I live and breathe in her, and have life and being" (1. 30) (the allusion being to Acts 17:28). It is in order to contrast a preoccupation with the empirical (past and present) and commitment to an ideal that Cervantes has Sancho ask the ape a question instead of Don Quijote, for Dulcinea's meaning can bear no association with the impasse of imitative and sycophantic bondage in the past, symbolized by the anomalous "divining ape" that cannot prophesy.

Speculation as to a real person who might be the bearer of the poet–persona's ideal of humanity in Garcilaso's poems is certainly irrelevant, for it constitutes an obstacle to what might otherwise be an inclination to see such poetry as embodying ideas of high generality, ideas of a philosophical, socio-historical, or meta-psychological nature. The primary artistic value of works such as Garcilaso's Sonnet 2 and *Canción* 1 is not that they represent personal experience on the part of the author. It is that, as tragic art, they constitute a quasi-religious spiritual exercise whereby people are assisted in comprehending their experiences in the world with resilient detachment as well as strong feelings of pathos, in that way overcoming emotions that dehumanize them and enslave the freedom of their thought and will. Resources such as elaborating

---

[60] Maxim Gorky, *Untimely Thoughts*, trans. H. Ermolaev (New York: Eriksson, 1968), 226.

along metaphorical lines the phenomenon that we today refer to as "masochism" made it possible for "mannered" lyrical poets in the High Renaissance to advance an ennobling secular spirituality in terms that were subtle, intriguing, quasi-ironic and, as a result, urbanely unsentimental, hence having what even today seems a distinct modernity of tone in their passionate, elegiac celebrations of the *religio amoris*.

4

The Death of Love's Hopes: Garcilaso's Sonnet 22 Considered in the Light of Phenomenological Ethics of Values

Both Garcilaso's Sonnet 22 and the work I will consider below in chapter 6, Fray Luis de León's "En la Ascensión," treat the general subject of a love that becomes a source of grief because the one who loves fears being the object of a depreciating attitude on the part of the beloved. In Fray Luis's poem, the transfiguration and ascension of Christ vest him with a superiority to his disciples that makes them dread the ontological gulf separating humankind and sovereign God and calls for an attitude of awed reverence that is hard to reconcile with the feeling of natural kinship that had united them to the beloved teacher and companion who had personally guided them toward a higher destiny. In Garcilaso's Sonnet 22, the obstacle to love's movement toward the realization of higher values is the lady's attitude of defensive modesty, which suggests to the persona that she does not notice him as a person, an individual, and hence shatters his hopes that he and the lady are or can be united by temperamental sympathy. On the other hand, one senses that the appeal of the lady's modesty may also cause the persona's hopes to be reborn, and his intense despair at the end of the poem is an indication that his love for her remains. Because of the variety of ways that its many ambiguities allow it to be interpreted, Sonnet 22 has been widely recognized as one of Garcilaso's more elusive poems; yet one is encouraged by its apparent simplicity. It runs as follows:

> Con ansia estrema de mirar qué tiene
> vuestro pecho escondido allá en su centro
> y ver si a lo de fuera lo de dentro
> en apariencia y ser igual conviene,
>   en él puse la vista, mas detiene
> de vuestra hermosura el duro encuentro
> mis ojos, y no pasan tan adentro
> que miren lo qu'el alma en sí contiene.
>   Y así se quedan tristes en la puerta
> hecha, por mi dolor, con essa mano,
> que aun a su mismo pecho no perdona;
>   donde vi claro mi esperanza muerta
> y el golpe, que en vos hizo amor en vano,
> *non esservi passato oltra la gona.*

[With extreme longing to see what your breast has hidden away in its center and to see if what is within matches what is without in appearance and being equal, I placed my eyesight on it, but your beauty's harsh stroke stops my eyes, and they do not proceed inward so far as to see what your soul contains within itself. And so they remain sad at the door made, to my sorrow, with that hand that will not give leave even to what is within its own breast; where I saw clearly my hope dead and the blow, which love dealt you in vain, "not having penetrated beyond your gown."]

The last line is a direct quotation from Petrarch's *Canzone* 23.

Sonnet 22 has recently been discussed in some detail by Daniel Heiple (*Garcilaso*, 241–50) and by Elias Rivers in his review of Heiple's monograph (*Calíope* 2 [1996]: 100–8, here 105–6). Rivers accepts Heiple's recognition of the contribution made by Rivers himself in his 1974 critical edition of Garcilaso's works (122–24), but he finally questions some of Heiple's observations on the basis of Antonio Gargano, *Fonti, miti, topoi*. The current consensus is that Sonnet 22 presents, in the context of an unexpected encounter between the persona and the lady, an opposition between the persona's initial intention to behold the lady's inner beauty and his own susceptibility to the power of her sensuous, outer beauty, which hinders the persona's efforts to reach his goal. Shortly before Rivers's edition appeared, Ana María Snell published an article in which she discussed Sonnet 22.[1] Snell's view of Sonnet 22 would seem to deviate from the interpretations of Rivers and Heiple in that she sees the lady's modest action of shielding her breast from the persona's scrutiny as having the effect of hindering the persona's Platonic interest in her. In fact, Snell regards that professed interest on the part of the persona as being primarily hindered from within by the persona himself, for she considers the persona's idealistic claims to be a subtle disguise for sensual desire and the poem's irony to be its central feature. Except for Gargano, who appears unaware of Snell's study, subsequent critics have concurred with Snell in considering the persona to be flirtatiously feigning innocence, and they have all (including Gargano) shared Snell's view that this sonnet describes a moment when the persona's interest in the lady as a spiritual person was effectively thwarted by the impression made on him by her physical beauty, the result being her rebuff and the persona's present despair. Rivers affirms: "A nuestro parecer, *de vuestra hermosura el duro encuentro* (v. 6) podría quizá ser un golpe de mano con el que se tapó la dama el pecho (vv. 9–10 y 13); ... Quizá más verosímil sea un sentido figurativo: su hermosura carnal era de por sí una cruel barrera para los ojos del poeta, quien quería verle el alma" (*Obras* [1974], 123) ["It seems to me that *de vuestra hermosura el duro encuentro* (line 6) could perhaps be a blow with the hand with which the lady covered her breast (lines 9–10 and 13); ... Perhaps more plausible would be a figurative sense: her carnal beauty itself was a cruel barrier for the eyes of the persona, who wanted to see her soul"]. According to Heiple,

> The lover, blinded by exterior beauty, could not see the interior virtue of his mistress, and in fact, in this external beauty he "sees" his hopes die: "donde vi claro mi esperança muerta." These hopes are

---

[1] The previous readings of the poem by El Brocense, Herrera and Tamayo are summarized by Rivers in his 1974 and subsequent critical editions of the *Obras completas* (122–23), by Gargano (33–36) and Heiple (243–46), who proposes a number of new, likely influences on Sonnet 22. Heiple mistakenly states (243) that Snell's interpretation expands on an idea advanced by Rivers. Actually, Snell's study appeared a year before the first, 1974 printing of Rivers' critical edition.

not the courtly desire of conquest, but the Platonic desire of an intellectually requited love. His love of sensual beauty and his inability to enter the door signify the death of Platonic love, further indicated by the fact that his love has not been reciprocated. Cupid's arrows have not passed the gown of the mistress, in the same way his vision, struck by her sensual beauty, could not pass the covering of the body. (*Garcilaso*, 248)

Like Rivers, Heiple would seem to assert that the primal power of the lady's physical beauty is represented as brutally arresting the persona's initial, more sublimated interest in her: "the irony of this sonnet indeed runs deep, for the door that closes out sensuality has become a door that shuts out the access to pure Platonic love" (246). Heiple considers the hand in the first tercet to be that of Cupid (246–50). Rivers disagrees with this interpretation, favoring instead Gargano's view that the hand is that of the lady. Although disagreement on this point has not led to differences between Rivers and Heiple as to how Sonnet 22 as a whole should be interpreted, my own reading of the poem must favor here the interpretations of Rivers and Gargano. It seems to me that because the words "por mi dolor" immediately follow "puerta hecha," it would be more likely that at that instant the persona is contemplating not a "door" (access) opened by love but a "door" that has been closed by the lady's resistance. In the present comments there is no need to dwell on differences among previous interpretations of this sonnet, since my main purpose is to consider the poem in a new perspective, one that is informed by the phenomenological ethics of values. It is, however, necessary that I set forth my own reading of the poem and explain the differences between it and the contemporary interpretive perspective on Sonnet 22 established by Snell, Rivers, Heiple, and Gargano.

Two elements in the interpretations by Rivers and Heiple cannot, I feel, be justified by the language of the poem itself, by the text. One is the assumption that in the brief period described by the poem, the persona at some point focuses his attention on the lady as an object of sensuous pleasure, even if such pleasure can be experienced visually. Another is that, even if the persona did turn his attention exclusively to the lady's physical beauty, his doing so would have had to conflict with his interest in her as a spiritual person. Although one can imagine that in the scene described by the poem these events might have occurred, I see no evidence in the text that supports the conclusion that either actually did. That the persona is cognizant of the beauty of the lady's breast or bosom is evident from the implications of lines 3–4: we are led to conclude that "en apariencia y ser igual conviene" (which I read as "matches ... in appearance and being equal" or, "matches in appearance and [possessing] equal being," filling a possible ellipsis) means "equal in beauty." Yet the persona's recognition of the physical beauty of the lady's bosom need not imply a diminution of his interest in her inner disposition and personality. The lines "... si a lo de fuera lo de dentro / en apariencia y ser igual conviene" do seem to mean that he wondered whether he could find in her an inner beauty that matched the beauty of her outward appearance. However, in order for these lines to be interpreted to mean that at the moment in question the persona was moved to make the comparison only by the impression made on him by her physical beauty, he must be thought of as referring to an equal *degree* of beauty. It is more plausible that "en ... ser igual conviene" refers to whether what is within the lady, her inner nature, has the same general *quality* as what is without. Also, if the question were one of degree (whether she is inwardly as beautiful as she is outwardly), his knowing the answer would involve the problem of applying the same standard of measure to types of beauty that are fundamentally different. That difficulty is eliminated if the persona is understood merely to be referring to whether she has a spiritual beauty that harmonizes with, corresponds to, her corporeal beauty, whether she *is beautiful both inwardly and outwardly* (cf. Socrates' prayer in Plato, *Phaedrus* 279B).

The specific sense assigned to the word "conviene" is clearly of fundamental importance. Does it mean "suits" in the sense of "is in keeping with" or in the sense of "matches"? What the persona seems to want to know is whether the lady's inward beauty is as appealing and inviting as her outward beauty; but since he has directed his sight at her breast it is not clear whether what he has in mind when he refers to "lo de fuera" is her outward beauty in general or specifically the outward beauty of her breast. Also, we do not know whether he is looking at her breast because it is the location of her heart, the seat of the emotions, or whether he is aware, at that moment, of the physical beauty of her bosom; and if it is the latter, we do not know whether he is conscious of the beauty of her skin or the beauty of her bust. Snell ("Tres ejemplos," 185) follows El Brocense in assuming not only that it is the latter but also that the lady's breast is uncovered. The indefinite "lo de fuera" can refer to her appearance in general, or ambiguously to both the outward beauty of her bosom and her appearance in general. In any case, the internal beauty that the persona hopes to glimpse in the lady must be much richer than a soul that is merely not at variance with the lady's external beauty, not inconsistent with it. On the basis of the words "en ... ser igual," we can conclude, as I have explained, that he must mean equal in kind (appealing and inviting). For this reason I have assigned to the word "conviene" the meaning of "matches" and not as "is suited to" or words to that effect. A definition of *convenir* in the *Diccionario de autoridades* is "Vale también pertenecer, ser a propósito y correspondiente a la naturaleza o calidad de alguna cosa" ["it also means to belong, to be fitting and corresponding to the nature or quality of something"].[2] Also, in line 4 the persona says that he wondered if the lady's inward beauty matches her outward beauty "en apariencia" [in appearance] and being equal. One can only question how the persona could have anticipated that her inward beauty could "appear" to him at all. Perhaps he was referring to the possibility of her providing concrete evidence of her sensitive humanity by displaying delicacy in relation to himself — as opposed to what actually happened, her assuming that his look constituted a threat.

In any case, the interpretation I propose, that the persona is concerned with whether the lady's inward beauty is compatible with her outward beauty, is also consistent with the perspective of Renaissance classicism, the aesthetic orientation with which Garcilaso has traditionally been most identified. Renaissance classicism was grounded in a humanistic concept of natural human innocence and an ideal of beauty based on the harmony of body and spirit (*kalokagathia*). That ideal is acclaimed, for example, in Castiglione's *Il Corteggiano*, a work which we know Garcilaso held in the highest regard. Judging by the excellence of Garcilaso's verse, there is every reason to believe that he consciously embraced the classicist standard of an equilibrium of formal perfection and substance, of subjective appropriation and objective content. On the basis of these considerations, it seems even more unlikely that he would posit a fictional situation in which the poet–persona's effort to behold a harmony of inward and outward beauty becomes thwarted by an inherent incompatibility between them.

The only element in Sonnet 22 that could conceivably lead one to conclude that the persona's interest in beholding the lady's inner being has been overpowered by her sensuous appeal is the word "duro," in line 6. Taken together with the word "encuentro" (as we shall see), the word "duro" is decisive in determining one's interpretation of the poem. Snell does not address the issue, but Rivers reads the word "duro" to mean "cruel" or pitiless, apparently in the sense that the lady's sensual ("carnal") appeal has the effect of abruptly quashing the persona's initial, spiritual interest in her by provoking in him the compulsive unrestraint of sensual appetite. As can be seen from the passage cited above, Heiple takes the same view, suggesting that the impact of the lady's bosom (in the physical sense) on the persona was such as to disorient him and send him reeling, as it were, in an attitude of sensual fixation that prevented him from

---

[2] *Diccionario de autoridades*, 3 vols. (Madrid: Gredos, 1990), 1: 577.

The Death of Love's Hopes: Garcilaso's Sonnet 22

being able to attempt to concentrate further on the lady's soul. I will argue, however, that this interpretation is not entirely cogent.

If "duro" is understood to mean "cruel" or "pitiless," then the interpretations of Rivers and Heiple seem possible. However, the word can also mean "severe" or "harsh," and when it is understood in this way, the persona can be seen as being brought up short, not — I wish to suggest — because of any inherent antagonism between spiritual beauty and sensual appeal but because of resistance met with in the lady's *modesty*. The protective function of sexual modesty is described by Max Scheler as follows:

> Modesty is, as it were, the "natural veil of the soul" in our entire sexuality. Nietzsche has justifiably emphasized Madame Guyon's words that modesty is "ce que enveloppe le corps." ... clothes are only a crystallization of shame. They are also a symbolization of shame for bodies made in the arts. However, in a phenomenological focus, shame must be compared to a refined aura of invulnerability and untouchability felt to be an objective guard.[3]

The lady's warding off the persona, probably in a reflex, causes *not him but her* to hinder love's claims, for she concentrates attention on the physical and then repels his attention because it is focused as it is. When the persona sustains a "duro encuentro" with her beauty that thwarts his look, he does indeed meet with sudden resistance to his forward advance. However, that resistance does not occur because the concrete sight of the lady's bosom caused the persona's initial innocent interest to be unexpectedly countered by a propensity in him that is incompatible with that innocence. The resistance that the persona encountered and that caused his experience of disillusionment is not an effect of her outer beauty but of a quality of her personality. Hers is a harshly defensive and precipitous modesty that peremptorily prevents him from glimpsing her spirit more fully. The lady's being portrayed in such terms is consistent with the tradition of allegorical motifs in courtly love literature. C. S. Lewis explains in *The Allegory of Love* (123–24, 364–66) that the quality of *Daunger* (danger) displayed by the lady as a result of her modesty is a formidable enemy of the lover and is personified as a *vilains* who is swarthy, huge, and hirsute. *Daunger*'s meaning

---

[3] Max Scheler, *Person and Self-Value*, trans. M. S. Frings and B. Noble (Dordecht: Nijhoff, 1989), 23–24.

is "the rebuff direct, the lady's 'snub' launched from the height of her ladyhood, her pride suddenly wrapped about her as a garment, and perhaps her anger and contempt" (124).

Another detail of language that appears to have gone unnoticed in previous readings of Sonnet 22 is the persona's use of the word "de" instead of "con" in line 6. The word "de," which is inconsistent with the translation "encounter with," forces one to conclude that the meaning of the word "encuentro" cannot be "encounter" in the sense of "meeting" but is rather "stroke, blow."[4] Rivers may have recognized that possibility, in his observation that the line "de vuestra hermosura el duro encuentro" could refer to a blow from the hand with which the lady covered her breast [*Obras completas*, 123]). But Rivers does not enter into details in relation to these issues, and on the basis of his other comments it seems more likely that what he had in mind was not that the "encuentro" is a blow but that the line is a subtle way of referring to the lady's action of blocking the persona's view by quickly shielding herself with her hand. That reading, that the lady (personified by her own modest beauty) assumes a "combatively" defensive attitude toward the persona's interest in her beauty, supports the conclusion that the circumstance causing the effects of her beauty to seem "duro" (harsh) to the persona is not the type of that beauty considered externally (for example, sensuous beauty) nor any passionately arresting susceptibility to the voluptuous on the persona's part but is rather a function of the lady's internal nature, evaluating tendency, and attitude of mind as these become evidenced in her action of guarding herself with her hand. Also, the word "detiene" (stops) in line 5 implies the presence of an active subject. Such a subject can, of course, only be the lady, who is represented by the synecdoche "vuestra hermosura." In any case, when the word "detiene" in Sonnet 22 is interpreted thus, the persona's respectful interest in the lady as a person is given as having been countered by a display of modesty on her part. This reading is consistent with the event referred to in the third stanza, the lady's shielding her bosom from the

---

[4] Whereas "encounter of" or "encounter from" would have sense as a translation of "encuentro de," "encounter with" does not; but if "encuentro" is translated as "encounter," "encounter with" is the only one that fits the situation. One definition that the *Diccionario de Autoridades* gives for "encuentro" is "el golpe que se da encontrando con alguna cosa" ["the blow that is dealt when one meets something in combat (or lights, descends upon something)"], followed by an example from *Don Quijote* 1.1: "Y le derribo de un encuentro, o le parto por mitad del cuerpo" ["And I'll knock him down with one stroke or I'll cut him in half"]: 2: 453.

persona's eyes — an action that she evidently performs with such insistence as to abort further communication between herself and the persona and thus end the encounter. Interpreting the second stanza to mean that the persona's own reaction to the lady's beauty is what hindered his attempt to behold her soul is inconsistent with this explanation given by the persona himself in the third stanza, if that stanza is understood as meaning, as I agree with Snell ("Tres ejemplos," 185) and Gargano (*Fonti, miti, topoi*, 42) that it does, that the lady covers her breast with her hand.

§

Now that I have introduced my own perspective with regard to Sonnet 22, let us consider the interpretation of Antonio Gargano. At present it stands as the uncontested, or "preferred," interpretation of Sonnet 22, having been accepted by Alicia de Colombí-Monguió in a review article on Gargano's monograph and approved of by Rivers in his review of Heiple.[5] With characteristic tact, Rivers, in the course of faulting Heiple for not having taken Gargano's book on Garcilaso into account, extols Gargano's interpretation of Sonnet 22 in spite of Gargano's having, in that same interpretation, taken issue with Rivers' own views on the poem. Rivers attempts no defense of his own point of view, presumably because a review article on Heiple's book was not an appropriate forum. Yet, as I shall explain, what differences exist between Gargano's interpretation and Rivers's do not seem to me necessarily to resolve themselves so clearly in Gargano's favor.

Gargano (*Fonti, miti, topoi*, 28) disagrees with Rivers's opinion that in Sonnet 22 the "disdain, or coy withdrawal" of the lady, whom Rivers had referred to as being "deliberately cruel," elicits in the persona not tragic suffering but "sophisticated frivolity" evidenced in his witty quotation of Petrarch in the last line (E. Rivers, *Garcilaso de la Vega, Poems: A Critical Guide* [London: Grant & Cutler, 1980], 26–28). Gargano considers Rivers's interpretation to imply that the poem lacks depth (*Fonti, miti, topoi*, 28–29), himself taking the view that Sonnet 22 is the account of a painful experience of frustration (41). It is my own view that the otherwise fine and suggestive analyses

---

[5] See Alicia de Colombí-Monguió, rev. of *Imitación y transformación: El petrarquismo en la poesía de Boscán y Garcilaso de la Vega*, by A. J. Cruz, and *Fonti, Miti, Topoi: Cinque Studi su Garcilaso*, by Antonio Gargano, *Kentucky Romance Quarterly* 38 (1991): 95–106 and Elias Rivers, "Garcilaso de la Vega and the Italian Renaissance: Texts and Contexts / Review Article," in *Calíope*.

of Sonnet 22 by Rivers and Gargano, as well as by Heiple and Snell, share the limitation of not recognizing the central issue, the lady's modesty. If the possibility of focusing on the lady's modesty ever did present itself to these critics, they may have been reluctant to place an emphasis on it because of not wishing to suggest that the persona intended to "fault" the lady or blame her for the impasse, for it is not clear from the poem that the persona has such an attitude. However, while it appears that in his poetic complaint the persona regards her modesty as excessive, her high degree of modesty could also be considered by him, as we shall see, to be an attribute of her beauty in the same way that self-value is a complementary attribute of the spiritual person. By this perspective the persona, upon beholding the inaccessible lady's elegant modesty, is actually more smitten by her than ever: hence his grief and his complaint. In fact, when he refers to "your beauty's harsh stroke," the lady's beauty, in addition to being a personification of the lady herself, can be seen (as I have already suggested) as a personification of her modesty, which is "harsh" and brutal not just because it repels the persona but to the extent that the persona finds it irresistible. When considered in that light, there are elements in Sonnet 22 that are reminiscent of the alternative reading of line 4 of Garcilaso's Sonnet 23. There, the appeal of the lady's beauty is seen as heightened by her restraining modesty:

> En tanto que de rosa y d'azucena
> se muestra la color en vuestro gesto,
> y que vuestro mirar ardiente, honesto,
> enciende el corazón y lo refrena . . .

> [While the color of your face displays rose and white lily, and your ardent, chaste look ignites the heart and restrains it . . .]

Gargano recognizes the importance of line 6, "de vuestra hermosura el duro encuentro," for a reading of the whole poem (*Fonti, miti, topoi*, 35), but he interprets that line to refer to the obstacle constituted by the arresting effect upon the persona's eyesight of the beautiful, unclothed hand with which the lady shields her bosom (38–40). When the persona is dazzled and hence stopped by the external, corporeal beauty of the hand, his spiritual vision is overpowered and he loses sight of the lady's "breast" in the specific internal sense of "soul," notwithstanding the ambiguity that the word "breast" also suggests "bosom" in the physical sense (50, cf. 40–41). Thus, line 13, "y el golpe, que en vos hixo amor en vano" ["and the blow, which love dealt you in vain"] refers to the persona's look and its failure to attain the desired results. But Gargano sees the failure not as being due to the lady's guarding herself from the persona's advances, as I do, but as being the result of his weakness, his not being able to avoid tearing himself away from the beauty of the lady's hand and proceed inward ("Lo sguardo ... dell'amante non ha saputo evitare de arrestarse troppo al di qua del cuore") ["The lover's look was incapable of avoiding being stopped to an extent he found regrettable before reaching [this side of] her heart": 41]. So it is, according to Gargano, that line 11, "que aun a su mismo pecho no perdona" ["that will not give leave even to what is within its own breast"], has the meaning that the lady's hand does not "pardon" her own breast in the sense that it will not allow it to be seen (40). The overall perspective offered by the poem, Gargano maintains, is that, far from any "cruelty" on the part of the lady being the cause of the persona's failure, the persona himself must bear the shame ("smacco": 39) and the guilt ("colpa": 51) for his error and consequent painful frustration (41). Gargano emphasizes the influence ("genealogia") of two poems by Petrarch (Sonnet 257 and Canzone 70) on Garcilaso's poem, even going so far as supporting his interpretation of Sonnet 22 by citing line 44 of Canzone 70 ("il bel che mi si mostra intorno") as though it were a line from Garcilaso's poem (50).[6] As I mentioned, de Colombí-Monguió agrees with the conclusions that Gargano draws on the basis of intertextual influences. The influence of these poems by Petrarch on Sonnet 22 is undeniable, but it is my view that the assumption (by Gargano or any other critic) that intertextual influences are so decisive as to determine or restrict even thematic dimensions of subsequent compositions must ultimately be regarded as arbitrary.[7]

---

[6] Colombí-Monguió quotes (rev. of *Imitación y transformación: El petrarquismo en la poesía de Boscán y Garcilaso de la Vega*, by A. J. Cruz, and *Fonti, Miti, Topoi: Cinque Studi su Garcilaso*, by Antonio Gargano, 101) the passage in which Gargano refers (*Fonti, miti, topoi*, 50) somewhat misleadingly to this line from Petrarch, but since she does so without including the quotation marks from Gargano's text, the line appears to be Gargano's paraphrase of a line from Garcilaso's Sonnet 22. The unintended effect is that, while she strengthens the case for Gargano's interpretation and for her endorsement of it, she also adds to the general confusion.

[7] Anne Cruz in "Spanish Petrarchism and the Poetics of Appropriation" (in *Renaissance Rereadings: Intertext and Context*, ed. Maryanne Cline Horowitz [Urbana: University of Illinois Press, 1988], 80–95) specifically seeks to correct the misconception that the imitation of model texts in Boscán and especially in Garcilaso is perfunctory.

Like other critics who have analyzed Sonnet 22, Gargano sees the poet–persona as having become transfixed by the arresting power of physical beauty; but, as I shall discuss further, he displaces that conclusion in a peculiar manner. Rivers, in the paragraph emphasized by Gargano, does not enter into details as to what he thinks obstructs the persona's original intention of beholding the lady's spiritual beauty, but we must assume that Rivers's explanation is the one I cited previously: that the lady's "carnal beauty was itself a cruel barrier for the eyes of the persona."[8] Gargano interprets Rivers's reference to "the lady's disdain, or coy withdrawal" to mean that the lady responded to a courtier's voyeurism with *pruderie* (*Fonti, miti, topoi*, 28). Actually, when Rivers discusses line 6 (*Obras completas*, 123), not only does he weigh two possibilities for an interpretation of line 6 ("duro encuentro" referring either to the blow with an open hand when the lady covers her breast or to the barrier constituted by her carnal beauty) without expressing a clear preference for either, but his words "coy withdrawal" do not by themselves have a definite meaning. "Coy" can mean either bashful or coquettish or a combination of both. Its most likely meaning in this context is a coquettishly assumed bashfulness. Now, "coyness" understood in this sense is the opposite of *pruderie* if by that term we are to understand "prudishness," i.e., overly modest behavior. Coyness in a woman is an affected modesty that is intended to spur the interest of the suitor by presenting to him the female's resistance with the covert intention of inviting the male to overcome it. It is not entirely clear from Gargano's use of the French word *pruderie* whether he is referring to the pseudo-modesty of coyness or to actual prudishness, but he probably means the former. He does make it clear (28) that he disagrees with Rivers's conclusion that a mundane instance of courtly flirtation is the subject of the poem. Gargano seems justified in his view if we consider that it is difficult to reconcile the light tone of the words "coy withdrawal" with what the persona in lines 10 and 12 refers to as the painful experience of his hope's death. If Sonnet 22 is not tragic, it is close to it, which is not to say that it does not also have an ironic and even humorous dimension as well. On the other hand, Rivers's idea of "the lady's disdain" would seem to go too far in the direction of emphasizing the deliberate nature of the lady's behavior: her action of fending off the persona's attention may seem brutal to the persona, and it may indeed constitute a

---

[8] Rivers states this view in his 1974 edition, 123, and it reappears in a new printing in 1981, a year after the publication of *Poems: A Critical Guide*, which contains the passage with which Gargano takes issue.

painful slight, but it need not be regarded as an act of disdain. Nor can I find in the poem a basis for regarding her modesty as being coquettish, even if it does have the effect of concentrating attention on herself as an object of desire. But Rivers's interpretation of the lady's being "deliberately cruel" and "disdainful" is not so inaccurate as Gargano claims if we see the lady as projecting her own preoccupation with the sensual (with the sensual preoccupations of others) onto the persona and as then rejecting him because of what she assumes to be his attitude. She would have placed her person at no significant risk if, before responding defensively, she had briefly hesitated in order to attempt to discern the nature of the persona's interest. Presumably, the persona would at that point have been able to satisfy his initial curiosity by seeing that the lady was not given to boringly mechanical behavior — that, indeed, her inner beauty *did* match her outer beauty. On the other hand, a defensive response on her part would not seem inappropriate if the persona's initial look at her breast revealed itself as a fixed gaze at her physical beauty, especially given the relatively austere official morality of the day. In that case Snell's view that the lady's reaction was justified ("Tres ejemplos," 185) would follow logically. But there is no basis in the text of the poem either for attributing indelicate behavior to the persona or, as I have mentioned, even for assuming that the lady's physical beauty in itself was, at that moment, the basis of the persona's interest.

The main weakness in Gargano's interpretation of Sonnet 22 is his view that the lady's physical beauty, which stops the persona's eyes, is the beauty of her hand. Considered in the abstract, such an explanation seems plausible enough, especially if we also postulate the context of a rarified cultural environment characterized by a high degree of restraint where sexual matters are concerned, or one so repressive as to impose rigorous norms of bodily shame. The problem is that the poem does not actually *say* that what consumes the persona's interest is the beauty of the lady's hand. It says "your beauty's harsh stroke stops my eyes." True enough, the poem does not say "your physical beauty in general" either. It is not even made clear from the language itself that those words are specific even to the extent of referring on the literal level to the lady's physical beauty. That much must be inferred, as it must be inferred that "your beauty" in that line refers to the lady as bearer of the value of her own beauty and, as its protector, author of the rebuff. But the poem strongly suggests, with the persona's eyes on the lady's breast and his reference to the beautiful appearance of what is without, that his consciousness of her physical beauty is not limited to a mere hand. One can only wonder where an interpretation that places such high value on the lady's hand could have come from. Perhaps it was influenced by Herrera's speculation, "o por ventura alaba la mano, que era tal que se enamoró della" (["or perchance he is praising her hand, which was such that he fell in love with it"]; Rivers, *Obras completas*, 122). True enough, the lady's corporeal beauty was recognized by the persona prior to the moment referred to in the poem. But it seems to me that the problem with the prior interpretations of Sonnet 22 by Herrera, El Brocense, and Tamayo — that the persona was distracted by the lady's physical beauty from his intention to contemplate her heart — is that the image of the poet–persona thus suggested is not an image of the elegant and sophisticated man whose voice is heard in the poem; it is that of a green, goggle-eyed youth. Could it be that Gargano posits the idea that the persona is in awe of the lady's hand in order to prevent the persona from appearing libidinous? If this was Gargano's intention, he attains that end, but our interest in the poet–persona as a vital personality is compromised in the process. Also, if the attention of the persona (of his "eyes," a figure of speech that represents him as a receptive subject) is arrested and fixed by the great enthusiasm that he feels for the beauty of the lady's hand, how can that same hand simultaneously cause him (his eyes) to be sad? And if the persona were able to suspend his enthusiasm for the beauty of the lady's hand to the extent of feeling sad, would he not also have the presence of mind to be able to proceed beyond the lady's external beauty (the beauty of her hand) and glimpse her inner person? That he was not able to do so is evident from the poem, but what prevented him? The explanation, I wish again to assert, is not that the lady's hand continued to absorb the persona's attention; it is that the lady herself averted his efforts to connect with her spiritually. There is no basis for holding the view that she wanted to prevent him from seeing that she did *not* possess the inner beauty he sought to behold. One can, however, conclude that with her hand she fended off the persona's attention.

But what specifically could have been her motive in doing so? In relation to this issue a series of troublesome questions emerge. Did she perceive his behavior as being forward? After all, he did have his eyes directed at her breast. He claims that he was not paying attention to her physical beauty, that he was attempting to look beyond it to see if her spiritual beauty matched it. But how was she to know that such was the case? Perhaps it is he himself who must assume responsibility for having offended the lady's modesty and provoked the response that he now complains has caused him so much pain. Or perhaps she did notice his reserve in regard to her sensual appeal and feigned a defensive reaction because her vanity was piqued or because she found his behavior to be too unaggressive. Or did she have some other reason for not wanting to encourage him? Was she married? Did she want to conceal her inner personality because she was naturally introverted? Answering such questions, of course, requires information that we do not possess, information concerning the lady as an individual and how she perceived her encounter with the persona.

One is tempted to conveniently dispel such quandary with a statement to the effect that the "point" of Sonnet 22 is to make us generally conscious of the intriguingly ambiguous nature of language and experience, that the poem "makes us think" and proves the futility of attempting to make one-sided interpretations and taking dogmatic stances. However, in my conviction that nothing is resolved in ambiguity, I wish to assert that interpretations are only possible if certain ground rules are established, facts that everyone can agree upon. In the case of Sonnet 22, I would first of all acknowledge that I do not consider the poem to be exclusively playful and ironic. The irony of the persona's being painfully repulsed by a delicate hand and of bitter despair being evoked in language that is wittily sophisticated and paradoxical correspond to only one dimension of this complex poem. When interpreted figuratively, the sonnet also has an earnest, even somber side. Given that perspective, I would hold that if the persona continues to be in great pain it must be because he loves the lady. If he loves the lady, it must be because he beholds in her at least the external evidence of an ideal ethos of personality.[9] We can surmise that there is an ideal ethos of individual personality that the persona discerns in her as a value of which she is the bearer, for it is this ideal ethos that the persona loves. On the other hand, there is no evidence on which to base any other conclusion where the lady is concerned. Hence one may conclude that any such speculations are not important to the theme of this particular poem. Because of a similar lack of information to the contrary, we must accept the persona's word as to the nature of his interest in the lady at the time of their encounter, and we must take the view that, even if the lady *is* married, the nature of his interest in her, as it is given in the poem, is as yet not such as to necessarily threaten the lady's virtue or reputation.[10] Also, the poem represents the point of view of the poet–persona, and it does

---

[9] By "ideal ethos of personality" I mean the individual–personal value-essence, the potential, ideal form of the distinguishing qualities (the value-character) of one unique person: see Scheler, *Formalism in Ethics*, 489–94; Hartmann, *Ethics*, 2: 342–46; and Werkmeister, *Hartmann's New Ontology*, 211.

[10] My recognition of the need for a ground rule whereby we take the poet at his word unless the poem provides information to the contrary is consistent with Deyermond's observations concerning the necessary means for overcoming certain difficulties that present themselves in interpreting narrative that is autobiographical or fiction that is presented through the eyes of the protagonist, as in the case of *Lazarillo de Tormes*. Referring to comments on troubles with irony in Wayne Booth's *The Rhetoric of Fiction* (Chicago:

not claim to represent that of the lady: we are thus justified in limiting the basis of our interpretation of the poem to information that the perspective of the persona is able to offer. On these general grounds we are able to narrow down the range of possible implications of the passage in question and arrive at the following view: in her exquisite and attractive modesty, the lady responded to what was presumably a proper and respectful interest in her on the part of the persona as though his interest in her had been of a different nature, although she may not have actually seen his attitude as being different at all. She may also have merely been startled.

If one does not assume that the beauty of the lady's hand monopolized the persona's attention merely on the basis of Gargano's observation that there was a tradition of such motifs, the idea of the persona's subordinating all interest in every dimension of the lady's beauty to a preoccupation with her hand seems quite preposterous. For that assumption would have to be based on the premise that the persona's initial interest in the lady's inner beauty was tentative at best, yet in the first words of the poem the persona declares that it was "con ansia extrema" ["with extreme longing"] that he felt moved to behold that beauty. If we transport ourselves imaginatively to the situation described, placing ourselves in the position of the persona and seeing through his eyes, we must naturally infer that he witnesses the physical presence of *the whole woman* — not just her hand or even the beauty of her body but also her face (likely her most beautiful physical feature) and her comportment. Actually, it is the eyes, not the breast, that are the "window to the soul," yet the lady's eyes are never mentioned, presumably because Garcilaso wanted to distinguish her attitude from the receptive attitude of the persona (who is actually identified with his eyes). When the persona says that he placed his eyes on the lady's "breast" in order to "see her inner nature," he is speaking figuratively. The only way that he could really "see" the lady's spiritual being would be in various manifestations of her personality, of her spiritual personhood ("person" being understood here as a unity of acts) — not only those that are able to be perceived sensorially at the same time that they are interpreted intellectually, but those that linger in mental images and become comprehensible only as they are

---

University of Chicago Press, 1961), 316–23, Deyermond notes that it is a well-established convention to accept the actions of the characters and the facts of the situation as the narrator states them unless there is warning to the contrary: *Lazarillo de Tormes: A Reader's Guide* (London: Grant & Cutler, 1973), 72–74, and idem, "The Corrupted Vision: Further Thoughts on *Lazarillo de Tormes*," *Forum for Modern Language Studies* 1 (1965): 246–49, here 246–48.

The Death of Love's Hopes: Garcilaso's Sonnet 22

contemplated retrospectively. How can the beauty of the lady's hand, unclothed and beautiful as it may be, compete with such a rich set of impressions? And how, if we do not see him as being repulsed by her, could her merely raising her hand make him forget every other dimension of her being? If he is not a green youth or effetely hypersensitive, delicate, and easily discouraged, it seems that it would have required considerably more than the lady's raising her hand for his interest in knowing her better to be thwarted.

But are we not now drawing conclusions about the character of the persona for which we have no real basis in the poem, conclusions such as we have already refused to draw about the lady? The difference here is that it is the persona who speaks, not the lady. Although aesthetic values are object-values, a poem is an act-value of the poet, an utterance of his voice. One can base justified inferences as to his mentality and attitudes on implications of style and, in that way, assess some behavior patterns that would be attributed to him as being more plausible than others. Garcilaso's lyric has a distinct personality, and it is different, in some respects, from the personality of, for example, Petrarch's lyric, with whom Gargano wants to closely associate Garcilaso. Whereas the serene melancholy of Petrarch in his *Canzoniere* is given at times to representing the persona's general disposition as being somewhat shrinking or languishing, Garcilaso's persona is more often recklessly impetuous and self-destructive. While in Petrarch love is often painfully timid and unassertive, love in Garcilaso is often an epic force. It was Karl Vossler who recognized in the style of Garcilaso a heroic character that contrasts with the more secluded and withdrawn idyllic style of authors like Petrarch.[11] Of course, the personas in the elegiac love lyric of both Garcilaso and Petrarch share their most important feature, a deep and tenacious anguish at not having attained a remote preferred value.

Gargano's notion of the captivating hand in Sonnet 22 may well suggest an additional general problem, or perhaps danger, in criticism that places a strong emphasis on intertextual influences. I have already mentioned the problem of assuming that subsequent authors have retained the thematic focus of the works from which they drew. A related fallacy is that in establishing the influence of some authors upon others it is possible to lose sight of the extent to which the authors who are influenced still managed to develop distinct and original literary personalities of their own.

---

[11] K. Vossler, *Introducción a la literatura española del Siglo de Oro* (Madrid: Cruz y Raya, 1934), 97–98.

§

Previous interpretations of Sonnet 22 have contemplated only the poet–persona's advance toward the lady and have ignored the second dynamic, which, from the persona's point of view, is the crucial issue: whether the actual essence of the lady is harmoniously directed ("matched") by her ideal essence and whether that ideal essence is as the persona envisions it. If such were the case, instead of being mechanically predisposed by conventional, bodily shame to avoid a disvalue by curbing the sex-drive and hastily fending off the persona, the lady might well have been prompted by less rigid (less "harsh") and more thoughtful feelings of psychic shame[12] to affirm the value of the love felt by the persona and to display a sensitivity to the requirement of a response of love — which is not to say that she should have *given* a response of love. She would thus have also displayed the autonomy of at least having the *potential* to advance toward the persona as well, even if, for whatever reason, she were not able to or did not want to do so. As Rivers and Heiple discern, Sonnet 22 presents an opposition between a sensitive regard for the spiritual person and the disruptive power of crude sexual instinct. But that opposition is not given in the poem as incompatible tendencies within the persona, as is generally thought; it is given in an opposition between the persona and the lady. It is not the persona who, on the occasion described by the poem, is represented as being determined by the material order of existence (sexual drive), but the lady. The purely sensuous sex drive differs from the spirituality of sexual love in being rooted in the physical order of nature, an order not directed by ends but mechanically and blindly ruled by cause and effect. Yet it is only through co-existing with the causally determined temporal process and minimizing conflict with it that the axiologically directed will is able to master natural causality and rise above it in order to actualize its own aims.[13] When such co-existence is hindered by subjection to rigid moral principles intended to guard against the "tyranny" of causal determinism, what was originally supposed to be avoided — determination by the tem-

---

[12] For a discussion of the distinction between "bodily shame" and "psychic shame," see Scheler, *Person and Self-Value*, 27, 69–70. My application of these terms bears the influence of concepts drawn from Scheler, *Formalism in Ethics*, 536, and Hartmann, *Ethics*, 2: 457–59.

[13] A discussion of the relation among the causal order, finalistic determination (determination of the means from the point of view of the end), and freedom of the will is in Hartmann, *Ethics*, 3: 62–80.

The Death of Love's Hopes: Garcilaso's Sonnet 22

poral process — is indirectly brought about. Such is the fallacy of severe morality, which in Garcilaso's day ranged from an oppressive asceto-monasticism to the teachings of Savonarola and Calvin.[14] In any case, one might say that the lady in Sonnet 22 was determined, if not by sensuousness directly, by a "presumption of sensuousness." The result of her conventional reflex of modesty is that the persona is prevented from seeing the contents of her soul, for that reflex also prevents her from revealing those contents.

Broadly speaking, the lady in Sonnet 22 represents ontological determination, not axiological determination, and the impasse of the encounter described in the poem represents microcosmically the general human plight of a failure to achieve a synthesis between those two equally important preferential trends.[15] That failure is "the death of hope," of the hope to fulfill the persona's, or (if the persona is seen as a metaphor) of "mankind's," human destiny. Seen allegorically, "the man/poet–persona" "longs to" transcend commitment to mere ideal being by setting down roots in the actual, just as "the lady" stands to transcend actual existence as such through the creative power of values. The persona does not conclude that the ideal essence of individual personality that he beheld in the physical beauty of the lady has no counterpart in the actual person, in her will's potential for self-determination through values, but rather that he was not able to discover whether it does or not. As he himself implies, his hopes of making that discovery, and perhaps his hopes for a love between them, perished in the impasse. For the persona to have gained such insight would have required that the behavior of the lady not impede the formation of spiritual ties between them.[16] For him to achieve his goal, the lady would have had to advance beyond herself to encounter the persona, not with defensive resistance ("harshness") but with sensitivity and moral solidarity. On the other hand, the situation depicted is not lacking in com-

---

[14] For a poignant exposé of the dehumanizing effects of repressive austerity in sixteenth-century Spain (the case of Fray Francisco Ortiz), see A. Selke de Sánchez, *El Santo Oficio de la Inquisición* (Madrid: Guadarrama, 1968).

[15] Related to this conclusion are Scheler's views concerning what he terms "the immanent tragedy of sexual love," which he regards as being necessitated by "extant coincidences between lower systems of values and those most generally accepted": *Person and Self-Value*, 64–66.

[16] The lady would have had to not refuse what Scheler refers to as "an act of love of ideal oughtness [of the good that ought to be]" corresponding to the persona's *worthiness* to be loved. What the lady does instead is to give scope to "the negative value lying in the non-being of the positive value of responding love": *Formalism in Ethics*, 537.

plexity, largely because the circumstances of the relationship and details pertinent to the encounter are described so elliptically. To say that the lady represents "ontological determination" (the order of natural causality) does not represent the situation from the lady's point of view. From her point of view, an attitude of distrust toward the persona may be justified on principle, for she could regard his possibly forward behavior as making *him* suspect of "representing ontological determination." Yet the poem, as has already been observed, presents the point of view of the persona, and it is from this point of view that it must primarily be interpreted.

The issue here is not one of my or the persona's attempting to assert the persona's right to command the lady's love, for there is no such right and that claim cannot be made by anyone. The lady's apparently brusque response may make life a little worse for the persona, but it causes no diminution in his love for her, precisely because, as one who loves, his intuitive insight directs his attention beyond her actual, empirical personality and focuses it on her ideal essence. Surely in this poem especially it is suggested that love's being "requited" and its value affirmed does not necessitate that love itself actually be reciprocated but (I repeat) merely that there occur a *psychic act* of "coexperiencing the *requirement* of a response of love" (Scheler, *Formalism in Ethics*, 536), an act of relating to another as a person with real being and an individual identity, a personal essence, and not as a preconceived stereotype. Yet such response implies the possible understanding of a felt love, an experience that conventional, collective moral norms and, in this case, the lady's precipitous adherence to those norms have effectively negated, at least temporarily. For, according to those norms, "the other" has no givenness as a *person* but is a member of a hostile alien force, " 'the enemy,' which is a complex of vital power" (Scheler, *Formalism in Ethics*, 314). But it would also be a mistake and an over-simplification for ourselves to carry an emphasis on normative considerations to the point of asserting that the poet's "point" in representing the situation described by the poem is merely that the lady is remiss and the persona unjustly wounded. Sonnet 22, which treats the subject of feminine modesty, ultimately participates in the tradition of a rhetoric of praise intended as an invitation to intimacy. As such, it is an eloquent tribute to a lady's extraordinary appeal and to the power of her beauty. Scheler observes,

> Just as shame is the gift of a noble human being to preserve the most valuable inner feelings and protect them from any admixture with the low or bad, so also shame is a token of the capacity to love and

> of a strong drive. People who have little shame and are not shy often
> have a cold and empty nature. Conversely, strong modesty reveals
> increased *passion*, for which reason shame is so attractive to a noble
> person. (*Person and Self-Value*, 70)

How are feelings of sexual modesty "a token of the capacity to love"? According to Scheler, having those feelings requires that one be capable of experiencing a tension between love, which is directed exclusively and discriminately toward one individual, and the purely sensuous sex drive, "the quantifying and generic principle of sexual relations" whereby one seeks relations with a multiplicity of members of the opposite sex with little regard for their identity as individuals (*Person and Self-Value*, 17, 70). The lady's experience of that tension is evidenced in her modesty, and the persona's sorrow at the end of the poem is likely the passion that the lady's modesty has aroused in him. Similarly, the persona's agony and desperation at the rebuff represent him in a morally noble light, for they attest to the strength and vitality of his passion, to the uncompromising and exclusive character of his value-preferences. It is implied that his drive wellings, his abundance of the sexual urge, are "composed into one passionate stream, and thus they enter directly into an intentional relation to a person, for *one* person" (*Person and Self-Value*, 70). However, drawing biological ("vitalistic") implications from the aesthetics of manners could lead to misplacing the proper emphasis in an interpretation of Sonnet 22. We must remember that the undercurrents of an extraordinarily vital sexual energy that can be inferred on the basis of the behavior of the persona and the lady are able to be postulated only because it is also possible to infer a will effectively to dam such drives, for the capacity to do so is itself a sign of noble character. Any display of a common *predisposition* to the quantifying and generic experience of sensuous pleasure would be incompatible with the presumed high moral standing, the appeal as persons, of the persona and the lady, as well as with the elevated language of the poem. Her aversion at the prospect of discovering a lack of modest restraint in the persona may well be what explains the lady's having been moved to end the encounter prematurely. As for the persona, if he sees her display of modesty as being a quality of her beauty, it would have to be a characteristic of both her inward and outward beauty and would, therefore, have the effect of baffling the persona's assumption of a dichotomy of those two types of beauty. Perhaps the harmony of both types of beauty in the lady is what has caused his intense grief, which is the grief of frustration of a love that has intensified because of the appeal of the lady's modesty. The persona states that his hopes died but not that his love died, and where there is love there is hope. One recalls the epigram, "Love can hope where reason would despair."[17]

Critics of Sonnet 22 would seem traditionally to have followed the example of the lady in the poem by seeing in the persona a predisposition for the sensuous that is not there — or, perhaps it would be better to say, one "that is not concretely evidenced in the poem," for in this work the poet can be thought of as deliberately baiting us as readers, subtly inducing our natural tendency to project our own preoccupation with the sensual on the persona. In the tradition of the unsettling complexity of mannerist, or mannered, style, the poet creates an ambiguity and then plays on it and uses it to make readers confront their own unconscious assumptions.[18] Certainly no seasoned reader of Garcilaso will be surprised by my advancing an interpretation of Sonnet 22 whereby the lady is assigned an ambivalent identity vis-à-vis the strivings of the

---

[17] "None without hope e'er loved the brightest fair; / But love can hope where reason would despair": *Thesaurus of Epigrams*, ed. Edmund Fuller (New York: Crown, 1943), 158, No. 2968.

[18] The failure to recognize the subtlety of this technique for what it is has had the result of preventing certain problematic elements in the language of Sonnet 22 from receiving the scrutiny they deserve. One such element is the word "conviene" in line 4 that I have discussed above. My reading of the sonnet has also been informed by my having made imaginative interpretations of the words "mano" and "perdona" in the first tercet, in the passage "essa mano / que aun a su mismo pecho no perdona." The hand, which is associated with activity and with the sense of touch, is a symbol of differentiating action. I would suggest that in this poem it can be regarded as an analogue of the will. The sense of line 11 must be that the lady's will, in brusquely repulsing the persona's making known his receptiveness to response in love and esteem, also stifles what is within itself, the word "perdonar" here meaning "to release" in the sense of "to permit to be shown" or "to reveal," i.e., "to give leave to." Taking "mano" to represent the lady's will, then, the meaning is that in her peremptory rebuff of him she is also forsaking her own highest propensities, i.e., she stifles her noble will and high breeding, her feelings of compassionate solidarity and the vitality of a passionately loving disposition. In line 11 the words "a su" ("its," referring to "hand" or "will") could not mean "her," since the persona addresses the lady directly and nowhere refers to her in the third person. What is left, of course, is only the last antecedent noun: "mano." Hence my reading: "that hand that will not give leave even to what is within *its* own breast." And I am interpreting the word "pecho" as primarily a synecdoche for "value feelings." One of the entries that the *Diccionario de autoridades* has for "pecho," is "se toma muchas veces por la parte interior dél" ["often taken for its inner part]: 3: 177.

persona. Far more uncharacteristic of Garcilaso would be what to date is the more established reading of this work, whereby the persona is seen to carry the obstacle to those strivings within himself. It is typical in Garcilaso for the persona's movement towards a higher determination through values to be brutally and categorically ("despotically") squelched by the determination of a lower, mechanical, finalistically contingent (accidental), yet "sovereign" natural causality. In Sonnet 22 the persona's experience of being peremptorily blocked by a standard of lower determination is effected by the lady, who diverts attention in the direction of the sensuous and parries his overture in a manner that the persona compares to deflecting Cupid's arrows. Perhaps Cervantes had Garcilaso's sonnet in mind when in *Don Quijote* he wrote the poem sung by fifteen-year-old Don Luis. Let us recall that Don Luis has disguised himself as a mule lad in order to pursue his beloved Doña Clara, the "star" he follows as a mariner of love "sin esperanza / de llegar a puerto alguno" ["without hope of arriving at any port"]. In one stanza Don Luis sings,

> Recatos impertinentes,
> honestidad contra el uso,
> son nubes que me la encubren
> cuando más verla procuro. (1. 43)

[Uncalled-for modesty and being overly chaste are clouds that cover
it (the star he follows) when I try hardest to see it.]

The themes of unfounded suspicion and mutual distrust figure prominently in *Don Quijote*, in the interpolated narratives. Similarly, in Sonnet 22 as elsewhere, Garcilaso reveals himself not as a puritanical moralist, even of the inspired, Neoplatonist variety, but as participating in a current of secular humanism that is rooted in a constructive interest in the realities of human experience. In Garcilaso, that interest is compatible with Renaissance Hellenism in that sensuous beauty is not represented as being an obstacle to personal love of the sexes; the obstacle is an undue emphasis on the sensuous that results from the view that sensuous beauty is "sinful" and its effects so corrupting that it is best banished from human consciousness altogether. The antimonastic spirit of early Reformism, which coincides exactly with Garcilaso's dates, is clearly suggested in such a perspective. Thus it is that Heine was able to observe, "The painters in Italy perhaps carried on a much more effective polemic against clericalism than the Saxon theologians. The voluptuous flesh in Titian's paintings — all of this is

Protestantism. The loins of his Venus are much more fundamental theses than those the German monk posted on the church door in Wittenberg."[19] The theme of the elusive lady whom the poet–persona pursues as he is only able to glimpse her in the distance is central to Garcilaso's love lyric. The persona's words from *Canción* 4, "voy buscando / a quien huye de mí como enemiga," could well refer to Garcilaso's own pursuit of the fleeing possibility of enjoying life in a world delivered from an austere morality that imposes subjection to appetite precisely through a repressive process of denying the senses their natural place in human experience. In broadly symbolic terms, the chastely demure lady in Garcilaso's lyric may be seen as standing for the causally determined and ultimately self-referential cyclical order of nature that incorporates and entraps "man" (humankind) — the axiologically determined, teleological entity — and yet remains unreconciled to him. In Sonnet 22 the persona makes clear from the beginning of the poem that what he originally hoped for was to pass beyond a sensuous experience. At the end he makes known his anxiety at having been frustrated in that attempt.

---

[19] Heinrich Heine, *Selected Works*, trans. Helen Mustard (New York: Random House, 1973), 142–43.

5
Ambivalent Love and the Birth Pangs of Individuation in Garcilaso, Fray Luis de León, Fairbairn, and Jung

In Sonnet 38, Garcilaso de la Vega presents a situation reminiscent of a number of his works (Sonnets 1, 6, 17), as well as of Petrarch's Sonnet 15; Ausias March's Cant 121.6; and Fray Luis de León's Sonnet 2. I will analyze Fray Luis's Sonnet 2 after considering Garcilaso's Sonnet 38. The scene of Sonnet 38 is a dreary road that the poet–persona has been traveling in pursuit of a lady. He stands immobilized by confusion and anguish, unable either to turn back or to continue because each alternative is as painful as the other. At first, this predicament seems not to present any particular difficulty to the reader; the persona's affliction seems to be a result of the lady's refusal to reciprocate, and he seems simply to be expressing the idea that he can neither flee her nor continue to pursue her:

> Estoy contino en lágrimas bañado,
> rompiendo siempre el aire con sospiros,
> y más me duele el no osar deziros
> que he llegado por vos a tal estado;

> que viéndome do estoy y en lo que he andado
> por el camino estrecho de seguiros,
> si me quiero tornar para hüyros,
> desmayo, viendo atrás lo que he dexado;
> y si quiero subir a la alta cumbre,
> a cada paso espántanme en la vía
> exemplos tristes de los que han caydo;
> sobre todo, me falta ya la lumbre
> de la esperanza, con que andar solía
> por la oscura región de vuestro olvido.[1]

[I am constantly bathed in tears, ever rending the air with sighs, and it pains me more that I dare not tell you that I have come to such a state because of you; seeing where I am and what has occupied me on the narrow road of following you, if I want to turn to flee you, I faint, seeing behind me what I left; and if I want to climb to the high peak, I am frightened at every step along the way by sad examples of those who have fallen; especially, I now lack the light of hope, with which I used to tread in the dark region of your forgetfulness.]

Yet upon closer examination several questions arise that a superficial reading of the poem cannot answer. When the poet–persona says that if he wants to turn to flee the lady he is unable to do so because what he sees behind him makes him faint, is he referring to what is "behind him" before he turns to flee or afterwards? What is it that he sees and why does he faint? What is the significance of the high peak that the persona says he does not dare to climb because of the many who have attempted to do so but have fallen? What are the broader implications of the experience that the persona is having at the moment of utterance, plunged in a dark abyss and trapped between two equally undesirable alternatives? Why has frustration in the situation described had such severe effects on the poet–persona, producing in him a degree of anguish that borders on the pathological? And how, finally, can one explain the com-

---

[1] Quotations of Garcilaso's poems are from Rivers, *Obras completas*, 162–63. Translations of Sonnet 38 and of critical commentary by Rivers or other scholars are mine.

patibility of, on the one hand, the spirit of courageous love-idealism that one senses to be the basis of part of the poem's aesthetic appeal and, on the other, the persona's helplessness and incapacitating, even morbid, despair?

As is so often the case in Garcilaso, before one can broach the terrain of thematic considerations it is necessary to address the problem of establishing the text — not so much considering textual variants as choosing among the many possible ways in which the text can be understood even on a preliminary basis, in spite of its logic and deceptive appearance of simplicity. The first stanza is quite clear: the persona makes it known that he is in great pain and is overcome with anxiety because of a lady to whom he cannot reveal his suffering. The second stanza is more problematic, especially in the last two lines. The persona states that when he considers where he is and what has occupied him on the narrow road of following the lady, if he tries to flee her he faints, seeing behind him what he left. The issue of what, exactly, the persona sees when he looks back that prevents him from fleeing is as elusive as it is important for a reading of the entire poem, for it provides a basis for interpreting the alternative to fleeing the lady, i.e., climbing to the "high peak." In preferring any single interpretation, one must be guided by the standards of coherence and logic of language, as well as by what will render comprehensible the persona's total dilemma and the overall theme of the poem. In any case, climbing to the high peak must be considered an alternative to fleeing the lady.

Apart from the fact that in the first line of stanza two the words "do estoy" ("where I am — on the narrow road of following you") can be understood to mean either "how much of the road is left" or "how far I have come," the words "lo que he dejado" ["what I left"] in line 8 can be interpreted in at least six possible ways, three of which have been identified prior to the present study. It is my view that of those three interpretations that have already been suggested by critics and editors, only that of Rivers is a viable possibility. Of the three new interpretations that I will suggest, I believe that one is preferable to that of Rivers while yet another is superior to any of the other five interpretations.

I will first mention those that have already been identified by other critics. Bienvenido Morros considers that by what the persona sees he has left when he wants to flee, he is referring to "un camino estrecho y difícil" ["a narrow and difficult road"],[2]

---

[2] B. Morros, ed., *Garcilaso de la Vega: Obra poética y textos en prosa* (Barcelona: Crítica, 1995), 62.

and he goes on to mention that Fernando de Herrera holds the narrow road to be the road of virtue. In fact, Herrera's explanation of the narrow road is given in relation to the first line of the following stanza — in reference to the road leading to what is given in the version in his edition as the "dificil cumbre" [difficult peak].[3] In any case, it would seem that Morros means that the persona's preoccupation with the lady herself has become displaced by his concern for the suffering involved in pursuing her. He is overcome by emotion and prevented from fleeing her because he considers how arduous his efforts to pursue the lady have been (the narrow road he would turn away from); that is, he reflects that by fleeing he would be abandoning the pursuit that he had endured so much to sustain. There are two problems presented by this interpretation as I understand it. One is that it would be illogical for the persona to be stating that he feels unable to renounce just the narrow road itself (not the lady) immediately after, in the first stanza of the poem, emphasizing the grief and frustration that he has experienced as a result of that same narrow road, even if one were to consider "do estoy" to mean "how far I have come." The second problem is that emphasizing the persona's concern for his own suffering diminishes his moral stature and aesthetic appeal by attenuating the reader's impression that he is transported beyond himself by an act of passionate willing.[4] The same objections can be raised to the interpretation made by Heiple (*Garcilaso*,152), who sees the persona as looking back to see if he could flee but as being "frightened by the trials he has left behind": such fright would seem to be more of an incentive to abandon the quest than a basis for his feeling reluctant to do so — especially if one interprets "do estoy" to mean "how much of the road left," as would seem consistent with Heiple's interpretation. Rivers states (*Obras completas*, 162–63) that the second stanza of Sonnet 38 is quite similar to the first stanza of Garcilaso's Sonnet 1. He also considers the "vía" [road] in line 10 to refer to the "camino estrecho" [narrow road] of line 6, and he sees the high peak as a place where the poet–persona would encounter the lady. Both Morros (*Obras poéticas*, 62)

---

[3] A. Gallego Morell, *Garcilaso de la Vega y sus comentaristas* (Granada: Universidad de Granada, 1966), 103, 366.

[4] I have already discussed, in relation to Scheler's ideas concerning passionate willing in general, fateful love's being rooted in the dangers of such willing (see above, p. 50). In addition, Scheler observes that as compared to the central feelings of happiness or unhappiness that accompany the willing and execution of acts, "the feeling-*state* that follows such [good or bad] willing as a *consequence* does not matter to the one who acts": *Formalism in Ethics*, 349–50.

and Heiple, the latter of whom refers to the persona's seeing if he will "continue the uphill pursuit" (*Garcilaso*, 152), coincide with Rivers on these last two points. As we have seen, Sonnet 1 presents a world of problems of its own, but when one compares the two stanzas in question, what appears to the common denominator that Rivers has in mind (especially given his citation of El Brocense's note) is the thought that the past the persona originally left in order to devote his life to the lady seems worse than the affliction he is experiencing in the present moment. I consider that interpretation to be questionable in the cases of both of those stanzas. However, by that reading lines 7–8 of Sonnet 38 would seem to mean that the persona is not able to abandon his effort to gain the lady's favor because he realizes that, if he were to do so, the situation he would go back to would be even worse than his present misery. That interpretation of why the persona cannot flee the lady seems quite sound, until one considers that the persona's "turning to flee" is a metaphor for resisting the lady's power; consequently, it cannot be assumed that what the persona "sees he left behind" refers to his situation in the past. The problem, then, with Rivers's otherwise cogent interpretation is that the only way it can be considered to clarify what the persona sees that would make him contemplate returning to the pursuit of the lady, now to the high peak, immediately after he says that he wants to abandon pursuit of the lady because it is causing him great suffering, is if one assumes that "tornar" [turn] and "huir" [flee] can be understood literally (in terms of a mental image of the poet following the lady and looking backward) instead of as a metaphor for resisting the lady's power. Nor does that reading explain why the persona does not follow some other course of action, one that is neither pursuing the lady nor returning to his former life. In a subsequent study Rivers expresses a view that is essentially the same as Morros's, that when the persona looks back he is frightened by the road: ". . . he is equally frightened by the lady herself and by the steep, dangerous road leading either away from her or towards her" (*Poems: Critical Guide*, 27).

The next two possible but unacceptable interpretations of what the persona looks back at and that prevents him from fleeing the lady have not, to my knowledge, been previously considered by critics. The first is that what the persona means by what he left behind ("lo que he dejado") is that when he considers the important sacrifices he made in order to pursue the lady in the first place, he is overcome by the recognition of his own rashness. The problem with that reading is, again, that if in the stanza to follow "climbing to the high peak" is interpreted to mean that the persona is somehow interested in resuming his quest, he cannot be seen to offer an explanation as to why, immediately after expressing the considerations that make him want to abandon that effort, he would want to resume the same course of action. The second possibility, which, in my opinion, is the best of the unacceptable ones, is along the lines of the one just given, with the difference that when the persona looks back at the sacrifices he made, he realizes that he has nothing to go back to. The strength of that interpretation is that the persona can now be understood to be compelled to resume his quest — because he forfeited so much in order to begin it, because he has sacrificed so much in order to persist in it, and because he now has no life besides it. The weakness of this interpretation is that although having nothing to go back to may move the persona to resume his quest, such a perspective would hardly provide him with the positive incentive implied in the words "if I *want* to climb to the high peak..." (my emphasis).

In my opinion, only one reading, one which has not been identified previously, is completely acceptable: it is that while the persona is in the act of turning away from the lady as he attempts to flee her, what he sees behind him before he has finished turning (sees "behind" him because he has turned his body away from her but still not his head) is the lady herself. It is the realization that he is actually leaving *her* behind that causes him to recoil and faint, for seeing her is also what prompts him, in the next stanza, to contemplate and even relish reaching her on the high peak. Given his deep but ambivalent feelings toward the lady, the persona's fainting would be a reaction to the accumulation of violent emotional strain that results from his wanting to flee her and pursue her and, at the same time, his not wanting to do either. He is unable to continue his quest because he wants to escape the lady's power and the suffering it brings him, yet so strong is his desire to gain her attention or favor that he cannot renounce his quest. He will suffer if he renounces it, but if he persists in it he will suffer no less. This perfectly incapacitating quandary is a recurring element in Garcilaso's poetry, perhaps the most notable instance of it being in lines 7–8 of Sonnet 1, "sé que me acabo, y mas é yo sentido / ver acabar conmigo mi cuydado" ["I know that I am dying, and I have regretted more seeing my love-anguish die with me"]. Few qualities are more deeply characteristic of Garcilaso's representation of anguish than his vivid metaphorical evocation of what is actually passionate willing as an impersonal, irresistible force that totally depletes the lover as it carries him to destruction.

Perhaps the explanation for criticism's not having previously suggested the interpretation I prefer for lines 7–8 is that it has been assumed that in lines 5–6 "do estoy" [where I am] means "how far I've come" and that "seeing (considering) where I am and what has occupied me on the narrow road of following you" refers to what the poet-persona considers when he looks back, thus constituting an explanation for why he says, in lines 7–8, that he does not want to flee the lady. I favor the view that "do

Ambivalent Love and the Pangs of Individuation

estoy" [where I am] means "how much of the road is left" and that lines 5–6 explain not the persona's reluctance to flee but his desire to flee. Another possible explanation for its not having been considered that the sight of the lady is what prevents the persona from fleeing is related to the significance of "la alta cumbre" ["the high peak"] and the problem of allegorizing the persona's dilemma in broad ethical terms that adequately represent the poem's thematic depth. Rivers, Morros, and Heiple all consider the "camino estrecho" in line 6 and the "vía" that leads to the peak and is referred to in line 10 to be one and the same, but whereas Morros cites Herrera's interpretation that the road leading to the high peak is the road of virtue without explaining or defending that view but also without taking exception to it, Rivers (*Obras completas*, 163) disagrees with Herrera's reading on the grounds that "quien ocupa la cumbre no es la virtud, sino la dama a quien sigue con tanta dificultad el poeta" ["the peak is occupied not by virtue but by the lady, whom the persona is following with so much difficulty"]. Actually, Herrera's reading is not inconsistent with the view that the lady is on the peak. There are circumstances that strongly favor seeing the lady as being located on the peak and seeing the act of reaching the peak as a triumph of "virtue" in the sense of moral strength or moral courage. The height of the peak and the extreme difficulty of reaching it effectively evoke, by analogy, a sense of the lady's hostile resistance; also, the natural association of the peak with an upper world of light and fecundity, in contrast to "la oscura región de vuestro olvido" [the dark region of your forgetfulness], easily prompts the conclusion that climbing the peak is a metaphor for gaining the lady's favor, for becoming worthy of doing so, or for both. Presumably, what Herrera means is that the steep road leading to the peak represents the challenge of achieving high moral status. We definitely know that the persona was cognizant of the lady when he pursued her on the narrow road and that the anguish of pursuing her is what has made him want to flee. An understanding of what the persona sees that makes him no longer able to flee must be arrived at by deduction. The only way it could have been the lady is if the persona somehow saw her differently from the way he saw her when he felt the urge to flee. Neither Rivers, Morros, nor Heiple considers the sight of the lady to be what prevents the persona from fleeing, but whereas Morros sees her as possibly corresponding to a high value, Rivers seems to see her as at best a temptation. It would seem, however, that in fact all three critics see her as ultimately a threat to the persona. Herrera sees the road to the high peak as the road of virtue but does not explain how that interpretation relates to other elements in the poem. Herrera's view may perhaps be interpreted to imply ambivalence in the persona's attitude toward the lady, but no critic has emphasized the crucial circumstance that the persona simultaneously holds two contradictory views of the lady: he sees her *both* as a danger to be fled *and* as a high value to be pursued.

I wish to suggest that the explanation for the paradox of the poet–persona's simultaneously seeing the lady as a threat and as a refuge from that same threat must be sought in the psychological sphere. There are several general premises upon which my examination of Sonnet 38 will be based. One is that Garcilaso followed Petrarch and the Catalan poet Ausias March in developing amatory lyric as a medium that lends itself to exploring the complexities of human psychodynamics. Another is a moderate version of the rather conventional assumption, but one that was most notably espoused by the New Critics, that the elements necessary for establishing the coherence of a text and deducing its broader implications are to be sought in elements of the text itself. The third premise is that as a Renaissance humanist frustrated by his dealings with a traditionalistic and despotic autocratic elite,[5] Garcilaso understood the psychological process whereby the exercise of moral autonomy confronts the individual with the need to overcome feelings of powerlessness, isolation, and fear.[6] Specifically, the focus of the present study concerns the obstacle that is presented in the fictional situation of the poem as the poet–persona's attitude of infantile identification with the lady, an attitude that he reveals in references to his own emotional state. As regards my methodological premises, my adherence to a New Critical approach is moderate because

---

[5] This assertion would have been only somewhat possible on the basis of what has been known about the political affiliations of Garcilaso's brother (who belonged to the rebellious *comunero* movement) and the poet's exile to an island on the Danube; but it is much more meaningful in the light of recent discoveries by María del Carmen Vaquero Serrano concerning the poet's lengthy relationship with a neighboring woman of the upper nobility who bore the poet an illegitimate son and whom the poet was probably unable to marry because her older brother was a *comunero*. (See M. del Carmen Vaquero Serrano, *Garcilaso: Aportes para una nueva biografía* [Toledo: Oretania, 1999], 73–75; idem, *Garcilaso: Poeta del amor, caballero de la guerra* [Madrid: Espasa Calpe, 2002], 134.) In any case, my interest in biographical data is only in its incidental correlation to interpretations that might be made of the spirit or tone of the poetry, not in its usefulness as a basis for interpretation.

[6] For an interesting discussion of the anxieties accompanying the process of individuation in the period of the Renaissance, see Erich Fromm, *Escape from Freedom* (1941) (New York: Holt, 1969), 40–49. Fromm's perspective differs from the one developed here partly because he addresses the ambivalent nature of freedom that is a result of the completed event of individuation, whereas I concentrate on ambivalence experienced during the process of individuation itself.

I freely combine an assiduous concern for the terms of the text with attention to historical circumstances that seem to have conditioned early modern lyric's distinctive personality and can probably be associated with the author's experience in life. The main problem with biographically-oriented criticism is that, given the complex, personal, and generally obscure nature of the relationship between author and text, there is little that such a critical approach *can* offer; it is not that in principle it has little *to* offer, since, as Norman Holland reminds us, codes or other symbolic orders ultimately cannot be isolated from the human being using them[7] — even if the author is anonymous, as in the case of *Lazarillo de Tormes*. I refer to biographical considerations, however, only insofar as such speculations are subordinate and correlate to implications that are already introduced by the coherence of the text and to the extent that they are based as much as possible on documented fact, as opposed to the myriad arbitrary assumptions that continue to plague criticism's excessive recourse to biography. In any case, I accept the view (advanced, for example, by Tolstoy) that authors create in their own image, but I certainly do not hold that fictional characters or poetic personas can always be analyzed in relation to their creators. My justification for drawing on analytic psychology in order to probe the complexities of fictional characters partly coincides with Henry Sullivan's view that the psychologically fantastic nature of individual subjectivity tends to be a fictional "virtual reality" in much the same way literary creations are,[8] but it is also simply that, regardless of how "scientific" one considers it, psychoanalysis offers effective and relevant means for exploring human mental processes and psychic experience, which are subjects of interest in their own right.

The degree of exaggeration expressed in the tears and sighs of the opening lines of Sonnet 38 fall just short of expressing an attitude of infantile identification. They are not so exaggerated and incongruous that they cannot be read as a conventional hyperbolic evocation of love–anguish. Emotionalistic helplessness suggestive of infantile identification is, however, found in lines 7 and 8, when the persona states that if he tries to leave the lady he faints. After already having suffered prolonged isolation and affliction in order to pursue the lady, the prospect of giving up his unhappy quest and forfeiting the consolation of even hoping for the lady's favor would seem to be more than the persona can bear. The peculiar irony here is that, in spite of having been met

---

[7] N. H. Holland, *The Brain of Robert Frost* (New York: Routledge, 1988), 179.

[8] H. W. Sullivan, "Don Quixote de la Mancha: Analyzable or Unanalyzable?" *Cervantes* 17 (1998): 4–20, here 12, 14, 16, 19.

only with the lady's attitude of rejecting indifference, the poet–persona still compulsively longs for her ready acceptance and is reluctant to seek her favor on any other terms, e.g., by "climbing to the high peak." In this poem the persona is not confronting the need to give up an actual proximity to the lady; he is forced to give up a consuming need for such proximity or for the illusion that it can be attained. To explain the attitude of infantile dependence and the regressive tendency, I will refer to the theories of the Scottish psychoanalyst Ronald Fairbairn, as well as to Carl Jung and other psychologists. Garcilaso's preoccupation with love relations may seem to make his interest in the psyche more narrow than the perspective of modern psychoanalysis; however, much of modern psychoanalysis, and especially proponents of object-relations theory such as Fairbairn, regard "love relations" (defined in broad terms but terms that are still clearly related to adult sexual love) to be a decisive if not the central component of human life. I invoke psychoanalytic theories because of their aptness for interpreting and describing complex mental states, but I do so with an awareness that they themselves are metaphorical systems no less than poetry; and in doing so I do not fear anachronism on the grounds that humanist artists in the early modern period certainly had the capacity to understand intuitively and depict the same phenomena that psychoanalysts found theoretical terms to describe many generations later. When I use terms from the phenomenological ethics of values of Nicolai Hartmann or Max Scheler, I do so with the same justification, since what those philosophers have been able to explain theroetically, Garcilaso perceived and depicted with an artist's intuition, as did other authors. It is well known that modern psychology and philosophy have drawn heavily from insights provided by literature.

§

The advantage of Fairbairn's approach to psychodynamics is that it is a tool for interpreting not only the post-natal origins of psychopathic behavior but also the anxieties of normal adults who have experienced problems in adaptation. Also, although fundamentally broad and simple, Fairbairn's theories lend themselves to complexity of the sort we encounter in Sonnet 38. Fairbairn holds that the fundamental fact of human nature is "love," a libidinal drive the goal of which is good object relationships that satisfy our needs to be treated as persons (including having our practical needs satisfied). The word "objects" in this context refers to other persons in the outer world, internalized others, or "bad" and "good" parts of others to whom one's ego relates after it has defensively split them off from an original frustrating or threatening "whole object" that it internalized in order to remove it from outer reality. The ego itself also splits into parts that have relationships among themselves and with their internal whole and part objects. Fairbairn considers the unsuccessful attempt to abandon the attitude of infantile dependence to be the ultimate cause of psychopathic personality disorders,[9] and he views psychopathology as the study of relationships of the ego with internalized objects. When the ego experiences anxiety because it confronts an object that is exciting but unsatisfying or threatening, it uses any or all of four techniques to defend itself by adapting ego structures toward that object: the phobic, the obsessional, the paranoid, and the hysterical. I will propose that the explanation for the gloomily self-destructive and diseased affect — the element of morbidity — in Garcilaso's Sonnet 38 must be sought in the poet–persona's attitude of infantile identification with the lady and his experiencing certain conflicts that Fairbairn sees as characterizing the transitional stage between infantile and mature dependence, specifically, the conflicts that accompany phobic and obsessional anxieties.

The perspective offered by Fairbairn's theory would suggest that the emotional crisis depicted in Sonnet 38 derives from the undifferentiated nature of the poet–persona's ego and the fact that he has transferred to the lady the same attitude of infantile dependence that a child has toward its mother. Fairbairn's explanation for this behavior and its hindrance of the persona's maturation process would be that he has reactivated a specific technique established in early life for regulating relationships with internal exciting and rejecting objects,[10] the classic example being the "good" and "bad," i.e., the present and absent, breast of the mother. The view that the lady in the poem is a rejecting object, however, presupposes that she is aware of the persona's interest in her, for if she does not know that the persona loves her, how can she be said to be rejecting him? Actually, the poem is ambiguous on the issue of whether the lady is aware of the persona's interest in her.[11] Perhaps the most likely explanation for that

---

[9] W. R. D. Fairbairn, *Psychoanalytic Studies of the Personality* (1952) (London: Routledge & Kegan Paul, 1976), 120.

[10] W. R. D. Fairbairn, "Observations on the Nature of Hysterical States," *British Journal of Medical Psychology* 27 (1954): 105–25, here 115. (Today exception would be taken to the term "hysterical.")

[11] The strongest argument in favor of the view that the lady is not aware of the persona is that there is no explicit evidence in the text that she is. It seems to me that the reference at the end of the poem to "vuestro olvido" [your forgetfulness] does not constitute such evidence, for "forgetfulness" in this context is less likely to mean a total lack of cognizance than it is to be a rhetorical figure for present disregard. The arguments for

ambiguity in the poem is that it serves to draw the reader into the poet–persona's experience of anxiety. Once the reader, like the persona, is in a position of experiencing anxiety over whether the persona is justified in considering himself a victim of the lady's aloofness, the reader can develop a sense of how the persona's paralyzing despair on that score serves to sabotage his capacity to meet the challenge of gaining the lady's favor. From the point of view of object relations theory, the basis of that anxiety, which would have led to the splitting off and internalization of the lady as bad object, would be that the persona's anti-libidinal ego is directing aggression toward the object of his libidinal ego, the exciting object, and toward the libidinal ego itself. Thus, object-loss becomes narcissistic ego-loss, as the split between the ego and its object develops into a split between the ego and the ego-ideal and the sudden loss of self-esteem threatens an otherwise healthy grandiosity.[12] What underlies the persona's anxiety, then, is his struggle to suppress his libidinal ego; but since his libidinal ego is

---

the opposing point of view, that the lady actually is aware of the persona, or even knows him, but is either refusing to recognize his worthiness to be loved or is refusing to reciprocate his love, are largely circumstantial but not unconvincing. The fact that the persona loves her itself suggests that he knows her. Given the sophistication and elevated character of this poetry, the persona's great enthusiasm for the lady is likely to have been prompted by a good familiarity with her finer human qualities, such as her disposition and elegance. Also, one is naturally inclined to imagine a collective setting frequented by the poet, such as the court, as the sphere where the persona and the lady have been in contact with each other, in which case she would likely have been aware of the persona's existence. Additionally, the reference to "what has occupied me on the narrow road of following you" (the biblical allusion in line 6 is of course to Matthew 7:14) suggests that for a good while prior to the moment of utterance the persona has been attempting to "serve" the lady in an effort to draw attention to himself, in which case it is likely that he would have succeeded at some point in making himself and his affection at least known to her, in spite of his stating in the opening stanza that he cannot bring himself to admit to her how much he has suffered on her account. On those grounds one could argue that it is likely that in the situation depicted the lady is aware of the persona's interest in her but remains aloof. (None of these arguments, of course, is based on enough textual evidence to seem conclusive.)

[12] See James S. Grotstein, *Splitting and Projective Identification* (New York: Jason Aronson, 1981), 24–25 on Freud's "Mourning and Melancholia"; and N. Gregory Hamilton, *Self and Others* (Northvale, NJ: Aronson, 1988), 230–34. The great seminal work on melancholy is Aby Warburg, *The Renewal of Pagan Antiquity*, trans. David Britt (Los Angeles: Getty Research Institute, 1999), 635–51; E. H. Gombrich, *Aby Warburg*, 2nd ed. (Oxford: Phaidon, 1986), 211–15.

regressive, that anxiety is also prompted by his struggle to abandon an attitude of infantile dependence on the exciting object. In general terms, such aggression against the self can be explained as a way of rendering tolerable ongoing ambivalence toward an internal object that one experiences as both exciting and rejecting. Ultimately, the attack of the persona's ego on its own unsatisfied libidinal needs — the persona's attack on his own love — can be seen as a defense against having a desire (for the lady's attention or favor) that he fears not being able to satisfy. It may well be that the lady's having previously assumed the role of rejecting object is what caused her to draw attention to herself as exciting object,[13] but we cannot be certain on the basis of the text that the lady as original, unsplit object in the outer world ever rejected the persona. There can be little doubt that the lady presented in the poem and referred to in the first stanza as the cause of the persona's grief is seen by the persona to be cruelly rejecting him, for in any case "she" is a fantasized rejecting object that is a product of the original lady's having been split and internalized as bad object by the persona's central ego. The persona's attitude of dependence makes him particularly vulnerable to the feeling that he is being rejected: "... dependence upon others makes for exceptional vulnerability, which in turn leads to a feeling of being neglected, rejected, and humiliated whenever the excessive amount of affection or approval demanded is not forthcoming."[14]

In applying Fairbairn's terms to an interpretation of the ambivalence expressed by the poet–lover in Sonnet 38, it should be noted that just as the mother who fails to satisfy a child libidinally becomes a "bad" internal object, the lady, who fails to satisfy the persona libidinally, is also "bad;" but she is also a "good" object insofar as, in a world full of harshness and disappointment, the persona relishes ready access to her sheltering warmth. All such fantasies on the persona's part, are rooted, of course, in

---

[13] In commenting on two cases of hysteria, Fairbairn notes, "It is interesting to consider the significance of the fact that, in the case of both these patients, it was the father who intervened and assumed the role of rejecting object. Doubtless, in assuming this role, both fathers drew attention to themselves in the role of exciting object likewise": "On the Nature of Hysterical States," 113. With the same perspective, María Pilar Manero Sorolla regards the traditional Petrarchist association of the lady with ice and snow as corresponding to the severity and disdain of the lady and so to that which spurs the persona's passion: "La configuración imaginística de la dama en la lírica española del Renacimiento: La tradición petrarquista," *Boletín de la Biblioteca Menéndez Pelayo* 68 (1992): 5–71, here 52.

[14] Karen Horney, *Our Inner Conflicts* (New York: Norton, 1945), 55–56.

his own unsatisfied need for a good object, but insofar as the lady is held to be satisfying and comforting, she plays a valuable role in furnishing him with a good state of mind and a starting point for integrating his ego on the basis of a loved and protected good object (Hinshelwood, *Dictionary of Kleinian Thought*, 170–71). Yet one's having a good object that is also bad because it is rejecting and frustrating places severe strain on one's capacity for endurance and on maintaining the illusion that the object offers ready acceptance. It is that circumstance that explains why the persona removes the traumatic factor, the original lady, from the world of outer reality and transfers it to the field of inner reality by internalizing her (Fairbairn, *Psychoanalytic Studies*, 110). After the persona idealizes the lady (placing her on the high peak) by his central ego's splitting off from her, removing from outer reality and repressing in the persona's unconscious those aspects of her that it finds threatening, the lady as "bad" internal object is able to exercise an influence on him that is immediate and absolutely compelling, since his conscious adaptation to the threatening bad object is now impossible. "Because an objective relationship is non-existent and out of the question, the libido gets dammed up and explodes in an outburst of affect."[15] The persona has internalized the "bad" object because he needs it, and it is because this need remains attached to it in the unconscious that he cannot bring himself to part with it; yet that need is also what confers upon the "bad" object great power over him (Fairbairn, *Psychoanalytic Studies*, 67–68). Since direct oral-incorporative action of the libido vis-à-vis the accepted object (the ego-ideal) is prevented by the lady's rejecting attitude, the persona now sees himself as being confronted by two choices: either to embrace the internalized unsatisfying, rejecting, "bad" lady and be at her mercy, or to remain objectless. The morbid dimension of the poet–persona's anxiety is a result of the fact that with the splitting of the persona's ego and the sabotage of his libidinal ego by his anti-libidinal ego, his fantasized relationship with a needed, exciting object becomes increasingly replaced by a relationship with an object that is not only unsatisfying but also rejecting (Guntrip, *Personality, Structure, and Human Interaction*, 283, 329). Seen from one angle, that morbid anguish is a result of the cathexis that his ego obstinately maintains with the frustrating yet exciting internalized object in spite of its having been attacked by his anti-libidinal ego; seen from another, it is a result of the bad state of mind that the persona experiences in relation to the object of the anti-libidinal ego, the

---

[15] C. G. Jung, *Collected Works*, trans. R. F. C. Hull, 20 vols. (London: Routledge & Kegan Paul, 1957–1979), 5: 471.

rejecting object, and a result of the fact that his need for a relationship with a good object remains unmet. He identifies with his internalized object to the point that he feels as though it were part of him or as though he were attached to it in the same way a baby is attached to its mother. Since he is absolutely dependent upon it yet also feels limited and confined by that same dependence, he regards her as a being from which he must not separate and, at the same time, as one from which he must separate.

The alternative to the poet–persona's remaining in the unequal relationship of infantile dependence represented by the confining narrowness of the road, in contrast to both the height of the peak where the lady is located and the unlimited scope above it, is his accepting the challenge of overcoming his own regressive tendencies and becoming worthy of the lady's favor. Until he can make the psychological transition toward claiming greater independence as a differentiated person, he will experience "a conflict between the progressive urge to surrender the infantile attitude of identification and the regressive urge to maintain that attitude" (Fairbairn, *Psychoanalytic Studies*, 43). He (his ego) thus experiences the anxiety of the phobic conflict of not knowing whether to flee from the power of the object upon which he feels dependent or to seek refuge in that power; for in the first case he feels threatened by perpetual isolation, and in the second case he feels threatened by being devoured and annihilated. He also experiences the anxiety of the more aggressive obsessional conflict concerning mastery or forcible control of the object: on the one hand he desires to expel the lady as a frustrating and rejecting bad object from which his ego needs relief, and on the other he desires to retain her as contents because she continues to allure him. In the first case, he fears being emptied or drained of the hope ("la luz de la esperanza") of attaining what he imagines the lady to offer, and in the second case he fears the bad state of mind that he experiences as a result of continuing his relationship with a bad object (Fairbairn, *Psychoanalytic Studies*, 43–44).

If the attempt is now made to apply Fairbairn's perspective to the problem of identifying the alternatives of progressive and regressive movement in Sonnet 38 and to match them with imagery in the poem, it would appear that the persona is faced with three possibilities: to continue to follow the lady on the narrow road, to turn and flee her, or to climb to the high peak. The basis for distinguishing between the first and third options will be discussed shortly. Because of the undifferentiated state of the persona's ego at the moment of utterance, his feelings of helpless dependence, and the bad, morbid state of mind that he is experiencing as a result of being bound to his relationship with a bad object, his continuing in his present state along the narrow road in pursuit of the tempting and exciting but unsatisfying lady must be regarded as movement in a regressive direction, the direction of maintaining a state of infantile dependence. In traveling that road, he is compulsively fleeing toward the power of the object and toward the illusion of refuge that it holds out to him. The second direction, fleeing from the lady, represents a desperate attempt on the part of the persona's ego to regard the internalized "bad" object as external and flee from its presence. Yet two important facts must be considered. First, he is unable actually to bring himself to flee; second, even if he were able to flee, that action would still be determined by the power of the object and, hence, would not be a function of the persona's independence. In fact, his impotent longing to flee the object is a result of his being unable to do so because the object is actually internal. Thus, that second alternative must also be seen to constitute a regressive tendency — what Jung refers to as the childish and passive fantasy of a mere dreamer. Such separation could, however, constitute movement in a progressive direction if the persona were able to renounce his attitude of infantile dependence and, instead of fleeing, freely depart. The third option, that of ascending the high peak, could lead to moral salvation for the persona if he could bring himself to embrace it, but because of his attitude of dependence he is psychically debilitated and unable to do so. If the lady is seen to be located on the high peak, the word "alta" in relation to "cumbre" takes on its full meaning of high moral attainment, for if the persona were able to conquer his fears and rise above the confining dark abyss of his present condition of susceptibility to primary dependence, the degree of independence that he would achieve would open up the possibility of his meeting the lady on an equal level and achieving a relationship with her that is a relationship with a differentiated object. In the interpretation I have considered to be less acceptable of what the persona left behind, the word "alta" mainly has the limited meaning of "remote" or "perilous." It may be that Rivers (*Obras completas*, 163, n. 9) does not consider the high peak to represent virtue because he favors that meaning of "alta." Yet insofar as strength of character and self-determination through values are conditions for the persona's reaching the lady, Herrera's view that the high peak represents virtue seems plausible.

"Climbing the high peak," to win the lady through his own attainments, then, not only is the only potentially progressive direction of movement but also is the only viable alternative left to the persona, since he is unable to flee the lady and is no longer motivated to pursue her on the narrow road. To regard that choice as preferable, however, is by no means a claim that it is necessary — for (as will be discussed below) if it were a necessity it would have no moral value, and the persona can also prefer to move in a regressive direction. In any case, I further propose that, contrary to the perspectives of Rivers (*Obras completas*, 163), Morros (*Obra poética*, 62), and Heiple (*Garcilaso*, 152), the "camino estrecho" [narrow road] is distinct from the "vía" [road] leading to the high peak. Whereas the former is the bad infinity of infantile dependence and corresponds to "la oscura región de vuestro olvido" ["the dark region of your forgetfulness"], the latter is the road of both self-conquest and individuation, the prize for traveling that road successfully being an encounter with the lady as differentiated object and, hence, the possibility of meriting her favor. The "camino estrecho" and the "vía" can also be seen as different aspects of the same road, the former being where individuality is born and the latter where it is fulfilled.

§

Turning now to Jung, an interpretation of Sonnet 38 in terms of Jungian psychology will afford the possibility of moving from Fairbairn's rather clinically oriented psychoanalytic perspective to an approach that is more mythopoeic and heroic, as is appropriate in an appreciation of aristocratic poetry. I could best suggest the relationship between my use of Fairbairn's theories and Jung's discussion of individuation with the observation that what Fairbairn refers to as the conflict between flight to the object and flight from the object is, in Jungian terms, a conflict between flight from individuation to the object and flight from the object to individuation. For Jung, individuation is the process whereby individual human identity comes to birth through a painful problem in adapting followed by the self-regulating effects of establishing polarities and balance between the conflicting opposites of consciousness and the unconscious, thought and feeling. What for Fairbairn would be the poet–persona's split internal object and its corresponding dynamic structures (the libidinal ego and the anti-libidinal ego) would be, in Jungian terms, the imago of the persona's ambivalent anima, his feminine unconscious, divided between a portion that is projected in an outer object (the lady) and a portion that remains unprojected. A way of understanding the ambivalent character of the anima is seeing it as a mother-imago with two halves: her lower half is the dimension where the persona's regressive libido seeks infantile attachment but is blocked from it by the incest taboo, and her upper half is her aspect as heavenly bride (Jung, *Works*, 5: 213–17).

Jung sees the development of genuine personality, whereby individual functioning and performance and the distinguishing qualities of one unique person achieve completeness, as being the result of experiences that produce tension or conflict between the opposed poles of consciousness and unconsciousness by bringing them together and, as a result, both differentiating and integrating them. For a male, such tension is between the male persona, or masculine conscious identity (the ego's socially accepted image), and its internal feminine counterpart, the anima. Individuation is the process of the ego's self-realization through overcoming the de-individualized states of its identifying itself too strongly with the collective (versus individual) contents of the persona or the anima, thus allowing the two to become integrated. The development of individuality requires, in addition to conscious, personal relationships with individuals upon whom the unconscious is projected, the coordination of thought and instinct (feeling) through "a psychic relationship to the collective unconscious" (Jung, *Works*, 7: 303). The attainment of individual consciousness (personality), the forward flow of psychic energy, and personal independence are a result of the self-regulating effects of establishing polarities and a balance between conflicting opposites. Yet in order to be raised to such a newer and higher level, a higher moral power, the individual must experience the ordeal of contending with final moral decisions that open up to him an abyss of confusion, deception, and despair.[16] Surviving such an ordeal requires, above all, overcoming the enemy within the self: the powerful force of the regressive tendency.

When a man meets stubborn resistance in his environment or is faced with the challenge of accomplishing some great work, he at first recoils, doubtful of his strength. The libido leaves the bright upper world of the persona and sinks into the darkness of its own depths where it finds a substitute for the upper world that it has abandoned. It streams back to a yearning for association with the source from which it originally flowed, the mother and memories of the paradisal state of infancy (Jung, *Works*, 5: 292, 304, 305).

> ... if he gets stuck in the wonderland of this inner world, then for the upper world man is nothing but a shadow, he is already moribund or at least seriously ill. But if the libido manages to tear itself loose and force its way up again, something like a miracle happens: the journey to the underworld was a plunge into the fountain of youth, and the libido, apparently dead, wakes to renewed fruitfulness. (Jung, 5: 293)

---

[16] C. G. Jung, *Works*, 7: 277, 53, 61, 75; idem, *The Integration of the Personality*, trans. Stanley Dell (London: K. Paul, 1940), 303.

When, through regression, the man reassumes the attitude of the son, his anima becomes identified with the dominating power of the mother, who corresponds to the subject's own regressive tendency. She may impair him with a sentimental attachment and a diminution of manly character, or she may restore his confidence, regenerate him, and spur him on to greater heights (Jung, *Works*, 9.1: 26–29, 70–71, 270–71). In the poem under consideration, insofar as the persona is susceptible to the childish attitude of a dreamer whose Eros remains passive, the lady — an anima-imago — is a danger that he must escape; but insofar as she constitutes a source of his inner strength by revealing to him the instinctive forces that remain locked up in his unconscious, she is that power without which his conscious personality is incapable of channeling its volitional energy in a definite direction. These two opposed aspects of the mother as anima-imago, then, correspond to the two aspects of the beloved lady with whom the persona in Sonnet 38 is found to be identifying at the moment of utterance. At that moment the persona may or may not be able to overcome his regressive libido's withdrawal into confinement and dependence in the dark abyss of hopeful surrender to the all-giving mother and mobilize a re-born progressive libido so as to brave the road of adaptation and development and return to the world of light. Garcilaso's poem depicts the psychological event of the poet–persona's struggle to overcome the spellbinding power of his own regressive tendency and to return with renewed energy to the challenge of overcoming the harsh resistance of the external world. We can recognize here a displacement of any or all of three myths: that of Theseus imprisoned in the underworld, that of Odysseus trapped on Circe's isle, and that of Orpheus failing to return to a life of fulfillment in the upper world because of turning to look back at Eurydice. The abyss, which contrasts to the high peak as inferiority does to superiority, is itself a mother archetype. Jung explains that enveloping, embracing, and devouring elements of symbolism point to the mother as object of the regressive libido seeking gifts of nourishment and protection. He also notes that events such as descent into the darkness of night or profound introversion or descent to the bottom of the sea where one is devoured by a whale-demon represent entry of the libido into the maternal depths of the unconscious where ritual death is followed by rebirth in places such as the church, the cave, or other instances of womb imagery (*Works*, 5: 340–46; 9.2: 11–12). The abyss of the unconscious mind is referred to in Garcilaso's poem in line 14 as "la oscura región de vuestro olvido" ["the dark region of your forgetfulness"] and the world of light is the "alta cumbre" [high peak], which represents the persona's triumph over his own death (the mortification of having been rejected by the lady) and his re-adaptation to the challenges of the real world through the coordination of thought and feeling. If one considers climbing to the high peak as a possibility that is opened up to the persona by fleeing the confining narrowness of the road along which he had been pursuing the lady as mother — as the place where the lady in her aspect of heavenly bride is located — the persona's facing the high peak can be seen as his confronting the prospect of realizing his ego-ideal. In any case, in the high peak "the ... reader will recognize at once the idea of a 'mid-point' that is reached by a kind of climb (mountaineering, effort, struggle, etc.)" (Jung, *Works:* 7: 223). The mid-point in question is, of course, a point between heaven and earth, the point at which the anima is transformed into a function of relationship between the conscious and the unconscious (Jung, *Works*, 7: 227).

In the case of Sonnet 38, however, it would be misleading to place too much emphasis on the power of progressive libido. The mid-point where the poet–persona finds himself at the moment of utterance is not the high peak; it is a point between possible courses of action which the persona feels incapable of pursuing. What stands out in this poem is not so much the prospect of a triumph over the regressive tendency, for at the moment represented in the poem such a triumph may seem more unlikely than likely. What is important is the persona's experience of futility, anguish, and despair. From a Jungian point of view, that anguish is the necessary precondition for integrating thought and feeling, or for what Fairbairn would refer to as uniting the splits in one's fragmented ego by uniting the splits in the objects to which the split ego is attached — more specifically in Jungian terms, it is the precondition for a man's overcoming the limitations of a one-sided identification with his persona, of his being unconscious of his feelings. If Max Scheler and Nicolai Hartmann are right in maintaining that it is in our feelings that we discern values, the importance of integrating emotional experience into psychic life can hardly be overestimated.[17]

---

[17] What Jungian analytic psychology refers to somewhat vaguely as a process of "integrating" emotional experience and conscious thought can probably be characterized more precisely in the terms of Antonio Damasio's physiological and neuropsychological hypotheses as a process of enhancing the positive effects and reducing the negative effects of the feelings of the emotions upon which reason inherently depends: *Descartes' Error* (New York: Avon Books, 1994), 245–46, 132–33, 143–44. What I have referred to as experiencing value-feelings would correspond to what Damasio characterizes as responding to an object by building (from memory) acquired and innate topographically organized dispositional representations, triggering and evaluative images, that activate body-bound responses of emotion and feeling (106, 162–63, 242–43). He thus refers to a "cortically based biological self embued with value" (244).

I have posed the question of how our perception in Sonnet 38 of the persona's helplessness and incapacitating despair can be seen to relate to the aesthetic appeal of the poem. The answer to that question is to be found in the principle that, contrary to causal, ontological necessity, the necessity of values subsists independently of possibility, i.e., even if a value is not attainable it is necessarily still a value. The formulation of the phenomenon in question that would have been known in Garcilaso's day is the Aristotelian principle, set forth in the *Nicomachean Ethics*, that virtue is incompatible with determinism (Sorabji, *Necessity, Cause, and Blame*, 245), "determinism" referring either to the inevitability of striving for a result or to the inevitability of the result itself. Not only does the moral worth of an act depend not on the success of the act but on the direction of the intention (Hartmann, 2: 81, 40), "the value of a mere Ought-to-be in something not completed stands in opposition to the value of completion; thus a value peculiar to the living tension towards something unattained — indeed to a certain degree the value in the inability to attain — stands in opposition to the value of attainment" (Hartmann 2: 86). However desperate and helpless the persona is, he is at least traveling the road, i.e., actively striving. In any case, the aesthetic appeal of presenting the persona as desperately continuing to strive for values that remain beyond his reach is that such a depiction implicitly affirms the value of such striving purely as an end in itself. The "heroism" thus represented is not the conventional heroism of effective action but is what I might paradoxically term "the heroism of potentially ineffective action,"[18] what Gorky referred to as "the madness of the brave ... the madness of those who, disregarding each and every resistance of reality, all its painful tortures, strive unswervingly to assert their will, to carry through their ideas under actual conditions, however trying these may be" (*Untimely Thoughts*, 181).[19]

The poet–lover in Sonnet 38, frozen in his tracks at the threshold of his own individuality, represents archetypally a universal human tendency to shrink from life's unbearable trials and uncertainties and thus forfeit all the unforeseen possibilities that come with meeting new challenges. Thus the poem articulates the integrated personality's need to wrench itself free from its infantile past and embrace its own destiny. After having sought refuge from disappointments in love, the persona is now driven

---

[18] On the contradictory relationship between heroism and the pursuit of ends, see B. Creel, *Don Quijote, Symbol of a Culture in Crisis* (Valencia: Albatros-Hispánofila, 1988), 89–90.

[19] Such a perspective offers us insight into the kinship of Garcilaso's poetry and Cervantes's *Don Quijote*, where Garcilaso is alluded to in 2.18, 48, and 70.

to ascend to a higher world because his love has been "a childlike and emotionally dependent relationship which, if it is not to end in frustration, must develop into something else."[20] Since the transition to a newfound individuality is a stage that is characterized by painful oscillation, it should not surprise us that this same oscillation was developed by Renaissance artists as an aesthetic value. Unresolved tension, contradiction, strain, and anti-classicist disharmony have been held by critics to be characteristics of mannerist style,[21] and in Arnold Hauser's words, as an aesthetic category "modern individualism, with its problematical nature, continually oscillating between revolt and conformism, now rebelling against ties, now putting itself in fetters, is a creation of mannerism" (*Mannerism*, 1: 36).

In sum, Sonnet 38 presents a situation in which the poet–persona has isolated one frustrating relationship from the rest of his life and is obsessively experiencing so much anguish in relation to that same frustration as to exclude all other possibilities. That predicament can be seen as the result of a process by which the persona's ego sabotages itself in order to defend itself against a personal need that it fears cannot be satisfied. The process itself can be understood more clearly if the persona's inner situation of emotional conflict is seen as a dramatization of his relationship with his objects. In general, the libidinal ego is characterized by needs and the anti-libidinal ego is characterized by aggression. In Garcilaso's poem the persona as libidinal ego identifies with the lady as exciting object; at the same time, his anti-libidinal ego identifies with the lady as rejecting object. The representation of the lady in negative terms, as assuming an attitude of cold aloofness towards the persona, dramatizes metaphorically the persona's defensive persecution of his libidinal ego by his anti-libidinal ego. The persona's regarding the lady as ambivalent, his identification of conflicting parts of his ego with her different aspects, has resulted in a debilitating split in his ego and a conflict vis-à-vis the object, thus causing him to oscillate between attitudes of yearning and renunciation. Also, this identification of the persona's ego with his internalized object explains why what would be his aggression toward a frustrating outer object has instead turned inward toward his libidinal ego and its object, the exciting object. The image of the repudiated exciting object is the remote lady, and the identification of the

---

[20] Northrop Frye, *The Secular Scripture* (Cambridge, MA: Harvard University Press, 1976), 154.

[21] See Wylie Sypher, *Four Stages of Renaissance Style* (Garden City, NY: Doubleday, 1955), 162–71; Jacques Bousquet, *Mannerism* (New York: Braziller, 1964), 53–54; James V. Mirollo, *Mannerism and Renaissance Poetry* (New Haven: Yale University Press, 1984), 121; and Arnold Hauser, *Mannerism*, 2 vols. (London: Routledge, 1965), 1: 23–27.

persona's libidinal ego with that repudiated object is naturally given as the persona's morbid self-repudiation and self-sabotage as a pretender to her favor. The attack of the persona's ego on its own unsatisfied need, i.e., the internal masochistic hindrance of the libidinal ego, is what explains the persona's attitude of helplessness and despair as well as his self-pity and his state of emotional castration and paralysis. Through the eclipse of areas of the persona's self that results from such repression, his center of gravity has come more and more to rest on others, so that the lady has become raised to a height (the high peak), idealized, and rendered in his eyes more and more fearful, needed, and necessary. As her opinion of him has come to have overwhelming power, he has become increasingly, even abnormally, affected by disregard and rejection: he has become hypersensitive (Horney, *Our Inner Conflicts*, 151–52). That extreme sensitivity to rejection is related to the attitude of despair referred to in the last stanza: the persona's self-contempt prompts his anxiety as to whether or not he will measure up to the idealized image of the lady. His fear of not being able to satisfy his needs, then, is a fear of not being worthy of having those needs satisfied. At bottom, the persona's hopelessness is a fear of individuation (Horney, *Our Inner Conflicts*, 184–85). In relation to the subject of hopelessness, Horney cites Kierkegaard's observation that all despair is fundamentally a despair of being ourselves (183).

Like Petrarch, the authors of love lyric in the Spanish fifteenth century, and poets such as Scève, Torquato Tasso, and Donne,[22] Garcilaso seems to have been interested in many of the same perplexing mental and emotional issues that have come to be the focus of psychoanalytic research in our own day, especially the problems of obsessed and phobic subjectivity. His work suggested that he was intrigued by the emotions associated with what has now come to be referred to as schizoid and depressive tendencies, the latter being roughly equivalent to what Garcilaso himself termed "el dolorido sentir" ["hurtful feeling"].[23] His interest in morbid emotional states was not exactly clinical, of course, since he gave those states a heroic cast and depicted them

---

[22] For a discussion of mannerism in Garcilaso, see Hatzfeld, "Literary Mannerism and Baroque in Spain and France," *Comparative Literature Studies* 7 (1970): 419–36, here 419–22; in Scève, Donne, and Tasso, see Mirollo, *Mannerism and Renaissance Poetry*, 151–52, 168–72, and 133–34 respectively. Also interesting in relation to the present study is Juliana Schiesari, "Mo(u)rning and Melancholia: Tasso and the Dawn of Psychoanalysis," *Quaderni d'Italianistica* 11 (1990): 13–27.

[23] Garcilaso never uses the word "melancolía" or "melancólico" in his poems, but he uses the word "triste" or a variant thereof over fifty times and "miserable" or a variant thereof twenty times.

with aesthetic ends, as did other mannerist poets in the Renaissance, who, like Garcilaso, were precursors of the Romantics.[24] Garcilaso explores the phenomenon of morbid subjectivity, but not with an interest that is primarily scientific and impartial. Is love in Sonnet 38 an ennobling experience in the Neoplatonist tradition? It could be argued that love in this poem is an experience that is more degrading than ennobling. Actually, if one is deprived of loving genuinely and of having one's love genuinely accepted, the consequences can be even worse than degrading — they can result in a disorientation and disintegration of the ego such as Melanie Klein refers to as "primary confusion" (Hinshelwood, *Dictionary of Kleinian Thought*, 169). Love in Sonnet 38 is degrading insofar as the lover's regressive tendency cannot be abandoned. If he can abandon that tendency, all of the anguish leading up to the event of his doing so becomes a necessary precondition for its occurrence, and the poetic depiction of anguish can then be clearly seen in a positive light, as valuable and ennobling pathos and a celebration of heroically stubborn love-idealism.[25] In the meantime, given the persona's oscillation, it is not clear whether his experience of love is degrading or ennobling.

In Garcilaso's Sonnet 38 the poet–persona stands paralyzed, torn between opposites, and both able and unable to achieve individuation, Jung's "mid-point" of a balance of power between the conscious and the unconscious minds (Jung, *Works*, 7: 229). Jung sees the coming to birth of genuine individual human identity as achieving "the desired 'mid-point' of personality, that ineffable something betwixt the opposites, or else that which unites them, or the result of conflict, or the product of energetic tension" (Jung, *Works*, 7: 230). What are the opposites between which the persona is torn in Sonnet 38? Certainly they are thought and feeling insofar as the persona's attitude toward the lady includes feelings of love and esteem as well as anxiety and

---

[24] See Mirollo, *Mannerism and Renaissance Poetry*, 33–35 on what he terms Renaissance "Angst-Mannerism"; Bousquet, *Mannerism*, 215–20 on melancholy as a pre-Romantic subject of Renaissance mannerist art; and Raymond Klibansky et al., *Saturn and Melancholy* (New York: Basic Books, 1964), 238–40 on the artistic treatment of melancholy as a tradition that was also cultivated in the Romantic era (based on the work and experience of Aby Warburg). On the antecedents of the Romantic movement in Spain's Renaissance, see the discussion of E. Allison Peers, *A History of the Romantic Movement in Spain* (1940), 2 vols. (New York: Haufer, 1964), 1: 1–13 on what he terms "the Romanticism of the Golden Age."

[25] On the pathos of melancholy in the early modern period, see Klibansky et al., 217–35, the influence on mannerism being mentioned on 233.

dependence and insofar as those feelings are counterbalanced by the knowledge that his only hope as an individual lies in the direction of autonomy and self-determination.

If the type of conflict represented in Sonnet 38 is characteristic of the transition from infantile to mature dependence and of personality's emergence from an undifferentiated state, it is logical that such poetry would have been written in the Renaissance, which was a historical period that was rich in aesthetically integrated and coherent human individuality at the same time that it knew both the dazzling allure and the sinister threat of dominating and frustrating parental figures — i.e., the wealthy and authoritarian representatives of patriarchal power. The type of conflict presented in Sonnet 38 becomes even more understandable in broad terms when one considers the cultural–historical crisis that existed in Spain in the early modern period, a period when society was at a crossroads between stagnation and change. That problem persisted in Spain into the twentieth century. It became more clearly understood with the Generation of '98 and continues to be perceptible, for example, in Antonio Machado's road imagery. With a perspective reminiscent of the persona's quandary in Sonnet 38, Jung (*Works*, 5: 83) speaks of the Scylla of world-renunciation and the Charybdis of its acceptance: each alternative removes some dangers while it introduces others. Developing a similar perspective, Hartmann speaks of morality's double face, symbolized by the head of Janus:

> In it the Ought sets up a backward-looking claim and at the same time one that is forward-looking — not temporally backward or forward, but axiologically. If the elementary values had an absolutely secure position in life, if a man of serious mind could always be absolutely certain even of himself . . . he could be exempted from the watchful glance backward upon the interests of the lower values and look solely forward to higher values, which lie before him waiting for fulfillment. (*Ethics*, 2: 459)

In Sonnet 38 the specific significance of the persona's conflict between proceeding forward and turning back is a conflict between on the one hand clinging to what offers the security of being familiar to him, even though it brings him mortifying confinement and humiliation, and on the other hand accepting the wager and venture of fulfilling the claims of personality. Renaissance love lyric's detailed exploration and analysis of the inner self played an important part in what Rafael Lapesa and others refer to as the fundamental event of the Renaissance, the discovery of the individual (*Estudios*, 220).

Renaissance lyric's contribution to the creation of individuality was not, however, limited to providing examples of individual awareness of self or of the process of attaining such awareness. As we can see in the work considered here, poets such as Garcilaso de la Vega can also allow us to observe first-hand the painful birth of individuality, to witness the precise moment of its struggle to come into being.

§

A conflict similar to the one treated in Garcilaso's Sonnet 38 is presented in Fray Luis de León's Sonnet 2, "Alargo enfermo el passo." The general purpose of the comments to follow will be to explore the implications of the conflict in Sonnet 2 and how that conflict's significance contributes to the poem's aesthetic value. As in the analysis of Garcilaso's Sonnet 38, I will first apply to Fray Luis's poem certain concepts from the microcosmic meta-psychological schemes of Ronald Fairbairn and Carl Jung and then apply concepts of Jung and others to suggest some macrocosmic cultural–historical, axiological, and aesthetic perspectives that seem applicable to that poem. The work is as follows:

> Alargo enfermo el passo, y buelvo, quanto
> alargo el passo, atrás el pensamiento;
> no buelvo, que antes siempre miro atento
> la causa de mi gozo y de mi llanto.
>   Allí estoy firme y quedo, mas en tanto
> llevado del contrario movimiento,
> cual haze el estendido en el tormento,
> padezco fiero mal, fiero quebranto.
>   En partes, pues, diversas dividida
> el alma, por huir tan cruda pena,
> desea dar ya al suelo estos despojos.
>   Gime, suspira y llora dividida,
> y en medio del llorar sólo esto suena:
> "Quándo volveré, Nise, a ver tus ojos?"[26]

---

[26] Quotations of Fray Luis de León's Sonnet 2 are from *Poesía completa*, ed. José Manuel Blecua (Madrid: Gredos, 1990), 237. Translations of Sonnet 2 are mine.

[Sick, I lengthen my step, and turn, as much as I lengthen my step, my thought backwards; I do not return, rather I ever look attentively at the cause of my joy and my tears. There I am, firm and still; but as I am carried by the opposite movement, like one stretched in torture, I suffer fierce grief, fierce harm. My soul, then, divided in diverse parts, to flee such cruel pain, desires to give to the earth these spoils. It moans, sighs, and weeps helplessly, and amidst the weeping only this is heard: "When, Nise, will I see your eyes again?"] (my translation)

Let us clarify from the outset that the words in line 6, "the opposite movement," apparently refer to the persona's continuing to go forward, as he was doing before he stopped and looked back at his beloved.

On a literal level, the terms in which Fray Luis presents his subject are highly expressive yet elliptical: they are "lyrical" in the sense that they invite a maximum of thought with a minimum of words. While we are struck with the extreme intensity of the persona's anguish, we are given no explicit details that might explain his having left his lady or any particulars concerning either her or their relationship. As the persona walks away from the lady, he turns his thoughts back to her, to whom he refers ambivalently as "la causa de mi gozo y de mi llanto." He then stops to think of her, and when he continues forward he feels agonizingly torn in two by the conflict between whatever necessity prompts him to depart and his urge to return. Feeling so much pain, he relishes death, and "his soul" cries and sighs like a helpless child. Still, he cannot renounce the memory of his beloved. Both his departure from Nise and his desire to return to her cause the persona's anguish, but the inner realities that underlie that anguish must be interpreted by the reader.[27] As I mentioned previously in relation to

---

[27] The only critics who have commented specifically on Sonnet 2 are F. Lázaro Carreter, "Los sonetos," 30, 36–37, and P. Ruiz Pérez, "Sobre los Sonetos de Fray Luis de León," *Edad de Oro* 11 (1992): 149–60, who coincide in interpreting the passion of the persona as an expression of mystical longing to achieve spiritual ascent, which they see symbolized by Nise. One might also mention the interpretation by Adolphe Coster, who sees in Nise an image of the Virgin Mary ("Luis de León," *Revue Hispanique* 53 [1921]: 1–468; 54 [1922]: 1–346), an opinion that has been rejected by Ángel C. Vega, ed., *Poesías de Fray Luis de León* (Madrid: Saeta, 1955); Félix García, ed. *Obras completas castellanas de Fray Luis de León* (Madrid: Editorial Católica, 1959), and Lázaro Carreter ("Los sonetos," 30). Leslie S. B. MacCoull has pointed out to me that there is significance in the

Garcilaso's Sonnet 38, Fairbairn holds that when the ego confronts an exciting but threatening object it uses any one or all of four techniques to defend itself by adapting ego structures toward that object: the phobic, the obsessional, the paranoid, and the hysterical. I will argue that the phobic structure best describes the conflict in Sonnet 2. Upon applying such theories to Sonnet 2, special attention must be given to the issue of whether there are grounds for asserting that the lady in that work can be said somehow to fail to satisfy the libidinal needs of the persona, since the applicability of Fairbairn's ideas to the poem rests on that premise.

Basing ourselves on Fairbairn's theories, we could speculate that, as in Sonnet 38, the problem that is the subject of the poem is the poet–lover's struggle to overcome an attitude of infantile dependence. We could further speculate that, as in Sonnet 38, the situation presented in Fray Luis's poem is that the persona's (central) ego responded to the problem of his attitude of dependence by splitting off from itself a "libidinal ego" and an "anti-libidinal ego" or "internal saboteur." The exciting (but threatening) object of the former is the lady, while the object of the latter is that aspect of the lady that constitutes a rejecting object from which the persona must separate himself in order to achieve an adult identity based on relationships with objects differentiated from the self. There is no basis in the text for concluding that the persona is departing because of some attitude or behavior on the part of the lady. But the text does allow the interpretation that the persona is experiencing frustration because of the unequal nature of the relationship and the persona's attitude of infantile dependence, of "primary (quasi-symbiotic) identification" with the lady. That the persona has such an attitude is suggested in two elements of the poem, line 12 and the metaphor of the rack. In line 12 ("[el alma] Gime, suspira y llora dividida" — in some versions "desvalida" substitutes for "dividida") ["It (my soul) moans, sighs, and weeps helplessly"] the persona displays not merely grief at loss or separation but an emotional insecurity that is almost totally incapacitating and hence incongruous and problematic. Given the lack of any explanation for the persona's departure, if he experienced only an ordinary degree of pain at separation, it would not be necessary to address the issue of the per-

---

name "Nise" insofar as Nysa was the name of the secret valley where the child Dionysus was raised by nymphs, the chief nymph also being named Nysa. Thus, she feels, a Dionysian, intoxicating quality is implicitly attributed to the lady. I would add along the same lines that such an implicit close association of Nise with Dionysus also suggests a daemonic, bewitching influence on the part of the lady, underscoring the poet's difficulty in overcoming his attachment to her.

Ambivalent Love and the Pangs of Individuation   147

sona's ambivalence and its implications. His departure would be a minus value, his return a plus value, and the point of the poem would be a celebration of the strength of the persona's love. But besides the incongruous degree of pain referred to in line 12, the severe pain that the persona expresses by describing himself as being "tortured on the rack" is a result of the fact that the object with which he is identified is equivalent to an incorporated object, so that separating from her and making the transition to what Fairbairn refers to as "mature dependence" is like separating from part of himself. According to Fairbairn,

> the great conflict of the transition stage . . . is characterized by both desperate endeavors . . . to separate . . . from the object and desperate endeavors to achieve reunion with the object. The anxiety attending separation manifests itself first as a fear of isolation, and the anxiety attending identification manifests itself as a fear of being shut in, imprisoned, or engulfed. (*Psychoanalytic Studies*, 43)

Hence "alargo . . . el paso" ["I lengthen my step"] contrasts with previous confinement. It thus seems reasonable to assume that the persona's ambivalent attitude toward the lady has its source in the persona's feelings of absolute dependence, and that the reason the poem gives no explicit reason for the persona's separation from the lady is that the abandonment of infantile dependence is a general necessity imposed by life and by the individual's natural evolution, both biological and psychic.

In lines 10 and 11 ("el alma, por huir tan cruda pena, / desea ya dar al suelo estos despojos") the persona implies that he is on the verge of dying. Is this reference to real death, or are his words mere hyperbole? If we further interpret Fairbairn's scheme and apply it — and adapt it somewhat — to the situation in Fray Luis's poem, the persona may be seen to be in an intermediate stage where he oscillates between infantile and mature dependence and to be experiencing the typical phobic conflict between flight *to* the power of the object and flight *from* it (*Psychoanalytic Studies*, 44–45). The main problem faced by the persona's ego, then, is that both his acceptance and his rejection of the object, both his libido and his aggression, constitute a threat to him. His only solution is to spend as much as possible of his store of aggressive hate toward the object that frustrates him (because of his excessive dependence) in attacking the libidinal part of his own ego that wants to depend on her (Fairbairn, *Psychoanalytic Studies*, 114–15). That is, the "central ego" assigns to one part of the ego (the libidinal ego) the task of being aware of (cathecting with) what the original, primarily dependent ego wants in its object and hopes to attain from it. In addition, it assigns to another part of the ego (the internal saboteur or anti-libidinal ego) the task of being aware of the original ego's frustrations (of the "rejecting character" of the object). The anti-libidinal ego then attacks the libidinal ego (by attacking the exciting object) while the central ego attacks both the libidinal and anti-libidinal egos and their objects. The central ego's object is the "accepted object," shorn of its exciting and threatening aspects. In any case, the result is that the original need to cathect with the needed, exciting but frustrating object becomes a regressive urge to cathect with what is now a rejected object, so that the original disturbing and regressive cathexis with a threatening object is depleted and replaced by a progressive urge to repudiate that same cathexis. Infantile dependence can now be overcome. However, if the attachment of the libidinal ego to its object is very strong, the anti-libido's assault can be required to be so violent that it destroys not just the libidinal ego's regressive portion but destroys the libidinal ego altogether. Since libido is the primary object-seeking life-drive, such a loss of libido is certainly a "death" of sorts. In Fairbairn's words, "This withdrawal of libido may be carried to all lengths. It may be carried to a point at which all emotional and physical contacts with other persons are renounced; and it may even go so far that all libidinal links with outer reality are surrendered, all interest in the world around fades and everything becomes meaningless" (*Psychoanalytic Studies*, 50). We may surmise, it would seem, that the death the persona fears is real, even if it is not physical.

When Jungian terms are applied in an interpretation of Sonnet 2, a reading would be as follows. For some unknown reason the poet–persona has to depart from the lady in whom he projects his anima and adapt to her absence. His undifferentiated ego is protected from the shock of the event by the following process. His libido, seeking renewed strength, streams back to a yearning for an earlier, more successful form of adaptation, a relationship of infantile dependence with the mother. The state of radical regression in which the persona finds himself is a result of his departure from Nise, yet his own development requires that he tear himself from that state and continue onward. In order to do so and re-direct libido towards a new object, the persona's ego now introjects Nise and identifies her with the threatening mother, who is really the persona's own regressive tendency. It is against this tendency that his ego now directs aggression, so that the persona's repudiation of the lady–mother becomes aggression against himself insofar as he clings to his former dependence: that is, aggression towards a threatening object becomes the self-affliction that he experiences when he continues walking onward. The power of the lady, who is now identified with the clinging mother, is manifested in the persona's intense regressive desire to return to her. The persona's ego has thus defensively redefined the situation: his unsuccessful efforts to attain satisfaction from an object that excites him have been re-cast as potentially successful efforts to escape an object that threatens him. The ego is thus protected from injury. In any case, it is in the situation in which the persona's libido is attempting to overcome the paralyzing effects of ready acceptance by the mother that the process of individuation would have to occur, thus making it possible for the personality (Fairbairn's "ego") to be raised to a higher moral power by channeling volitional energy in a definite direction and returning to the challenges of adapting to the real world.

Critical perspectives based on the theories of Fairbairn and Jung have many characteristics in common. Infantile dependence and regressive libido are elements that are prominent in both. Fairbairn's "exciting, needed object" is Jung's "mother," and Fairbairn's anti-libidinal ego that attacks the exciting object, thus sabotaging libidinal ego, is the progressive libido that must tear itself loose from the mother. Fairbairn's "threatening, frustrating, or rejecting object" is, in a Jungian interpretation of Sonnet 2, the beloved lady who initially threatened the persona with his own dependence. The beloved lady whom Jung sees as a projection of the persona's anima is Fairbairn's "original object." For both Jung and Fairbairn, acquiring a differentiated identity involves unifying the splits in one's personality: what for Jung is overcoming regression and reemerging to the upper world of light, again adaptively facing the contradictory realities of the outer world and doing so as a whole, integrated, self-realized ego, is for Fairbairn the transition from infantile dependence to mature dependence with both a greater independence of the integrated ego and "the substitution of a whole object for a part object" (*Psychoanalytic Studies*, 48). In this connection, it would seem logical to deduce that in the last line of Fray Luis's poem, "¿Quándo volveré, Nise a ver tus ojos?" ["When, Nise, will I see your eyes again?"], two eyes symbolize unity; and, since Nise is the persona's unconscious (his anima) and his eyes look at hers, his seeing her eyes has the significance of the persona's integration of the order of the unconscious into consciousness. The process of overcoming disintegration of the ego must be accompanied not just by a psychic relationship to the collective unconscious and (as Fairbairn would say) the integration of the internalized objects with which various parts of the ego have relationships, but by conscious, personal relationships with whole persons, unitary egos in whom the unconscious is projected (Jung, *Works*, 7: 303).

It would perhaps not be unjustified to speculate that Fairbairn's scheme owes a certain debt of gratitude to Jung. On the other hand, in certain respects Fairbairn's theory is fundamentally different from Jung's and is even its opposite. In both Fairbairn and Jung the ego performs an adaptive and integrative function, but in Fairbairn the ego renders the original object less desirable by turning ego against libido and causing a portion of libido to be *suppressed*. In Jung, on the other hand, the process of adaptation and integration, which is equivalent to individuation, entails a progressive *liberation* of unconscious libido (of psychic energy of the unconscious) after a necessary regressive phase of recovering unconscious values that were previously excluded from the conscious process of adaptation. In Fairbairn the central (moral) ego and the anti-libidinal (primitive talion) ego function as powerful equivalents to Freud's super-ego. In Jung's scheme there is no super-ego, or censor, that is a separate agency exercising a progressive inhibitory function; there is merely the inhibition to which potentially progressive unconscious values are subjected as a result of the exclusive directedness, the one-sidedness, of conscious contents — in a man's case the inhibition of feeling by thought (Jung, *Works*, 8: 34).

Which of these two perspectives, Jung's or Fairbairn's, seems best suited to interpret Fray Luis's poem? In comparison with what for Fairbairn is the guiding influence of the ego's interests, the independent initiative that for Jung is exercised by libido makes his perspective more heroic and romantic. This quality is undoubtedly related to the importance of myth in Jung's ideas, since the characters of myth have heroic attributes and often are direct personifications of libido. In Fray Luis's poem, the persona's intense agony is not a result of his standing still in a state of indecision as he "looks back" mentally; it is a result of progressive movement of libido, of his being "llevado del contrario movimiento" ["carried by the opposite movement"]. The poet–persona in Sonnet 2 is, therefore, more an exponent of developing libido such as it is conceived by Jung. Fairbairn's perspective is more Protestant; it implies a distrust of the ascending dynamic of libido, and his theory has no mechanism for the recovery of lost libido nor for the strengthening of libido. Also, Jung's perspective is more "Renaissance" and humanistic in that it postulates an enhancement of the innate creative powers of human personality. The "integrated personality capable of adaptation" as Fairbairn conceives it strikes one as being a personality that is still perhaps somewhat infantile in the sense that it is de-libidinized and therefore lacking in direction, if not docile — even if it is less dependent. Fairbairn's integrated state is reminiscent of the relatively blunted condition in which Sireno in Montemayor's humanistic romance *La Diana* finds himself after drinking the wise Felicia's narcotic *agua mágica*.

It is interesting that in spite of the thematic similarities between Garcilaso's Sonnet 38 and Fray Luis's Sonnet 2, Fray Luis's poem is imitative of Garcilaso's poem only in the broadest sense. On the literal level Fray Luis actually reverses the terms of

Garcilaso's poem. Whereas in Sonnet 38 the persona is threatened by his longing for proximity to the lady, in Fray Luis's sonnet a previous proximity to the lady is what the persona is striving to overcome. It is also interesting that, unlike Fray Luis's Sonnet 2, in Sonnet 38 Garcilaso goes beyond utilizing a temporal dynamic of past and future and a spatial dynamic of distance and proximity of the persona to the lady by adding the vertical dynamic of "above" and "below," placing the lady above the persona. By doing so and representing the lady as being dominant and aloof, Garcilaso is able to introduce the additional thematic dimension of the persona's struggle with feelings of impotence and persecutory anxiety. It may well be that Fray Luis's Christian perspective made him reluctant to represent "above" in critical terms, a speculation that is born out by other of his poems such as "Noche oscura." On the other hand, in his poem "En la Ascensión" (discussed below in chapter 6) Fray Luis does seem to represent "above" in a such a light, and it is a poem that shows a strong influence of Garcilaso. In any case, in Fray Luis's Sonnet 2 the lady is threatening but not because of her threatening superiority. A trait that both that poem and Garcilaso's Sonnet 38 share is that the poet–persona can be understood to be struggling to abandon an illusory emotional security that had been promised by an attitude of infantile identification. Both poets portray that struggle as being an instance of what is today referred to as the "schzoid position," which need not be considered "abnormal" insofar as splits in the ego at some level are a universal human phenomenon (Fairbairn, *Psychoanalytic Studies*, 8).

A drawback in applying Fairbairn's and Jung's theories to these poems is that explaining the persona's ambivalence in terms of conflicting needs (freedom and security) associated with infantile dependence draws attention away from the poems' aesthetic value insofar as such value derives from the portrayal of mature, exemplary strength of character — qualities that do not have to be thought of as being compromised by the sincere candor with which the personas reveal their pain, even if that pain does assume quasi-pathological, morbid and "modern" proportions. On a level where less attention is paid to subtle details in these poems, a reading that is preferable in some respects is made possible by applying John Bowlby's attachment theory. Bowlby considers the differences between that theory and theories based on the principle of dependence to both complement the latter, psychoanalytic approach and to offer new insights.[28] One could equally say, for example, that the presence of a heroic dimension

---

[28] John Bowlby, *Attachment and Loss*, 3 vols. (New York: Basic Books, 1969–1980),

especially in modern manneristic works is in no way necessarily incompatible with the presence in them of a satiric dimension. The inconsistency between such dimensions can itself become one dimension of their subject. Attachment, Bowlby maintains, is not a pathological state, and, unlike dependence, it implies an enduring bond and is necessarily associated with strong feeling.[29] One could answer that dependence assumes pathological proportions to only the extent that it endures into adulthood, in which case the illusory bond of dependence is both enduring and emotionally charged, but in the discussion of a relatively romantic literary work that emphasizes heroic attitudes, the possible advantages of the more "positive," "affirming" character of attachment theory is undeniable. Attachment theory's emphasis on intense emotion also combines well with an approach to these poems that seeks to comprehend their aesthetic appeal in terms of value theory. If one were to see the greatest aesthetic appeal of Sonnet 38 and Sonnet 2 as being rooted in their evocation of the emotional depth and strength of feeling of the personas, both poets can be seen as achieving an effect of high emotional intensity through counterposing two values of similar grade, the claims of one being contrary to the fulfillment of the other. Those two values are love of the nearest (of the lady in her aspect of offering a secure proximity) and love of the remotest (the lady in her aspect of an ideal object of striving), the lady assuming the character of a remote value more the more the persona withdraws from her or con-

---

1: 234, and idem, *The Making and Breaking of Affectional Bonds* (1979) (London: Routledge, 1995), 131–32. One could note that Bowlby's emphasis on the positive, affectional character of attachment bonds is especially applicable to the forms those bonds assume in Mediterranean cultures, as opposed to the forms of those bonds experienced in Northwest Europe and the Anglo-Saxon world. I am indebted to Leslie S. B. MacCoull for this point.

[29] See Bowlby, *The Making and Breaking of Emotional Bonds*, 131–32 and idem, *Attachment and Loss*, 3: 40, where one reads,

> Many of the most intense emotions arise during the formation, the maintenance, the disruption and the renewal of attachment relationships. The formation of a bond is described as falling in love, maintaining a bond as loving someone, and losing a partner as grieving over someone. Similarly, threat of loss arouses anxiety and actual loss gives rise to sorrow; while each of these situations is likely to arouse anger. The unchallenged maintenance of a bond is experienced as a source of joy. Because such emotions are usually a reflection of the state of a person's affectional bonds, the psychology and psychopathology of emotion is found to be in large part the psychology and psychopathology of affectional bonds.

templates doing so. In any case, alternating back and forth between affirming the one value and then the other (between staying or trying to stay close to the lady and fleeing her or trying to flee her) has the cumulative effect of heightening the emotional pitch of these poems. If their aesthetic value is seen in these terms, two principles noted by Hartmann apply. On the one hand, the moral value in the intention of the ideal rises in proportion to the strength of that intention and the disposition to which it gives rise; on the other hand, "love of the nearest is on a small scale what love of the remotest is on a large scale" (*Ethics*, 2: 328–29). Hence, affirming both the nearest and the remotest can be comprehended as ideals and hence as values of similar grade, love of the far distant simply being more exceptional than love of the nearby.

Surely an important source of the aesthetic value of Fray Luis's sonnet, from a more complex thematic point of view, is that it explores the divided and contradictory role of the libidinal ego (roughly equivalent to what in Fray Luis's day was referred to as "*voluntad*," "will") in human mental and emotional processes. In this regard, Sonnet 2 can be seen as a precursor to the investigations of psychodynamics that have been carried out by psychoanalysts such as Jung and Fairbairn. It also anticipates the modern "ethics of values" of theorists such as Hartmann, in whose *Ethics* one reads, for example, statements such as the following: "All courage to act is ... fortitude in suffering, in the bearing of consequences, of disaster and guilt" (2: 247). There is no need to explain the relation of such concerns to the revival of tragic art in the Renaissance, a period when the development of personality, of human differentiation and greatness, was valued more than ever. But above all, we find Fray Luis's poem appealing not because of its clinical interest but because of the sheer intensity of libido that it depicts — an intensity that is "fateful" as a result both of the great power exercised by Nise and the persona's capacity to oppose that power with even greater resolution of his own. Fray Luis's Sonnet 2 goes beyond the conventions of a poetry of praise in the courtly-love tradition by depicting a man struggling to become an individual and embrace his destiny. The central issue in the poem is whether the persona can recover sufficient intensity of libido for his libido to survive after it has renounced that part of itself that has a relationship of infantile identification with the object from which it is separating. In drawing that conclusion I combine the views of Jung and Fairbairn.

6

The Despondence of Orphaned Humanity:
Love's Protest against Sovereignty
in Fray Luis de León's
"En la Ascensión" and in Garcilaso

It is common and legitimate practice for critics to shed light hypothetically on certain aspects of a work by suggesting correlations between those aspects and biographical data concerning its author, and it is particularly tempting to do so in the case of a figure whose life experience is as striking as is that of Fray Luis de León. Our perception of Fray Luis has been made more vivid by Aubrey Bell's important biographical study, in which Fray Luis's long imprisonment is explained as resulting in part from the courageous forthrightness that was a marked characteristic of his personality. Bell writes:

> That his enemies expected that a man so excitable as Luis de León and so frank would implicate himself irremediably under arrest was evident, and they, rather than the Inquisition itself, must bear the odium for his long imprisonment. Here was a professor with many enemies, not mealy-mouthed, a keen supporter of the Jew Grajal, bold and even rash in his statements of doctrine, fiery in his denunciations, a man of invincible spirit, who, after weary months of im-

prisonment, kept telling the Inquisitors what it was their duty to do, and demanding that his accusers should be summarily punished. And this man was regarded as an oracle in the Schools. If one cannot excuse the continual delays, one can at least understand that the local Inquisitors should be not unwilling to protract his trial and had changed their opinion of July 1572, that 'importa la brevedad' ['expediency is indicated'].[1]

As Manuel Durán writes, "there was no trace of timidity in him."[2] Fray Luis's famous ode on the Ascension, in which Christ is addressed in a tone of reproach for having left his flock, seems naturally susceptible of an interpretation relating it to the spirited personality of its author, and so it is that in 1946 Karl Vossler stated (without elaborating further on the subject) that if in writing that poem Fray Luis temporarily forgot the religious significance of the Ascension it is "una prueba de que la emoción ante las cosas eternas que sentía el poeta era mucho más fuerte en él que su erudición de comentarista de la Biblia" ["proof that the emotion the poet felt toward eternal things was much stronger than his erudition as a commentator on the Bible"].[3] It would perhaps be more appropriate to the breadth of meaning suggested by "En la Ascensión" for an interpretation of it not to rely on biographical considerations as much as Vossler's does, but for the poem to be interpreted in broader terms that at the same time correlate successfully with such considerations. However, except for Vossler's brief comment, readings of "En la Ascensión" have tended to run directly counter to our general impression of Fray Luis. Instead of addressing the attitude of dissent that the poem expresses, critics have tried to see in it sentiments that are not really in keeping either with our impression of the temperament of Fray Luis, whom Bell (*Luis de León*, 11) has compared to Savonarola, nor with the language and spirit of the text. The observations to follow will propose an alternative reading of "En la Ascensión." By coming to terms with the poem's tone of reproach, my interpretation departs from most of the previous interpretations by being, I believe, more consistent with our general sense of Fray Luis's personality. My interpretation is also consistent with that of Manuel Durán and Miguel Atlee, who, without entering into further details, write,

---

[1] A. F. G. Bell, *Luis de León* (Oxford: Clarendon Press, 1925), 60–61.

[2] Manuel Durán, *Luis de León* (New York: Twayne, 1971), 35.

[3] Karl Vossler, *Fray Luis de León*, trans. Carlos Clavería (Buenos Aires: Espasa-Calpe, 1946), 98.

"Angustia, deseo de evadirse, son evidentes, junto con un reproche a un Dios que se aleja y no consuela" ["Anguish, a wish to escape, are evident, together with a reproach of a God who is going away and offers no consolation"].[4] I will also relate a broad, metaphorical interpretation of the crisis represented in Fray Luis's poem to elements of the poetic tradition cultivated by Garcilaso de la Vega and the themes of death and rebirth.

What is considered to be the final version of "En la Ascensión" is five stanzas long. The view expressed by José Llobera[5] and repeated by Colin Thompson,[6] that the poem expresses the viewpoint of Christ's disciples, seems accurate (especially because of the cloud's being addressed, and the pronoun "nos," in the last stanza), though the poem could also be considered to be representing the point of view of humanity as a whole. The first stanza expresses anguish prompted by feelings of abandonment and reproachful vexation at Christ's (imputed) preference for a happier, safer, and more exalted state than that in which he is leaving his faithful disciples:

> ¡Y dejas, Pastor santo,
> tu grey en este valle hondo, escuro
> con soledad y llanto!
> Y tú, rompiendo el puro
> aire, ¿te vas al inmortal seguro?[7]

[And you leave, holy Shepherd, your flock in this deep, dark valley with solitude and tears! And you, breaking into the pure air, depart for the safety of immortality?]

---

[4] Manuel Durán and Miguel Atlee, *Fray Luis de León: Poesía* (Madrid: Cátedra, 1985), 118.

[5] P. José Llobera, ed., *Obras poéticas del maestro Fray Luis de León*, 2 vols. (Cuenca: Talleres Tipográficos del Seminariano, 1931–1932), 1: 279.

[6] Colin P. Thompson, " 'En la Ascensión': Artistic Tradition and Poetic Imagination in Luis de León," in *Medieval and Renaissance Studies on Spain and Portugal in Honour of P. E. Russell*, ed. F. W. Hodcroft et al. (Oxford: Society for the Study of Medieval Languages and Literatures, 1981), 109–20, here 112–13.

[7] All quotations from "En la Ascensión" are from *Poesías de Fray Luis de León*, ed. Vega, 519–21; translations are mine.

The second stanza reiterates the sense of abandonment, adding to it feelings of deprivation, desolation, and even disorientation:

> Los antes bienhadados,
> y los agora tristes y afligidos,
> a tus pechos criados,
> de Ti desposeídos,
> ¿a dó convertirán ya sus sentidos?

[The once fortunate and now sad and afflicted, raised at your breasts, dispossessed by you, where will they now turn their attention?]

The next stanza again emphasizes the disconsolate state of those facing the absence of the being who had inspired them:

> ¿Qué mirarán los ojos
> que vieron de tu rostro la hermosura,
> que no les sea enojos?
> Quien oyó tu dulzura,
> ¿qué no tendrá por sordo y desventura?

[What will the eyes that saw the beauty of your face behold that will not be troubling to them? To those who heard your sweetness, what will not seem dull and unfortunate?]

On a more practical note, stanza four, while possibly referring to an incident in Christ's life,[8] expresses concern that a world (or the Church) engulfed in violence and confusion will be left helpless without the principle of a higher order capable of guiding it in a good direction:

---

[8] Edward Sarmiento, ed., *The Original Poems of Fray Luis de León* (Manchester: Manchester University Press, 1968), 87.

> Aqueste mar turbado,
> ¿quién le pondrá ya freno?
> ¿Quién concierto
> al viento fiero, airado?
> Estando tú encubierto,
> ¿qué norte guiará la nave al puerto?

[This troubled sea, who will restrain it now? Who will bring harmony to the wild, angry wind? With you hidden, what north star will guide the ship to port?]

The final stanza, addressing the cloud bearing Christ upwards, returns to an element introduced in the first stanza, the contrast between heaven and earth, wealth and poverty, power and impotence, splendor and gloom:

> ¡Ay!, nube envidiosa
> aun de este breve gozo. ¿Qué te aquejas?
> ¿Dó vuelas presurosa?
> ¡Cuán rica tú te alejas!
> ¡Cuán pobres y cuán ciegos, ay, nos dejas!

[Oh, cloud, jealous even of this brief pleasure. What afflicts you? Where are you flying with such haste? How richly you depart! How poor and how blind, oh, you leave us!]

The tone of joy in the four stanzas added to the end of what seems to be an earlier version of the poem[9] has the effect of largely dissipating the paradoxically irreverent

---

[9] Those verses are transcribed as follows from Vega's edition by José Manuel Blecua, ed., *Fray Luis de León: Poesía completa* (Madrid: Gredos, 1990), 212, who also does not accept their authenticity:

> Tú llevas el tesoro,
> que sólo a nuestra vida enriquesía,
> que desterraba el lloro,
> que nos resplandecía
> mil veces más que el puro y claro día.

tone of reproach that stands out in the shorter version. Since the inclusion of those stanzas vastly simplifies the problem represented by the poem's tone of complaint (they compensate for that tone) there is a natural tendency to regard them as authentic. Their authenticity has been accepted by Antolín Merino, Edward Churton, James Fitzmaurice-Kelly,[10] and Edward Sarmiento (*Original Poems*, 87). Dámaso Alonso[11] and Ángel Custodio Vega (*Poesías*, 523) favor the view that the stanzas were written by Fray Luis, who later deleted them, Vega preferring the briefer version because of its "mayor viveza, rapidez y misterio" ["greater liveliness, swiftness and mystery"] (521).

   ¿Qué lazo de diamante,
ay, alma!, te detiene y encadena
a no seguir tu amante?
¡Ay, rompe y sal de pena!
Colócante ya libre en luz serena.
   ¿Qué temes la salida?
¿Podrá el terreno amor más que la ausencia
de tu querer y vida?
Sin cuerpo, no es violencia
vivir, mas no lo es sin Cristo y su presencia.
   Dulce Señor y amigo,
dulce Padre y Hermano, dulce Esposo:
en pos de Ti yo sigo,
o puesto en tenebroso
o puesto en lugar claro y glorioso.

[You bear the treasure that only enriched our life, that banished weeping, that shone on us a thousand times more than the pure and bright day. What bond of diamond, oh soul! detains and enchains you to not follow your beloved? Oh, break away and emerge from sorrow! Your are being placed free in serene light. Why do you fear departing? Does earthly love have more power than your love and life? Without a body living is not violence, but not without Christ and his presence. Sweet Lord and friend, sweet Father and Brother, sweet Husband: behind You I follow, whether I am in a dark place or in a place that is bright and glorious.] (my translation.)

Cf. Senabre, "La oda," 86–88. The allusions are to Statius, *Thebaid* 4.534–535; Philippians 1: 23; 2 Corinthians 5: 8; cf. Revelation 14: 4. I am indebted to Leslie S. B. MacCoull for these and other classical, scriptural, and patristic references in this chapter.

 [10] For the opinions of Merino, Churton, and Fitzmaurice-Kelly, see Sarmiento, ed., *Original Poems*, 87.

 [11] See Dámaso Alonso, "Vida y poesía en Fray Luis de León," in idem, *Obras completas* 2: 789–824, here 832.

The burden of justifying the poem's tone of anguished protest would seem to be felt more by those who deny the authenticity of the additional four stanzas. However, José Llobera (*Obras poéticas*, 277–78), José Manuel Blecua (*Poesía completa*, 212), and Felix García (*Obras completas castellanas*, 1461) do not accept the authenticity of the four stanzas but also do not address the problematic character of their tone. Other critics who do not accept the authenticity of the additional stanzas include Karl Vossler (*Fray Luis de León*, 98), Oreste Macrí, Diego J. Figueroa (whose rejection is implicit), Ricardo Senabre, and Colin P. Thompson. Macrí rejects the four additional stanzas on the grounds that the New Testament, to which Fray Luis, as a biblical scholar, would have been faithful, is "sparing and severe in evoking feelings of joy and pain," and he explains the unusual tone of the poem by observing that the tragic pathos of man abandoned in a dark vale of tears figures prominently in the Old Testament, particularly in the book of Job.[12] Diego J. Figueroa makes no mention at all of the longer version of the poem (one therefore assumes that he discounts its authenticity) and explains the work's "pessimistic" tone as being the consequence both of an orphaned humanity's ascetic fear of worldly temptation's threat to self-perception and of the need to counteract that threat with the presence or vision of Christ's image.[13] Like Francisco Martínez de la Rosa,[14] Ricardo Senabre expresses surprise at the tone of the poem's beginning, yet whereas Martínez de la Rosa ignores the problematic character of that tone, Senabre explains it by seeing Fray Luis as writing in the "más afectiva y dramática" ["more affective and dramatic"] tradition of St. Bernard, from whom Senabre quotes passages expressing a mood similar to the mood in Fray Luis's poem. One such passage is "¿Cómo me dejaste sin despedirte de mí, cuando hermoso en tu gala, Rey de la gloria, te retiraste a las alturas de los cielos?" ["How did you leave me without saying goodbye to me, when beautiful in your finery, King of Glory, you withdrew to the heights of heaven?"].[15]

---

[12] Oreste Macrí, ed., *Fray Luis de León: Poesías* (Barcelona: Editorial Crítica, 1982), 78–79. (The expression "valley of tears" is well known from the Marian antiphon "Salve Regina.")

[13] Diego J. Figueroa, "La 'Oda a la Ascensión' de Fray Luis," *Religión y cultura* 10 (1965): 211–28, here 211, 219–21.

[14] Martínez de la Rosa is quoted by Llobera, *Obra poética*, 279–80.

[15] Ricardo Senabre, *Tres estudios sobre Fray Luis de León* (Salamanca: Universidad de Salamanca, 1978), 76–80, 94–96. The original is Bernard, *Sermo in Ascensione Domini* 2.4, PL 183. 303 A–B: "Quomodo me dereliquisti insalutatum cum formosus in stola tua res gloriae in alta coelo num te recepisti?".

Colin Thompson has published the most important recent study of "En la Ascensión." Continuing the line of reasoning of Macrí and Senabre, Thompson discounts the authenticity of the additional stanzas and points to antecedents in Judeo-Christian tradition of man's anguished helplessness and God's apparent indifference, particularly in facial expressions of fear and awe in iconographic tradition (an influence suggested to him by Bell). He interprets the poem as a faithful if imaginative re-creation of the biblical story of the Ascension and sees its "apparently pessimistic" tone in the depiction of confusion resulting from a lack of faith on the part of the disciples and their consequently mistaking ascension for abandonment ("Artistic Tradition and Poetic Imagination," 110–13).

The trend of modern interpretations of "En la Ascensión," then, has been to contradict such early reactions to the poem as that of Guillermo Junemann, who repudiates its elegiac tone as "falso" because it is inconsistent with the intimate joy that he claims was actually felt by the disciples upon witnessing the ascent of Christ.[16] Vossler (*Fray Luis de León*, 98) and Macrí (*Poesías*, 78) also refer to "un teólogo" who was astonished that the Ascension could awaken feelings of despair and abandonment (bearing in mind John 16:16–30). Have the arguments of critics, especially Vossler, Figueroa, Macrí, Senabre, and Thompson, been successful in defending Fray Luis's poem against such reservations? Have they been able to justify the poem's spirit of anguished reproach in terms that are convincing?

The possibility cannot be discounted that there are two authentic versions of the poem, but even if both versions are by Fray Luis, we are still faced with the problem of explaining the tone of the briefer version. It is, after all, the more generally credited version and hence the more deserving of attention. Vossler's explanation, that Fray Luis was carried away by his subject, has the serious defect of implying that the writing of the poem was not in every way a deliberate act: an unlikely theory, even if it has the advantage of emphasizing the sincerity of the emotions that the work expresses. Figueroa's approach patently ignores the feelings of abandonment in the poem and with them the attitude of reproach, i.e., the work's most distinctive features. Once the notes of grief and apprehension are thus isolated from their source, he proceeds to represent them in conventional terms as "pessimism" and "fear" on the basis of the loosest definition of those terms, even if such a perspective finds some support in Luke 24:37. Macrí, Senabre, and Thompson all would obviate the necessity of confronting the

---

[16] Junemann's views are quoted by Llobera, *Obras poéticas*, 278.

surprising sense one feels of the profoundly legitimate character of the poem's tone of anguished protest by placing the poem in the referential context of a broad tradition of religious orthodoxy and, in that way, suggesting that there is nothing very surprising about the work after all. Thus, those critics provide answers to the questions raised by the poem without attempting to address specifically the problematic terms of the poem itself or reconciling the contradictory elements of those terms (in spite of minute textual analysis in the case of Senabre and Thompson).

The refusal to address Fray Luis's poem on its own terms has led to a variety of difficulties. Macrí's justification (adduced by Senabre and Thompson) for denying the authenticity of the additional stanzas could be used to deny the authenticity of the shorter version of the poem as well, for if the additional stanzas' tone of extreme joy is not in keeping with the New Testament (notwithstanding Revelation 14:4; 2 and Corinthians 5:1–8), the tone of extreme pain in the short version is, according to Macrí himself, not in keeping with it either. Similarly, the passages from St. Bernard cited by Senabre,[17] although they constitute a clearly direct influence on Fray Luis, do not represent, either in nature or degree, the same attitudes of desolation and helplessness or necessarily the nuance of reproach present in Fray Luis's poem. The claim of an influence from the Old Testament is more convincing, and the probable existence of such an influence on "En la Ascensión" is summarily pointed out by both Macrí (*Poesías*, 79) and Thompson ("Artistic Tradition and Poetic Imagination," 112). Here, particularly in the book of Job, one finds an agonized sense of abandonment and, if not the same emphasis on helplessness, a similar anguish in the face of God's apparent indifference to the plight of his creatures. One may also note that, like the disciples, Job reproaches the deity for arbitrariness in the exercise of his sovereignty. Yet, again, it is possible to question the extent to which pointing out the presence of these elements in the book of Job can be considered to contribute to an interpretation of their meaning in Fray Luis's poem, for there are important differences. Job's affliction is so extreme as to resemble a punishment for sins, and he feels abandoned by a just God

---

[17] Note the allusion to Psalm 24:7–10. The remaining passages by St. Bernard cited by Senabre are as follows: "Pero si bien lo pensáis, hermanos, ¡cuánto dolor y temor ocuparía los apostólicos pechos cuando le vieron desviarse de ellos y levantarse sobre los aires! . . . Bendiciéndoles, caminaba al cielo, estremeciéndose acaso aquellas entrañas de singular misericordia al dejar a los suyos afligidos . . ." (*Tres estudios*, 79). The original is Bernard's *Sermo in Asc.* 2.3, PL 183. 302C–D: "Quid tamen putatis, fratres . . ."; "Benedicens ergo eis ferebatur in coelum . . .".

precisely because he has not sinned. Here God is a being who commands awed respect as one who retains an attitude of proud superiority to human beings. In Fray Luis's poem the disciples feel abandoned because their beloved teacher (God in his aspect as the sacrificed Son), whom they have known as a friend and companion in suffering, is removing the comfort and guidance of his actual presence among human beings (cf. John 16:5–7) to occupy an exclusive, superior realm in the heavenly kingdom. The two situations are fundamentally different. It is true that both Job and the disciples can be seen as displaying confusion as a result of a lack of faith. Yet whereas the circumstance is central to the book of Job, which ends with a resolution in the form of God's rebuke of Job or perhaps just of Job's friends, in "En la Ascensión" the issue of faith, if it is present at all, is subordinate to the immediate, human experience of bitter grief at being deprived of the presence of a beloved companion. Hence, the direct comparison of this poem to the book of Job has the misleading effect of suggesting that the poem's passionate expression of grief and solitude is the temptation of a faithless pessimism. As we shall see, however, the comparison can prove fruitful in other ways.

If we attempt to use Thompson's Warburg-like association of "En la Ascensión" with iconographic tradition to shed light on the poem's more problematic elements, that approach also proves inadequate. For to justify those elements by placing the poem in a broad context of treatments of the same subject in other works only draws our attention away from the problems in Fray Luis's text, bypassing the literal value of certain key elements of language (the reproach) and hence bypassing Fray Luis's particular treatment of the subject. Instead of explaining those problematic elements, such an approach substitutes less problematic ones ("fear and awe" or "prayer and devotion" ["Artistic Tradition and Poetic Imagination," 110]) for them, specifically opposing William Empson's and Jonathan Culler's view that critics must preserve as much of the literal meanings of metaphors as possible.[18] Also, Thompson's contention that Fray Luis was above all depicting an anguish that was the result of the disciples' confusion and lack of faith discounts the authenticity of the poem as an expression of feelings with which the author himself could identify. As I mentioned earlier, it ought by no means to be a foregone conclusion that in this poem, any more than in his ode "Noche serena" (with which it has a great deal in common), Fray Luis does not give expression to anxieties that he himself experienced. So in keeping would his doing so

---

[18] Jonathan Culler, *Structuralist Poetics* (Ithaca, NY: Cornell University Press, 1975), 183.

be with our general impression of Fray Luis and his outspoken personality that Coster,[19] Vega (*Poesías*, 519), Macrí (*Poesías*, 47), and Figueroa ("La 'Oda a la Ascensión'," 215) have assumed Fray Luis to have written "En la Ascensión" sometime during the five years he spent in inquisitorial prisons.[20] There are certainly grounds for the view that a truly great lyrical poem is not just an exercise in language or based on thought but involves an expression of an artist's own feelings.[21] That view does not depend on the assumption that a poem is autobiographical in nature, at least demonstrably. Also, an element that we expect in the works of classic authors (and Fray Luis is a classic author in every sense of the term) is the ideal quality of the genuine, and a mere ironic representation of faithlessness would conflict with that expectation. Llobera recognized the fallacy of discounting the authenticity of the feelings expressed in "En la Ascensión" when, in response to Junemann's denial that the disciples of the Savior could experience pain upon seeing him return to heaven, he wrote, "A eso se responde que si los Apóstoles se alegraron de la gloria de su Señor, no por eso dejaron de afligirse por la ausencia de su divino Maestro" (["The reply to that is that if the Apostles were glad of the glory of their Lord, that was not a cause for them to fail to feel affliction at the absence of their divine Teacher"]; *Obras poéticas*, 278). Of course, Llobera's words still do not constitute a cogent explanation for the intensity of the poem's protest against what almost seems to be regarded as a complacent betrayal of loving trust.

§

---

[19] Coster's thoughts on this subject (from "Luis de León") are paraphrased in detail and interpreted by Félix García, *Obras completas castellanas*, 1460.

[20] Thompson states ("Artistic Tradition and Poetic Imagination," 113) that Bell considers "En la Ascensión" to have been written while Fray Luis was in prison, but in the sources I have consulted Bell places the writing of that poem after the prison years (*Luis de León*, 241).

[21] To this effect Tolstoy writes "... the chief property of art is the contagion of others by the feeling which the artist experienced..." (*What is Art?* [Philadelphia: Henry Altemus, 1898], 160). Without believing that Tolstoy's opinion is the last word on this subject (it corresponds to what M. H. Abrams refers to as "the expressive theory" of literature [*Doing Things with Texts*, 11–17], I am more inclined to credit a classic literary artist's views on such matters than the "death of the author" principle of theorists like Barthes and Foucault, although the specific point argued by that principle also has its share of validity, even if it is overstated.

A satisfactory interpretation of "En la Ascensión" should account for the inordinate degree not just of grief but of bitterness that the poem expresses at its outset and that underlies the whole. The second and third stanzas convince us that the bitterness expressed is inseparable from the love that the disciples feel for Christ. The love between Christ and his disciples was more than just an emotional bond; it grew strong in their having joined together and striven in pursuit of the benefit of humanity (cf. John 13:14–17, 14:18–19, 15:12–17). It was that cooperative relationship that the disciples saw imperiled by Christ's imminent absence (cf. John 16:5–6) (also John 14: 27–28). Fray Luis's lengthy commentary on the book of Job expresses the attitude that the faithful can be deprived of their assurance of God's desire to cooperate with them personally without that occurrence reflecting upon them in a negative way. Traditionally, the divine intervention or theophany at the conclusion of the book of Job is interpreted as an indignant denial of Job's right to question the ways of God; however, in the epilogue God exonerates Job and criticizes Job's friends for not having said of him the thing that was right, as his servant Job had. Fray Luis's interpretation is consistent with the epilogue: he writes that although Job deserves his rebuke for having addressed God with "cierta demasía de palabras" [a certain excess of words], his cause is nevertheless "buena y justa" [good and just].[22] The feelings of deprivation experienced by Christ's disciples must have been in some ways even more disorienting than those experienced by Job. The strain on Job's awed respect for an Old Testament God of objective command is compounded in Fray Luis's rendition of the Ascension by the disciples' being deprived as well of the concretely personal experience of Christ's presence. The explanation for the boldness with which the disciples address Christ, then, must be sought in the specific character of the relationship between Christ and his disciples. Words that might be disrespectful when addressed by Job to God himself are not necessarily so in addressing the Son, whom the disciples know as a beloved companion ("amado" is a term to which Fray Luis dedicates a chapter in his *Nombres de Cristo*). In his comments justifying in principle Job's words of despair (but censuring their propriety when directed to God), Fray Luis writes, "en un alma por una parte herida tan crudamente, el dolor y la buena consciencia y la seguridad que della nace cría naturalmente una sancta osadía, que entre amigos se sufre y se perdona" (["in a soul injured in part so cruelly, pain, good conscience, and the security born of the

---

[22] Quotations from Fray Luis's *Exposición del Libro de Job* are from *Obras completas castellanas de Fray Luis de León*, ed. García, here 1233.

latter, naturally breeds a blessed boldness, which among friends is suffered and pardoned"]; *Obras completas*, 1233). That same justification is even more applicable to the tone of reproach with which the disciples address Christ as a companion in "En la Ascensión."

It is in the personal love felt for Christ by his disciples, as well as in the frustration of that love, that one also finds the specific source of the bitterness underlying the disciples' reproachful attitude. One is immediately struck by a familiar authenticity of feeling in those elements of Fray Luis's poem, a sense of having heard something similar elsewhere. One recalls lines such as the following:

> Pues en una ora junto me llevastes
> todo el bien que por términos me distes,
> lleváme junto el mal que me dexastes;
> si no, sospecharé que me pusistes
> en tantos bienes porque desseastes
> verme morir entre memorias tristes.

[Since in one hour you took from me all the good that by degrees you gave me, take from me together the bad that you left me; if not, I will suspect that you placed me in so many goods because you wanted to see me die amidst sad memories.]

and

> Mas ¿qué haré, senora,
> en tanta desventura?
> ¿A dónde iré si a vos no voy con ella?
> ¿De quién podré yo agora
> valerme en mi tristura
> si en vos no halla abrigo mi querella?

[But what will I do, madam, in so much misfortune? Where will I go with it if not to you? Of whom will I be able to avail myself in my sadness if my complaint finds no protection in you?][23]

---

[23] All quotations from Garcilaso's poetry are from *Obras completas con comentario*,

These passages are, of course, from Garcilaso, from Sonnet 10 (9–14) and *Canción* 2 (15–19) respectively. Here also are depicted emotions that accompany the experience of being deprived of the presence of a loved one. "Nonsense!," those who want to guard Fray Luis from imputations of secular frivolity will exclaim. What relation could there be between Garcilaso's amorous passion and the disciples' pure, spiritual love of Christ? Without necessarily claiming to be identifying a direct influence of Garcilaso on Fray Luis, drawing attention to qualities that Fray Luis's poem and works by Garcilaso have in common may, in spite of their obvious differences, shed some light on the essential significance of both. In all of Garcilaso's poems that represent the anguish resulting from frustrated love the problem of the loved one's absence is implicit; but in some poems he treats that subject explicitly. An example is Sonnet 9, which begins

> Señora mia, si yo de vos ausente
> en esta vida turo y no me muero,
> paréceme que offendo a lo que os quiero
> y al bien de que gozava en ser presente. (1–4)

> [My lady, if I last in this life in your absence and do not die, it seems to me that I offend how much I love you and the good that I enjoyed in being with you.]

In Sonnet 37 the persona touchingly compares himself to a stray dog "whose master had withdrawn from its presence":

> A la entrada de un valle, en un desierto
> do nadie atravesava ni se vía,
> vi que con estrañeza un can hazía
> estremos de dolor con desconcierto:
>   aora suelta el llanto al cielo abierto,
> ora va rastreando por la vía,
> camina, buleve, para, y todavía
> quedava desmayado como muerto.

---

ed. Rivers; translations are mine. The allusion in the second quotation is of course to John 6:68.

> Y fue que se apartó de su presencia
> su amo, y no le hallava, y esto siente:
> mirad hasta dó llega el mal de ausencia.
>   Movióme a compasión ver su accidente:
> díjele lastimado: "Ten paciencia,
> que yo alcanzo razón, y estoy ausente."

[At the entrance of a valley, in a desert where no one crossed or was seen, I saw that a disoriented dog agonized with disconcertment: now letting out cries to the open sky, now dragging itself along the road, walking, turning, stopping, and even falling in a faint like one dead. And it was that its master went away from its presence, and it could not find him, and it senses this: look at the extent of what can be caused by suffering from a loved one's absence. Seeing his illness moved me to compassion: in pain, I said to him: "Be patient; while I can reason, I too am afflicted by absence."]

It may seem ridiculous to suggest a comparison of the dog in this poem to Christ's disciples, but if it is so it is because the liberty of such a comparison conflicts with the exalted character of a religious subject, not because it lacks a fundamental validity. Sonnet 26, on the other hand, could almost have been written by the disciples themselves, except for the last line:

> Echado está por tierra el fundmanento
> que mi bivir cansado sostenía.
> ¡O quánto bien s'acabó en solo un día!
> ¡O quántas esperanças lleva el viento!
>   ¡O quan ocioso está mi pensamiento
> quando se ocupa en bien de cosa mía!
> A mi esperança, assí como a baldía,
> mil vezes la castiga mi tormento.
>   Las más vezes me entrego, otras resisto
> con tal furor, con una fuerça nueva,
> que un monte puesto encima rompería.
>   Aqueste es el desseo que me lleva

> a que desee tornar a ver un dia
> a quien fuera mejor nunca aver visto.

[Dashed to the earth is the foundation that sustained my weary life. Oh, how much good came to an end in one day alone! Oh, how idle my thought is when it is concerned with my well-being! My torment punishes my vain hope a thousand times. Most of those times I surrender, other times I resist with such furor, with a new strength, that would split a mountain placed above it. This is the desire that leads me to want to see again one day whom it might have been better never to have seen.]

The last line expresses a degree of "sancta osadía" (blessed daring, a concept corresponding to the patristic παρροδία) that is perhaps beyond what the disciples would either venture or consider appropriate in addressing the merciful Christ.

What, then, can we say is the common denominator of "En la Ascensión" and the poems by Garcilaso? What is the source of anguish common to them both? If it is true that in the works I have cited by both poets anguish has its source in frustrated love and that those works can be seen to share a common ground, there must have been a concept of love broad enough to fit the works of both poets and that also could have been known to them both. That concept can be found in the most likely place, in Plato's *Symposium*, where love is defined as "birth" or "creation" and is implicitly compared to poetry, which is defined as "calling something into existence that was not there before" (*Symposium* 205B: *Collected Dialogues*, ed. Hamilton and Cairns, 205). Max Scheler has elaborated the Platonic concept, defining love as a movement that tends to the enhancement of value on the basis of an idealized paradigm of value that love sets up for the person actually present.[24] Applying the same Platonic emphasis on the creative value of love to the works under consideration, one may note that in both "En la Ascensión" and the works of Garcilaso I have considered there is a protest against the impairment of love's viability as a creative force, against the loved one's withdrawal of his/her actual presence from a movement towards higher values after having inspired an idealized paradigm of potential value in the lover and, in that way,

---

[24] Max Scheler, *The Nature of Sympathy*, trans. Peter Heath (London: Routledge, 1954), 154.

given that movement direction. In the poems by Garcilaso the prospective value aspired to by the lover is the fulfillment of the ideal ethos of individual personality of the beloved, while in Fray Luis's poem that prospective value is the triumph of divine justice, harmony, and universal love. In any case, the loved one's denial of his/her actual presence is a crucial element. As Llobera noted, the greater significance of Christ's ascent to heaven may have been known to the disciples, but it was not able to console them in their affliction. The disciples may be confused, as Thompson observes, but they are not confused about the fact that Christ will no longer be actually present in their lives. That circumstance is the source of their helplessness and hence anguish: "Genuine superiority ... is utterly impotent if it does not derive efficiency from the cooperation of those who are of the same mind" (Hartmann, *Ethics*, 2: 197). Faith is important as a necessary substitute for a cherished actual presence, but it can never really replace that actual presence. The absence of a cherished object may not be its complete loss, but it is different enough from the power generated by that object's living, concrete presence for the prospect of such absence to prompt despair, especially at the very moment of its departure.

And where is the lady who is referred to in Garcilaso's poems? In *Canción* 4 he writes, "... voy buscando / a quien huye de mí como enemiga" (["I am seeking the one who flees me like an enemy"]; 81–82). Unlike what one encounters in Petrarch's *Rime*, for example, concrete references to the lady beyond an occasional allusion are rare indeed. Garcilaso refers to her again in *Canción* 4: "De los cabellos de oro fue texida / la red que fabricó mi sentimiento ..." (["From golden hair was woven the net made by my feeling"]; 101–2). In Eclogue 2 we read "¡O hermosura sobre'l ser humano, / o claros ojos, o cabellos d'oro ..." (["O beauty above human being, O clear eyes, O golden hair"]; 19–20). She seems clearly to be elevated beyond his reach, if only by his praises. In *Canción* 1 he writes, "Vuestra soberbia y condición esquiva / acabe ya ..." (["May your pride and aloof temperament now cease"]; 14–15).

I would not myself be so bold as to assert that the imperious lady who, like a queen, fails to heed the yearning adoration of Garcilaso's persona has a clear parallel in the ascending Christ. Yet the note of complaint in Fray Luis's poem cannot be ignored. The disciples are experiencing a mutation in their relationship with their God. As Jorge de Montemayor writes in his poetic adaption of Savonarola's commentary on the psalm "Miserere Mei Deus" (Psalm 50 [51], a work whose emphasis on the wretchedness of the self makes it similar in spirit to the other poems cited here), "... quien pasible bajó, subió impasible" (["he who descended passible ascended impassible"]; *Segundo cancionero espiritual* [1558], fol. 234v).[25] He who had been a companion in suffering, truly a personal God actually present, is now abstracting himself and becoming depersonalized. He does so in order to reassimilate with a majestically esoteric, divine power (the Godhead), a power whose sovereignty and hence superiority, independence, and distance in relation to others makes it naturally resistant to the consciousness of affinity that Ficino saw as the reason for love.[26] It was that same sovereignty that lent itself to being misrepresented by those at whose loveless hands Fray Luis himself experienced so much affliction during his life.[27]

Just as such a consciousness of affinity can cause love to increase, circumstances that negate feelings of affinity can cause love to diminish. In this connection, the models of analytical psychology suggest additional possibilities for interpreting "En la Ascensión" along metaphorical lines. The separation anxiety displayed by the apostles in Fray Luis's poem seems to be a consequence of the threat that Christ's rebirth as a divine being poses to their attitude of identification and affinity with him. Whereas the anxiety expressed by the disciples is not likely to be derived from their fear of not being equal to Christ, the terms in which the situation is depicted — Christ rising on a cloud (Acts 1:9) as the disciples look up at him and address him — are such that the disciples seem to be reacting against feelings of self-contempt that are prompted by Christ's position of superiority, his being "above" them. They, being "below," feel undervalued, belittled, emasculated, inferior (Adler, *Neurotic Constitution*, 341–42). There is an obvious relation between such separation anxiety and the representation of Christ as a nursing mother:[28] the eventual removal of the disciples (or of humanity)

---

[25] This is an important patristic nuance, more than appears here. Compare Bernard's *Sermo* 57.2, PL 183. 681 B–C.

[26] See P. O. Kristeller, *The Philosophy of Marsilio Ficino* (Gloucester, MA: Peter Smith, 1964), 111.

[27] With an interpretation similar to my suggestion that in "En la Ascensión" Fray Luis expresses his own anguish in that of the Apostles, Antonio Carreño has seen the experiences of Job in Fray Luis's verse adaptation of the book of Job as paralleling Fray Luis's own death and rebirth in altered form as he made the transition from prison to freedom: " 'Las voces de mis duelos' (XIII, 38): El *Libro de Job en tercetos* de Fray Luis de León," in *San Juan de la Cruz and Fray Luis de León: A Commemorative International Symposium*, ed. M. M. Gaylord and F. Márquez Villanueva (Newark, DE: Juan de la Cuesta, 1996), 33–53, here 52.

[28] For background on the history of the image of Christ as the nursing mother, see

from the presence of their beloved leader and provider was as inevitable as a child's separation from its mother. Adult love's natural tendency regressively to rekindle attitudes of comforting dependence such as one had toward one's parents and to direct them towards a surrogate is the basis for the feelings of ambivalence toward the loved one expressed in "En la Ascensión,"[29] an issue that, as we have seen, is also important in Fray Luis's Sonnet 2 and Garcilaso's Sonnet 38. The process of achieving individual identity and emotional independence requires abandoning the regressive lure of identification with an undifferentiated object. The pain of that event makes it comparable to a "death" as well as to a "birth": the former in the depressive state resulting from the trauma of loss of the object and the latter in the birth trauma of forfeiting a state of symbiotic dependence. Both of these traumas experienced by the disciples can be seen to be expressed in their words of anguish.

Freud has shown that the morale of a group depends upon the authority of the super-ego through which the bonds that unite individuals into a group are forged and maintained. Fairbairn observed that a loss of morale among soldiers in wartime could be precipitated by nervous tension: traumatic situations favoring the return of internalized bad objects could cause the appeal of the super-ego, which bade soldiers to serve their country, to be replaced by acute anxiety (Fairbairn, *Psychoanalytic Studies* 81, 167). If in Fray Luis's "En la Ascensión" Christ is viewed as the super-ego that binds together the disciples, Fray Luis's poem can be seen as an example of the above-mentioned process of a loss of morale, in this case of the morale that sustained Christ's group of followers. When Christ's absence favored a return of internalized bad objects (Christ's enemies, represented metaphorically as the "mar turbado" [troubled sea] and the "viento fiero" [angry wind]), the release of acute anxieties replaced the security of

---

Joseph F. Chorpenning, "Christ the Nursing Mother in Fray Luis de León's "En la Ascensión," *Journal of Hispanic Philology* 11 (1987): 199–204. The image was famous from its use in St. Bernard's Commentary on the Song of Songs, a biblical book Fray Luis commented on three times: see Thompson, *The Strife of Tongues*, 26–35, 60–61, 104–21 esp. 108; Fray Luis de León, *Cantar de Cantares de Salomón*, ed. José Manuel Blecua (Madrid: Gredos, 1944); and cf. Max Engammare, *Le Cantique des Cantiques à la Renaissance* (Geneva: Droz, 1993).

[29] For observations on the contradictory and, hence, manneristic character of "En la Ascensión," see the analysis of Denise Bonnafoux, " 'En la Ascensión' de Fray Luis de León," in *Mélanges a la Mémoire d'André Joucla-Ruau*, ed. Chalon Paul et al. (Aix-en-Provence: Université de Provence, 1978), 491–500.

identification with the super-ego/Christ and caused its status, the faith in its authority and benevolence, to be shaken. Such a collapse of the authority of the super-ego is evidenced in a deterioration of a sense of duty on the part of the disciples: when they ask who now will restrain the troubled sea and guide the ship (Peter's bark; cf. John 21:3–14) to port, it is implied that to some degree they have ceased to see those responsibilities as being their own. Feelings of smallness, inferiority, and vulnerability have released defeatist tendencies, and perhaps even some degree of a nagging depreciation (reproach) motivated by resentment. Above all, it has prompted an attitude of immobilizing despair, of an at least temporary regressive resistance to the uncertainty and dangers of the need for self-reliance that is being imposed upon them from without. Perhaps Fray Luis saw the broader significance of his treatment of the subject of the Ascension in the skeptical implication that Christ's ascension into heaven imposed upon humankind the need to claim its own destiny, a challenge that it has been less than anxious to accept.[30] From that point of view, the strife and injustice of the world (important themes in other of Fray Luis's poems) would be understood as an additional instance of the situation I have noted in Garcilaso's Sonnet 2: the persona–lover (or humanity as a whole) seeking to become reconciled with his frustrations by seeking refuge in the womb (or the abyss of the world) and refusing to be reborn and grow beyond himself.

---

[30] Thus Rudolf Bultmann, *The Gospel of John: A Commentary*, trans G. R. Beasley-Murray, R. W. N. Hoare, and J. K. Riches (Philadelphia: Westminster, 1971), interprets Jesus's words to the disciples in John 16.4b–11, in particular 16.7b ("It is expedient for you that I go away . . .") as a revelation intended to set the believer free: "The certainty which it gives is not the continuation of the present — of something that has in fact already gone by — but the eternity of the future" (560). "Freedom as eschatological gift signifies for him [man] the opening of the future, of himself as a future phenomenon, a new thing" (437).

7
Moral Disfranchisement as Ironic Rebirth in Lazarillo de Tormes

The protagonist of *La vida de Lazarillo de Tormes y sus fortunas y adversidades* (*The Life of Lazarillo de Tormes and his Misfortunes and Adversities*) (1554) would seem to be less a rogue himself than a victim of the roguery of others. This feature of the work is partly what makes the *Lazarillo* different from other picaresque novels. It is harder to assert that this book affirms the entertainment value of the protagonist-narrator's moral apathy or petty chicanery because in the first five of the novel's seven chapters that same narrator establishes a critical perspective whereby his own youthful innocence is contrasted with the baseness of other characters, which it accentuates.[1] Thus, the cynical parsimony and abusive neglect, not to mention the crass hypocrisy, of Lazarillo's masters, particularly the blind man and the priest from Maqueda, are placed

---

[1] For reasons such as these (because the *Lazarillo* is removed from a preoccupation with delinquency), Alexander Parker does not classify the *Lazarillo* as a picaresque novel but as a precursor of that genre: *Literature and the Delinquent: The Picaresque Novel in Spain and Europe* 1599–1753 (Edinburgh: Edinburgh University Press, 1967), 28–29. For a discussion of controversy surrounding the issue of the *Lazarillo*'s compatibility with the term "picaresque," see Robert L. Fiore, *Lazarillo de Tormes* (Boston: Twayne, 1984), 1–7.

in a satirical light partly by the fact that they cause affliction to the protagonist. The simple fact that Lazarillo departs from the company of the seller of indulgences and the constable when they are operating a confidence game, even though the narrator (Lázaro, who is now an adult) gives no real explanation for his having left, has a similar effect: Lazarillo is made to appear less "knavish" than they are. Is our impression of the innocence of the youthful Lazarillo only a result of rhetorical manipulation on the part of the fictional narrator, whom by the end of the novel we come to know as not being very scrupulous? True, Lazarillo never "makes anything of himself" by developing a skill or learning to perform a socially valuable service that requires any significant effort. In the one period in his life in which he actually did "work" for a living, in any real sense of the term — in chapter 6, when he transported water with a mule — he left that work as soon as he had earned enough money to buy a suit of clothes that made him feel "above" such an occupation.[2] Lazarillo's revenge on the blind man or his having stolen food from the blind man or the priest from Maqueda, or his having been, in some small degree, party to deceitful means of selling indulgences are not reprehensible enough to make Lazarillo the child seem to be a "rogue" (pícaro). In the first two instances the blind man and the priest deserved what Lazarillo did to them, and in the third Lazarillo was too young to know what he had initially involved himself in.

Certainly the main moral aberrations with which we associate Lazarillo are the ones presented at the end of the book. There the adult Lázaro explains that he is employed as a town crier announcing the daily price of wine and that he has accepted an arrangement whereby he enjoys the patronage of an Archpriest in exchange for marrying one of the Archpriest's servants and renting a house nearby. The reader gathers that the arrangement has been made so that the Archpriest can maintain illicit

---

[2] The adult Lázaro's lack of motivation to invest labor in a real skill may be attributable to the degradation of his having been brutally exploited in this occupation, by the Chaplain who lent him the mule. It took him four years to save enough money to buy the old, used clothes with which he was able to "dress honorably." On the satirical implications of the figure of the Chaplain in chapter 6 of the *Lazarillo*, see Stanislav Zimic, *Apuntes sobre la estructura paródica y satírica del "Lazarillo de Tormes"* (Madrid: Iberoamericana, 2000), 77–79. For analyses of that chapter that are also critical of the narrator-protagonist, see George A. Shipley, "Lazarillo and the Cathedral Chaplain," *Symposium* 37 (1983): 216–41, and idem, "Lazarillo de Tormes Was Not a Hardworking, Clean-Living, Water Carrier," in *Hispanic Studies in Honor of Alan D. Deyermond*, ed. J. S. Miletich (Madison, WI: Hispanic Seminary of Medieval Studies, 1986), 247–55.

relations with Lázaro's wife, who is said to have had three illegitimate children. At this point the relatively high social norm that had previously been established by the innocent boy seems to plunge, as the narrator reveals himself to be consciously opportunistic and contemptuous of his own honor as well as able to be intimidated by his hypocritical wife (who went into a rage when Lázaro expressed his suspicions). Lázaro, now an exploiter himself,[3] assumes the posture of claiming not to believe those allegations about his wife, though they have been made repeatedly to him by his friends. In that situation, Lázaro is contributing to the same type of circumstance of which he as a child had been a victim, the need to survive as an orphan. In any case, these latter instances of moral neglect are surely regrettable forms of human degradation and even violence perpetrated by Lázaro (but also by his wife and the Archpriest), both against himself and possibly against children born out of wedlock. The fact that such indignities go uncensored and unpunished in the book has produced two general reactions among scholars. Some see that neutrality as a symptom of the unsuspecting ignorance of the protagonist–narrator, while others see it as a function of his cynicism. These two different interpretations of the author's motives in presenting in impartial terms the situation of the adult Lázaro correspond to two possible interpretative approaches to the novel as a whole. The view that the protagonist–narrator is ultimately an unsuspecting victim is the basis for the view that the work is a poignant and disturbing exposé of a brutal and degrading society and the story of a young man's struggle to survive in that society. The view that the protagonist–narrator disgusts us by compliantly learning from an unscrupulous world, shamelessly assimilating to it, and then deviously eliciting sympathy for himself with his self-justifying life story, is the basis for the view that the *Lazarillo* is a work in which satiric irony completely dominates. Since the grotesque irony thus perceived in the work is morally ambiguous or even cynical, it leaves those who read the work in those terms two choices: either to reject it outright because of its cynicism, or esoterically to maintain that the good one can see in it consists in the fact that it makes us object to it so much,

---

[3] My interpretation of Lázaro's situation differs from that of M. J. Woods, who denies that Lázaro is pandering on the grounds that the marriage "procures nothing which he [the Archpriest] could not enjoy before" and that the Archpriest "does all the exploiting there is to do": "Pitfalls for the Moralizer in *Lazarillo de Tormes*," *Modern Language Review* 74 (1979): 590–98, here 591. Apart from Lázaro's description of the gifts he and his wife receive from the Archpriest, the arrangement affords the latter a veneer of respectability at the same time that he has his mistress close by.

since it crassly affirms, on however pathetic a scale, an ethics of opportunism and manipulation as a means of advancing in the world.

Which of these two readings should have primacy? Should we accept uncritically the persona of the protagonist–narrator, his presenting himself as a hapless young victim of life's brutality who nevertheless managed to achieve a position of security in life? Or should we take a critical attitude toward the protagonist–narrator and regard him as an adult who is responsible for his attitudes and behavior and who, though he may have achieved relative "success" in his abject world, is ultimately a victim of self-degradation? Should we see the sufferings in life of the protagonist–narrator (both the youth and the adult) and his eventual self-accommodation and moral complacency as brutal effects of a hostile environment, or should we see the robust yet pathetic self-portrait of an innocent waif and floundering adolescent as having been intended by the author to be interpreted as a ploy by which that same protagonist–narrator seeks to manipulate readers and gain their sympathy, that is, as a satirical indictment of the society to which the protagonist has assimilated and now represents, a society that hypocritically and cynically exploits the egoism that is precipitated by poverty? In the first case, the claims of temporally vulnerable, physical human nature meet with indulgent sympathy: fundamental — material and practical — values are seen as having primacy, and higher values are regarded as luxuries that are beyond some people's reach but that, fortunately, are relatively dispensable. In the second case, human nature is held to a higher standard: higher values are seen as having primacy, and the protagonist–narrator's concessions to material success are regarded as leading him to a situation that is tragically hollow and meaningless. The first perspective is analogous to a mother's caring interest in the isolated individual; the second perspective reflects a just judge's impatience toward a being who betrays his greater human destiny.

The scholars in the second group, who see the satirical perspective of picaresque literature as ironically indicting the picaresque protagonist himself, implicitly base their position on the premise that the point of view that picaresque literature expresses is essentially the same as that of the picaresque (roguish) protagonist–narrator. For example, Gregorio Marañón considers the picaresque novel to be immoral and pessimistic, and he objects to the negative light in which it presents Spain; Américo Castro refers to the picaresque's reality-destroying style based on a "negative idealism" whereby all that is great, noble, and beautiful is replaced by that which is worthless; and José Ortega y Gasset sees the picaresque's ridiculous foreshortening of society, its irreverent attitude toward everything (social classes, professions, etc.), its corrosive negativism, and its blind eye for anything that is of superior value or worthy of optimism as being motivated by plebeian resentment.[4] If Ortega y Gasset, the author of *The Rebellion of the Masses*, seems biased by an elitist attitude, it is interesting to compare his views on this subject with those of Maxim Gorky, whom it would be very difficult to classify as an elitist. Gorky considers the picaresque to be "true bourgeois literature" that reflects the tastes, interests, and practical morals of those to whom it caters. He writes, "The bourgeoisie have admired the thief's adroitness and the murderer's cunning with the same relish as they do the detective's shrewdness." Gorky says that this literature, which exalts petty chicanery, "creates a liking for adroit knaves and encourages the urge to steal" (*On Literature*, 237–38). I will return to Gorky's comments shortly. Whereas the adverse judgements of the picaresque are understandable in relation to novels such as Mateo Alemán's *Guzmán de Alfarache* and Francisco de Quevedo's *El Buscón*, works in which the author seems deliberately to seek to provoke a reaction of disgust in the reader, in the case of *The Life of Lazarillo de Tormes* one cannot help wondering whether such condemnation is altogether appropriate. It is also interesting that those who take exception to the picaresque do not deny that it has a definite satirical dimension where the various secondary characters are concerned. What they object to is the absence of a clear satirical perspective in relation to the protagonist

---

[4] See Gregorio Marañón, "Sobre la novela picaresca,"in idem *Obras completas*, ed. A. Juderfías (Madrid: Espasa-Calpe, 1966), 1: 1019–27; Américo Castro, Introduction to *La vida de Lazarillo de Tormes*, ed. Everett W. Hess and Harry F. Williams (Madison, WI: University of Wisconsin Press, 1948), V–XII; and José Ortega y Gasset, "La picardía original de la novela picaresca," in idem, *Obras completas*, 6th ed. (Madrid: Revista de Occidente, 1957–1962), 2: 121–25. Other, more recent studies in which the protagonist-narrator and even the book itself are viewed with various degrees of what is overall an ever-increasing amount of skepticism are L. J. Woodward, "Author-Reader Relationship in the *Lazarillo de Tormes*," *Forum for Modern Language Studies* 1 (1965): 42–55; Howard Mancing, "The Deceptiveness of *Lazarillo de Tormes*," *PMLA* 97 (1982): 225–32; Peter Dunn, "*Lazarillo de Tormes*: The Case of the Purloined Letter," *Revista de Estudios Hispánicos* 22 (1988): 1–14; Víctor García de la Concha, *Nueva lectura del Lazarillo: el deleite de la perspectiva* (Madrid: Castalia, 1981); and four studies by George Shipley, "The Critic as Witness for the Prosecution: Making the Case against Lázaro de Tormes," *PMLA* 97 (1982): 225–53; idem, "The Critic as Witness for the Prosecution: Resting the Case against Lázaro de Tormes," in *Creation and Re-Creation: Experiments in Literary Form in Early Modern Spain*, ed. R. E. Surtz (Newark, DE: Juan de la Cuesta, 1983), 105–24; idem, "Lázaro and the Cathedral Chaplain"; and idem, "Lazarillo de Tormes Was Not a Hard-working, Clean-Living, Water Carrier."

and, hence, generally in relation to moral laxity, which they see as being dubiously exploited for entertainment purposes.

Those authors and critics who explicitly or implicitly approve of the *Lazarillo* tend to subordinate a concern for the work's problematic semantic dimensions to an appreciation for its anti-clerical and social satire and its innovations in the area of literary art: its realism, but also features that I will mention below in relation to Cervantes. Qualities in the *Lazarillo* that appeal to modern, democratic taste are the unpretentiousness of its story about a person who would generally go unnoticed, and the modesty represented by its anonymous authorship. Ultimately, however, a generally "approving attitude" toward the *Lazarillo* will tend to rest, as I have said, on the view that the novel expresses a critical attitude primarily toward a society that degrades the protagonist, who is seen primarily as a victim. The admirers of the *Lazarillo* (or perhaps all of us inasmuch as we approve of the work) see the protagonist–narrator as possessing qualities that the book ridicules or laments but that in any case inspire pity for him — for he can be seen, at least partly, as a victim of society, even if his dishonor is part of his punishment.[5] Yet still, one also wonders whether those who sympathize with the *Lazarillo*'s protagonist uncritically truly object to Lazarillo's experiences of brutality or whether they themselves in their heart of hearts are content to enjoy certain of the benefits of a hierarchical society that is all too similar to the society of

---

[5] Examples of studies in this group, in which the *Lazarillo* is read as naturalism and the protagonist–narrator is viewed with what is ultimately an attitude of sympathy, are Claudio Guillén, "La disposición temporal del *Lazarillo de Tormes*," *Hispanic Review* 25 (1957): 264–79; Raymond Willis, "Lazarillo and the Pardoner: The Artistic Necessity of the Fifth *Tractado*," *Hispanic Review* 27 (1959): 267–79; Bruce Wardropper, "El trastorno de la moral en el *Lazarillo*," *Nueva Revista de Filología Hispánica* 15 (1961): 441–47; Alan Deyermond, "The Corrupted Vision: Further Thoughts on *Lazarillo de Tormes*," *Forum for Modern Language Studies* 1 (1965), 246–49; Francisco Márquez Villanueva, "La actitud espiritual del *Lazarillo de Tormes*," in idem, *Espiritualidad y literatura en el siglo XVI* (Madrid: Alfaguara, 1969), 67–137, cf. 30–38; Didier Jaén, "La ambigüedad moral del *Lazarillo de Tormes*," *PMLA* 83 (1968): 130–34; Francisco Rico, *La novela picaresca y el punto de vista*, (Barcelona: Seix barral, 1970, repr. 1973); Woods, "Pitfalls for the Moralizer in *Lazarillo de Tormes*"; Douglas Carey, "*Lazarillo de Tormes* and the Quest for Authority," *PMLA* 94 (1979): 36–46; Georgina Sabat de Rivers, "La moral que Lázaro nos propone," *Modern Language Notes* 95 (1980): 233–51; Joseph Ricapito, Introduction to *Lazarillo de Tormes* (Madrid: Cátedra, 1985), 11–85; and Pamela Waley, "Lazarillo's Cast of Thousands or the Ethics of Poverty," *Modern Language Review* 83 (1988): 591–601.

Moral Disfranchisement as Ironic Rebirth 181

which they perceive Lazarillo to be a victim.⁶ If the latter is the case, their attitude of approval of the work expresses their ambivalence toward an inhumane and hypocritically apathetic respectability by which they themselves feel sullied, and enthusiasm for the *Lazarillo* assumes, to some degree, the significance of a sort of purification of the self, a purging of bad conscience. Oddly enough, however, there is no melodrama in the *Lazarillo*, no factitious appeal to emotions of a pathetic identification with victims of human suffering. Given its ironic detachment, one truly must wonder whether or not the author of the *Lazarillo* ever even thought of having his protagonist elicit pity.

Although readers are naturally under the impression that their response to the *Lazarillo* is a function of qualities in the book, whether they approve of the ethical perspective presented by that novel or view it with impatience is to a large extent a result of the way they themselves are oriented ideologically, or, to put it differently, it depends on one's "criteria of adequacy" of an interpretation to a text, and these are largely a function of one's background.⁷ To be more specific, those who take exception to the *Lazarillo* for being morally equivocal or for implicitly condoning the baseness with which it seeks to entertain probably see the adult Lázaro as having betrayed his innate propensity for higher values and human dignity. As what might be termed "romantics," they are likely to feel that the *Lazarillo* lacks idealism, and their perspective is based, probably unconsciously, on the assumption that human beings have a natural capacity for right behavior. That view could be seen as corresponding to the Platonist principle that "memory" is the cognitive process whereby the mind supplies intelligibility to outer reality, the "truth" of which is always that which mind itself projects. From that perspective, moral virtue is evidenced in the subject's capacity for the apprehension of intelligibles, or timeless truths, and the absence of virtue is a deficiency of the subject. In the contrasting, implicitly approving view of the *Lazarillo*, any transgressions that Lázaro–Lazarillo might be accused of are mere peccadillos in

---

⁶ This question of the hypocrisy of the reader's condemning the social environment that afflicts Lazarillo while failing to see a connection between that fictional environment and the social environment of which the reader is a part is related to the issue of our turning away in disgust at the man Lázaro has become while we fail to see corruption in ourselves. See the mention by Deyermond (*Lazarillo de Tormes: A Critical Guide* [London: Grant & Cutler, 1973], 94) of the relationship between that latter theme and the "Coco" joke in chapter 1 of the novel.

⁷ Louise M. Rosenblatt, *The Reader, the Text, the Poem: The Transactional Theory of the Literary Work* (Carbondale, IL: Southern Illinois University Press, 1998), 123–24, 129.

the light of the empiricist and deterministic belief that baseness on his part was a mechanical effect of material causes, that he lacks self-esteem because poverty condemned him to a subhuman existence. As "realists" and perhaps Aristoteleans, they base their perspective on some version of the assumption that the mind is a *tabula rasa* and that what Lazarillo became is no fault of his own but is strictly what life made of him. Whereas the "Platonists," we could say, want to assign responsibility and accountability to the protagonist of the *Lazarillo*, the "Aristotelians" do not: for them he is like a chip of wood swept along by a flood.

The idea I wish to propose is that the author of *Lazarillo de Tormes* deliberately shocks us with a dry and ironically detached perspective that is radically Aristotelian and empiricist in that the protagonist never shows any sign of independent judgement, initiative, or maturity, even as an adult. Such lack of character is another instance of the picaresque's distortion along negative lines, the inversion of the tendency of romance so often observed by critics. Yet since in general idealism arouses an attitude of skepticism and skepticism arouses an attitude of idealism, the effect of that deterministic perspective is that readers react along idealistic lines by taking the opposite stance and feeling impatient with Lázaro's lack of self-respect, especially towards the end of the work. In that way the moral purpose of the book is achieved, for base opportunism and passive compliance are condemned but without any trace of a moralistic or didactic attitude ever being suggested by the author.

Gorky's above-cited adverse judgement of the picaresque raises important issues. Not only is he one of the great world authors, but he also specialized in depicting precisely the class of people who populate *Lazarillo de Tormes*, people of the type he referred to in such terms as "the barefoot brigade" and "human debris." Gorky's deep sympathy and yet realistic view of the poor is revealed in many superb stories such as "Chums," "Evil-doers," "In the Steppe," and "Twenty-Six Men and a Girl" and in novels such as *Orphan Paul* and *The Three of Them*. Perhaps he objected to the picaresque's exploiting actions motivated by baseness or malevolence for their entertainment value instead of situating those actions in a definitely critical perspective. In his own works, Gorky avoided that element of the picaresque, as did Cervantes. His stories "Evil Doers" and "The Affair of the Clasps" are perhaps the best examples. Gorky may also have objected to presenting poor people as both base and ridiculous, and to the possible implication that the poor are typically both base and unworthy of respect. When in his own fiction he presented the poor in negative terms, he did so with the purposes of pointing out the degrading effects of poverty and showing how it contributes to social chaos. He wrote about the plight of middle-class individuals as well, in stories such as "A Sky-blue Life" and novels such as *Matvei Kozhemyakin*, *Foma Gordeyev*, and *The Artomonov Business*. How well did Gorky know *Lazarillo de Tormes*? He writes, "Commencing with the figure of Thyl Eulenspiegel, who belonged to the late fifteenth century, with Simplicissimus of the seventeenth century, then Lazarillo of Tormes, Gil Blas, the heroes of Smollett and Fielding right down to Maupassant's *Bel-Ami* ..." (*On Literature*, 237). He seems to think the *Lazarillo* appeared in the seventeenth century instead of the sixteenth century (in fact 1554). Perhaps he was confusing it with Mateo Alemán's *Guzmán de Alfarache* or Francisco de Quevedo's *El Buscón*. On the other hand, Gorky probably did know the *Lazarillo*: the first Russian edition of it was published in 1775, and there was an edition published in 1930, four years before Gorky presented the comments I have cited to the First All-Union Congress of Soviet Writers, in 1934.[8] Pedro Salinas even considers Gorky to have been influenced by the *Lazarillo* (Ricapito, *Bibliografía razonada*, 112). Indeed, there seems to be much in the *Lazarillo* of which Gorky would approve. To test the validity of Gorky's comments, let us further consider adverse judgement of *Lazarillo de Tormes* and try to determine to what extent it is justified. I will begin with the arguments against the *Lazarillo*, and then I will counter these with arguments in its favor.

As we have seen, the main objection to picaresque works like the *Lazarillo* expressed in reservations such as those cited above is that they present human degradation uncritically, that is, that the moral apathy displayed by the protagonist, who is also the first-person narrator, is affirmed by the author and the novel as a whole. Américo Castro, whose view of the *Lazarillo* can be better described as ambivalent than as negative, says:

> The work is ironic and sarcastic in tone, rather than didactic or moralizing. ... In the *Lazarillo* criticism and doctrine are the least important element; its decisive value lies in the vitality of its characters ... The "realism" so often attributed to the *Lazarillo* is more than a little suspect ... The tattered picaros that everybody could see in sixteenth-century Spain ... cannot be equated with Lázaro de Tormes, Guzmán de Alfarache, or Pablos the "Buscón." The latter

---

[8] See Joseph V. Ricapito, *Bibliografía razonada y anotada de las obras maestras de la picaresca española* (Madrid: Castalia, 1980), 388, 276.

> are artistically important not for the fact of being picaros but for their unique manner of envisaging life — their own lives and the world around them. Such data of actual reality as are present only serve as ingredients to build up an artistic, independent, and autonomous reality . . . Thus the normal hierarchy by which values are assessed is inverted and the pit of degradation becomes "the summit of all good fortune." This typically picaresque intuition and understanding of life is in no way interpolated as a moral commentary; it is integrated into the very experiences of Lazarillo. (Introduction to *La vida de Lazarillo de Tormes*, 9–12)

Certainly Castro would not have taken the view that the *Lazarillo* does not imply moral commentary if the human degradation that it depicts were perceived by Lazarillo or other characters in that work as experiences of violence or even death. Thus an important basis for the view that the picaresque represents degradation uncritically is that the tone of the picaresque is ultimately comic. Experiences that the requirements of tone in a different genre would cause to be represented as painful are in the picaresque introduced as sources of amusement, for comedy does not evoke pain as being real or severe. Indignities are also a source of amusement in satire, but there the author's aggressive denunciation of certain types of behavior is made more clear by elements of treatment, such as plot development, that foment indignation in the reader. The characteristic of the picaresque that has a disorienting effect is that by unabashedly depicting low behavior, rather than question that behavior, it seems to become a party to it and even encourage it. The issue that presents itself in this regard is whether a work can legitimately be considered to affirm what it is depicting merely because it makes it an object of aesthetic interest without either overtly censuring that behavior or implicitly qualifying interest in it, for example by presenting it in an unappealing light.

A reader's willingness to be amused by events such as Lazarillo's degradation at the end of the novel does indeed seem questionable. But can we conclude, as Américo Castro did, that in the *Lazarillo* "the normal hierarchy by which values are assessed is inverted and the pit of degradation becomes 'the summit of all good fortune'?" If such an "inversion"[9] were really to take place, the view the work represents would be that

---

[9] Wardropper ("El trastorno de la moral en el *Lazarillo*") fully develops the idea, originally introduced by Castro, of the inversion of values in the *Lazarillo*.

Moral Disfranchisement as Ironic Rebirth 185

what is generally considered virtuous is actually base and what is base is virtuous. But in the *Lazarillo* — in the final chapter, for example — is what is base really considered virtuous, or is it merely seen as preferable to the more demeaning alternative of poverty? After the life he has led, can we realistically expect Lázaro the town crier to do anything that might jeopardize his "soft job" and his "respectable" place in the community? That perspective may well have been present in the mind of the work's author. In his *Eudemian Ethics* (2.8, 1225a19)[10] Aristotle treats some actions that are performed from the "excusing factor" of fear of a greater evil as constituting a category of involuntary (pardonable) action (Sorabji, *Necessity, Cause, and Blame*, 259).

Let us briefly consider some contemporary instances of works that, notwithstanding the more sordid degree of the depravity depicted in them, are ethically equivocal in ways that are not entirely unlike the picaresque. Three films come to mind: *Bonnie and Clyde*, *In Cold Blood* (the film version of Truman Capote's documentary novel), and *Natural Born Killers*. All of these films contain "shock appeal" based upon the fact that they depict baseness with no evident critical perspective; they rather exploit the sensational appeal of violence and crime. Is the *Lazarillo* comparable to works such as these? In them the normal moral hierarchy is inverted to the extent that moral values are not respected in the least. Spectators may believe that the depction in those films of an aberrant indifference to healthy values was motivated by satirical or "realistic" intent, by a desire to protest such behavior. However, given the commercial interests that drive the film industry, it is hard not to suspect that these films, like many of the characters in them, exploited instances of human degradation for the sake of amusement or material gain. Lazarillo's moral compromise was surely motivated by modest material gain, but the author of the book is protected from being suspected of the same motives in writing it by the circumstance of remaining anonymous. The claim that amusement was the author's objective may seem confirmed by Maxime Chevalier's analysis of the attitudes toward the *Lazarillo* in the sixteenth century and the conclusion that at that time the *Lazarillo* was seen as entertaining, an *obra de burlas*.[11] On the other hand, those findings do not contradict the likelihood that there existed

---

[10] Editions of Aristotle's *Ethics* were published in Spain in 1493 and 1509 (see R. R. Bolgar, *The Classical Heritage and its Beneficiaries* (Cambridge: Cambridge University Press, 1954), 509; also F. Edward Cranz, *A Bibliography of Aristotle Editions 1501–1600* (Baden-Baden: Koerner, 1984), 172–75.

[11] M. Chevalier, *Lectura y lectores en la España de los siglos XVI y XVII* (Madrid: Turner, 1976), 180.

sensitive readers who saw in the work dimensions that were overlooked by the majority of its readership. Sensitive readers of the *Lazarillo* can also be entertained by it without losing sight of its social implications. Yet it would seem difficult for sensitive spectators of the films I have mentioned to be entertained by them, for the only way one can justify being entertained by scenes of gratuitous and brutal violence is by telling oneself "this is only a movie." As Richard Gerrig observes, "fictions will fail to have a real-world impact only if readers expend explicit effort to understand them as fictional."[12] There are several considerations that make it difficult to compare the *Lazarillo* to the three films mentioned above. The main victims in the *Lazarillo* are poor wretches who struggle in circumstances of dire poverty. The Squire whom Lazarillo serves in Toledo was not originally a victim of poverty, but he is destitute when we know him, and we sympathize with him, in spite of the fact that he abandoned Lazarillo in order to escape his creditors. These downtrodden characters are not interested in amassing fortunes, but rather seek to defend themselves from hunger. It is true that theirs can be seen as an ethics of cynicism, parasitism, and petty chicanery, but their lives are so abysmal that the novel can hardly be seen to be romanticizing them along sensationalistic lines. Also, in the films I have mentioned there is much gratuitous violence, and it is of an extremely brutal nature. The *Lazarillo* is on a completely different plane. Here the focus is on a docile, apparently vulnerable youth who is met with harsh reality at every turn.[13] Apart from the humor, which can be thought of as having been introduced to counteract a tone of pessimism, the book makes relatively few concessions to the sensational, and whatever brutality it presents is both unextreme and sparingly described, more so than in other picaresque novels. The most profoundly shocking form that brutality assumes in the *Lazarillo* is the absence of experiences of human kindness on the part of the protagonist, except in the brief time he spent with the Squire. But even there, the Squire exploits Lazarillo, on however pathetic a scale, and can be seen as being too needy himself to be expected to care very much about others. In this respect, the *Lazarillo* has none of the contrast between two

---

[12] R. J. Gerrig, *Experiencing Narrative Worlds* (New Haven: Yale University Press, 1993), 240.

[13] I am aware that in establishing which information constitutes a valid basis for interpretation, I am taking the fictional narrator, Lázaro, at his word, a decision that may seem problematic. On Deyermond's comments, in reference to the *Lazarillo*, on the convention of accepting the facts as the narrator states them unless there is reason to do otherwise, see above, chapter 4, n. 9.

worlds that Arnold Kettle observed in Dickens's *Oliver Twist*, between the dark, brutal world of the workhouse, the funeral, and the thieves' kitchen and the light and comfortable world of the Brownlows and Maylies.[14] In the *Lazarillo* the stark brutality of existence is an unrelieved prison of unmet needs.

Perhaps there is a tendency for readers to be misled by the quality in the *Lazarillo* that Lázaro Carreter has referred to as its "jocose epidermis" (quoted in Chevalier, *Lectura y lectores*, 178), the naive comic quality of a surface that encloses more serious and problematic dimensions within. Cervantes may well have taken that element from the *Lazarillo* and applied it in ways of his own. But another important lesson that Cervantes would seem to have learned from the *Lazarillo* is the inconspicuous way in which Lazarillo manages to resist the degrading effects of a brutal existence. As amusing as the mishaps suffered by the poor lad may be, behind them lurks an extremely sinister reality, that which has been emphasized by José Antonio Maravall and Anne Cruz in their studies of the picaresque[15] — the experience of living in a state of constant material need. The effects of insufficient caloric intake on the brain are well known. Whereas others may aspire to more elevated goals, the fulfillment of their potential as individuals, for Lazarillo merely having food and lodging that he can rely on is a genuine triumph. When he speaks of "arrimarse a los buenos" ["associating with good people"], he is referring to people who have food and enjoy security in the world. Given his needy state and the point of view that goes along with it, he is not referring to people who are altruistic or have fulfilled their potential as individuals. Separated from his mother when he was young and never meeting anyone who took a real interest in him, he lived without love and without proper guidance, even from those who ought normally to have been expected to provide it, the priests and the "exemplary" nobility represented the Squire — people who, whether they knew it or not, were desperate for love and guidance themselves. In these circumstances, it seems inhumane indeed to judge Lazarillo's behavior very harshly. Again, the author of the *Lazarillo* could well have had this idea in mind as a formal principle. In *Nicomachean Ethics* 2.1–3 and 10.9, Aristotle recognizes upbringing and the enormous influence of

---

[14] A. Kettle, *An Introduction to the English Novel*, 2 vols. (New York: Harper & Row, 1960), 1: 130–31.

[15] See José Antonio Maravall, *La literatura picaresca desde la historia social* (Madrid: Taurus, 1986), 138–63, and Anne Cruz, *Discourses of Poverty: Social Reform and the Picaresque Novel in Early Modern Spain* (Toronto: University of Toronto Press, 1999), 39–74.

other people in forming our initial habits as "excusing factors" (what we would call "mitigating circumstances") in the assignment of guilt (Sorabji, *Necessity, Cause, and Blame*, 266–67).[16]

It is hardly possible to minimize the seriousness of Lazarillo's radical emotional deprivation if one considers the emphasis that a psychoanalyst like Fairbairn places on the fundamental importance of establishing satisfactory object relations early in life and on the disorders in ego-development that can result from a child, like Lazarillo, feeling that he is not really loved as a person and that his own love is not accepted (Fairbairn, *Psychoanalytic Studies*, 55). Jung tells us that wandering, the restless urge that never finds its object, is a symbol of longing for the lost mother, i.e., for the experience of being treated like a person (*Works*, 5: 235, 205). Jung also notes that just as hunger represents the need for love, ravenous hunger describes man's repressive instinctuality at the stage where the parents have a predominantly nutritive significance (*Works*, 5: 339). We may recall that after leaving his mother, the first woman with whom Lazarillo has a relationship significant enough for him to mention is his wife, who indirectly nourishes him by being the circumstance for his having gainful employment. She thus fills the role of the mother he had prematurely lost, the nourishing mother. Before her, his only relationships were with father figures, whom Jung regards as representing the world of moral commandments and prohibitions (5: 260). Should it surprise us that in no circumstances Lazarillo will allow his relationship with his wife to be threatened, that he clings to it at any cost? The empiricist view that Lazarillo was a product of circumstances clearly indicates an attitude of compassion towards him. To condemn Lazarillo–Lázaro would seem almost as pointless as condemning the weather, because he is as ontologically determined as he is undifferentiated and guided by his basic instincts. As a matter of fact, the innate kindness of this "pícaro" can actually be seen as a tribute to the Renaissance-humanist doctrine that affirms natural human goodness! Psychologists often assert that the result of the deprivation of mother-love and of the love-hunger to which it leads is retaliatory aggression (Guntrip, *Personality, Structure, and Human Interaction*, 282–83, 402). Let us note that, far from becoming aggressive, for all the frustration and suffering experienced by him, Lazarillo–Lázaro

---

[16] Examples of such passages from the *Nicomachean Ethics* are the following: "... building well makes good builders, building badly, bad ones. If it were not so, no teacher would be needed, but everyone would be born a good or bad craftsman. It is the same, then, with the virtues" (1103b 10–14), and "As we have said, then, someone who is good must be finely brought up and habituated ..." (1180a 15–16) (trans. Irwin, 292–93).

never develops a disposition that is vengeful, resentful, anti-social, or even bitter. He never displays malicious feelings or even a callousness toward others,[17] and as narrator he sustains a naive yet witty resilience of language, as opposed to any tendency towards morbidity or melancholy.

Does such resilience justify the conclusion that the protagonist–narrator is relatively courageous? In some ways he reminds us of the ridiculous and yet sublime Don Quijote, who, in spite of repeated disappointments, is mysteriously immune to discouragement and despair throughout almost the entire novel. Of course, Lazarillo–Lázaro does not emulate legendary heroism and nobility of character, as Don Quijote does. But the synthesis in him of naive innocence and a firsthand knowledge of the brutality of life, his capacity for remaining fundamentally good and generous in his attitude toward others in spite of life's harsh blows (a point emphasized by Waley in "*Lazarillo*'s Cast of Thousands"), may well have been a valuable model that Cervantes found in the *Lazarillo* and gave to Don Quijote. Another influence of the *Lazarillo* on Cervantes may appear in what in the *Quijote* has been termed "perspectivism," the possibility of contemplating human experiences in relative terms, with different angles of vision. What is commendable and a form of instinctive rectitude (if not "nobility") for Lazarillo — for example, not becoming ruthless or a thief — is not what is commendable for Amadís de Gaula, but it represents an accomplishment nonetheless. Perhaps Lazarillo is, relatively speaking, as worthy, in a way, of commendation as traditionally

---

[17] Stanislav Zimic has noted that the same lack of malevolence, and actually an attitude of sincere affection, characterizes not only Lazarillo the youth but also the members of his family. It is not until Lazarillo goes out into "respectable society" that he encounters violence and baseness and eventually resorts to deceit and cunning: *Apuntes sobre la estructura paródica y satírica de "Lazarillo de Tormes,"* 36, 37, 40. I would emphasize how each stage of what Zimic refers to as Lazarillo's "metamorfósis gradual" (["gradual metamorphosis"]: 40) until he arrives at a state of cynical amorality (48) is almost incongruously limited in degree, at least in the way it is represented by the fictional narrator. Yet this type of nuance does not go unrecognized by Zimic, who notes that Lazarillo's trickery is a "reacción desesperada" ["desperate reaction"] to the trickery of those who victimize him (52), and he notes as well the noble altruism with which Lazarillo pretends to believe that the home of "darkness and gloom" to which a corpse was being conducted was his own house, thus feigning foolishness in order to amuse and distract his anguished master, the poor Squire (55). This last rhetorical theme, Leslie S. B. MacCoull informs me, is a Cynic topos much used in hagiography.

recognized heroes. After all, he is "real," whereas heroes are mere myths and are thus exempt from prosaic concerns such as having to feed themselves or stay warm.

Gilman has seen *La vida de Lazarillo de Tormes* as actually being the story of the moral death of that character,[18] yet how can Lazarillo die morally if he never really lived morally? How can he have lost honor that he never had? Instead of seeing the situation at the end of the book as a moral death, perhaps it should be seen as a situation in which Lazarillo is further victimized, in which his fear of poverty has been taken advantage of once again. Judging Lazarillo as an adult is complicated by the fact that, as I have mentioned, his apparent emotional deprivation prevented him from maturing normally and, hence, completely. It is for that reason that Lázaro the adult does not maintain appreciably higher standards of self-value than did Lazarillo the child. Much of the subtlety and difficulty in interpreting this novel is obviously a result of the fact that whereas the child is the dominant persona and the dominant character in the novel, he and his perspective are represented by the persona of the protagonist as an adult. It is the adult who narrates the story of his own life, and it is through his eyes that we see the child and view the circumstances that arrested the evolution of his sense of self-worth. The elements from the child's life that the adult selects tend to serve the purpose of making it known, as is stated in the title and prologue, that "vive un hombre con tantas fortunas, peligros, y adversidades" ["there is a man who lives with so many misfortunes, dangers, and adversities"] (95).[19] Perhaps the *Lazarillo* can best be understood as an elaborate effort on the part of the fictional narrator to elicit the sympathy of the reader and thus vindicate himself in relation to the situation presented at the end of the book. That situation, which Lázaro himself experiences as his rebirth as a respectable member of the community, is actually the event of his complete moral disfranchisement. From that point of view, the association of Lázaro with Lazarus, the man who came back from the dead, takes on double irony. What Lázaro erroneously perceives to be moral vindication through social rebirth actually brings with it a deepening of moral degradation. The difference between "moral death" and "moral disfranchisement" is, in my mind, that "moral death" refers to a definitive loss of *stature* as a moral being, whereas "moral disfranchisement" means deprivation of moral accountability, of one's claim to be able to be guided by free

---

[18] S. Gilman, "The Death of Lazarillo de Tormes," *PMLA* 81 (1966): 149–66.

[19] Quotations from the *Lazarillo* are taken from *Lazarillo de Tormes*, ed. Joseph Ricapito (Madrid: Cátedra, 1985). Translations are mine.

choice, and, hence, of one's very *identity* as a moral being.[20] The novel describes the life of one whose basic needs (human and material) were never met and who, therefore, never evolved a sense of his own identity or dignity as a person, a sense that he had the ability to choose his own actions. Oddly enough, Lázaro considers his situation at the end of the book to constitute a triumph. It is clearly a triumph over hunger, but in every other sense is only an ironic triumph, and the shocking point of the book can be seen as being that the reduction of people to an animal existence can be compatible with "human nature," in the most abject sense of that term. The novel illustrates that in general people can actually be reduced to the satisfaction of their material needs and live for little else. That circumstance makes it difficult to attribute guilt to Lázaro, or rather it makes pointing out his guilt seem sanctimonious. To quote Nicolai Hartmann,

> As to the question of guilt it is important to arrive at the final ground for it, its super-individual, social ground. This question coincides with that concerning joint responsibility. For if the criminal acts from need, he is of course not excused, but the guilt then falls not upon him alone; it touches those also who tolerate the public condition which engenders or prolongs the need. (*Ethics,* 2: 236)

By placing the adult, Lázaro, beside the child, Lazarillo, this subtle work makes us conscious of the fact that although the adult should assume responsibility for having higher standards in life than the child did, he was evidently not able to do so, or at least he did not believe himself able to. Lacking moral autonomy and power, he remains an eternal child.[21] The work also places the psychologically deprived eternal

---

[20] "He who pardons a guilty person, compromises him spiritually. He denies his accountability. The presumption in washing away guilt, in discharging it, the admission of 'mitigating circumstances,' is at bottom a moral disfranchisement and a degradation of the man" (Hartmann, *Ethics,* 2: 145).

[21] By maintaining that Lázaro–Lazarillo remains a child, I do not wish to imply that he did not "develop" or "come into being" morally in any way. I agree with Wardropper ("El trastorno de la moral" 446–47), Willis ("Lazarillo and the Pardoner," *Hispanic Review* 27 [1959]: 267–79, here 277–78), and Deyermond (*Lazarillo de Tormes: A Critical Guide,* 72) that he becomes corrupted. What I wish to assert is that he does not grow or evolve from a lower, worse state to a higher, better state. He is never bad and he never becomes significantly "good" in the sense of pursuing higher values or performing good deeds. At most he was once pure, and "he who is pure does not actualize; his ethos is not in the

child, Lázaro, beside the adult fictional society of which Lázaro has become the satirical image, thus making us conscious of the fact that if the society does not assume responsibility for Lazarillo–Lázaro the child, it is negligent in the same way that Lázaro is toward himself. Yet in fact, if the fictional society does not assume responsibility for the Lazarillo–Lázaros of the world, who were never given the means to feel responsible for themselves, the society becomes worse than Lázaro because it cannot claim to be *unable* to assume more responsibility than he does. Is this perspective a function of the text or of the democratist social-historical perspective with which we, in the present day, read the work? Does the text promote the value of compassion? I believe that it does both implicitly, by the critical view of the cruelty that Lazarillo suffers at the hands of certain of his masters, and explicitly, in the compassion that Lazarillo feels for the Squire. Lazarillo is never loved by anyone. Thus the question is implied: ought he not to be loved by the reader either, even after it is "too late" for him to develop a sense of his own identity as a moral being?

The *Lazarillo* affirms, I believe, the "Aristotelian" perspective that as a victim of a brutal world, a moral casualty, Lazarillo-Lázaro's humiliation should be understood and indulged, and although he is "guilty" of not being better, the baseness to which, in his low self-esteem and moral ignorance, he himself comes to contribute should not cause him to be judged harshly. We view him as a child, and we hope that by our considering him to be good he will become good. Thus, our "Aristotelian" love for him as one who is above all determinable is, in principle, an investment in his future development. That such expectations have only limited efficacy when applied to fully developed adults such as we wish Lázaro were is expressed by Jung in the context of his observations on the figure of the "trickster":

> The disastrous idea that everything comes to the human psychology from the outside and that it is born a *tabula rasa* is responsible for the erroneous belief that under normal circumstances the individual

---

pursuit of ends" (Hartmann, *Ethics*, 2: 216). In relating Lázaro–Lazarillo's having the social position of a child to his lack of power, I mainly have in mind Adlerian psychology, which sees the life of the individual as a struggle to overcome a situation of being dominated, inferior, and powerless. Wardropper has observed that what Lázaro really wanted was power ("The Implications of Hypocrisy in the *Lazarillo de Tormes*," in *Studies in Honor of Everett W. Hesse*, ed. W. C. McCrary and José A. Madrigal [Lincoln, NE: Society of Spanish Studies, 1981], 179–86, here 185).

is in perfect order. He then looks to the state for his salvation, and makes the state pay for his inefficiency. He thinks the meaning of existence would be discovered if food and clothing were delivered to him gratis on his own doorstep, or if everybody possessed an automobile. ... As a result of these prejudices, the individual feels totally dependent upon his environment and loses all capacity for introspection. ... He has not yet made the discovery that he might be capable of spontaneous ethical impulses, and of performing them. ... (*Works*, 9.1: 267)[22]

By compassionately affirming Lázaro's worthiness to be loved and expressing our solidarity towards him, we thus return to a "Platonist" perspective, for such worthiness to be loved tacitly presupposes spiritual personhood, Lazarillo's identity as an individual. That presumption of the human identity of the Lazarillos of this world would obviously be meaningless without the existence of circumstances that will allow people to rise above an animal level. In that sense, the distinction I have made between the Aristotelian and the Platonist perspectives is accurate only *grosso modo*. As can be seen by referring to Aristotle's *Ethics*, taking into account the powerful influence of one's environment in shaping the person's behavior is not inconsistent with a recognition of the role of innate character or with assigning some degree of blame, the existence of "excusing factors" notwithstanding. But a work of literature is not a court of law, in spite of the many similarities that exist between plot structures and legal argumentation. In modern literature the complexity of life is the preferred subject matter, whereas legal issues must be viewed as being relatively "black and white."

Surely Gorky did not fully appreciate the *Lazarillo*. In his powerful story "In the Steppe," a fictional narrator, a student who is represented as a patient in a hospital with the author (who is a character in the story and the primary fictional narrator), recounts events in which he murders and robs a sick carpenter. He describes how he and a soldier had been wandering in a state of near delirium from starvation on the vast Russian steppe, where they encountered the carpenter dying of fever and longing for his family, desperate for human solidarity. When the story (within a story) is over, the author asks the narrator if he ever thinks about the carpenter. "As you see — or as you

---

[22] For a modern rebuttal of the *tabula rasa* doctrine, emphasizing the deleterious effects of that doctrine and the potentially liberating effects of superseding it, see Steven Pinker, *The Blank Slate: The Modern Denial of Human Nature* (New York: Viking, 2002).

hear," the man answered. "And there was nothing more?" the author asks. The man smiled. "What ought my feelings to have been in such a case — do you mean that? I was not to blame for what happened to him, just as you are not to blame for what has happened to me. And nobody is to blame for anything, for all of us alike are — beasts of the same kidney."[23] Part of the irony here is in the fact that the self-complacent and affectedly worldly-wise narrator, who repudiates the principle that human beings ought to feel responsible for their fellows, is, as he speaks, enjoying the good fortune of being cared for in a hospital. More importantly, however, Gorky's story illustrates the grim reality that when human beings are reduced to a struggle for existence, the loss of individual human identity that results leads to the obliteration of human solidarity and to a mass ethics of egoism. In Scheler's words, "there is no solidarity in the social unit of the mass because the individual does not exist at all as an experience and therefore cannot possess solidarity with others..." (*Formalism*, 527). Lazarillo–Lázaro lives in a dimension in which there is no human solidarity. He never becomes the object of a sense of responsibility that extends beyond the individual person's concern for himself, an object of kindness or devotion, and he never developed a sense of his own human dignity. His entry into what should have been adult life is represented as a hideous parody of complacent respectability, as it brings with it a heightening of his degradation. That degradation now extends to self-degradation as his insecurity and fear of squalor and hunger continue to be exploited, by another representative of God and the Church. In his life story Lázaro offers no examples of noble character, but it can be said in his defense that, as a man of the masses, he gave the world no less than he received. In that respect, the reader is challenged to match him, and the modern state is as well.

---

[23] Maxim Gorky, *Twenty-Six Men and a Girl and Other Stories* (New York: Avon, 1957), 165.

8

The Agony and Apotheosis of Innocent Love: Bernardim Ribeiro's Book of Sorrowful Longing

The literary personality of Bernardim Ribeiro (1482?–1552?) argues forcefully for the view that what is recognized as genius in an author is that which is absolutely unlike anything else. Ribeiro's fame does not rest on his cultivation of the eclogue, by which he introduced Renaissance pastoral into Portugal; for successful as he is as a writer of eclogues, that form is highly conventional and admits of relatively little originality on the part of the individual artist. Ribeiro's masterpiece is his prose work, *Menina e Moça* [*Young Girl*], the exceptional beauty of which has attracted yet also perplexed readers for centuries. Critics have had little success in fathoming the work's mysteries, much of their effort having been spent just on debating its classification.[1] I would

---

[1] The most ambitious relatively recent attempt to interpret Ribeiro is Helder Maçedo's laudable *Do significado oculto da "Menina e Moça"* (Lisbon: Moraes Editores, 1977). It is the first attempt to approach the work as an extended metaphor, and in so doing it broaches Yatesian subjects that, because of their difficulty, are too often overlooked, such as Cabalism, Gnostic dualism, Catharism, Sufism, and Illuminism. However, Ribeiro and

describe *Menina e Moça* as a unique blend of chivalric romance, the sentimental novel, and elegiac pastoral romance, the narrative assuming its vivid naturalness by virtue of a delicately patient, gentle, and plebeian interest in familiar detail, seemingly for its own sake, similar to the descriptive and psychological realism developed much later along more naturalistic lines in the prose fiction of Ivan Turgenyev and Anton Chekhov.

But what is there about *Menina e Moça* that is so "mysterious?" Most obvious is its elliptical plot. Although the work was first known by another title (*Livro das Saudades*) [*Book of Sorrowful Longing*], the fact remains that the character whom we expect to be the protagonist and who states that the book is to be of her making, Menina, is neither the protagonist nor the fictional narrator, in spite of the fact that the second chapter begins with the words "em que a donzela vai prosseguindo sua história" ["in which the maid continues her story"]. We never find out who Menina is or what happened to her, or who her "amigo verdadeiro" [true lover] was or what happened to him, but instead find the story abruptly transferred to a different narrator, to "uma dona do tempo antigo" [a mistress of olden times], who is lamenting what seems to be the loss of her son. But who he was and what happened to him, or who Dona [Mistress] is and what happened to her, we never learn. Also, in the only edition recognized as entirely the work of Ribeiro (Ferrara, 1554), the novel ends abruptly, in the middle of Dona's second long narrative and in the middle of an intercalated tale told by the knight Avalor. The last words are "Laus Deo," words which traditionally mark the author's intention that the work be considered completed. The fact that we seem to have been prepared for such an occurrence in the work's prologue, where Menina tells us, "Ainda que, quem me manda a mim oulhar por culpas nem desculpas, que o livro ha-de ser do que vai escrito nele? Das tristezas nam se pode cantar nada ordenadamente porque desordenadamente acontecem ellas . . ." (["Though, who bids me to pay attention to guilt or excuses, for the book is made up of what's written in

---

the analysis of his novel easily become lost in the difficulty of these materials; also, there are many important and puzzling elements in the narrative that this study does not account for. The essential, early and basic critical study of *Menina e Moça* is António Salgado Júnior, *A "Menina e Moça" e o romance sentimental no renascimento* (Aveiro: Gráfica Aveirense, 1940). Also very valuable because they place the attainments and shortcomings of all previous critical opinion on Ribeiro in perspective are the three essays on Ribeiro in Eugenio Asensio, *Estudios portugueses* (Paris: Fundação Calouste Gulbenkian, 1974): "Una nueva edición de *Menina e Moça*," 189–97; "Bernardim Ribeiro a la luz de un manuscrito nuevo: Cultura literaria y problemas textuales," 199–223; "El *Romance* de Bernardim Ribeiro 'Ao longo da ribeira': Texto nuevo e interpretación," 225–42.

it? Nothing orderly can be sung about sadness, because its occurrence is itself disorderly"]: 5, ll. 11–14])[2] makes it no less disorienting. Also mysterious is the extreme tension between the bucolic setting and the inward strife of the characters, but this element is already present in Sannazaro's *Arcadia*, though to a much lesser degree, and in Garcilaso's eclogues. In his *Diana*, Montemayor also does not evoke the bucolic setting, making the lack of natural beauty mirror the unfulfillment and disharmony experienced by the characters. The difference in Ribeiro is that he both evokes the beauty of nature and intensifies the tone of tortured melancholy to such a pitch that it seems to acquire ritualistic overtones. And, unlike Montemayor, that atmosphere is not relieved periodically by interpolated comic narratives. When Dona's narrative begins, the reader expects to escape into a world of adventure, but, along with his two protagonists, Bimarder and Avalor, Ribeiro renounces chivalry's heroic aspect in favor of its romantic aspect; and just before the reader's idle curiosity might finally receive the facile gratification of witnessing a heroic rescue, the book ends. There is little of the sensational in this work and hence little of what might be considered sheer entertainment, in spite of its extremely colorful, even exotic, blending of genres and motifs.

Most unusual of all, however, is an effect that seems to have first been achieved — though, as compared to *Menina e Moça*, as hardly more that a suggestion — in the highly original *Arcadia* of Sannazaro.[3] In pastoral literature we are accustomed to a vision of nature as a divinely sanctioned order, a heavenly, eschatological, idyllic world of finality and spiritual certainty,[4] and the patriarchal security of "the good Shepherd whose pastoral world sees no winter."[5] Yet into this Christian–pastoral and comic–romantic setting, Ribeiro introduces a flood of the tragic atmosphere and images that we associate (in the Ptolemaic scheme) with the cyclical sublunary world, with nature

---

[2] For this and future references to the text of *Menina e Moça*, see *História de Menina e Moça*, ed. D. E. Grokenberger (Lisbon: Studium Editora, 1947); translations are mine. The most recent edition is *História de Menina e Moça: reprodução facsimilada da edição de Ferara, 1554*, ed. José V. de Pina Martins (Lisbon: Fundação Calouste Gulbenkian, 2002).

[3] See J. F. Alcina, "Poesía neolatina y literatura española en los siglos XVI y XVII," in *Acta Conventus Neo-Latini Abulensis*, ed. R. Schur et al., MRTS 207 (Tempe, AZ: MRTS, 2000), 9–28.

[4] C. G. Jung, *Man and His Symbols*, 143–45.

[5] Frye, *Anatomy of Criticism*, 121.

as a fallen and chaotic sphere⁶ subject to demonic reversal and fullness followed by decay, the sphere of painful temporal experience, or "Mudança" (mutability): in short, the vision of the Orphic-agricultural religion the mysteries of which Christianity was supposed to have dispelled. In Ribeiro, when one expects images of order and friendship ("a história dos dois amigos" ["the story of the two friends"]), he finds irrational law and the isolated or betrayed individual; what is conventionally an Arcadian haven or garden, the pastoral world of a community of domesticated animals, is invaded by a sinister forest and ravaged by beasts of prey; instead of Arcadia's social equivalent, the world of houses and palaces, characters stray in solitude or inhabit secluded rocks; confronting the river as a generative principle is the sea as an image of flood and destruction.⁷

The theme that is central to *Menina e Moça* and that gives the work its unity is the opposition of fertility and sterility and the isolation of social sentiment in a world hostile to it. The fertile, healthy, or honorable (principled) personality is chiefly represented as the characteristically feminine capacity for devotion in love ("o bem amar"), which, when unrequited, assumes the concrete form of "tristeza," or melancholy. That social norm is introduced and established at the beginning of the work by the figures of Menina and Dona. Dona introduces her narrative by reviling the present age of sterility ("Se os homens nunca acostumaram agravar as donzellas, muito fora de sentir, mas das cousas costumadas, quem se deve agravar?" (["If it weren't customary for men to wrong women, it would be very regrettable, but who should feel wronged by things that are customary?"]; 19, ll. 11–13) and the eclipse of the romantic by the heroic virtues, which in her youth were said to be joined harmoniously in the same personality, in the chivalrous idealism of devout courage: "... cuidava eu que hum cavaleiro apostamente armado sobre seu fermoso cavallo pela ribeira de hum rio deste gracioso campo passando, nam podia hir tam triste como hua delicada donzella, em alto apossento, acostada ao seu estrado, entre paredes. . . ." ([I imagined that an elegantly armed knight on his beautiful horse riding along the shore of a river in this lovely countryside, could not be as sad as a delicate maid, in a high apartment, lying down in her bedroom, between walls . . .]; 18, ll. 16–20). But since that age, times have changed:

---

⁶ Frye, *Anatomy of Criticism*, 205; cf. C. S. Lewis, *The Discarded Image* (Cambridge: Cambridge University Press, 1964), 3–5, 95.

⁷ Frye, in *Fables of Identity*, 19–20, suggests terms close to these as distinguishing the patterns of the tragic and comic visions of the human, animal, vegetable, and unformed worlds.

> Quantas donzellas comeo jaa a terra com as soidades que lhe deixaram cavaleiros, que comeo outra terra com outras soidades? Cheos sam os livros de historias de donzellas que ficarom chorando por cavaleiros que se hiam e que se lembravam ainda de dar d'esporas a seus cavallos, porque nam eram tam desamorosos como elles. (19, ll. 17–22)

[How many maidens has the earth already swallowed along with the longings left them by knights, whom the earth somewhere else swallowed with other longings? Books are full of stories about maids who were left weeping by knights who were leaving and who still remembered to spur their horses, because they [their horses] were not as unloving as themselves.]

Her story, she says, is of two "amigos" (which can mean "suitors"), legendary heroes of that same locale, in whom "se encerrou a fe que em todo los outros se perdeo" ["dwelt the faith that was lost in all the others"]. This, she believes, is why other men betrayed them and had them killed: "... creo que por isso ordenarom outros homens de os matar a treiçam, porque se nam pareciam maamente com elles. Que o mal nam tam somente aborreceo o bem, mas nam quisera ainda que ouvera ahi lembrar-se" (["... I think that is why they ordered other men to betray and kill them, because otherwise they would make them look bad. Because evil not only abhors good but does not even want to have to remember it"]; 20, ll. 3–6). The main body of the novel consists of not one but two separate "histórias" [stories] in which Dona tells of the exemplary devotion of two knights, Bimarder and Avalor, who abandoned the profession of arms to be near the women they loved, and who, when forced to be separated from those women, preferred instead to renounce life itself. Dona, then, contrasts to the norm of the hyper-masculine and callous present the examples of virile heroes who, as opposed to renouncing love for war, renounced war for love. This standpoint is consistent with the sixteenth-century vogue of Reform evangelism and the pacifist, or rather irenicist, spirit of the *Philosophia Christi* as it was expounded by Erasmus and others in opposition to "el farisaísmo tiránico" ["tyrannical phariseeism"].[8] By the end

---

[8] See Marcel Bataillon, *Erasmo y España*, trans. A. Alatorre (México: Fondo de Cultura Económica, 1966), 142–46 and passim. For an interesting parallel see J. J. Sánchez

of the decade that evangelism would be persecuted as heretical.

Ribeiro's technique, in *Menina e Moça*, of incorporating pastoral motifs into what is essentially a secular poem of exile was only relatively new. Sannazaro in the *Arcadia* and especially Ribeiro himself, in his eclogues, had already developed pastoral along those lines, and these were followed by Garcilaso's eclogues and Montemayor's *Diana*, which was written at approximately the same time as *Menina e Moça*. The prototype for Renaissance pastoral literature is the Jewish song of exile, Psalm 137, *Super flumina*, "By the rivers of Babylon." During the High Renaissance that psalm was translated and paraphrased by poets throughout Europe. The adaptations of that psalm by Portuguese authors (particularly Camões and Montemayor) were by far the most ambitious and original.[9]

As for my interpretation of the specific thematic purpose Ribeiro had in writing a work utilizing the pastoral setting as a non-idyllic poetic metaphor, I will attempt to support that interpretation with: (a) evidence that poets and humanists who moved in courtly circles, such as Ribeiro,[10] personally experienced the type of isolation to which I referred and that such experience was related to the fashion for pastoral literature; and (b) consideration of the character of literary taste fashionable in Ribeiro's day, particularly that of amatory literature in the courtly-love tradition. Then, perhaps, a closer examination of *Menina e Moça* will bear out my interpretation.

§

During the years that Jorge de Montemor (the author "Montemayor") spent as a resident at court (which would have been during Bernardim Ribeiro's lifetime and in a period when the Portuguese and Spanish crowns were united through marriage), he wrote two letters that express the anxieties he experienced while living in a courtly

---

Gázquez, "Juan Ginés de Sepúlveda, un hispano a la altura del siglo XVI: Lutero y Erasmo," in *Acta Conventus Neo-Latini Abulensis*, ed. Schnur, 575–83.

[9] For a survey of poetic versions of Psalm 137 in Renaissance Europe, see Creel, *The Religious Poetry of Jorge de Montemayor*, 146–65.

[10] One of the few assumptions generally made about Ribeiro is that he belonged in his youth to the courtly circles that produced the *Cancioneiro Geral* of 1516, a collection to which he was himself a contributor. See B. Creel, "Ribeiro, Bernardim," in *Encyclopedia of the Renaissance*, ed. P. F. Grendler, 6 vols. (New York: Scribner, 1999), 5: 340–41.

setting. One is to Diego Ramírez Pagán and the other is to Jorge Meneses.[11] In both letters he refers to the court as a "mar de divisiones" ["sea of divisions"] that fosters favoritism, gossip, sanctimony, corruption, backbiting, and smug self-conceit. But what one discerns most clearly in Montemor's dissatisfaction is his disenchantment with a world dominated by the whims and vain pretenses of people whose culture and intellect are inferior to his own, some of whom actually felt contempt for learning. To Ramírez Pagán (whom he calls Dardanio, as though they were shepherds in an eclogue) he writes:

> ¿Gustas, Dardanio, di, deste innocente
> estudiantejo, nescio y confiado,
> que quiere en alabar hazerse gente?
> ¿Gustas, también, del cortesano inchado,
> muy visto y muy leido en las *Trezientas*
> y que a Boscán dos vezes a passado,
> Que se quiere poner con vos en cuentas
> (señor, no va este verso bien medido),
> y de una necedad, llega a quinientas?
> Y el otro, que se halla muy corrido,)
> porque otros ve escrevir, y sonetea,
> y luego está por si de amor perdido.
> Su dama sea muy vieja, nescia y fea,
> luego es otra Minerva, es otra Helena,
> y allá la vio en un prado en Galilea.
> Es cosa para mí de tanta pena
> ver estos poetillos remendados,
> que pienso ya en pregon poner la vena. (398, ll. 31–49)

[Dardanio, do you like this naive little student, silly and self-confident, who wants to become respectable through flattery? Do you

---

[11] For the letter to Ramírez Pagán, see Francisco López Estrada, "La epístola de Jorge de Montemayor a Diego Ramírez Pagán," in *Estudios dedicados a D. Ramón Menéndez*, 387–406. For the letter to Jorge Meneses, see *El Cancionero del poeta George de Montemayor*, ed. Angel González Palencia (Madrid: Sociedad de Bibliófilos, 1932, repr. 1942), 427–30. Translations of passages from the letters are mine.

also like the puffed-up courtier, very visible and well read in the *Trezientas*[12] and who has gone over Boscán[13] twice, who wants to question your meter (sir, this verse is not well measured), and from one silly thing reaches five hundred? And the other, who finds himself very embarrassed, because he sees others write, and he writes sonnets, and is soon lost in love of himself. His lady, though she may be very old, silly, and ugly, is immediately another Minerva, another Helen, and he saw her there on a meadow in Galilee. For me it is so pitiful to see these little patched poets that now I am thinking of applying my talent to the vocation of a town crier.]

In his letter to Jorge Meneses, recalling the types at court, he writes:

> Vereis otro que infinge de prudente
>   sin dar razón querer que lo que afirma
>   valga, porque lo afirma solamente.
> No pone alli Aristoteles su firma
>   cuando es Philosophia, ni Augustino
>   se (sic) es sacra Theología lo confirma.
> El solo es quien lo dize y es tan fino
>   que no creerá otra cosa, ni es bastante
>   ningún sabio a metelle por camino.
>   (*Cancionero del poeta George de Montemayor*,
>   ed. González Palencia, 428–29)

[You will see another who pretends to be cautious without wanting to recognize that what he is asserting has value only because he is

---

[12] A reference to *El laberinto de Fortuna* by Juan de Mena (1411–1446), otherwise known by the title of *Las Trezientas* (the three hundred) because of the approximate number of stanzas of which it is composed.

[13] A reference to Juan Boscán, an eminent poet and a friend and contemporary of Garcilaso de la Vega. A "boscán" came to be the term with which one referred to the first edition of Garcilaso's poetry, which was an addition to the edition of the works of Boscán published in 1543, the year before the year of Boscán's death.

asserting it. When it is philosophy Aristotle does not sign it, nor if it is sacred theology does Augustine confirm it.]

In these attitudes one recognizes the confidence that Renaissance humanists felt in their own cultural and intellectual superiority as compared to those who isolated, despised, and ultimately persecuted them, namely, the agents of a tyrannical theocracy seconded by the counterreformist Church.[14]

As an alternative to a world governed by dubious temporal authority and insincerity, Montemor proposes, stylistically of course, the pastoral life:

> Pasemos, pues, señor mas adelante
> ......
> De la vida campestre ora tractemos,
>   en las ribeiras verdes nos metamos,
>   que todo lo demas olvidaremos. (ed. González Palencia, 429)

[Well, let us, Sir, move forward: ... Let us now treat life in the country and place ourselves on green shores, for we shall forget all else.]

And to Ramírez Pagán:

> Dexemos, pues, pastor estos cuydados;
> escrivanse Dardanio y Luscitano,
> como siervos d'amor tras los ganados. (398, ll. 49–51)
> ......
> Allí serán, pastor, nuestras vezinas
> Marfira y mi Marfida, y gustaremos
> de contemplar pastoras tan divinas. (400, ll. 109–111)

---

[14] For an excellent portrayal of the conflict between learned humanists and other sectors of sixteenth-century Peninsular society, see Marcel Bataillon, "Humanismo, erasmismo y represión cultural en la España del siglo XVI," *Erasmo y el erasmismo* (Barcelona: Editorial Crítica, 1983), 162–78; also, Sánchez Gázquez, "Lutero y Erasmo."

> [Let us leave, then, shepherd, these cares; let Dardanio and Luscitano [Montemor] write each other like slaves [serfs, servants] of love behind their flocks ... and, shepherd, Marfira and my Marfida will be our neighbors there, and we will enjoy contemplating such divine shepherdesses.]

But, he warns, even the pastoral life is not free of danger:

> Mas guarde hos Dios d'ver entrar un manto,
> un rostro y ojos bajos, quel primero
> que assi lo ve, hos jura que es un sancto.
> Y el es un lobo en trage de cordero;
> quitaros ha el bonete con risilla
> y da luego del ojo al compañero.
> O, quien dixesse: ¡Hay-de ti, Castilla ... !
> Mas yo, Jesus, que digo: guarda fuera
> que no se usa verdad, ni es bien dezilla. (400, ll. 136–144)

> [But may God keep you from seeing a robe enter, a face with low eyes, whom the first to see it thus swears to you it is a saint. And it is a wolf in sheep's clothing; he will take off your cap with a little laugh and then wink at his companion. Oh, I wish I could say, "Poor you, Castile!" But, Jesus, I say: watch out, truth is not in use, nor is it convenient to speak it.]

The image of the robed monk, a wolf in sheep's clothing[15] with the appearance of a saint, snatching off Ramírez Pagán's university cap with smug arrogance as though to demand such a gesture of courtesy and then winking at a companion is all too suggestive of the vigilance and disrespect that humanists were subjected to by a malevolent, inquisitorial element at court. It is reminiscent of lines from Sannazaro's *Arcadia*:

---

[15] Often a satirical reference to a Cistercian, as in Bernard of Cluny, *De contemptu mundi* 2. 720–728, trans. R. E. Pepin (East Lansing, MI: Colleagues Press, 1991), 118–19.

> Two goats and two kids by his malice
> > that traitor thief stole from my flock:
> > > so avarice holds the governance in the world.[16]

And what is the attraction of the pastoral life? Again, in Sannazaro's *Arcadia* Opico recalls the Arcadia of his youth:

> Then the highest Gods did not disdain
> > to lead sheep to pasture in the woods;
> > > and, as we do now, they too would sing.
> One man could not grow wrathful toward another:
> > the fields were common and without boundaries;
> > > and Plenty caused her fruits always to spring forth anew.
> There was no iron, which today is seen to terminate
> > our human life; and there were not those tares
> > > from which it comes that every war and evil is germinated.
> These raging madnesses were not to be seen;
> > the people had not learned how to litigate,
> > > by which the world must now pull itself to pieces.[17]

In the midst, then, of one's experience of a tormenting tension between nature and civilization, the adoption of pastoral conventions gave an author the incentive to harmonize the healthy, sincere, truthful, immutable aspect of his own being, that is, his soul, with the fertility and innocence of an uncorrupted setting that mirrored the best in himself, that resisted corruption and hypocrisy, and remained, as it were, in a state of eternal springtime. The pastoral dimension thus becomes a projection of the poet's own soul. Lured by the idyllic harmony of that dimension, which reflects the poet's candor, he is drawn away from himself, yet, paradoxically, in a process of radical introversion, which is escape only in the sense of being entry into a dimension where he can relieve his feelings and express a discontent that would have been offensive to court etiquette. In his letter to Jorge Meneses, Montemor writes of the court:

---

[16] Jacopo Sannazaro, *Arcadia and Piscatorial Eclogues*, trans. Ralph Nash (Detroit: Wayne State University Press, 1966), 20.

[17] Jacopo Sannazaro, *Arcadia*, trans. Nash, 67.

> ¿Quien puede lo que ve disimulallo
> y el grave descontento en todo estado,
> e aquella sed de siempre acrescentallo?
>
> (ed. González Palencia, 427)

> [Who can dissemble what he sees and the somber discontent in every circumstance, and that thirst always to increase it?]

The result is the strangely introverted literature in a pastoral setting so peculiar to sixteenth-century Peninsular literature, including what Jorge de Sena has referred to as "o pastorilismo silepsista de Bernardim Ribeiro."[18] The emergence of such a literature is not gratuitous. It vividly depicts the experience of nations cut off from the rest of Europe and the isolation and consequent efforts of the Peninsula's cosmopolitan humanists to survive culturally and psychologically by retiring to the only free sphere that was left, the creative sphere. Referring to Spain, J. H. Elliott writes:

> Early sixteenth-century Spain was Erasmian Spain, enjoying close cultural contacts with the most active intellectual centres of Europe. From the 1550's there was a chilling change in the cultural climate. The *alumbrados* were persecuted, Spanish students were forbidden to attend foreign universities, and Spain was gradually sealed off by a frightened monarch from contact with the contagious atmosphere of heretical Europe. The conscious transformation of Spain into the redoubt of the true faith may have given an added intensity to Spanish religious experience under Philip II, but it also served to cut Spain off from that powerful intellectual current which was leading elsewhere to scientific inquiry and technical experiment.[19]

---

[18] Jorge de Sena, "Maneirismo e Barroco na poesia portuguesa dos séculos XVI e XVII," *Luso-Brazilian Review* 2 (1965): 29–53, here 36. If the term "silepsista" here is not a mistake for the "solipsista," solipsistic, by "syllepticistic," or sylleptic, Sena would seem to be referring to a writing style that uses images having a literal and metaphorical sense at the same time.

[19] J. H. Elliott, "The Decline of Spain," in *Crisis in Europe, 1560–1660*, ed. T. H. Aston (New York: Basic, 1965), 167–93, here 187. Actually, persecution of the *alumbrados* began much earlier, in 1525. Those persecuted in the 1550s were often accused of being

We have only to imagine the Peninsular "Arcadia" not as the Vergilian Golden Age, uneclipsed by time or death, but as a redoubt within a redoubt, or as a place of refuge from the place of refuge. For in *Menina e Moça* pastoral motifs are incorporated only as a metaphor for withdrawal from the anxieties of experience. The pastoral setting is never depicted for its own sake, never inhabited by the reader. Ribeiro's artistic solution is not the passive romanticism of a barren introspection into the self, even less so than any work in the Renaissance tradition of sentimental love literature, which conceives introversion in very special terms, as a longing for union with an ideal of goodness and beauty outside the self and represented by the beloved. *Menina e Moça* begins on a note of unprecedented, even fatalistic disenchantment, but that tone is largely abandoned after the introductory chapters in favor of a more active romanticism and a displaced version of the heroic mode.

Adoption of the pastoral mode did not furnish authors with a means to exercise freedom of expression in the modern sense. That freedom was relative; it was freedom only to express "heterodox" emotions (not thoughts), and it was generally purchased by authors at the cost of arraying their works in a shroud of obscurity, the tactic of Hamlet. Yet it is this same obscurity that makes much of Renaissance literature so highly suggestive. Some of the seemingly illogical and elliptical elements of such literature, often referred to in the present age as "manneristic," have been mentioned above and will be discussed again shortly. However, the most interesting and generally misunderstood ingredient of that obscurity (not to say "obscurantism") was that which donned a mask of absolute candor and came to constitute a fashion in literary and rhetorical taste that not only was consistent with but indeed was recognized as the better part of courtly etiquette itself: the age-old codified rhetorical idiom of courtly love.

According to the canons of that tradition, the character of romantic love is basically paradoxical: whereas it represents love as a joyous triumph of the "gentle heart," it was also the source of the most excruciating pain. Now normally the anxieties of love would be attributed to a fear of rejection or to frustrated desire and that would be the end of it. But in the literature of courtly love, it is part of the joy of love to be

---

alumbrados or Lutherans but were generally Erasmians, Catholic Reformists with Protestant leanings, or exponents of a spiritualized and personal piety reminiscent of all of the above, including the spirituality of the *alumbrados*, Lutheranism, and Augustinianism of a highly traditional sort. Elliott, by the way, indicates that, contrary to widespread belief, the social and economic crisis experienced by Spain is now seen as a general problem of European societies of the time (*The Decline of Spain*, 171–72).

sad, which, though psychologically accurate, is a paradox. It becomes a rhetorical stance, and the starting point for centuries of amatory lyric, of one of the richest traditions in world literature. Maurice Valency translates a characteristic stanza written by Rigaut de Barbezieux as follows:

> I am sad, I am happy; often I sing, often I sorrow, now I grow thin and now I put on flesh, for love has divided himself in my heart into joy and sadness; in laughing and in weeping, in dreaming and in playing. Love shows me his qualities in the midst of laughter and tears. (*In Praise of Love*, 157)

This concept of love is also introduced in *Menina e Moça*: Dona tells Menina, "... segundo entendo devem-vos aprazer as cousas tristes, como me vos a mi dezeis" (["... as I understand what you are telling me, sad things must please you"]; 14, ll. 14–15) and later describes herself as "amiga da tristeza" (["a friend of sadness"]; 16, ll. 5–6). A grateful acceptance of the inconveniences of one's devotion to the beloved was part of a fashion in refined taste. It represented the degree of one's inclination for devotion to an ideal of beauty and virtue. Love must always be deep and painful and a source of destruction. Thus Ribeiro's "Egloga IV (Chamada Jano)" begins,

> Un pastor, Jano chamado,
> de amor da fermosa Dina,
> andava tam tresportado
> que por dita nem mofina,
> nunca era outro seu cuidado:
> Segundo o bem que queria
> tam pouco do mal se guardou,
> que vendo a Dina, um dia,
> logo da vista cegou,
> que dantes d'alma não via.[20]

---

[20] Bernardim Ribeiro, *Obras Completas*, ed. Aquilino Ribeiro and M. Marques Braga, 2 vols. (Lisbon: Libraria Sa da Costa, 1950), 2: 91.

[A shepherd named Jano, out of love for the beautiful Dina, was in a state of being so moved, no matter how happy or unhappy he was he never had another care: So well did he love, he guarded himself so little from harm, that seeing Dina one day, he soon lost his eyesight, whereas before he could not see with his soul.]

On one level, of course, the image of physical disruption conveys the sense of how the lover dies figuratively and is reborn with a completely new psychic orientation, the lady being his cynosure. But I believe that it is also suggested in the literature of this tradition that the obstacles to love, which cannot help reminding one of a repressive and authoritarian atmosphere (the aforementioned "sterility"), render most impractical and perilous precisely those impulses that are the most pleasurable and voluntary. "O amor, que é, se nam vontade?" (["what is love if not will?"]; 48, l. 16). In the tradition of heroic romance and romance epic (from the *roman courtois* to treatments of the Orlando theme to *Menina e Moça*), the element of risk implied in the conflict between the individual strivings of love and collective expectations is the basis for combining heroic and amatory motifs as love becomes an inspired form of militance.

Since Boccaccio is the father of the sentimental novel (*Elegia di madonna Fiammetta*), it would be well in this study to exemplify the latter point with a passage from his works. In the *questioni d'amor*, which appears in the *Filocolo*, Galeone asks the beautiful and wise Fiammetta whether it is to a man's own good to fall in love. Fiammetta answers that there are three kinds of love. The first is virtuous love, good, upright and loyal, the love that links man to God. It reminds us of the "chaste felicity" that Fiammetta, the protagonist in the much later *Elegia*, enjoyed with the man whom she married dutifully at an early age before ever having fallen in love ("until furious Love with a secret kind of unknown fire, and never felt by me before, entered into my tender and young breast"). The second is love for delight: "that to which we are most subject and our god to whom we pray for our gratification."[21] This is the type of love that must be considered to answer Galeone's question. The third type of love is love for utility. Being exploitative, it depends on the presence of changeful Fortune and is rather "more a form of hate than love." (These comparisons are derived from Aris-

---

[21] This and the following quotes from the *Filocolo* are from Giovanni Boccaccio, *Thirteen Most Pleasant and Delectable Questions of Love*, trans. Harry Carter (New York: Clarkson N. Potter, 1974), 88–95.

totle's *Nicomachean Ethics*, 8. 3–8, 1156a 6–1159b 24.) Considering the second type of love, it is characterized as a cruel tyrant and an instigator of vice to be fled and reproved. The only reason we submit to love's power, pursue the wanton pleasures he affords, and even worship him is that it is unlawful not to. He is violent, devoid of reason, and the heart wherein he lodges is forever embittered by shame, anguish, passion, grief, and complaint of the same. "Who but fools will then encourage that love be followed?"

It is not very difficult to interpret the subtle irony in these words. Here the implicit denunciation of real, not figurative, corruption and despotic tyranny is coupled with a tacit affirmation of that which seems to be denounced. The first type of love is admirable, but it is not intriguing nor interesting. It is too strictly correct, too ruled, and too dull. The third type of love is out of the question. And what of the second? That type of love is denounced to the point of persecution, yet (we somehow know) with a knowledge on the author's part that any persecuted idea acquires a certain tinge of nobility and elicits sympathy. Hence, romantic love, which, through Fiammetta, Boccaccio seems to be discouraging, is actually encouraged. "Since we are caught in his nets, . . . it is better for us to follow him and be guided submissively to his pleasures." Here is an example of the profound "transvaluation of values" by means of which Renaissance secular culture unseated the asceto-monastic traditionalism of the Middle Ages. This tacit celebration of the ecstasy of love–passion, ironically projected as an experience only of agony, is what gives the literature of complaint in the courtly-love tradition, even the most mournful, its subtle gaiety and its charm. One of Heine's "Reflections" is "For in the last analysis the world is right — and forgives the flame so long as it is strong and genuine, and burns long and bright" (*Poetry and Prose*, 653).

There will always be something splenetic in the despondency of the thwarted lover. For this reason a lover's patient devotion is the more laudable, and — when there is not sufficient cause — his haughty impatience the more a sign of vulgar frailty. In *Menina e Moça* the contrast between these two types of love is exemplified in the intercalated narrative told to Avalor when, after attempting suicide for the second time, he is swept ashore and then awakened by the cries of a lady. She explains that she was seduced by the tears of a man with whom she remained for four years, until she distinctly sensed that he was in love with another woman. She ran into the forest, and he followed her insisting that she was wrong. To endear her to him he took out a hunting net she had made for him and in which she had woven some initials. As she looked at it somehow her hands became entangled in the net. When she would not yield to his pleadings, he became angry and walked away, saying "Pois me nam quereis creer, quando vos nam peze, eu farei que me creais, quando vos nam possa deixar de pezar" (["Since you don't want to believe me when it causes you no regret, I'll make you believe me when it can't fail to cause you regret"]; 134, ll. 11–12). Perhaps he did not notice, she explains, that her hands were still tied. Since that day she had wandered and was about to perish from exposure when she saw Avalor. But in contrast to her impatient lover, she did not want to take vengeance on him, only on the other woman: she tells Avalor, ". . . o dom que de vos aceitei, nam he para que me vingueis delle, que lhe nam quis tam pouco bem que lhe possa ainda querer este pequeno mal, mas quero-o para que me vingueis della" (["the gift that I accepted from you is not so that you avenge me on him, for I never loved him so poorly as to still be able to wish him this petty ill, but I want it so that you will avenge me on her"]; 135, ll. 4–7).

To interpret such an episode in abstract terms, that is, as an opposition between the idealism of faithful devotion on the one hand and the capacity for sanctimonious or arbitrary violence on the other is not to diminish the personal significance of romantic love. On the contrary: it is to recognize the central place that erotic love occupies in the human psyche and the relationship of that love to every important aspect of human experience. When one considers the unrelenting insistence with which poets worked and reworked the conventional motifs of courtly-love literature over a period of five centuries, one is left with the impression that such literature, especially as it developed under the influence of Renaissance Neoplatonism, was meant to refer to even more than love relations between men and women. Perhaps it was this intuition that led Maurice Valency to write of the *stilnovisti*, "Ultimately, this poetry has little to do with women" (*In Praise of Love*, 210); and of Jaufre Rudel he writes: ". . . the poems which Rudel sings of his far-off love do not permit us to decide whether *amor de lonh* is sacred or profane, concrete or abstract, a mood or an aspiration; whether the far-off lady is an ideal of unattainable happiness, or the Blessed Virgin, or simply a lady who lived on the other side of the sea" (126). The success of pastoral literature, which can look back on two thousand years of uninterrupted development, is due largely to the fact that it came to serve as a vehicle of romantic sentiment. Speaking of pastoral literature in general, Arnold Hauser writes, ". . . there is probably no other subject-matter that has occupied the literature of Western Europe for so long and maintained itself against the assaults of rationalism with such tenacity" (*Social History of Art*, 3: 18).[22]

---

[22] For general background and interesting perspectives on Renaissance pastoral, see

§

Courtly-love literature developed the concept of love as an external power that cannot be resisted, as the "torture of a mortal by a god who inspires him."[23] The most elaborate development of that theme was in the story of Amor and Psyche, widely read on the Iberian peninsula in the sixteenth century in Apuleius's *Metamorphoses*, or *The Golden Ass* (first translated into Spanish in 1513).[24] That story provides us with the starting point in a mythopoeic analysis of *Menina e Moça*'s most vivid images and their relation to the aforementioned central theme of the isolation of fertility, or social sentiment, in an environment hostile to it.

After Psyche violated Eros' command not to attempt to see him, suddenly she found herself on a lonely rock on the summit of a mountain. So Menina appears at the beginning of the novel, isolated on the summit of a mountain, the bride of an invisible Love, contemplating the bitterness of her fate, and seeing the land below drop into a vast ocean. Psyche first goes to a nearby river where she attempts suicide. So Menina goes to a river in the fertile valley below. There she listens to the doleful song of a nightingale (an image of herself, as well as of fecundity and freedom) that suddenly dies, falls through the leafy branches of a tree, and is carried downstream by the river. The sterility-fertility symbolism is further reinforced by Menina's contemplation of a boulder (a symbol of sterility) obstructing the flow of the water (a symbol of fertility): "aquelle penedo... enojando aquella agua que queria hir seu caminho" (["that boulder ... annoying that water that wanted to go its way"]; 13, ll. 12–13).

Paul Alpers, *What is Pastoral?* (Chicago: University of Chicago Press, 1996), esp. 77–93 on pastoral convention and 122–23, 349–60 on the *Diana*; Jane Tylus, "Pastoral on the Continent," in *Encyclopedia of the Renaissance*, ed. P. F. Grendler, 6 vols. (New York: Scribner, 1999), 4: 413–17; Heather Dubrow, "Lyric Forms," in *Cambridge Companion to English Literature 1500–1600*, ed. Kinney, 178–99, here 193–96; Michelle O'Callaghan, "Pastoral," in *Companion to English Renaissance Literature and Culture*, ed. Hattaway, 307–16.

[23] Edgar Wind, *Pagan Mysteries in the Renaissance* (New Haven: Yale University Press, 1958), 145.

[24] The 1513 translation was by López de Cortegana. It was again translated in 1543 by Alonso Fuentes (?). See Bolgar, *The Classical Heritage and Its Beneficiaries*, 527. For Apuleius in the Renaissance, see Stephen Harrison, "Constructing Apuleius: The Emergence of a Literary Artist," *Ancient Narrative* 2 (2002), http://www.ub.rug.nl/an/anvol02prelharrison.pdf.

Menina then meets the "dona do tempo antigo," who, like herself, is wandering as an exile in a hostile world, alienated from the order of nature. Dona is lamenting the loss of her son, who, we are given to understand (20, l. 21–21, l. 2), was a True Lover like the "dois amigos" [two friends/suitors] of whom she tells her story. On one level, the old woman simply represents the sterility of the present age, that interpretation being further reinforced by her statement to the effect that her misfortune is the world's or everyone's, having been deprived of her son: "a grande minha desaventura levou a todo mundo a meu ... filho" (["my great misforutne took my son from everyone"]; 11, ll. 3–4). On another level, however, "todo mundo" [everyone] is represented by Menina, and Dona's son is a symbol of Love and of general fertility, i.e., a Dionysus figure while Dona can be seen as an analogue of Persephone. According to Orphic legend, which was widespread in the Renaissance,[25] Persephone was (by Zeus) the mother of Dionysus (Dionysus Zagreus), who was killed by the Titans.[26]

Dona's first story is about a knight named Bimarder, a name that is generally interpreted as an anagram of Ribeiro's own name (Bernardim) but that seems also to encourage the interpretation *bem arder*, i.e. well-inflamed (by love). When he sees the beautiful Aonia (from *agonia*, the state of love-melancholy?, or from *aionia*, eternal?) mourning her dead sister, he renounces his service to Aquelisa (whose name Helder Maçedo associates with *Ecclesia*)[27] and changes his name (it had been Narbinel) so as to stay near Aonia and not be identified. One night his horse is chased by a pack of wolves into a stream and devoured. There are several ways to interpret the symbolism of that image, but it seems most consistent with the romantic mode of the work not to interpret it in strictly Neoplatonic terms — the horse as a symbol of lust and the wolves as the retributive messengers of Satan — but to interpret the horse as representing, like the nightingale, fertility and freedom and the wolves simply as an image of the perverse and diabolical. Hence the horse is an image of the hero himself, who, we have been told, was to meet with a similar fate. Bimarder then joins a group of shepherds, who live in constant fear of wolves, but prefer wolves to hunger. Avalor becomes known as "o pastor da frauta" ["the shepherd with a flute"]. The flute is widely honored in myth and ritual as a phallic symbol with influence over fertility and is for this reason played at betrothals, courtships, weddings and rites of fertility and

---

[25] See Wind, *Pagan Mysteries, passim*; Brumble, *Classical Myths and Legends*, 48–52.
[26] See W. C. Gutherie, *Orpheus and Greek Religion* (New York: Norton, 1966), 82–83, 107–9.
[27] Maçedo, *Significado oculto*, 89.

healing. In Greek art the flute is an emblem of Dionysus,[28] of whom both Bimarder and Avalor are representatives. Like Diana in Montemayor's novel, Aonia's father married her against her will to a wealthy neighbor. The general thematic import of Bimarder's devotion in love and in the impossibility of love has been discussed above. Although in romantic literature love had gotten the better of heroism before (e.g., in *Amadís de Gaula*), this degree of reversal of traditionalistic priorities signals an important shift away from the cold belligerence of the Middle Ages, pointing toward Céladon in d'Urfé's *L'Astrée* and the eventual reassertion of feminine emotion in the ideals of sensibility developed during the Enlightenment.

Dona next tells the story of Avalor, whose name reminds one of the word *avalar*, to endorse, or make good a promise. Now that the theme of the opposition of fertility and sterility is firmly established, Ribeiro concentrates almost all his attention on depicting the scrupulous innocence and timidity of the two lovers: Avalor and Armina (the daughter of Aonia's sister). The setting of this story is the court ("onde se nao custumam senam prazeres, verdadeiros ou fingidos" ["where people are accustomed only to pleasures, real or feigned"]; 98), although Avalor rarely enters the palace and it is not described to the reader. Avalor was committed to the service of one *senhora deserdada* [disinherited lady], who had come to court to ask for the assistance of knights after the land that she was to inherit upon her father's death had been stolen from her (an Arthurian motif). She is highly regarded by the King. But Avalor is seduced by Armina's modesty, by the way she lowers her eyes. His life now becomes a constant torment. At first he is torn between the *senhora deserdada* and Armina, but a vision of a delicate maiden visits him in a dream and explains to him the difference between devotion as an inspired sentiment and devotion as the mechanical performance of a duty, between a will that acts in the expression of an amorous impulse originating subjectively and a will that acts in conformity with an external command. Avalor now devotes himself to Armina, but before the two lovers are able to overcome their timidity and confess their mutual love, the envious gossips at court discover Avalor's feelings, thereby embarrassing Armina, who feels forced to return to the home of her father. Avalor is told by one of the vain courtiers that she is of the sort that cannot be loved because she is "tanto do outro mundo" ["so much of the other world"], which I believe is meant as a reference to her modesty, neither understood nor appreciated

---

[28] E. S. Whittlesey, *Symbols and Legends in Western Art: A Museum Guide* (New York: Scribner's, 1972), 116.

at court. Avalor tries to follow her but cannot. In desperation he eventually throws himself into the sea and, without knowing it, is washed ashore in the area where Menina and Dona are conversing.

At the end of the novel (that is, of the Ferrara edition) there are two reiterations of the water-stone symbolism. As Avalor is washed ashore, he tries to hold onto some rocks jutting out of the water. The sea pounds on the rocks and sweeps over them "como que se armava pera se vingar daquelles penedos que estrovo lhe faziam as suas agoas" (["as though it were arming itself to avenge itself on those boulders that were blocking its tide"]; 25, ll. 16–17). While unconscious, Avalor hears a voice saying, "E nam te acordas, Avalor, que o mar nam soporta nhua cousa morta?" (["And don't you remember, Avalor, that the sea won't tolerate anything dead?"]; 127, ll. 5–6) (cf. Revelation 20:13). Later, when Avalor begins the story of this father's defense of a lady who had been abused, brutally mocked and then abandoned by a local tyrant, he says that his father found her "acerca de hua fonte que de hum penedo daquella cerra sahia" (["near a fountain that issued from a boulder of that mountain range"]; 136, ll. 2–3). A rock swept by water, representing the emotional tension and frustration of the forsaken lover, is one of Ribeiro's favorite symbols. It also occurs in his Ecloga I:

> Sentava-me em um penedo
> que no meo d'agoa estava;
> então dali só, e quedo,
> a minha frauta tocava.[29]

[I was sitting on a boulder that was in the middle of the water; then from there, alone and still, I played my flute.]

But the most important image at the end of *Menina e Moça*, from a structural standpoint, occurs when Avalor regains consciousness, hearing a woman call out in distress:

> E sendo elle acerca de huns arvoredos grandes que sobre aquella alta
> rocha muito mais altos estavam, ainda olhou e vio ao pee de hua
> antiga arvore estar com as mãos atadas hũa donzella, segundo

---

[29] Ribeiro, *Obras*, 2: 9.

pareceo, nos cabellos que soltos tinha e toda a cobriam." (128, ll. 11–15)

[And while he was near some big groves on that high rock that were themselves much higher than it was, he still looked, and at the foot of an ancient tree he saw, with her hands tied, a maid, as it seemed, amid her undone hair that completely covered her.]

Dona is apparently referring to a great rock in the vicinity of herself and Menina, a rock analogous to the place, if not the same, where we found Menina at the novel's beginning. In the previous age of greater fertility, she explains, that rock was surrounded by forests whose trees were much taller. But most significant is that again there is introduced the image of the abandoned wife, who in this case is a figure reminiscent of the abandoned Andromeda tied to a rock by the seashore and awaiting rescue. At this point, in spite of its apparently truncated ending, the narrative, in both plot and theme, has gone in a complete circle.

Elements of manneristic dissonance in *Menina e Moça* that I have already mentioned are its exotic fusion of genres and the tension between the beauty of its natural setting and the extreme inward strife of its characters. Other such elements are its counterpoint between fantasy and realism and between archaism and realism, and its association of love and death. In addition to previously mentioned instances of unexpected ellipsis, the unresolved, obscure ending of Ribeiro's novel is manneristic as well, for the work breaks off at the beginning of what promises to be, from a sensationalistic point of view, its most thrilling episode. The resulting effect is that the reader is troubled, as one's effort to find a facile interpretation of Ribeiro's narrative is frustrated. Art critics and now literary critics use the words "troubled" and "unsettling" in describing manneristic style: "troublesome" might be a more appropriate term, from an epistemological point of view. The elliptical elements in *Menina e Moça* frustrate the reader and force upon him or her to an extraordinary degree a thematic appreciation of the text. For Ribeiro's novel, unlike, for example, the novels of Diego de San Pedro and Montemayor, does not seek even to appeal to the reader as a sample of courtly manners. Such structural techniques are not unique to *Menina e Moça*. That work is one of several sixteenth-century Peninsular pastoral romances that end on an unresolved note, promising, in some cases, a continuation that was never written. Such endings make it difficult to classify works as "entertainment literature": hence the tendency of much criticism to attempt to explain them instead in terms of an author's biography. The truncated ending, however, served the deliberate purpose of hindering the readers' tendency to dismiss a work by situating it in a neat system of classification, of frustrating the desire to dismiss a work by means of a conventional point of view. Why should we hesitate to consider that such is the case? It has been noted that such features of the nineteenth-century Romantic hero as homeless wandering, estrangement, restlessness, aimlessness, feelings of isolation, and anarchism[30] are expressions of rebellion against the refuge of a neatly-ordered rationalism and retrograde social convention. Why, in the case of sixteenth-century authors, do we overlook the traditionalism of social attitudes and the hypertrophic rationalism of scholastic theology and attribute many of the characteristics of that early romanticism to a "reaction" (not a rebellion) against classicist stability, as though that stability even existed outside of an artistic vacuum? Placing under the obscure and very broad heading of "mannerism" elements of style that are original, unexpected, or unusual ought not to be used as a substitute for attempting to interpret those elements and the purposes they serve, as is done in case of modern movements such as Romanticism and modernism. The sixteenth century especially has been noted for the modernity of its culture, in works such as Henri Hauser's *La modernité du XVIe siècle*, originally published in 1930, and Arnold Hauser's *Mannerism: The Crisis of the Renaissance and the Origin of Modern Art*, from 1965.

What can be said of the reasons for *Menina e Moça*'s censorship by the Portuguese Inquisition in 1564? Apart from its untamable libidinous morality and skepticism of spirit, which must simply have gone against the axiological grain of the counterreformist Church, the work contains certain elements that are characteristic of the doctrine of *iluminismo*, or Catholic reformist spirituality.[31] There is the denigration of works, a sensitive issue when the institution of penance and the *satisfactio operis* were under fire from Protestant elements throughout Europe. When Lamentor sends his daughter Armina off to court, he tells her, "de quem desseja com maa tençam ou de quem desseja com boa, d'ambos sam as obras iguais ... pois Deus soo o conhecimento das tençois dos homens gardou pera si ..." (["the works of those who intend good and of those who intend evil are the same ... for God kept the knowledge of men's intentions

---

[30] Hauser, *Social History of Art*, 3: 212.
[31] Bataillon, *Erasmo y España*, 703 defines *iluminismo* as "the revolutionary expression of a general tendency toward an internal and inspired religion, a tendency that Catholicism makes its own with very great danger" (my translation). See also Creel, *Religious Poetry of Jorge de Montemayor*, 36–37.

for himself alone"]; 100, ll. 2–9). Similarly, the maiden who appears to Avalor in his dream speaks of the difference between "vontade por força d'amor, e outra por amor forçado dada" (["willing out of the strength of love and another given out of forced love"]; 103, ll. 19–20). The same distinction between what could be interpreted as referring to sincere piety on the one hand and a hypocritical piety of external devotions on the other is expressed in the following words: "Que querer bem, e nam verdadeiro, pode-se dissimular e finger, mas dissimular ou encobrir o bem que quer alguem, nunca ninguem o soube fazer, que o quisese verdadeiramente" ["Loving much and not truly can be dissembled and feigned, but dissembling or concealing how much one loves is something no one who loved truly ever knew how to do"]; 117, ll. 25–118, l. 3). Also, the suicide attempts of Avalor might have been dimly viewed, since in Catholicism suicide is considered a mortal sin. Cervantes's difficulty in integrating, after Trent, the suicide of Grisóstomo in the *Quijote* is well known. The most profoundly "revolutionary" quality of *Menina e Moça*, however, is that by conceiving a tragic sense of life that arises from love's being regarded as the only truly important value, the spirit of the work militates against the repressive atmosphere of distrust and enmity that was fomented by what have been characterized as domineering and fanatical elements in the Reformation–Counter-reformation struggle.[32]

In sum, in its portrayal of the afflictions of tragic love, Ribeiro's novel both captures and places in a critical perspective the climate of violence and repression that by the middle of the sixteenth century came more and more to be directed against the opponents of authoritarian dogma, particularly those who favored cultured humanism and a civic-minded and evangelical emphasis on compassionate and tender humanity. Perhaps the Inquisition and the censorship of works such as *Menina e Moça* ought not to be regarded as aberrations of the times but rather as phenomena that erupted at a moment (by no means unique) when circumstances happened to favor the whims of a sterile and authoritarian element that exists in all societies in all ages, the narrow and psychologically sedentary element that resents inspiration and fears individuality. *Menina e Moça* represents a triumph of the inspired individual psyche isolated at a time when true emotional fervor and honorable sentiment courageously strove to survive. By means of a sentimental ethics and a cult of sensitivity to suffering humanity (which in Ribeiro's novel is always what kindles romantic love), Renaissance humanism sought systematically to oppose the cold fanaticism that was rampant in Europe in the

---

[32] See now John W. O'Malley, *Trent and All That* (Cambridge, MA: Harvard University Press, 2000).

The Agony and Apotheosis of Innocent Love 219

sixteenth century. Ribeiro's novel celebrates the sixteenth-century equivalent of the eighteenth-century man of sensibility, the good man inspired by feminine beauty, the man of feeling, the man of beautiful sentiments. Melancholy in this work (*Livro das Saudades*) is one such beautiful sentiment. It is the melancholy of the chaste and humble heart. Yet the sentiment of melancholy is of different types,[33] some of which betray a gloomy surliness or callous malevolence, cloaked though they may be in altruism or the appearance of piety. The distinction between these two general types of sentiment — healthy inspiration and pernicious fanaticism — is crucial to an appreciation of *Menina e Moça*, for the isolation and destruction of beautiful sentiment by arbitrary power is the subject of the book. At the very end of the final chapter, when the victimized woman whom Avalor's father had met near a fountain leads him into the castle where she had been held captive, he sees coming towards him

> hum cavaleiro grande, ao parecer de grande esforço, fermosamente armado, em hum fermoso cavalo com sua lança na mão, e escudo embaraçado a ponto d'aver batalha e chegando onde meu pai estava, dezia elle que *com demasiada ira* disse escontra a donzella que o alli trouxera, estas palavras: LAUS DEO. (140, ll. 5–10; my emphasis)

> [a tall knight, seemingly of great strength, beautifully armed, on a beautiful horse with his lance in his hand and his shield on his arm, on the verge of entering into battle, and arriving to where my father was, he [my father] said that *with too much anger* he [the knight] said before the maiden who brought him [my father] there, these words: PRAISE GOD.]

In the world of *Menina e Moça* the will to power, which occasions tragic suffering, is metaphorically contrasted to an almost morbidly self-abnegating devotion to the pursuit of ideal love. The culture of sentiment thus generated by Ribeiro's colorful and highly original narrative contributed powerfully to making unrelieved suffering in love — "saudade," or sorrowful longing — not only a sign of distinction but the basis of a distinctly Portuguese romantic and secular ideal of morality.

---

[33] See Louis I. Bredvold, *The Natural History of Sensibility* (Detroit: Wayne State University Press, 1962), 55–59.

9
Chaste Love as Metaphorical Death: Montemayor's "Nicodemist" Vindication of Human Passion in the Diana

For a literature offering reflective withdrawal from life's complexity, Iberian Renaissance pastoral's appeal for the readers of its day is a phenomenon that is surprisingly resistant to being explained in simple terms. It has been the triumph of a sequence of articles concerning Spain's first pastoral novel, Jorge de Montemayor's *Los siete libros de la Diana* (the first known edition is of 1559), that scholars have for some time acknowledged the existence of dimensions in Spanish pastoral that are not easily discernible to the twentieth-century eye.[1] Yet those readers who appreciate the remarkable modernity and substantive universality of Renaissance literature may feel that a fundamental question has still not been answered: how could a period producing

---

[1] See in particular B. W. Wardropper, "The *Diana* of Montemayor, Revaluation and Interpretation," *Studies in Philology* 48 (1951): 126–44; T. A. Perry, "Ideal Love and Human Reality in Montemayor's *La Diana*," *PMLA* 84 (1964): 227–34; and C. B. Johnson, "Montemayor's *Diana*: A Novel Pastoral," *Bulletin of Hispanic Studies* 48 (1971): 25–35.

timeless works that are found interesting today largely because of their realistic depiction of life (in Spain works such as *La Celestina, Lazarillo de Tormes,* and *Don Quijote*) have seen a vogue for a literature as artificially innocent and stylized as the pastoral? That question emerges with particular clarity in relation to the *Diana,* in which the conventional, lyrical sentimentality of the framing narrative and a comic–romantic urbanity of tone in the series of interpolated narratives in the tradition of the Italian *novella* exist side by side. How could the interest that sixteenth-century readers had in the stark conventionality and childlike naiveté of the former even compare with their interest in the risqué secularism and wittily skeptical spirit of the latter? What was the axiological basis for the widespread acceptance in the Renaissance of the literary style that has been recently referred to as "pastoral spirituality"?[2] Is it more than just a style?

First a few words on the extent of the *Diana's* popularity in its day. Francisco López-Estrada notes, in relation to the *Diana's* "amazing success," that enthusiasm for pastoral spread from courtly circles into the incipient middle class (*Libros de pastores,* 481–82). While the success of pastoral was not as great as that of the romances of chivalry, by the end of the sixteenth century that readership far surpassed being a minority. In Spain the success of the *Diana* had been exceeded only by that of *Amadís de Gaula* and *La Celestina.* Before the end of the sixteenth century, Montemayor's novel received seventeen editions in Spain.[3] In the dedication of the Lisbon 1624 edition, it is stated that the fame of Montemayor was so great that "there was not a house in which the *Diana* was not read, nor a street in which its verses were not sung, nor a conversation in which its style was not extolled." Outside of Spain the *Diana*, rapidly translated into French, English, Italian, and German, arguably enjoyed a vogue com-

---

[2] See Francisco López Estrada, *Libros de pastores en la literatura española* (Madrid: Gredos, 1974), 1: 480.

[3] The first two varorium critical editions of the *Diana* were both published in 1996, one edited by Julián Arribas (London: Tamesis) and the other by Juan Montero (Barcelona: Crítica). Arribas (119) convincingly argues that the number of editions of the *Diana* that has been traditionally calculated to have been published is much underestimated. He also maintains that the undated Valencia (1559?) edition could not have been the first, whereas Montero (LXXX–LXXXII) holds that there is no evidence for the existence of an earlier edition. Eugenia Fosalba, *La Diana en Europa: ediciones, traducciones e influencias* (Barcelona: Universitat Autònoma de Barcelona, 1994), also considers the first edition to be the undated Valencia edition, which, on the basis of a cogent analysis of circumstantial evidence, she calculates to have been published in late 1558 or 1559: 19–36, 86.

parable only to that of *Don Quijote*. It served as the model for the *Arcadia* of Sir Philip Sidney, who also translated some of its poems; it provided the plot for Shakespeare's *Two Gentlemen of Verona*; there are clear influences of Montemayor's novel in both the main plot of *A Midsummer Night's Dream* and in *Twelfth Night*; and John Donne took his motto "antes muerto que mudado" (["death before inconstancy"], from the *Diana*, 14).[4]

It is interesting to compare the enthusiasm for the *Diana* in the sixteenth century to views commonly held of it today. The standard for the adverse modern judgment of the *Diana* as representing a style that is passé and lacking in vitality was set by Marcelino Menéndez Pelayo. He expressed regret that in the *Diana* Montemayor did not or could not free himself from the imitation of Petrarch, that the work is excessively sentimental, enervating, and effeminate in tone, and that a "falso bucolismo" underlies the feebleness of the work, the author of which has no eye for nature.[5] Menéndez Pelayo's reservations about the *Diana* raise serious questions. If his judgment has a valid basis, how can we account for the *Diana*'s success? There are clearly two possibilities: either the *Diana* represents an aberration of taste in a period that was also extremely rich in literary culture, or sixteenth-century readers of the *Diana* were drawn to it by values for which Menéndez Pelayo and those modern readers who share his opinion have relatively little feeling. I will explore the latter possibility.[6]

Probably because of its stylized neo-paganism (the pastoral setting, pagan gods and temples, nymphs, satyr-like beasts with huge shells for shields) and because the cultured speech of Montemayor's shepherds matches the historical circumstance that in the High Renaissance pastoral masquerades were a favorite form of recreation at court, the success of the *Diana* is usually attributed above all to its relatively frivolous appeal as a literature of fashionable, aristocratic entertainment. Some critics emphasize the didactic value of such entertainment. López Estrada, for example, considers the appeal

---

[4] All textual references to the *Diana* are to Jorge de Montemayor, *Los siete libros de la Diana*, ed. Francisco López-Estrada, 5th ed. (Madrid: Espasa-Calpe, 1970). Translations are mine. For discussion of Montemayor's influence on John Donne, see George Williamson, *A Reader's Guide to the Metaphysical Poets*, 2nd ed. (London: Thames and Hudson, 1974), 53.

[5] Marcelino Menéndez Pelayo, *Orígenes de la novela* (1905), 4 vols. (Madrid: Bailly Bailliere, 1925), 1: 437, 441, cf. 436.

[6] For more recent perspectives on Renaissance pastoral, see Paul Alpers, *What is Pastoral?*; Jane Tylus, "Pastoral on the Continent"; Heather Dubrow, "Lyric Forms"; Michelle O'Callaghan, "Pastoral."

of pastoral to have a basis in the nobility's need to foster mature love relations among young men and women at court (*Libros de pastores*, 491). Bruno Damiani considers the *Diana*'s appeal to have resulted from its importance as a source of moral and sentimental refinement. Both recognize the importance of the vogue for Neoplatonic love doctrine to the success of the *Diana*, as to that of the lyrical poetry current at the time; but they also see such Neoplatonism, and pastoral itself, as corresponding mainly to a fashion of the day, that is, as essentially ephemeral, even if possessing cultural value.[7]

A more esoteric explanation for the *Diana*'s success, as an expression of Renaissance Neoplatonism, has been offered by Juan Bautista Avalle-Arce. He sees the *Diana* as both representing and propounding Neoplatonism: the former in the presentation of a "quintessentialized" existence in which pastoral reality is rendered abstract and ideal by being stripped of normal temporal circumstances, the latter in the different exempla of love as a sentiment devoid of sexual appetite.[8] Yet Avalle-Arce also sees this intellectual basis for the *Diana*'s appeal as being a localized, sixteenth-century phenomenon, a curiosity of the times. Other critics emphasize the value of the *Diana*'s originality as fictional art and that it possessed added appeal because it could be identified with the prestigious vogue of Italian humanism.[9] With still another point of view, Menéndez Pelayo saw the *Diana*'s success as being attributable to its use as a manual for the elegant conversation and Petrarchan conceits of courtiers who had come to regard the romances of chivalry as being brutal and antiquated. It represents, in his view, a "puro dilettantismo estético" (*Orígenes de la novela*, 1: 435, cf. 385). Another common opinion is that the appeal of the *Diana* can be explained by the alternative that it offered to the hypocrisy and formalism of life at court. Apart from being a conclusion following naturally from the essential character of the pastoral setting as a retreat from the anxieties of social life, that view was encouraged by Hugo Rennert's study on Montemayor in which he emphasizes the author's frustrations and

---

[7] See López Estrada, *Libros de pastores*, 484, and Bruno M. Damiani, *"La Diana" of Montemayor as Social and Religious Teaching* (Lexington, KY: University of Kentucky Press, 1983), 1–4, 41–43. Also see Barbara Mujica, *Iberian Pastoral Characters* (Washington, DC: Scripta Humanistica, 1986), who equates Montemayor's interest in unrequited love with the vogue for Neoplatonism.

[8] Juan Bautista Avalle-Arce, *La novela pastoril española* (Madrid: Revista de Occidente, 1959), 62–63, 68.

[9] See Johnson, "Montemayor's *Diana*," passim, and Amadeu Solé-Leris, *The Spanish Pastoral Novel* (Boston: Twayne, 1980), 49 respectively.

disillusionments while Montemayor was resident at court.[10] In a recent study, Elizabeth Rhodes sees parallels between the general outlook represented in the *Diana* and affective yet orthodox currents of Catholic religiousness such as that of the relatively conservative mystical movement known as "recogimiento."[11]

Whereas all of the above explanations for the *Diana*'s appeal among its sixteenth-century readers may (and some definitely do) have a basis in fact, none of these theories by itself, nor even all of them together, can account for that work's enormous popularity in its day. There is, of course, a sense in which all cultural developments correspond to what is "fashionable," but merely to point out the character of such

---

[10] Hugo J. Rennert, *The Spanish Pastoral Romances*, 2nd ed. (Philadelphia: University of Pennsylvania Press, 1912), 31–32.

[11] On the relatively conservative nature of "recogimiento" as compared to "dejamiento" (both of which were tendencies of the "alumbrado" movement), see Bataillon, *Erasmo y España*, 171–74. On the basis of observations concerning isolated examples of Montemayor's religous writings, Rhodes seeks to account for the melancholy tone of the *Diana* by arguing that pastoral literature resembles mystical piety because it contains features such as the self-examining contemplative life and pessimistic withdrawal from the world: *The Unrecognized Precursors of Montemayor's "Diana"* (Columbia, MO: University of Missouri Press, 1992), 76–77, 117. Her recognizing the need to account for the acute suffering of the characters in Montemayors's *Diana* is well taken, especially since many critics do not give the feature of intense melancholy in that work the attention and explanation that it requires. Substantiation of Rhodes's thesis, however, would require systematically proving that a broad sampling of Montemayor's religious writings, which are almost all poetry, in fact reveals characteristic traits of "recogido" mysticism. Montemayor is sixteenth-century Spain's foremost author of lay religious lyric, and his *Cancionero espiritual* and *Segundo cancionero espiritual* were repeatedly proscribed by the Inquisition (see Creel, *The Religious Poetry of Jorge de Montemayor*). Substantiation of Rhodes's thesis would also require taking into account such issues as whether tragic or elegiac works such as the *Diana* are, in fact, essentially "pessimistic" (as opposed to skeptical, in the tradition of pagan rationalism, and even ultimately festive); the differences between an orthodox, asceto–monastic, religious renunciation of worldliness and the *Diana*'s radically non-penitential and worldly, though austerely idealistic, secular affirmation of the value of the love of the sexes; the optimistic nature of Christian mysticism; and the gaiety of the *Diana*'s intercalated narratives. In short, it would be necessary to prevent an emphasis on "elements of the text that critics have generally chosen to avoid" (Rhodes, *Unrecognized Precursors*, 5) from detracting from the essences of both the *Diana* and orthodox religion and from the differences between the two. On the other hand, Rhodes states that she seeks not to reveal Montemayor's intentions in writing the *Diana* but only to illuminate certain facets of the text (1).

developments as fashions is not to explain them. The question remains: *why* was a particular development fashionable? It was Freud's view that there are organic grounds for changes in our ethical and aesthetic ideals (*Collected Papers*, 5: 286).[12] The basis for the widespread interest in Montemayor's *Diana* must, it would seem, be sought in deeper levels of that work's significance and in its relation to the changing culture of its day. The present study argues that, as a Renaissance humanist and a lay Catholic Reformist, Montemayor sought to oppose the doctrine of Original Sin not only in his religious poetry[13] but in the *Diana* as well. Thus, below the surface of the *Diana* Montemayor uses certain subtle strategies that are calculated both to combat that doctrine and to neutralize conservative opposition to his book. Those strategies are revealed in the quality in the *Diana* that Rhodes (*Unrecognized Sources*, 84) has aptly characterized as "the metaphorical death caused by human love" (the incapacitating agony that is represented as accompanying the love of the sexes) as well as in the *Diana*'s advancement of the rather contrived idea that the uncontrollable intensity of passionate love is not necessarily related to physical impulses, even in its source and origin. Once Montemayor uses those means to appear superficially to accommodate the traditional prejudice that sexual love is sinful, an adverse fate, on a deeper level he proceeds to combat that same prejudice by implicitly introducing the modern view that passionate sexual love and the physical desire that it generally includes are by no means at variance with naive innocence of heart. In that regard, Montemayor might be characterized as deploying in his *Diana* a strategy analogous to what I call Nicodemism (see below), using that term in a figurative, non-religious sense. In a work concentrating on passionate adult love relations he introduced a tone of gloomy melancholy and conspicuously minimized the overt influence of sensual impulse, emphasizing instead an ideal of "chastity" (*honestidad*). Because those qualities, considered superficially, appear consistent with the traditionalistic, curialist depreciation of human sexuality, they draw attention away from what beneath the surface of the *Diana* is an enthusiastic celebration of the passionate love of the sexes. Other instances in the period of Nicodemism — in the proper, religious sense of that term — are Juan de Valdés and Louis de Berquin, whom José Nieto and Marcel Bataillon see, respectively, as having delib-

---

[12] See now Steven Pinker, *The Blank Slate: The Modern Denial of Human Nature* (New York: Viking Press, 2002).

[13] See Creel, *The Religious Poetry of Jorge de Montemayor*.

erately simulated adherence to a then-orthodox Erasmism in order to draw the Inquisitors' attention away from their Lutheran leanings.[14]

§

Notwithstanding subtly disorienting appearances completely to the contrary, the essential and most innovative feature of the *Diana* is its frenzied Hellenism, its delirium of pagan joy, freedom, and love of life. It was this quality that made it novel, placing it in radical opposition both to the traditional, official austerity of asceto–monastic Christianity and to the stable harmony of High Renaissance classicism. On a superficial level, the "modernity" of the *Diana* is, on the one hand, in its attainment of the calm clarity, the sensitivity, and the fresh, harmonious simplicity of spirit that characterize the style of High Renaissance classicism and, on the other hand, in its "manneristic" breach with that same classicism of style by means of the emotionalistic subjectivism of its characters, their mood of inward strife, the ambivalence of erotic feelings, and the insoluble contradictions and "Byzantine" lack of formal consistency in its plot (not-

---

[14] See José Nieto, *Juan de Valdés and the Origins of the Spanish and Italian Reformation* (Geneva: Droz, 1970), and Bataillon, *Erasmo y el erasmismo*, 153, 253, 256–57. Another famous instance of the issue of Nicodemism in the period is Calvin's *Excuses à Mesieurs les Nicodémites* (1544). Nicodemus was a Pharisee who was interested in Jesus and visited him secretly. The term "Nicodemite" is defined in the *Oxford English Dictionary* as "one who resembles Nicodemus; a secret or timid adherent." I use the term "Nicodemism" to refer to the practice of consciously cloaking a controversial deeper intent with an orthodox exterior. It is thus analogous to Peers' concept of "eclecticism," which he regards as serving as a bridge in the transition from Classicism to Romanticism in Spain, a means by which authors could placate the stricter Classicists while they brought to light the merits of Romanticism. Peers defines "eclecticism" as "a self-conscious movement . . . not to be taken as covering the gradual appearance of Romantic tendencies among the neo-Classical traits. . . . For the purposes of this History, we should not describe as an Eclectic a writer like Cadalso, in whose work we can find traces of the Classical and the Romantic, since there is no proof, or even indication, that he was conscious of the duality" (*Romantic Movement in Spain*, 2: 74–75). The quality shared by "Nicodemism" and "eclecticism" as Peers defines it is their strategic character, which is indicated by the presence in a work of prominent, irreconcilable contradictions from an ideological point of view, though the pressures of a repressive, dominant official culture often required that such contradictions be subtly concealed.

Chaste Love as Metaphorical Death 227

withstanding its structural symmetry emphasized by Wardropper).[15] Certainly the *Diana*'s spirit of estrangement from a purely classicist stability in art contributed much to what must have been perceived as that work's originality. In the *Diana* there is a deep and constant tension between a tone of exuberant, secular gaiety, most obvious in the subplots, and the tortured love–melancholy repeatedly expressed by almost all of the characters in the framing narrative. The element of melancholy would seem to negate the comic–romantic aspect of the novel and, by its sheer intensity, produce a tone that is predominantly elegiac and a tragic, non-Neoplatonist, "fatalistic acceptance of the power of love" as an irrational force subverting the human will (Solé-Leris, *Spanish Pastoral Novel*, 38). Green considers the irrational character of love as seen in the *Diana* to have been over-stressed by critics. He points out that entrance into the Temple of Diana in Book Four of the novel is limited to those who have remained chaste and faithful to their true loves, a stipulation that conflicts with love's being conceived as "irrational," not just in the sense of being ruled by appetite but in the sense of being "fated" (*Spain and the Western Tradition*, 2: 327–28). The issue is of crucial importance for an interpretation of the novel and has far-reaching implications for an understanding of the *Diana*'s relation to the culture of the period.

The prominence with which lovesickness is treated in the *Diana* is what has caused many critics to regard Montemayor's concept of love to be medieval and fatalistic.[16] The perturbations of love in the *Diana* are so severe that love in that work would indeed appear to be a hostile and hence negative phenomenon. The characters even claim as much. Yet Montemayor goes to considerable lengths to emphasize his view that the emotional depth and intensity of love passion is not a function of the ethical quality of love's source and origin: "aquel excesso y ímpetu no es más propio del amor deshonesto que del honesto" (["that excess and impetus is not more a quality of unchaste love than of chaste love"]; 97). Actually, the very structure of Montemayor's novel is organized in such a way as to demonstrate the qualities that love ignited by instinctive sensual desire, "amor loco" [insane love], and love based on esteem, i.e., inspired by spiritual beauty — "amor bueno," "verdadero," or "honesto" [good, true, or

---

[15] See Wardropper, "The *Diana* of Montemayor."

[16] See, for example, Solé-Leris, *Spanish Pastoral Novel*, 37 and Green, *Spain and the Western Tradition*, 1: 174 (n. 45)–175 (where courtly love and Neoplatonism are compared in terms of their "negative side"); R. O. Jones, *The Golden Age: Prose and Poetry* (London: Ernest Benn, 1971), 59; and Avalle-Arce, *La novela pastoril española*, 67–68.

chaste love] — have in common. A brief survey of the sequence of central plot motifs will illustrate this point.

The *Diana*'s central thematic motif, that which establishes its social norm, is the deep and constant devotion to an ideal of feminine beauty. That devotion is introduced in the character of Sireno and is compounded in the identical devotion of his fellow-shepherd Sylvano. In them there is illustrated a love born of "reason," i.e., the contemplation of the lady's mental qualities and beauty of subjective spirituality — "amor que ... nace de la razón y del verdadero conocimiento y juyzio, que por solas sus virtudes la juzgue digna de ser amada" (["love that is born of reason and of true knowledge and judgement, that by her virtues alone judges her worthy of being loved"]; 198). They also illustrate the above-mentioned principle that a love born of reason and a chaste will can also produce uncontrollable passion. This is a principle that Castiglione, in his *Courtier*, advances with the idea that (in the language of Juan Boscán's translation of 1553) "nuestra alma es en estremo inclinada a los sentidos" (["our soul is in the extreme inclined to the senses"]; 243).

The love of Sireno and Sylvano is immediately contrasted to the frivolous, transitory, and sensuous infatuation of irrational love, "amor loco" [insane love] inspired purely by the sight of the loved one. It is represented by Selvagia, Ysmenia, Alanio, and Montano. The love between Selvagia and Ysmenia establishes a second high social norm, this time in the realm of the sensuous: the two fell in love with such force that they did not take time even to establish one another's sexual identities. Yet the discovery of the situation causes no feeling of shame in either of them precisely because the sensuous (visual) appreciation of corporeal beauty that stimulated their mutual infatuation was alien to a self-seeking, narrowly gratifying sensual impulse (pure sexual instinct). For that reason sexual differences are not important.[17] When we meet

---

[17] Referring to Ficino's theory of love, Kristeller writes: "Since love between two persons is conceived as a mutual love, although free from any sensual element, the difference between the two sexes, which actually determines erotic relations in the ordinary sense, loses its basic importance. ... Not only man and woman but also two men or two women may be united by a sentiment of love" (*The Philosophy of Marsilio Ficino*, 277). Although nothing could be more improbable in a work that sought to exonerate the passionate love of the sexes by attributing to it a childlike innocence that was alien to the dictates of a self-conscious sensuality, critics persist until the present day in ignoring Montemayor's "manneristic" technique of playing on readers' expectations for purposes of challenging their propensity for naive innocence. The primary form of that innocence in the *Diana* is a passionate yet sexually neutral and disinterested enthusiasm for human

Selvagia, her love for Alanio, who is by then married to Ysmenia's sister, has deepened and turned to pain. We perceive that the depth of her passion vests her with a dignity comparable to that of Sireno and Sylvano. To remove any possibility of doubt as to the elevation that may be attained even by a love originating in a turmoil of dazed sensuousness bordering on sensuality, as did Selvagia's, that love is contrasted to the brute voluptuousness of the three wild men, who are killed by Felismena.

In the character of Felismena, we are presented with a second superior alternative to the love born of the eyes (the first alternative having been presented by Sireno and Sylvano). Felismena, who, as another model of exemplary devotion, has been wandering for a year in quest of the fugitive Don Felis, was able to be moved to fall in love with him only by the sincerity of one of his letters. In Felismena's story of the betrayal of her love by Don Felis, there is presented, in the character of Celia, another example of a passion of uncontrollable strength. So overwhelmed is Celia by love for Felismena, who is disguised as the valet of Don Felis, that the agitation produced by "his" absence causes her to have a stroke and die. Such a fate, nevertheless, was probably regarded

---

beauty understood to be manifested emotionally and psychologically as well as physically. Because such enthusiasm also operates powerfully in sexual love, in which sensual experience figures prominently, in the *Diana* it assumes an ambiguous character. Such elements of complexity make it possible to view the *Diana*'s "Nicodemism" not merely as a stylistic and ideological strategy but as a step in the direction of modern realism. In any case, some critics have, in my opinion, "taken the bait" and quite unhesitatingly asserted that it is homosexual desire that underlies the relations between Selvagia and Ysmenia (see, for example, Montero, ed. *La Diana*, 46, n.217, where those relations are referred to as "un franco caso de lesbianismo" ["a clear case of lesbianism"]). Menéndez Pelayo, who expressed horror at this passage in Montemayor's novel, would seem to have held that view himself. Perhaps an argument in support of the naive sexual innocence of Selvagia and Ysmenia could be based on a parallel between the *Diana* and the twelfth-century Byzantine romance *Hysmine and Hysminias*, which enjoyed great popularity during the Renaissance beginning with the Italian edition of 1550 and the French edition of 1559 (see Ingela Nilsson, *Erotic Pathos, Rhetorical Pleasure: Narrative Technique and Mimesis in Eumathios Makrembolites' Hysmine and Hysminias* [Uppsala: Uppsala University Library, 2001], 13 nn.14, 24). Apart from the presence of the same character name in both works and the extreme Byzantine convolution of plot in this episode of the *Diana*, at the end Makrembolites's work Hysmine is proven to be a virgin, in spite of the fact that Hysmine and Hysminias were enabled to meet as lovers by the latter's pretending to be Hysmine's brother (Nilsson, *Erotic Pathos*, 49, 292–93).

as evidence of a passion born mainly of a love of corporeal beauty and therefore unable to mitigate sensual desire through the contemplation of spiritual beauty.[18]

Like Felismena, Belisa, whom we meet next, also fell in love with spiritual beauty, that of Arsileo, with his "discreción, gracia y gentileza" ["intelligence, wit, and gentility"] and "buenas partes" [good qualities], revealed to her in the poetry that his father, Arsenio, was proffering as his own. But she fell in love with Arsileo's corporeal beauty as well, his "hermosura" [beauty]. Thus, her love is the composite of the loves of Sireno, Sylvano, and Felismena, on the one hand, and of Selvagia and Celia on the other. Also (as in the tradition of Petrarchan lyric), far from the death of Arsileo lessening the love she feels for him, it purifies that love, strengthens it, and increases it.

"Aquel excesso y ímpetu no es más propio del amor deshonesto que del honesto; antes es una propiedad de cualquiera género de amor" (["that excess and impetus is not more proper to unchaste love than to chaste love; it is a property of any kind of love whatsoever"]; 197). The *Diana*'s episodes illustrate that view (paraphrased from León Hebreo), which differs from more conservative Renaissance views on love such as those expressed in Pietro Bembo's *Gli Asolani* (1505): "Sono adunque due . . . le strade dell'animo . . . : l'una della ragione, per la quale ogni naturale movimento s'incamina; l'altra delle perturbazioni, per cui hanno i non naturali a'loro traboccamenti [eccessi] la via" (*Prose e rime*, ed. C. Dionisotti, 407) ([. . . "there are two roads before the soul: one that of reason, along which all the natural instincts move; the other that of the perturbations, by which the unnatural ones proceed to their destruction"]; trans. R. B. Gottfried, *Gli Asolini*, 98).

As I mentioned previously, the view that Montemayor's emphasis on love's anguish is retrograde and medieval has gained considerable acceptance: Solé-Leris, for

---

[18] Castiglione, *El cortesano*, trans. Boscán, 244–45: ". . . asi que por huir el tormento desta ausencia y gozar sin ninguna pasión la hermosura, conviene que el Cortesano, ayudado de la razón, enderece totalmente su deseo a la hermosura sola, sin dejalle tocar en el cuerpo nada, y cuanto más pueda la contemple en ella misma simple y pura, y dentro en la imaginación la forma separada de toda materia . . . acordándose siempre que el cuerpo es cosa muy diferente de la hermosura, y que no solamente no le acrecienta, mas que le apoca su perfición. . . ." ([". . . thus it is that to flee this absence and enjoy beauty without any passion, the Courtier, aided by reason, would do well to direct his desire totally toward beauty alone, without allowing it to extend to the body at all, and as much as it can to contemplate beauty in itself, simple and pure, and in his imagination the form separated from all matter . . . remembering always that the soul is very different from beauty, and that the soul's perfection not only does not increase beauty but reduces it . . ."]; my trans.).

example, holds that Montemayor represents all "love" (sensual desire as well as sexual love) as being antagonistic to reason and that his doing so is the basis of a traditionally medieval, fatalistic view of love (*Spanish Pastoral Novel*, 37). Actually, Montemayor's conception of sexual love as containing a fundamental sensual ingredient without being reducible to it is peculiarly modern. It thus differs from both a rigid ecclesiastical morality's tendency to equate sensual desire and sexual love and subordinate the latter to the institution of marriage[19] and from rigorously dualistic Neoplatonic idealizations of love (Ficino, Bembo, Castiglione). The more modern view, as expressed, for example, by Ribot in his *The Psychology of the Emotions* (available in English as early as 1906), is that "sexual instinct remains the center round which everything revolves; nothing exists but through it" (256). Ribot's view would seem to be that sexual love necessarily presupposes an essential element of physical desire, which is far from equating true love and sensuality. Castiglione cautions against such an equation in the fourth book of his *Courtier*. Both Castiglione and Montemayor would seem to have been influenced by Ficino's view that the human soul is simultaneously inclined upward by a desire for God and downward by its natural appetite towards its own body, the latter desire being free from moral reproach (Kristeller, *Philosophy of Marsilio Ficino*, 194–95). The concept that is both stated and illustrated in the *Diana* is that the lower senses can contribute to the emergence of a lofty if disruptive emotion of love, not that they can give rise to a lofty sensuality. Since there is no reason to assume that Montemayor equates sexual desire, as an element of sexual love, and sensual desire, there is no basis for assuming that he considers intense sexual desire *per se*, even when it is emotionally consuming, to be at variance with man's dignity as a spiritual being. Even Aristotle (*Nicomachean Ethics* 8, 1156a32–1156b6; 9, 1167a4–8) distinguished between simple sexual appetite and erotic passion in the sense of intense interest in the beloved, desire for his/her presence and company.[20] Montemayor's approach to the distinction between appetite for physical sexual gratification and a more generalized passion is based on an exquisite ambiguity similar to that found in León Hebreo's treatment of the subject. León Hebreo distinguishes between "carnal passion" and "spiritual passion," yet he goes on to state that whereas the first type of passion ceases upon attainment of its object, in the second case carnal delight actually causes passion to increase:

---

[19] See Scheler, *Person and Self-Value*, 69.
[20] See *Nicomachean Ethics*, trans. Terence Irwin (Indianapolis: Hackett, 1985), 397 in Glossary under "erotic passion, erotic love, *erōs, erōtikos*."

> ... el amor de los amantes cuyas penas cesan con la ganancia de la carnal delectación no depende de la razón sino del apetito carnal; ... sus penas y pasiones son carnales y no espirituales, como las inmensas de admirable penetración y de intolerable pungimiento que sienten los amantes cuyo amor depende de la razón. Estos tales, por el deleite carnal no consiguen remedio para su dolor, ni se les mitiga que después de tal unión son mucho mayores y más incomportables. (*Diálogos de amor*, ed. P. Carmelo Sanz [Madrid: Atlas, 1960], 44)

> [... the love of lovers whose pain ceases with attainment of carnal delight does not depend upon reason but upon carnal appetite; ... their pain and passion is carnal and not spiritual, like those immense ones of admirable penetration and intolerable severity that lovers feel whose love depends upon reason. These latter attain no remedy for their pain from carnal delight nor is it mitigated, for after such union it is much greater and more unbearable. (my trans.)]

So first a rigid distinction between the two types of passion is established on the basis of the object of each, but then, when it is stated that the object of carnal passion can be that of spiritual passion (though without altering the essential spiritual nature of the latter), that distinction is effectively negated: negated, that is, inasmuch as carnal delight is no longer considered an object unworthy of "spiritual passion." The crux of this "ambivalent," or, better, "equivocal" representation of sexual love as both instinctive, bodily, hedonistic sensual desire and a broad, innocently inspired sexual (procreative) desire directed toward an entire personality, including that personality's physical manifestations, is the somewhat sophistic concept, also taken by Montemayor from León Hebreo, of love that is born of reason but does not allow itself to be governed by it: "aunque el perfecto amor sea hijo de razón, ... no se deja gobernar por ella" (["even though perfect love is a child of reason ..., it does not allow itself to be governed by her"]; 197). What the *Diana* posits, then, beneath its celebration of "chastity," is an affirmation of sensuous nature as not inconsistent with human spiritual pursuits and as even being a component of them. In this regard Montemayor departs from the orthodox Neoplatonic (not Platonic!) theory of a Ficino, whereby love is a desire for beauty, which is something in which "the lower senses have no part" (Kristeller, *Philosophy of Marsilio Ficino*, 265).

Chaste Love as Metaphorical Death 233

In Montemayor sadness at unfulfillment in love is not a mere result of ungratified sensuality, that is, negative in a "medieval" (rigorously Christian) sense. The "fate" of that unfulfillment does not have any implications for the ethical value of love *per se*. On the contrary, the more perfect love is, the more agonizingly passionate it becomes: "quanto más perfecto es, con tanto mayor velocidad y enagenamiento de sí mismo, va a buscar la persona amada" (["the more perfect it is, the greater the speed and abandon with which it goes in search of the beloved"]; 196). Such affliction, far from being unworthy of those who experience it, is a sign of one's refinement and lofty character: "en estos casos de amor . . . el ánimo generoso y el entendimiento delicado . . . lleva grandíssima ventaja al que no lo es" (["in these instances of love . . . the generous/noble spirit and delicate intelligence . . . has great advantage over that which is not generous/noble or delicate"]; 170). Love is a noble virtue: "como el amor sea virtud y la virtud siempre haga assiento en el mejor lugar, está claro que las personas de suerte serán muy mejor enamorados que aquéllas en quien ésta falta" (["insofar as love is virtue and virtue always settles in the best place, it is clear that persons of noble descent will be in love better than those in whom this is lacking"]; 170). Yet the nobility of the lover is not equivalent to nobility of social rank any more than shepherds are aristocrats; it is a privilege of noble character: "los que sufren más son los mejores" (["those who suffer the most are the best"]; 167).

§

It is clear that for Montemayor love, which may be conditioned by sensual desire, constitutes above all an ideal of moral value-being the usual outward sign of which is unhappiness. The *Diana* is a powerful contribution to a sophisticated erotic–sentimental literature that was much valued in the Renaissance and that advanced a "cult" or vogue of suffering in love, a fashion in taste whereby outward disharmony was a sign of inward harmony, external indignity suffered a sign of internal dignity sustained. It was a cult of chaste innocence vulnerable to disillusionment and hence of youth, since optimistic youth is most subject to disillusionment. That cult is symbolically represented in Montemayor's novel by the mythological figure of Diana, goddess of both chastity and childbirth and protectress of innocent, youthful vigor. Chaste innocence was primarily an ideal of ingenuous character, since "honestidad" (modesty, purity, chastity) was not limited to sexual purity. Nor was such ingenuousness an exclusively pagan ideal: note, for example, that in Spanish the word "santo," in addition to its religious meaning of "holy" (blessed) or "saintly," can mean "simple," or "artless," i.e., ingenuous. The wretchedness of the lover mattered insofar as he/she were unhappy and might even be destroyed physically by the sheer intensity of that unhappiness; but such suffering in the *Diana* is nevertheless a matter of such ultimate indifference that the detachment of the lover's will to love from an incapacitating lovesickness is emphasized with ostentation, the degree of which corresponds to the degree of nobility of character of the one who suffers. Sylvano sings, "Amador soy, mas nunca fuy amado" (["a lover am I, but never was I loved"]; 16). In the ethos of the *Diana*, as in Christianity, pain is pain and woe, yet (in spite of appearances to the contrary) it may be suffered happily,[21] since the love for which it is suffered is identical with goodness. In the *Diana* the agony of love–melancholy, far from bespeaking an essential deficiency, is possible only insofar as love is present in an individual in an unusual abundance and only if that love is pure and ingenuous in nature. Max Scheler has noted that, in general, realizability by or in a volitional act is not an essential condition of moral value-being. Suffering on a peripheral stratum is compatible with positive feelings at the deepest stratum; bliss and despair are independent of changes in happiness and misfortune: "for every willing that is given as good willing is accompanied by central feelings of happiness.... The feeling-*state* that follows such willing and acting does not matter to the one who acts" (*Formalism in Ethics*, 349–50).

The axiological dimension of the *Diana* is aristocratic and vitalistic. Its ethos emphasizes character-values and the importance of goodness, nobility, feelings of sympathy, and morals of love and sympathy based on feelings of sympathy as belonging to the essence of life and constituting its fullness.[22] As such, its most characteristic feature is the archetypal motif of the willing sacrifice of a common and morally insignificant personal well-being,[23] the renunciation of practical eudaemonism in an

---

[21] See Max Scheler, "The Meaning of Suffering," trans. Daniel Liderbach, in *Max Scheler (1874–1928): Centennial Essays*, ed. Manfred S. Frings (The Hague: Nijhof, 1974), 121–63, here 159, 161. In Wilde's "The Selfish Giant," when the Giant asks "who hath dared to wound thee?" the Child replies, "Nay, these are the wounds of love."

[22] See Scheler, *Formalism in Ethics*, 307, also 277–81.

[23] Nicolai Hartmann has criticized Scheler's view that well-being (or biological or vital values in general) may be classified by degree in terms of the contrast between the noble and the common. Hartmann argues that while well-being is a genuine life-value, it approaches the common more than the noble (*Ethics*, 2: 194–95). In a footnote in his *Formalism in Ethics* Scheler states that well-being does not coincide with vital values in

affirmation of the vital value of the noble, of uncommon goodness (good willing, or humanity — represented by love)[24] as an ideal of moral value-being. Insofar as such sacrifice is recognized as a *sine que non* of moral value-being ("to be or not to be"), it is indeed comparable to a "fate." But, as in the case of Christ's Passion, it is so only as regards the life of the body, for what is consciously defied by such suffering is the necessity of mechanical conformity to the order and demands, the egoism, of sensuous being.[25] From that point of view the cult of suffering in love could be seen as a conscious stylistic pose that had the value of masking and at the same time esoterically suggesting a central core of happiness, gaiety, and even bliss.[26]

It would be an error to see expressed in the *Diana* the stoic concept of "fate" as a force that degrades the lover by undermining the free action of his will. For Montemayor "fate" corresponds at most to the Boethian concept of fate as the disposition or interconnection of the particular as determined on a general basis by providence, or even to the Augustinian ideal of subordination to the truth of eternal law (love of the Good), which is also the essence of both freedom and happiness.[27] The shepherd

---

general: "the value of well-being is determined by the extent to which the individual or the community, which can be in a good or bad state, is *noble* or *base*" (106, n. 83).

[24] For Ficino's views characterizing humanity as universal love (the love of men for men), see Kristeller, *Philosophy of Marsilio Ficino*, 113 f.

[25] Hegel discusses the infinite grief and death, the negativization of sensuous and finite individuality as the condition for its conversion into universal spirituality (independent and free spiritual subjectivity) and for the absolute satisfaction of the latter: see his observations concerning "The Religious Domain of Romantic Art" (*Aesthetics*, trans. Knox, 1: 536–39, cf. 522). Scheler, who distinguishes between a vital–aristocratic ethos and a utilitarian–democratic ethos, takes issue with Nietzsche's view that all morals of love and sympathy are consequences of declining life. Scheler holds that not only is sympathy with other life-processes consistent with a conception of life as a tendency to power, but "communities become diseased or senile to the degree that egoism becomes their ruling principle" (*Formalism in Ethics*, 307, cf. 278–79).

[26] For a development of this view in relation to the courtly love tradition, see chapter 8 above.

[27] For Boethius's clarification of the relationship between providence and fate, see *The Consolation of Philosophy*, Book 4, prose 6; for Augustine's views on true freedom see Mary T. Clark, *Augustine, Philosopher of Freedom* (New York: Desclée, 1958), 55, 57, 128–29, 178; also Maryanne Djuth, "Liberty" and "Will," in *Augustine Through the Ages*, ed. A. D. Fitzgerald (Grand Rapids, MI: Eerdmans, 1999), 495–98, 881–85; and on Boethius's synthesis of the stoic and the Christian concepts of fate see Edmund Reiss, *Boethius*

Filemón says, "quando yo nací y aun ante mucho que naciesse, los hados me destinaron para que amasse a esta hermosa pastora . . . y a esta causa, e respondido con el efecto de tal manera que no creo que ay amor como el mío . . ." (["When I was born and even long before I was born, fate destined me to love that beautiful shepherdess, and to this cause I have responded with such effect that I believe there is no love like mine"]; 261). For the morally (and hence artistically) initiated readers of the day, the manneristic, Arcadian wilderness of the *Diana* — a wilderness because the lovelorn can have no eye for nature (a point missed by Menéndez Pelayo) — was seen to be in reality a sumptuous garden of rich and tenacious vitality. The unabashed, turbulent sensuality of such innocence (innocence attested to in a simultaneous sacrifice of personal happiness)[28] is completely compatible with such a spiritually Edenic, metaphorical setting, for although the frustration of desire is agonizing on one level, it is exhilarating and intoxicating on another. Alexander Bain, in *The Emotions and the Will*, writes: "The excitement at its highest pitch, in the torrent of youthful sensations and ungratified desire, is probably the most furious and elated experience of human nature."[29] The wretched state of the lovers in the *Diana* is "wretchedness" only on a peripheral stratum; beneath it lies a central joy and vitality. The *Diana* is considered to be the first genuinely modern pastoral romance. In that regard it is a prototype of the modern novel of unrequited love. Understanding its paradoxes can help explain why the passion and beauty of feeling of such characters as Werther and Emma Bovary, however morbid it may appear, suggests anything but a vital decadence.

The *Diana* can be seen to reflect secularizing humanism's shift away from theocentric religious morality toward a morality that, while it is markedly idealistic and non-utilitarian, is, at the same time, boldly anthropocentric. By presenting in secular terms the Christian–evangelical idea that the act of love, having a value that is independent of its object, is the highest good, and by celebrating (esoterically, as pseudo-

---

(Boston: Twayne, 1982), 122–23. Boethius's *Consolation* was widely read in the vernacular in Europe (including Spain) by the sixteenth century (Bolgar, *Classical Heritage*, 328 and 526–27), and the late fifteenth and first half of the sixteenth centuries saw five editions of Alonso de Cartagena's translations of Seneca containing a long commentary in which de Cartagena, basing himself on the authority of Boethius and St. Augustine, discusses Christian views on fate: K. A. Blüher, *Seneca en España* (Madrid: Gredos, 1983), 138–39, 597.

[28] Lawrence Durrell: "Real innocence can do nothing that is trivial: and when it is allied to generosity of heart, the combination is the most vulnerable of qualities under heaven."

[29] Alexander Bain, *The Emotions and the Will* (New York: Appleton, 1976), 138.

erotic suffering) the vital and hence autonomous[30] value of such love, Montemayor's novel implicitly postulates the modern concept that the human individual alone is the autonomous bearer himself of the moral good. In that way (among others) the *Diana* can be seen to represent an individualistic reaction against what used to be seen as rigid ecclesiastical culture's official "prototypal form of the conception of life as dominated by authority,"[31] and even against Christian heteronomy in general, whereby the object of ethics, the moral good, is seen to be outside of man, in God.[32] Recognizing this principle makes it possible to appreciate the general, culturally renovating impact of modern literature, the "modernizing" influence of its emphasis on the human individual as an object of artistic and hence intrinsic interest, i.e., as an object the embodied meaning of which may be contemplated and enjoyed for its own sake and not for its practical, cognitive, or existential implications.[33] In the long passage in Book Five of the *Diana* roughly paralleling a passage from León Hebreo's *Diálogos de amor*, Felicia at one point insists that love born of reason is disinterested and has no object other than loving the person for him/herself: "no tira a otro fin sino a querer la persona por ella misma, sin esperar otro interesse ni galardón de sus amores": (["the goal toward which it draws one is none other than loving the person for him/herself, without expecting any other interest or reward from one's love"]; 198). The closest parallel to that passage in the León Hebreo text is in Sophia's objection that the sufferings of lovers are caused more by a desire for the thing not possessed than by "true love for it": "más ayna proceden del desseo de la cosa no avida, que del propio amor della" (["they proceed more speedily from desire for a thing not possessed than from true love for it"]; *Diálogos de amor*, ed. Sanz, 44). If one were to discount Hebreo as Montemayor's source for the concept of loving a person "for him/herself," another more likely possibility not considered by critics is Aristotle. In his treatise on friendship in

---

[30] Scheler discusses "the peculiarity and autonomy of vital feelings" in *Formalism in Ethics*, 339–40.

[31] Ernst Troeltsch, *Protestantism and Progress* (1912), trans. W. Montgomery (Boston: Beacon, 1966), 150, 153. Also see E. Walser, "Les publications de la Bibliothèque Warburg," *Revue de Litterature Comparée* 7 (1927): 352–58, here 356–57 for a synopsis of a study by A. Doren that views the cultivation in the Renaissance of an interest in the goddess Fortuna as an expression of rebellion against divine authority (very dated). Recently see Brumble, *Classical Myths and Legends*, 123–26, s.v. "fortune."

[32] Manfred S. Frings, Introduction to Scheler, *Person and Self-Value*, xiv.

[33] For such a definition of aesthetic contemplation see L. A. Reid, *A Study in Aesthetics* (New York: Macmillan, 1954), 43.

the *Nicomachean Ethics*, he distinguishes between "incomplete friendships" for utility and pleasure and the "complete friendships" of good people: "only good people can be friends to each other because of the other person himself; for bad people find no enjoyment in one another if they get no benefit" (1157a 18–20; trans. Irwin, 215).

It will be asked how an idealized regard for the human individual as an object having purely autonomous, intrinsic value can be considered inconsistent with what we have referred to as "Christian heteronomy" in the sense of a conception recognizing the object of ethics as being outside of the individual. For does not the Christian love his neighbor with a charitable, disinterested love? The issue of whether or not Christian morality is ultimately disinterested is more complicated that it may seem, partly because there are different types of Christianity, that is, more than one fundamental Christian ideal of moral culture. One would ultimately have to maintain that where disinterestedness itself (free forgiveness of sins, freely-given grace) is the ideal revered, Christianity is truly disinterested. Such a spirituality is affirmed by Montemayor in those portions of his religious poetry that celebrate omnipotent grace and deprecate the merit of works.[34] Yet the question may remain as to whether or not there is a self-seeking element in such an apparently disinterested cultivation of virtue, some longing for personal happiness through salvation. Hartmann skeptically views Christianity as a form of other-worldly eudaemonism that "simply lacks the individualistic and egoistic note":

> Eudaemonism is reflected most clearly in Christian asceticism, anchoritism and martyrdom. To lay up treasure for oneself in heaven is for the Christian in fact the supreme concern, and is not by any means a mere figure of speech. Even St. Paul's justification by faith, which opposes all salvation by works and every human merit, does not change the matter. Whether it be due to grace or merit, the same glory of the Beyond is the thing yearned for. (*Ethics*, 1: 136)

Max Scheler believes that eudaemonism is a reaction against an essential pessimism and that Christianity's optimistic view of life renders it incompatible with eudaemonism. He considers the philosophy of stoicism, and the outlook of the ancients in general, to be fundamentally eudaemonistic (*Person and Self-Value*, 162). However, just as the

---

[34] See Creel, *The Religious Poetry of Jorge de Montemayor*, 113–19.

"true freedom" that the stoic sought through impassivity can be considered a form of happiness, the element of pessimism in Judeo-Christian thought can be considered an essential characteristic of Christianity, even if that element is more characteristic of ecclesiastical than of evangelical Christianity. In any case, in the *Diana* Montemayor posits an ideal of the lover who is unhappy yet gladly accepts his unhappiness insofar as that unhappiness is a consequence of truly loving. Such an ideal is not eudaemonistic nor optimistically Christian, and stoic serenity is a matter of indifference to it. It rejects any object beyond the nature of its own value-being and therefore represents a departure from ecclesiastical Christianity's tendency to assign virtue a motive, that of the desire to escape the unhappiness of imprisonment in fallen nature. Of course, in other ways, even beyond the obvious emphasis on disinterested, freely-given love, the *Diana* is profoundly Christian, perhaps primarily in the passionate tone of the work. "The Christian is not a stoic. The passions of the soul are for him not despicable. For him the highest values are objects of the highest passion ..." (Hartmann, *Ethics*, 1: 137).

§

It is known that the *Diana* was a work highly appreciated by women of its day. One need not seek far to discover the basis for that acceptance. The *Diana* extols feminine virtues and the ideals of feminine beauty to a degree that borders on the strenuous. It is appropriate to such a work that the center of gravity in the plot and the setting for its moment of epiphany is the Temple of Diana, where the reader finds apotheosized, enshrined in a sort of pantheon and processionally eulogized, in the "Canto de Orpheo," a long series of remarkable women of the day.[35] Unsatiated romantic and feminine love-idealism is a characteristic feature of the *Diana* as it is of Renaissance high culture generally. The Provençal aristocracy's enthusiastic celebration of feminine beauty and the love of women had ended abruptly in the thirteenth century with the crusade against the Albigensians, but European court culture during the three centuries to follow saw a revival of the markedly feminine character of courtly romanticism. The renewed appreciation of women and devotion to them has been seen as typical of Renaissance culture.[36] To some extent that development may be seen as paralleling the

---

[35] Narciso Alonso Cortés presents exhaustive identification and genealogical information on these women: "Sobre Montemayor y 'La Diana'," in idem, *Artículos históricos-literarios* (Valladolid: Imprenta Castellana, 1935), 127–40.

[36] See Jean Delumeau, *La Civilization de la Renaissance* (Paris: Artaud, 1967), 438–

emergence of a Christian-humanist, irenic[37] opposition to the patriarchal tyranny of the old, violent heroism and to the ethic of savage honor as it was reinforced by monarchic authoritarianism[38] and the emergence of national wars. In his religious poetry Montemayor can be seen to expound an anti-authoritarian, anti-bellicose, irenic theology of modest piety in the Erasmian tradition.[39] Thus, in the *Diana*, which celebrates the feminine virtue of a tender, solicitous humanity in male and female characters alike, the association of the central motif with Orpheus is not without reason. It was Orpheus who, as he sang his grief for Eurydice, caused the Furies to weep: touching the heart of Persephone, his song, in Milton's words, "Drew Iron tears down Pluto's cheek, / And made Hell grant what Love did seek" (*Il Penseroso*, 107–8). The irenicism of the Christian humanists was different from modern pacifism in two ways: first, it was not a categorical opposition to bearing arms under any circumstances but rather permitted their use in situations of inevitable necessity (think, for example, of the killing of the three armed wild men by the fully armed shepherdess Felismena and of the latter's rescue of the wounded knight Don Felis from his attackers). Second, instead of assuming the form of a negative precept, it is an affirmation of peace and of the social temper that operates towards it.

To appreciate fully the irenic character of the *Diana*, one need only contrast the lovelorn shepherd to the heroes of the romances of chivalry and to those heroes' capacity for violence. The only character in the *Diana* to display a capacity for physical force is Felismena, whose martial prowess was visited upon her as a result of a curse. An effective warrior, if he is of heroic character, will necessarily have what would at best be a capacity for a beautiful and legitimate indignation, however restrained that capacity may appear. Yet indignation, the basis of revenge (which, according to Menéndez Pidal, is the central theme of epic),[40] is an ingredient that is conspicuously and

---

39; for more recent views see Joan Kelley, "Did Women Have a Renaissance?" in eadem, *Women, History, and Theory* (Chicago: University of Chicago Press, 1984), 12–50; Margaret L. King and Sarah Covington, "Women," in *Encyclopedia of the Renaissance* 6: 317–28.

[37] See Bataillon, *Erasmo y España*, 88, 401, 409, 494–95.

[38] See A. W. O. von Martin, *Sociology of the Renaissance* (New York: Harper & Row, 1983) 65; Maravall, *Poder, honor y élites en el siglo xvii* (Madrid: Siglo XXI, 1979), 85; and Creel, *Don Quijote, Symbol of a Culture in Crisis*, 2–24.

[39] See Creel, *The Religious Poetry of Jorge de Montemayor*, 188–94.

[40] Ramón Menéndez Pidal, *De Cervantes y Lope de Vega* (Buenos Aires: Espasa-Calpe, 1948), 11–12.

peculiarly absent in any form in the *Diana*, even in the tale of Abindarráez and Jarifa. In his commentary on Plato's *Symposium*, Ficino writes, "He who loves another, but is not loved by another, lives nowhere. Therefore the unloved lover is completely dead. Nor will he ever revive unless indignation should revive him" (trans. Jayne, 55). Indignation is precisely the quality for which the solitary, wandering characters of the framing narrative of the *Diana* have no capacity. In their stubborn idealism they are incapable of indignation and therefore must love irrevocably. In this regard, it is interesting that in *Don Quijote*, which is a parody of the chivalric romance (of the romance epic), and, in part, a satire of militarism, one of the salient ridiculous traits of the protagonist is his tendency to become gratuitously indignant.[41] When at the end of the novel he regains his "sanity," he renounces being a warrior and wants to become a shepherd. In order for the shepherds of the *Diana* to be cured of their ideal devotion — of their concentration on a single individual to a degree of contraction that results in virtual suffocation[42] — the process must be accomplished by means in which a natural indignation plays no part, for that emotion would violate the ethos affirmed by the work. But categorically to negate or neutralize particular love passions that are supposed to be distinguished by being "immutable" would also be inconsistent with that ethos. Hence the impasse, the emotional parenthesis, of Sireno's condition at the end of the work. The Priestess Felicia's "agua mágica" has a salutary effect where desire is redirected, as in the case of Selvagia and Sylvano. Yet for Sireno its effects remind one more of the ambivalent, numbing effects of a frontal lobotomy. Diana tells him, "Estraña libertad es la tuya" (["yours is a strange freedom"]; 274). At the end of the *Diana*, Sireno wanders unfulfilled and puppet-like in the false paradise, the "feigned Arcadia" (to use Cervantes's and Tirso's term)[43] of the novel. It is logical that in a work celebrating love passion, a resolution based on suspension of that same passion should lead to an ending in a minor key.

If one were to consider the traditionalistic curialist conception of life as conformity to a finite, temporal order (the worldly authority of the Church) as reflecting, to some degree, a principle of empirical monism, the *Diana* can be seen to be offering an

---

[41] See Creel, *Don Quijote, Symbol of a Culture in Crisis*, chapt. 2.

[42] Bain (*The Emotions and the Will*,137) refers to "the contracted mode of feeling" as being the favorite of Romance.

[43] See Creel, *Don Quijote, Symbol of a Culture in Crisis*, 62–69 on the episode in *Don Quijote* (in 2. 48) of the "Fingida Arcadia" (feigned Arcadia) and its broader thematic implications. Tirso de Molina for his part wrote a play entitled *La fingida Arcadia*.

alternative to that conception in its ethic of Neoplatonic dualism.[44] In the former case ideals themselves have no reality and moral activity is only another form of self-interested activity. In contrast, the idealistic ethos of Neoplatonism posits the reality of ideals of morality and the attainment of inner harmony through freeing the self from everything external and transitory and achieving purification of the mind. Love in the *Diana* recognizes no authority but its own ideality; it is a "law unto itself," independent even of the attainability of its object. It is its own object. That feature alone would be enough to make the *Diana* depart radically from the teleological character both of a piety of religious observances and of the warrior ethos of the heroic quest. The "irenic" temper of the *Diana* can thus be seen in more than just the tenacious solicitude and disinterested good willing of its characters; it is in the "chastity" of an ultimate detachment from finite reality in general, including mechanical stimuli to the senses. The pristine, super-sensuous innocence and the languishing ingenuousness of the *Diana* are fundamentally contrary to the sensationalism of war and the sado-masochistic voluptuousness of war's violence and aggression. For that reason the *Diana* is (as Menéndez Pelayo noted) contrary to a literature of martial violence.

There is another way, one related to the foregoing and that I briefly mentioned earlier, in which the figure of the lovesick shepherd can be seen to suggest a reaction against rigid authority and the aggressive will to power and to be contributing to Christian humanism's tendency to effect a secularization of piety. It is in the way that the *Diana*'s ideal of an ecstasy of chaste (not categorical) denial of the self, in the broad sense of subordinating the temporal, sensuous aspect of one's being, offers a positive alternative to rigid patriarchal feudalism's religious counterpart, negative asceticism. Perhaps it is not too much to speculate that the irenic spirit and the exaltation of feminine beauty in the *Diana* were indirectly related to the disrepute in which church monasticism found itself in the sixteenth century, an era that Erasmus in *The Complaint of Peace* characterized as one in which miters and helmets agreed and joined together to carry out "Bellona's business."[45] As diametrically opposed as Christian asceticism and the love of war seem to be on the surface (and as Lucka maintains they

---

[44] For discussion of the opposition between dualism and monism, see Emile Durkheim "The Dualism of Human Nature and its Social Conditions," in *Emile Durkheim on Morality and Society*, ed. R. N. Bellah (Chicago: University of Chicago Press, 1973), 149–63.

[45] Erasmus, *Querela Pacis*, ed. O. Herding, in *Opera Omnia Desiderii Erasmi Roterodami* 4.2 (Amsterdam: North-Hollabd, 1977), 83: "Bellonae rem agunt."

are),⁴⁶ they can both become manifestations of (in Freudian terms) the aggressive instinct. In military action (if it is not purely defensive in character) the aggressive instinct is turned sadistically outward. Similarly, when ascetic purification goes beyond being the acceptance of peripheral pain and suffering out of love of one's spiritual self and in the interest of concentrating one's spiritual vision on the central (spiritual) goods of life, and instead assumes the form of emulating an ideal of voluntary self-affliction of pain and suffering out of a "moral" hatred and contempt of the body,⁴⁷ the same aggressive instinct asserts itself, but here it is turned masochistically inward. At the time when the *Diana* was written, such negative asceticism, based on military obedience and on the accentuation and discipline of the passions (as opposed to the Erasmian ideal of an inner freedom achieved through their negation), had been revived by Ignatius Loyola and the young Jesuit order.⁴⁸ That Montemayor, as an exponent of the Catholic-reformist brand of piety, was particularly sensitive to the oppressively deprecatory spirit of penitential monastic asceticism based on servile fear and sought to propagate a spirituality that was an alternative to it is evidenced in his religious poetry (Creel, *Religious Poetry of Jorge de Montemayor*, 212–29). In his religious poetry, Montemayor can also be seen implicitly to reject the doctrine of Original Sin by equating original sin with personal sin (Creel, *Religious Poetry of Jorge de Montemayor*, 166–72, 232). I have argued that the *Diana* opposes an oppressive asceticism by affirming the fundamental aspect of man's nature as a sensuous being: in the *Diana* the individual is conceived of as being uncorrupted by original sin. An elaborate prose love poem, the *Diana* celebrates individual human beauty; it has none of "the fundamental desire of depreciating the individual" that asceticism rests upon (Ribot, *Psychology of the Emotions*, 325). I have further maintained that in the *Diana* love-melancholy is not an essential or true melancholy but is the outward designation of a central bliss and vitality that are themselves a result of an essential goodness (good willing), a disposition to love. Freud explains "true" love-melancholy as a form of sadomasochistic revenge upon the lost loved one, as hatred of the object turned round upon the self. He considers sadomasochism to be generally tied to the action of the

---

⁴⁶ Emil Lucka, *The Evolution of Love*, trans. Ellie Schleussner (London: George Allen & Unwin, 1922), 40.
⁴⁷ Scheler, *Ressentiment*, 103, and idem, "The Meaning of Suffering," 161–62.
⁴⁸ Bataillon, *Erasmo y España*, 44–48, 589–91, and his introduction to Erasmus's *Enquiridion*, ed. Dámaso Alonso (Madrid: Revista de Filología Española, 1971), 7–84, here 76–78, where he contrasts the Ignatian and Erasmian spirituality and concepts of piety.

sexual instinct. In Freud's view, the sexual instinct (libido) has the task of making the aggressive (death or destruction) instinct harmless to the individual by turning it towards the objects of the outer world and causing it to assume the form of the instinct of destruction, of mastery, the will to power. In the sexual function the aggressive instinct assumes the form of "true sadism," i.e., the exercise of power or violence upon some other person. Of course, the instinct of sexual love, Eros, is not identical with sadism. In any case, when part of the instinct of destruction or mastery is not displaced outwards but rather is turned round upon the subject, it becomes masochism, or sadism towards the self. In the state of love–melancholy, the attachment of the aggressive instinct to the sexual instinct, and its displacement outwards, is repressed. Hence, in his anger, the lover takes revenge upon the lost loved one "by the circuitous path of self-punishment."[49]

If my analysis of the *Diana* is valid, love–melancholy there is distinguished precisely by the paradoxical tenacity with which the frustrated libido's strivings are proud of remaining positive, healthily erotic, and essentially alien to angry indignation, which does not assume even a repressed form.[50] It is "melancholy" that is represented as being devoid of aggressive, sadomasochistic self-punishment, and it is in this quality that Montemayor's tearful exaltation of vigorous innocence offered its sixteenth-century readers a positive, secular, and lay "asceticism" that was an alternative to an official, ecclesiastical monastic ideal (decried by Christian humanists in the Erasmian slogan *Monachatus non est pietas*)[51] founded upon repression of the sexual instinct and on hatred and contempt for the body. Of course, I do not wish to suggest that all of ecclesiastical asceticism is of the rigid, repressive variety.[52] The best tradition of such asceticism strives for the inhibition of that part of the libido devoted to externalizing aggression so that the entire quantity of the libido may be preserved for the encour-

---

[49] Freud, *Collected Papers*, 2: 260; 5: 230, 347; 4: 162.

[50] Consistent with this perspective is the observation by M. Gillette: "The notion [on the part of the shepherds and shepherdesses in the *Diana*] that their suffering ennobles them as lovers sustains them in their melancholy. . . ." in idem, "Foolish Fancies? Maybe Not. Symptoms of Melancholy in *La Diana*," *Romance Notes* 39 (1998): 95–102, here 101.

[51] See Marcel Bataillon, Introd. to Erasmus, *Enquiridion o manual del caballero cristiano*, ed. Dámaso Alonso (Madrid: Revista de Filología Española, 1971), 36–37.

[52] Eloquent observations concerning ecclesiastical monasticism seen in a favorable light, as "grand moral" and "monasticism of the great style," were made as early as in Oswald Spengler's *Decline of the West* (1922), trans. C. F. Atkinson, 2 vols. (New York: Knopf, 1926–1928), 2: 272–74, 335–39.

agement of positive emotional ties via the "erotic," or life-affirming, instinct (in this case, devotion to a personal God). Yet that inhibition, or discipline, can be too strict (a rigor too easily confused with piety), causing the repression of Eros, or sexual love (which could otherwise be healthily sublimated as personal love, i.e., as fulfillment of one's ideal self through devotion to another),[53] and forcing sexual instinct, cut off from an object, to flourish the only way it can, by turning inward upon the self as masochism. The *Diana* counters a negative principle with a positive one. Negative asceticism's concept of self-denial out of penance for man's fallen state regards the love of the sexes, insofar as it is derived from sensual desire, as being sinful and identifies piety with the restraint of that desire if not its suppression. In contrast, the Neoplatonic ideal of "chaste" innocence, asserting the super-sensuous moral autonomy of human beings, is based on an erotic life-affirmation that is also complemented by the Christian notion of resurrection of the flesh, by the Catholic doctrine of consecration of the material (transubstantiation), and by Christian spirituality's conception of the inner harmony of the faithful (paralleled in the *Diana* in the figure of the devoted lover).

Instead of conceiving human beings negatively, as uncorrupted, such an ideal offers a positive conception, that of human innocence, thus asserting both the legitimate place of human beings in the world of nature and their dignity as spiritual beings governed by reason (soul). Regarded in this way, human beings are possessed of an autonomous independence from both non-spiritual and non-sensuous being. Rigid ecclesiastical morality's ethic of doctrinaire piety and religious observance is thereby rivaled by a secular, individualistic ethic of moral freedom that is actually closer to the liberal spirit of medieval urban democracy (an element of the continuity of medieval culture in the Renaissance) than to the austere and hieratic tenor of life under the new, theocratic monarchies, the rigidity of the latter ("refeudalization") being a conservative–"medievalistic" response to the threat of a new individualism.[54] Whereas rigorously ascetic traditionalism attempted to make a negative feeling-state (the human fall from grace) the source of positive values,[55] the new, Renaissance temperament is derived from a positive feeling-state (affirmation of natural human goodness). Whereas the former is based on objective command, conformity of the mechanically-ordered

---

[53] Hartmann (*Ethics*, 2: 370–75) uses such concepts to characterize personal love.

[54] See Maravall, *Poder, honor y élites*, 5.

[55] In Scheler's *Formalism in Ethics* see the section introduced with the heading "All Volitional Directions toward the Realization of Positive and Comparatively Higher Values Originally Arise from Positive Feeling-States as Sources" (348–53).

parts to the whole, social pressure, duty, and order, the latter is based on human love, voluntary action, personal values, on accommodating the independence of freely-inspired, organically-ordered parts, with their extravagance of individual aspirations, on good willing (the only real source of positive values), and on an ideal of realizing the fullness of positive value-feeling.[56] The *Diana*, then, though it signals a preference for greater leniency in the cultural sphere, would seem to be less a symptom of a new leniency in the socio–political sphere than a reaction against a new rigidity.[57] Just as the positive striving of romantic love (absolute preference for one person and no other) became, in the Renaissance, the primary means by which literature postulated a new ethos idealizing the self-dependent autonomy of the individual, the despondency of love–melancholy (persisting in love despite a failure to realize love's ends) acquired the value not of an unfortunate fate but rather of a misfortune that does its bearer honor: the lover's tenacious solicitude was regarded as an elegant triumph over a tyrannical contempt for sentimental culture as represented in the callous indifference of the beloved. Subjection to a cruel, alien will was well known to a society emerging from the age of feudalism, and elegiac love literature provided an opportunity to condemn such cruelty energetically on the pretext of a purely personal aim, that of overcoming the resistance of a disdainful lover. As that literature became fashionable and its humanizing influence grew stronger, love–melancholy came to be regarded, paradoxically, as the force of a new freedom: the greater the agony, the greater the force with which one was considered to be inspired.

But still, it may be asked, are not the lovers in the *Diana* imprisoned in love? Are they not the very image of a bitter unfreedom, "medievally" and allegorically represented as a "fallen" worldliness? In the *Diana* love is repeatedly referred to as a state that is not only alien to freedom but that brings with it the loss of freedom. How, then,

---

[56] See Durkheim on mechanical vs. organic solidarity: *The Division of Labor and Society* (1899), trans. W. D. Halls (New York: Free Press, 1984), 60–61, 83–85; Henri Bergson on the distinction between the "closed" and the "open" types of society: *The Two Sources of Morality and Religion* (1932), trans. R. A. Audra and C. Brereton (Garden City, NY: Doubleday, 1956), 266–68; and Werner Sombart concerning "A fundamental deviation between two types in modern society" in *Quintessence of Capitalism*, trans. M. Epstein (London: Unwin, 1915), 1: 205–9.

[57] The view that the emergence of High Renaissance culture in the Atlantic powers coincided with an erosion of individual freedom is posited in broad terms, in relation to the belated vogue for Italian Renaissance culture in those nations, by Jorge de Sena, *Estudos da literatura portuguesa* (Lisbon: Edições 70, 1981), 1: 61–63.

can love–melancholy in the *Diana* be characterized as the force of a new freedom? The same contradiction seems to exist in Ficino's observation, "What is more voluntary than love? It is the first, highest, perpetual disposition of will and so operates that we cannot desire not to love" (Kristeller, *Philosophy of Marsilio Ficino*, 270). How, one may wonder, can the absence of willpower be seen as a disposition of the will?

In loving, the lover freely sacrifices his or her freedom as the ultimate free act. The lover "freely" sacrifices it in the sense of doing so intentionally, in an act that is not subject to external rule or control. The "freedom" thus sacrificed is exercise of the power of choice, i.e., exercise of will directed by intellect. One can voluntarily surrender one's judgment (of another or of the practical implications of one's own actions) and hence one's will, and doing so can constitute a free act, an act of willing. Hence the meaning of Ficino's words quoted above. Love prevents the true lover from wanting to resist its power, so that loss of "freedom" becomes forfeiture of the absolute spiritual independence by which the individual's practical "reason" (as distinguished from Pascal's *raisons du coeur*) secures individual well-being. Relinquishing that source of a form of self-dependent autonomy will cause the commonplace, undignified suffering of powerlessness,[58] the type of suffering that critics have so readily identified as pervading the world of the *Diana*. Yet that loss is accepted for the sake of a higher value, i.e., the value of growth stimulated by love's vision of the ideal and by the increment of vitality that the ideal inspires.[59] Thus the lover accepts pain and suffering (consequences of the exemplary degree of differentiation of his value-feeling and hence capacity for perceiving the fullness of differences through which individual value-qualities are feelable)[60] in order to exercise a new, different form of self-dependent autonomy, that which accompanies an increase in vigor and vital value-being in the actual core of the person and an increase in life itself. The growth thus achieved brings with it more suffering, yet pain that is not only not a negative value but is noble insofar as pain is an inevitable accompaniment of life's progress (both of the life of the individual and of life in general).

Beneath the surface, the seemingly wretched characters of the *Diana* are not only blissful and love truly, as only the blissful can love, but they enjoy a new, higher freedom of subjectivity in that their willfulness is unrestricted by a dependence upon any-

---

[58] See Scheler, "The Meaning of Suffering," 131.
[59] See Scheler, "The Meaning of Suffering," 134.
[60] Scheler, *Formalism in Ethics*, 306.

thing external. Although it is true that the lovers in the *Diana* are absolutely determined, they are absolutely determined by themselves and from within. They are initially inspired, or inflamed, by the beauty (ideality) of a loved one, but just as their love takes on a life of its own that is independent of the presence, reciprocation, or attainability of its object, the pain resulting from the unfulfillment of that love is itself determined not by the object but by the state of the subject. Bembo expresses this latter concept with the words "non è altro l'amaro dell'animo, che il fele delle passioni che l'avelenano" (*Prose e rime*, ed. C. Dionisotti, 351) (["bitterness of the mind is only that venom with which the feelings poison it"]; trans. R. B. Gottfried, *Gli Asolini*, 43). It is the "unredeemed," lovelorn state of the shepherds in the *Diana* that gives them their distinctive significance. The solitary, lovesick, but rhapsodically devoted shepherd exactly and graphically personifies the new, morally autonomous human being: Montemayor's shepherd is the image of "modern man" from a non-worldly, secular, Renaissance point of view.

The frustration of lovers in the *Diana* thus assumes a peculiar character: as heroic passion, it is conceived of as a sublime force that cannot be explained by the limiting character of external circumstances but rather is self-determining and is able to endure eternally. That same frustration is the mark of an élite of personal culture (a principle of "noblesse oblige" in the sense of "obliges to love") whose bearers are proudly martyred to passions that cannot be deferred by any obstacle. For the members of that élite of sufferers in love, the finitude of externality (love's not being answered by love on the part of the other) does not constitute an insuperable barrier but rather is the point of departure for an internal dissatisfaction, a straining from within and an anguish to which the lover gratefully yields, relinquishing every trace of commonplace well-being, of consolation in anything external. The lovers in the *Diana*, merry lords of their own noble plight, wander free and dejected in a disconsolate stubbornness, exhibited as a sort of private "*Weltschmerz.*" I am speaking, of course, of the innocent, Renaissance prototype of the problematic (morally-ambiguous) aesthetic of "surrender to impulse"[61] that nineteenth-century Romanticism advanced in relation to the tenet of man's natural goodness.

Because love's fixation on a particular individual came to assume the character of an absolute ethical value, it was not possible for that value to be determinable by any

---

[61] This concept is used to characterize "Romantic doctrine" by Winters, *In Defense of Reason*, 8.

contingency of the natural world, be it by a chance circumstance, such as the beloved's presence or absence, or even by whether or not love was reciprocated. The largely haphazard and possibly even frivolous character of "love bonds" and the degree to which they are trivialized by being determined by chance encounter, far from rendering sexual love unsuitable as a subject for this new literature advancing personality and its demands as non-contingent ideals, actually served to enhance to a greater degree romantic style's most distinctive feature, the paradox of "absolute contingency," i.e., the raising of the "purely" individual (humanly typical, as opposed to essentially idiosyncratic, ends and actions of highly individualized personality)[62] to the level of a supreme value.[63] Thus the supernatural character of Felicia's magic philtre (the only possible means in the *Diana* of restoring a lover's emotions to their normal tranquility) serves to emphasize the degree to which that which is individual, personal, and even private — and can seem to be even idiosyncratic and ultimately contingent — has been poetically rendered as a value that is non-contingent and absolute.[64] That Renaissance culture is characterized by a triumph of individualism is widely recognized.

§

As innovative as Renaissance culture was, it would be misleading to suggest that the ideals of moral culture advanced by the *Diana* represent a sudden departure from the past, including what I have referred to as Montemayor's secular "Nicodemist" strategy as a humanistic cultural renovator. The unbounded subjectivism of the *Diana*'s characters can also be seen in the religious individualism that was an aspect of mysticism (mainly Franciscan) and of late-medieval lay religion (e.g., the *Devotio moderna*), yet the *Diana* had its secular antecedents as well: consider the elegiac love lyric in the tradition of Petrarch (e.g., Garcilaso) and Ausias March (whom Montemayor

---

[62] For observations concerning the distinction between typical vs. eccentric individual passion see Georg Lukács, *Realism in Out Time*, trans. J. and N. Maude (New York: Harper & Row, 1964), 30–31.

[63] I have freely adapted Hegel's concept of "supreme contingency" and given it a broader meaning. See Hegel, *Aesthetics*, 1: 568.

[64] Instead of attempting to interpret the significance of Felicia's "agua mágica," critics often cite the distaste expressed for that motif by the Priest in *Don Quijote* (1. 6). That character's attitude, however, is consistent with the likelihood that he, as a priest, would not be sympathetic with pagan magic. For that reason, to identify his views with those of Cervantes, as many critics have done, may certainly entail a fallacy.

translated), or the sentimental romance in the tradition of Boccaccio and Diego de San Pedro. Although such literature must have seemed innocent enough in its way to many of Montemayor's contemporaries (and still does in our own day), it was not without its "heretical" implications. For centuries it had been taught that Original Sin confronted human beings impersonally as an invincible fate imposed from without. Yet Renaissance man conceived his fate as a circumstance that could arise from within, as a result of the contemplation of innocent human beauty, and in that way he stood in fundamental opposition to the premise of Original Sin. Also, literature in the courtly-love tradition was fond of representing life without union with the beloved as a living hell, a metaphorical death. Insofar as such love contained an element of sexual desire and the lovers were not officially married (as they never were), it is implied that sin and "salvation" (which can be considered to be analogously represented as attainment of the loved object) are not incompatible. It was Luther, of course, who expressed that view explicitly, in his skeptical view of conventional piety and his teaching of the power of faith to justify. Such faith had its secular counterpart in the lover's tireless devotion in works such as the *Diana*. Luther also had transcended the view of the sinfulness of the physical impulses — particularly the idea that sexual pleasure is the original sin. That same attitude is undeniably implied in the *Diana*, as is the Lutheran view that the union of the sexes in spiritual marriage is the school of the highest morality.[65]

It would appear that the "unliberal" elements of the counterreformist clergy fulminated against the *Diana*. In Portugal the novel was completely prohibited by the Inquisitorial Index of 1581 and continued to be proscribed until 1624. In Spain the *Diana* was never censured, possibly because it had contributed so greatly to Spain's national glory throughout Europe. But that it had its enemies is indicated by the following words from a letter written by Fernando de León, a Jesuit on the Inquisition's district tribunal in Valladolid, to the Consejo Supremo in Madrid: "Ultimamente desearía que por servicio de Nuestro Señor se pronunciase acerca de la *Diana* de Montemayor que por el dulce estilo se entiende sea uno de los más perniciosos libros para la juventud de cuantos se leen"[66] ["Finally, I would request that out of service to

---

[65] See A. von Harnack, *History of Dogma*, trans., N. Buchanan, 7 vols. (New York: Russel, 1958), 7: 194, 200–1; William H. Lazareth, "ELCA Lutherans and Luther on Heterosexual Marriage," *Lutheran Quarterly* 3 (1984): 235–68, esp. 265: ". . . Luther extolled marriage as the Christian's highest social calling."

[66] Archivo Histórico Nacional, Madrid, Legajo 4435, no. 5. For a lively discussion of

Our Lord a pronouncement be made on the *Diana* of Montemayor, which by its sweet style can be inferred to be one of the most pernicious books for youth of all those that are being read"].

If such an attitude was typical of the view of the *Diana* held by members of the clergy, it can suggest to us the basis of some of the irony in the witty passage towards the end of *Don Quijote* where Don Quijote proposes that he, Sancho, and their friends change their names and become shepherds (2.67): the priest, he suggests, could change his name from "*cura*" (priest) to "Curiambro." Yet, as so often occurs with Cervantes, this irony has an additional twist. In contrast to the severe and intolerant attitude of the *eclesiástico* (in the home of the Duke and Duchess), who would undoubtedly have considered the *Diana* to be idle nonsense, the priest who is Alonso Quijano's friend speaks highly of the *Diana*. Cervantes's avoidance of stereotypes and drab conventionalism in any form makes him a worthy successor of the author of *Los siete libros de la Diana*.

---

additional reasons for dim views having been taken of the *Diana* in the sixteenth century by conservative "guardians of morality" — its challenge to the male and female stereotypes of the period — see Rhodes, "Skirting the Men: Gender Roles in Sixteenth-Century Pastoral Books," *Journal of Hispanic Philology* 11 (1987 [1988]): 131–49.

10

Finite Reality's Rebirth as Poetic Imagery: Theoretical Implications in Don Quijote's Idea of Enchantment

After defeating the Knight of Mirrors, the Bachelor Sansón Carrasco, Don Quijote puts the tip of his sword above his prostrate adversary's face and orders him to confess that the knight he previously claimed to have defeated "no fue ni pudo ser" ["neither was nor could have been"] Don Quijote de la Mancha but was an illusion created by enchanters (2. 14).[1] Part of the irony of that incident lies in the fact that the character who pronounces those words, Alonso Quijano, "neither is nor can be" Don Quijote either. The character "Don Quijote" is precisely an illusion, and the "enchanter" who created him is Miguel de Cervantes, whose supreme feat of magic is that his illusory hidalgo seems to depart from the order of reality as we generally know it by actually being not just more interesting than people in real life but more significant for a new understanding of the real world. Even when what Don Quijote sees is obviously a

---

[1] Passages from *Don Quijote* have been taken from Miguel de Cervantes, *El ingenioso hidalgo don Quijote de la Mancha*, ed. Martín de Riquer (Barcelona: Juventud, 1968); translations are mine.

figment of his imagination, we as readers are more interested in what he sees than in what is really there. At times Don Quijote defends his perceptions with a surprising earnestness and lucidity. He explains the existence of elements of the real world that are incompatible with his fantasies by claiming that they are illusions that enchanters have maliciously created in order to confuse people. Hence, for example, the windmills are not just giants but are giants cleverly made to look like windmills. Don Quijote rebels against such deceitful illusions, and he does so on the level of the very act of perception. When Don Quijote considers a barber's basin to be the legendary Helmet of Mambrino in enchanted form, what he perceives is a fabulous helmet that he has seized in battle and that is worthy of his own identity as a knight and champion of the tradition of high courage. So is an inn a castle, the packsaddle of a mule the fine harness of a steed, a flock of sheep an enemy army, a watermill a fortress, a rough peasant lass Dulcinea del Toboso, the Bachelor Sansón Carrasco, the Knight of Mirrors, etc. If they appear otherwise, Don Quijote thinks, it is because they are "enchanted," i.e., they have been transformed into deceitful sensory images. It is evident that Don Quijote's tendency to see a world that is subject to being subverted by sinister forces, instead of a world of pre-given, neutral objectivity that is to be regarded with optimistic impartiality, is not the result of a simple incapacity on his part, for Don Quijote is able to see what he alone sees and what others see as well. As a result, it becomes more difficult to dismiss his delusions as mere entertaining frivolity. Our attention naturally turns to the differences between Don Quijote's perception of the world and that of everyone else in the novel, the differences between — in E. C. Riley's words — poetic myth and historico–empirical actuality.[2]

Criticism generally recognizes that in the *Quijote* Cervantes explores the dual character of human nature and the ethical and aesthetic implications of the relationship between human being's physiologically real and psychologically fantastic aspects. Perhaps it is not too much to suggest that Cervantes introduced Don Quijote's obsession with enchantment and the complex process whereby Don Quijote sees what is there yet also what is not there to serve as a clue to how his novel can be seen to convey a meaning. The prominence of the enchantment motif alone (it is the most frequent topic of discussion in the novel, being spoken of by Don Quijote and Sancho more

---

[2] E. C. Riley, *Don Quijote* (London: Unwin, 1986), 170.

than a hundred times)[3] and the peculiarly esoteric manner in which Don Quijote regards empirical reality with suspicion because he considers ideal conceptions to be a basis for skepticism are themselves enough to imply that ideas on the subject of enchantment point to more than the fantastic and gratuitous delusions of a mind warped by romances of chivalry and to suggest that the concept of enchantment has a bearing on deep thematic dimensions of the novel. Critics have long noted, like Riley, that enchantment itself is an important thematic motif in the *Quijote*,[4] but studies of it have

---

[3] Richard L. Predmore, "La función del encantamiento en el mundo del Quijote," *Anales cervantinos* 5 (1955–1956): 63–78, here 75.

[4] Previous studies of enchantment in *Don Quijote* have not related it to theories of perception or knowledge nor attempted to interpret enchantment in broad, figurative terms as I do, by regarding it as a metaphor for epistemological realism. Actually, they have tended to be descriptions instead of interpretations. If Ortega y Gasset's brief observations on windmills had touched on the subject of enchantment instead of being confined to illusion, they would be an exception in this regard. He sees Don Quijote's "abnormality" to be the normal human cultural tendency to assign a sense to things regardless of their materiality: *Meditations on Quixote*, trans. Rugg and Marín (New York: Norton, 1961), 143–44. Castro does not explore the enchantment motif separately or analyze it in any detail. When he does refer to it, he sees it as a means Cervantes used to introduce the theme of the fallibility of the senses and the possibility of appearance being interpreted differently by different individuals, i.e., as supporting the ambiguous and relativistic conception of truth that he considers fundamental to the novel as a whole: *El pensamiento de Cervantes* (Madrid: Revista de Filología Española, 1925), 83, 390. Spitzer, like Castro, sees enchantment as the condition for Don Quijote's seeing things differently from others and, hence, as expressing the "perspectivism" advanced by Castro. He also sees Don Quijote's tendency to substitute fantasies for a monotonous and limited reality as expressing a healthy and heroic, although unrealistic, rebellion against the established order: *Estilo y estructura en la literatura española* (Barcelona: Crítica, 1980), 306, cf. 292–93. Alberto Navarro González sees the concept of "evil enchanters" as functioning to allow quixotic belief to be sustained: "La locura quijotesca," *Anales cervantinos* 1 (1951): 273–94, here 278. Likewise, Predmore characterizes enchantment in the *Quijote* as being the principle by which Don Quijote explains to himself the disturbing fact that people and things seem so often to be what they really are; hence, it is a means of maintaining his illusions and of explaining that for which he has no explanation ("Encantamiento," 67–68, 77). Avalle-Arce, on the contrary, sees enchantment as an intrusion that threatens Don Quijote's willfully created ideal vision of the world: *Nuevos deslindes cervantinos* (Barcelona: Ariel, 1975), 374. Ruth El Saffar regards enchantment as the means Don Quijote uses to protect what she terms his sanity as he becomes increasingly confused at his inability to rely on sense-perception and reason to explain the strange incidents that befall him: *Beyond Fic-*

been mainly descriptive. It has not been the subject of serious analysis or interpretation on a philosophical plane, and the implications of exactly what Don Quijote himself thought about enchantment have been overlooked altogether.

The usual interpretation of Don Quijote's idea of enchantment is that its function is primarily practical. Enchantment is seen as a means that Don Quijote uses both to render his world more fabulous, like the world of the chivalric romance, and to defend that fantasy world from the encroachments of empirical fact. That view seems essentially accurate, but it would seem that the romances of chivalry provided no more to the enchantment motif than a point of departure. Predmore, for example, has pointed out in "Encantamiento" that Cervantes's use of enchantment in the novel is quite different from the part that it plays in the romances of chivalry. Not only is enchantment in the *Quijote* almost without exception the work of anonymous enchanters (whereas enchanters are completely identified in the romances of chivalry), in the *Quijote* enchantment serves specifically to make it possible for characters (Don Quijote and Sancho) to maintain their illusions, to evade responsibility, and to provide explanations where rational explanations are lacking (77). Predmore observes that for Don Quijote himself enchantment has the function of defending his illusions from the

---

tion: *The Recovery of the Feminine in the Novels of Cervantes* (Berkeley: University of California Press, 1984), 111. Maureen Ihrie distinguishes between enchantment in Part 1, where it expresses Don Quijote's assurance that his mistaken sense-perceptions are accurate, and Part 2, where they are the means whereby he discounts accurate sense perceptions as being mistaken: *Skepticism in Cervantes* (London: Tamesis, 1982), 59–60. Like Navarro González and Predmore, Howard Mancing considers enchantment in the *Quijote* to be a way for Don Quijote to rationalize his defeats and thus to sustain his chivalric vision: *The Chivalric World of "Don Quijote"* (Columbia, MO: University of Missouri Press, 1982), 46. Edwin Williamson recognizes that Don Quijote's madness does not involve a crude distortion of visual perception and sees his distortions (presumably what Don Quijote would attribute to enchantment) as "a kind of perverse misreading of everyday situations caused by a desire to make them fit his chivalric obsession." Believing things to be superior to their actual appearances, Don Quijote seeks "to identify the romance potential concealed within the humdrum reality he is forced to live in so as to draw it out for others to see": *The Halfway House of Fiction: "Don Quijote" and Arthurian Romance* (Oxford: Oxford University Press, 1984), 96–97. Daniel Eisenberg notes that because of Don Quijote's insistence that enchantment changes appearances, it is impossible to convince him that he is in error, just as it is impossible to determine whether what one sees is reality or the product of enchanters' distortions: *A Study of Don Quijote* (Newark, DE: Juan de la Cuesta, 1987), 171, 173.

need to reconcile them with the real world and that they accomplish that end specifically by changing appearances (66, 77–78). Perhaps criticism's reluctance to analyze Don Quijote's own notions about enchantment or to interpret enchantment in broad figurative terms (even if it is sometimes interpreted thematically) is another instance of what Américo Castro characterized in 1925 as criticism's established tendency to take the view that Cervantes's work is not problematic (*El pensamiento de Cervantes*, 15). If a more ambitious study of enchantment in the *Quijote* were to prove revealing, it would certainly not be the first discovery of unexpected dimensions in what one critic has referred to as Don Quijote's *gigantesca locura* [gigantic madness].[5]

The bizarre, seemingly farcical character of Don Quijote's behavior in relation to what he calls enchantment is certainly one of the most difficult features of that character to reconcile with an attempt to explain his thematic significance in serious terms. On the other hand, extravagant, quasi-grotesque motifs are not uncharacteristic of the manneristic literature of the High Renaissance. One thinks, for example, of the stark artificiality and archetypal, elegiac atmosphere of the Spanish pastoral romance, the emergence of which was largely due to "maverick" intellectual, Neoplatonist influences. It is logical to associate the emergence of a doctrinaire subjective idealism in Renaissance literature with the vogue for Neoplatonism. Renaissance Neoplatonism is best known today as a somewhat localized if refreshing, secular moral idealism based on a spiritualized concept of sexual love. Actually, it was a source of a new, widespread independence of spirit and speculative rationalism, especially as it combined with nominalism and the voluntaristic teachings of St. Augustine. It was an entire metaphysical system, and it provided an alternative to the official, Aristotelian–scholastic tradition. What is often overlooked, however, is that whereas in the period prior to Renaissance humanistic learning a real knowledge of Aristotelian doctrines was thought to have been restricted to members of the clergy, the sixteenth and seventeenth centuries are a period of intense interest in Aristotle,[6] many of whose works were becoming

---

[5] Francisco Márquez Villanueva, "La locura emblemática en la segunda parte del *Quijote*" in *Cervantes and the Renaissance*, ed. Michael D. McGaha (Easton, PA: Juan de la Cuesta, 1980), 87–112, here 106.

[6] The classic study is Charles B. Schmitt, *Aristotle and the Renaissance* (Cambridge, MA: Harvard University Press, 1983); followed by *Aristotelismus und Renaissance*, ed. E. Kessler et al. (Wiesbaden: Harrassowitz, 1988). See now *Humanism and Early Modern Philosophy*, ed. Jill Kraye and M. W. Stone (London: Routledge, 2000), and *Renaissance Readings of the Corpus Aristotelicum*, ed. M. Pade (Copenhagen: Museum Tusculanum, 2001).

available in vernacular translation for the first time (Bolgar, *Classical Heritage*, 308–10). Hence there was also an interest in rereading Aristotle and in establishing the points of contact between his teachings and those of Plato.[7] Renaissance thought bears evidence of widespread interest in Platonist and Aristotelian theories of knowledge and perception.[8] That Cervantes was aware of those theories is generally accepted by Cer-

---

[7] See J. Monfasani, "Marsilio Ficino and the Plato-Aristotle Controversy," in *Marsilio Ficino: His Theology, His Philosophy, His Legacy*, ed. Michael J. B. Allen et el. (Leiden: Brill, 2002), 179–202; also Kristeller, *Studies*, Chapt. 4, "The Scholastic Background of Marsilio Ficino" (35–97). Also, in *Renaissance Thought* Kristeller goes to considerable lengths to draw attention to modern scholarship's fallacy of not recognizing the presence of a flourishing tradition of Aristotelianism throughout the Renaissance period (33–47, 50–57, 61, 114–16), pointing out that Neoplatonism itself was a synthesis of Platonism, Aristotelianism, and stoicism (51). He writes, "We have learned through recent studies that the chief progress made during the latter fourteenth century in the fields of logic and natural philosophy was due to the Aristotelian, and more specifically, to the Occamist school at Paris and Oxford. During the fifteenth and sixteenth centuries, university instruction in the philosophical disciplines continued everywhere to be based on the works of Aristotle; consequently, most professional teachers of philosophy followed the Aristotelian tradition, used its terminology and method, discussed its problems, and composed commentaries and questions on Aristotle." Kristeller attributes the emphasis on the importance of Neoplatonism and the neglect of Aristotelianism to historians' tendency to, like journalists, "concentrate on news and to forget that there is a complex and broad situation which remained unaffected by the events of the moment" (34). In advancing the view that Platonist and Aristotelian influences coexist in Cervantes's writing, I do not, however, wish to suggest that Renaissance humanists did not attack the Aristotelian–scholastic tradition. Many of them did; on the other hand, Ficino did not (see Kristeller, "Florentine Platonism and Its Relations with Humanism and Scholasticism," *Church History* 8 [1989]: 201–11 and idem, *The Philosophy of Marsilio Ficino*, esp. 14), for Platonism and Aristotelianism coexist in his philosophy, as in León Hebreo's *Diálogos de amor* (see Kristeller, *The Philosophy of Marsilio Ficino*, 236, and León Hebreo, *Diálogos*, ed. Mazo del Castillo, 224–25). Also, according to D. W. Hamlyn, the empiricist theory of knowledge developed by Aquinas is incorrectly attributed to Aristotle. Hamlyn points out that the context of Aristotle's discussion of sense-perception in *De anima* has been misinterpreted, since (unlike that of Plato) it is not epistemological but is intended to elucidate concepts of the philosophy of mind (that the acquisition of intellectual knowledge, like sense-perception, is a process from potentiality to actuality): see *Sensation and Perception* (London: Routledge & Kegan Paul, 1963), 17–18. Hamlyn's observations would seem to provide additional evidence for the view that there is less of an antagonism between Plato and Aristotle on epistemological concerns than is commonly thought.

[8] See H. Mikkeli, "The Aristotelian Classification of Knowledge in the Early Sixteenth

vantes scholars, largely on the basis of a quotation from Book IV of *La Galatea*, where a character refers to "that opinion of the one who said that the soul's knowledge is the memory of what it already knows" [Plato's *Meno*] and "the other, better opinion of the one who asserted [Aristotle] that our soul was like a *tabula rasa*" ("el que dijo que el saber de nuestras almas era acordarse de lo que ya sabían ... el otro mejor parecer del que afirmó que nuestra alma era como una tabla rasa").[9]

A concept that was especially important to Platonism, with which it originated, but was also important to Aristotelianism is the concept that ideas do not exist only as mental constructs but that they have a real, though non-material, existence in the physical world. Ideas are what make sense objects "real" in the sense of intelligible, i.e., objects of consciousness. In contrast to the modern, empiricist epistemological conception of the possibility of establishing a rational correlation of material nature viewed objectively as a causal mechanism, Plato and Aristotle both taught that knowledge requires transcending a mere awareness of sense-data, that to know is to have knowledge of ideas, or concepts, which are the intelligible forms of objects in the physical world. Whereas Plato maintained that there exists a separate, more truly real world of ideal, universal forms of which particular sense objects are imperfect reflections, Aristotle held that the objects of our senses have real, external, independent existence and that it is in knowing particular objects that we know the universal or ideal. The Aristotelian maintains that, in perceiving, the mind abstracts ideas from sense objects, in which they inhere. The Platonist sees ideas, or universals, as having an existence that is separate from particular objects, which are themselves instances of universal ideas — in perceiving the objects of the physical world the mind assigns ideas to them by subsuming sense impressions under concepts. Thus for Plato the world that we know is a vast projection of universal and self-subsistent mind. Not only is the spiritual faculty able to act on matter and organize a world in which our ideals and

---

Century," in *Renaissance Readings of the Corpus Aristotelicum*, ed. Pade, 103–27.

[9] Miguel de Cervantes, *La Galatea*, in *Obras Completas*, ed. Ángel Valbuena Prat (Madrid: Aguilar, 1967), 605–767, here 704. Francisco López Estrada suggests that Cervantes's source for this passage is Huarte de San Juan's *Examen de ingenios para las ciencias*: see Miguel de Cervantes, *La Galatea*, ed. Francisco López Estrada (Madrid: Cátedra, 1999), 452. Some critics (such as Felkel and Moreno Baez: see Felkel, "Aristóteles, Santo Tomás y la percepción sensorial en el *Quijote*," 195–96) have felt that the preference expressed in this passage by the unnamed knight and friend of Darinto for the latter, Aristotelian theory over the Platonist theory can be identified with a preference on Cervantes's part, but such a view is pure speculation.

values are objectively real, but mind's preeminence is secure because matter cannot act upon mind or alter ideal being. The entire Platonist metaphysic can be seen as an elaborate means of emphasizing the creative and synthesizing capabilities of mind. Even in Aristotelianism the mind does not assume a passive role in the perception of objects but actively apprehends ideas or forms that are present in objects. However, what needs to be emphasized for purposes of the present study is that in both Plato and Aristotle knowledge depends on the conceptual activity of the mind and that in the Platonist theory of knowledge the mind assumes not only an active role, but also a creative role: by means of what Plato calls "memory" it supplies the concepts or memory-images that make sense objects intelligible (Hamlyn, *Sensation and Perception*, 16).

I wish to suggest that Cervantes elaborated the enchantment motif in the *Quijote* in such a way as to make Don Quijote incarnate the Platonist concept of mind exercising its capacity to "remake reality" creatively. Cervantes illustrates that creative process first by setting up in Don Quijote's behavior the Neoplatonist, activist model of perception as an assigning of meaning to sense impressions. Cervantes then has Don Quijote greatly exaggerate the free activity whereby mind assigns to an object a concept that has ordinary descriptive reference by having Don Quijote first assign and then (applying an Aristotelian principle) abolish such a descriptive concept on the grounds that it is an illusion and finally proceed beyond the empirical realm altogether and, by projecting ideal values, replace the descriptive concept with another one, one that endows the object with mythopoeic significance. The process is rendered in vivid, dramatic terms by Don Quijote's having the idea that sense impressions (created by "enchanters") are deceitful illusions, or "phantasms" — an idea taken from Aristotelian–Thomist epistemology.[10] When the eccentric hidalgo claims, for example, that the barber's basin he sees is the Helmet of Mambrino made by evil enchanters to look like a barber's basin, Cervantes is pointing out to us the fundamental, dissenting, "non-observant" aspect of the process whereby the creative mind, willfully turning its back on the ordinary descriptive concepts with which we refer to objects, creates a metaphorical language that gives them new meaning and that posits new, more valuable ways of looking at the world. The broadly comical incongruity of seeing an ordinary barber's basin as a legendary helmet is a subtle means of acknowledging metaphor's

---

[10] For a recent study see William Mark Smillie, "Phantasia: In Defense of Thomas Aquinas' Account of Imagination," Ph.D. diss., University of Notre Dame, 1992.

characteristic "tension between semantic congruence and incongruence"[11] and underscoring the "deviant" character of metaphorical language and of the creative faculty in general. The creative process as it is characterized by Cervantes is very similar to Gadamer's idea of "concept formation"[12] (Weinsheimer 237–40, Ricoeur 147), referred to by Ricoeur in relation to his theory concerning the role of imagination in the creation of metaphor, which I shall discuss below. Don Quijote, himself an idea made real and a novel, highly suggestive metaphor, is, in part, a fictional projection of Platonist and Aristotelian theories of perception cast in psychological terms.

§

When considered in the light of the Neoplatonist theory of knowledge, certain of Don Quijote's attitudes vis-à-vis enchantment appear less paradoxical. In the Neoplatonist view, the ideal world of eternal essences, forms, or "Ideas" — the intelligible world — is concealed by the empirical world of appearances and change, the phenomenal world that can be known by the senses. Speaking to Sancho in the Sierra Morena mountains, Don Quijote says, "andan entre nosotros siempre una caterva de encantadores que todas nuestras cosas mudan y truecan, y las vuelven según su gusto" (["here is a throng of enchanters always among us who change and switch everything and alter it according to their pleasure"]: 1. 25). In a world in which sense impressions are misleading, what, one may ask, could be the basis of certainty? The answer to that question is given when the silk merchants whom Don Quijote has ordered to declare that Dulcinea del Toboso, Empress of La Mancha, is the most beautiful maiden in the world protest that they cannot pay homage to someone whom they have never seen, and Don Quijote says that if they saw her their confession would have no value: "la importancia está en que sin verla lo habéis de creer, confesar, afirmar, jurar y defender" (["what is important is for you to believe, confess, affirm, swear, and maintain it without seeing her"]: 1. 4).[13] For Don Quijote what is real is what is true, but "truth"

---

[11] Paul Ricoeur, *Freedom and Nature*, trans. E. V. Kohák (Evanston, IL: Northwestern University Press, 1966), 146.

[12] Joel C. Weinsheimer, *Gadamer's Hermeneutics* (New Haven: Yale University Press, 1985), 237–40; Ricoeur, *Freedom and Nature*, 147.

[13] A parallel to this passage is Jesus's words to Thomas in John 20:29: "Blessed are they that have not seen, and yet have believed." The exaggerated use of juridical language in Cervantes's passage achieves an ironic effect by contrasting the subjectivity of devout faith with the law's requirement that testimony have an empirical basis.

Finite Reality's Rebirth as Poetic Imagery 261

is not empirical knowledge, nor is it merely based on a non-rational fideism; it is cognizance of the real value of a suprasensible ideal. He tells Sancho, "bástame a mí pensar y creer que la buena de Aldonza Lorenzo es hermosa y honesta" (["for me it is sufficient to think and believe that the good Aldonza Lorenzo is beautiful and chaste"]: 1. 25). Truth here is not the mere fantasy of a wish-fulfillment dream: it is a function of an epistemological and ethical freedom from the claims of the sensuous or material, a matter of axiological priority. One could wonder whether Don Quijote's censuring of empirical reality by claiming that it is mendacious and instead asserting the truth of the books of chivalry is not Cervantes's way of parodically inverting the humanists' practicalist intolerance of the books of chivalry on the grounds that they were "mentirosos" [lying].[14] Following the Platonist model, Don Quijote draws from memory the ideas, or memory-images, with which he supplants ordinary descriptive concepts, memory here being the fund of images that Don Quijote has gathered from the romances of chivalry. Nor can material being alter Don Quijote's fantasies, which — seen in the Platonist perspective — belong to the impervious order of ideal being.

The mechanism whereby Don Quijote misconstrues the contents of the physical world is not triggered by faulty sense perception, but rather is conditioned by the combative aspirations of his moral will. He sees his mythical world as being under assault by forces that would debase it and trivialize it by imposing the banality of a literal empiricism conditioned purely by sense impressions, factuality, and practical interests. In Don Quijote's view, sense impressions are something to rise above; they are not, I repeat, phenomena to which he turns a blind eye. When Sancho will not agree with his claim that he has been placed in a cage by enchanters, Don Quijote tells him confidently (as though he were addressing superficial readers of the novel), "Tú, Sancho, verás cómo te engañas en el conocimiento de mi desgracia" (["You, Sancho, will see how you are mistaken in your understanding of my misfortune"]: 1. 48). He does not deny that he sees himself in a cage. He says, "yo me veo enjaulado" (["I see myself caged"]: 1. 48). What he denies is that he must willingly accept the dictates of sense knowledge and be reconciled to them. He denies that the empirical fact should take precedence over a moral priority and that the mind's capacity to project a different reality must be subordinated to natural necessity, a claim which he considers

---

[14] See Alban K. Forcione, *Cervantes, Aristotle, and the Persiles* (Princeton: Princeton University Press, 1970), 13 for bibliography on criticisms of the books of chivalry, as well as his discussion on 13–27. For a more recent treatment of the subject, see Daniel Eisenberg, *A Study of Don Quijote* (Newark, DE: Juan de la Cuesta, 1987).

false and misleading, a malicious fabrication intended to confuse the moral sense by placing it under a spell. He says,

> yo sé y tengo para mí que voy encantado y esto me basta para la seguridad de mi conciencia; que la formaría muy grande si yo pensase que no estaba encantado y me dejase estar en esta jaula perezoso y cobarde, defraudando el socorro que podría dar a muchos menesterosos y necesitados de mi ayuda.
>
> [I know and am persuaded that I am enchanted, and that is sufficient for the safety of my conscience; for I would be greatly burdened if I thought that I was not under a spell and allowed myself to be in this cage lazy and like a coward, defrauding those who are distressed and in need of the help I could give them.] (1. 49)

In implying the existence of an antithetical relationship between the moral will and empirical fact, Don Quijote's incongruous attitudes hint at the author's suggestion that, in general, the enthusiasm and integrity of subjective motivation can depend, to some extent, on an artificial and even self-conscious denial of outward reality. Except towards the end of the novel, Don Quijote is invulnerable to depression because he refuses to take seriously those threats that a less heroic cast of mind might find intimidating. He is grandiose in his projections but modest in what he actually requires to satisfy his demands of life. The reason is that his truth is conative, based on the strivings of the will, and hence independent of the actual realization of values.[15] The reality that Don Quijote opposes, that he sees as being perpetrated against him by his enemies the enchanters, and that he denounces as unreal, is the reality of a commonplace natural necessity that, when asserted in absolute terms, would obviate moral strivings by rendering them not just unviable but meaningless.

As Américo Castro has pointed out, the Neoplatonist theory of perception was skeptical, rationalistic, relativistic, and anti-dogmatic (*El pensamiento de Cervantes*, 82–90) in much the same way that "poststructuralist" theories are today. Castro held that in writing the *Quijote* Cervantes was reacting to an authoritarian dogmatism that

---

[15] On moral value-being's independence of realizability in a volitional act, see Scheler, 348–50.

was based on the scholastic–empiricist claim that sense-perception plays a necessary role in providing us with reliable knowledge. In contrast, Castro maintained, Cervantes's novel offers an innovative, prismatic vision of life's complexity, of a world where reality is unstable and wavering and is full of uncertainties, deceitful appearances, and problematic differences of opinion and in which knowledge is relative, differing according to the point of view of the individual observer. Castro believed that for all his geniality, the stability of his moral vision, and notwithstanding the restrained character of his skepticism, in the *Quijote* Cervantes presents a *Weltanschauung* that is impressionistic, relativistic, and ambiguous. Not only is a basin a helmet, it is also a basin-helmet (*El pensamiento de Cervantes*, 75–122). Spitzer characterized what Castro called "relativism" as "perspectivism." The Neoplatonism that these critics have perceived as underlying Cervantes's outlook is not moral idealism but the speculative and critical rationalism of Neoplatonist epistemology. I wish to suggest that within that same, general Neoplatonist framework, Cervantes developed the enchantment motif originally furnished to him by the novels of chivalry and that he did so as a moral idealist as well. As we shall see, Cervantes added to his synthesis the concept of the *phantasma*, which comes from the Aristotelian theory of perception — a concept that today we know as the principle of transcendental–phenomenological reduction set forth by Husserl. Husserl intended that principle to be a means of suspending our ordinary awareness of objects in order to make possible a transition to a reflective attitude. In making Don Quijote a fictional vehicle of the Neoplatonist theory of perception and introducing the Aristotelian–Thomist principle that sense impressions, or *phantasmata*, are dream images, delusions, Cervantes elaborates the enchantment motif on a scale that leaves the materials he received from the novels of chivalry far behind.

Indeed, it is hard to see how Cervantes could have relied on the romances of chivalry alone for the idea of an appearance that is illusory because of its limiting, material particularity and for the idea of rendering such an appearance significant, as Don Quijote does, by abstracting it from the conditions of concrete individuality and altering it in order to apprehend it in terms of a broader, more universal frame of reference. Plato had held that knowledge is always of the self-subsistent universal; all we ever really know about the sensible world is our idea of it through judgment by the mind, since reality consists of mind, not matter. It was Aristotle who, in the *De anima*, originally posited the view that sense-knowledge and intellectual knowledge are essentially distinct. Sense-knowledge recognizes only matter itself with its individual qualities, while intellectual knowledge has for its object the essence of material things. Intellect depends on sense-perception because forms have a being only in things. Hence intellectual knowledge follows upon sensation. The active intellect makes sense-representation, or "*phantasma*," capable of being known in a universal, intellectual likeness through a process of abstraction (*De anima* 431a–432a; trans. Hicks, 139–45). Thomas Aquinas also distinguished among (a) appearance, or "phantasm," the sensory image that results from the body-sense experience of a material thing yet without our awareness of such a sensation (i.e., without intelligibility, understanding); (b) "material intelligence," or sensing such an image only in its particularity, i.e., passively and knowingly experiencing only the sensation of the individual image; and (c) active apprehension of things in their universal aspects: "dematerializing" a thing so as to see beyond its particularity and understand it conceptually, spiritually (*Summa Theologica*, Question 79, articles 2–3; trans. Suttor, 149–57).[16]

---

[16] Américo Castro has shown that Cervantes was influenced by the Neoplatonist theories of Bembo, Erasmus, and Castiglione (*El pensamiento de Cervantes*, 85–90). What evidence is there that Cervantes was familiar with Aristotelian–Thomist epistemological theories distinguishing between sense-experience and intelligibility and could have had them in mind when he elaborated Don Quijote's ideas on the subject of enchantment? In general, the premises of the present study are consistent with Forcione's thesis that through the figure of Don Quijote (his ideas and actions), Cervantes sought "the liberation of art from the mimetic theories that dominated the mainstream of literary theorizing of the sixteenth century" (*Cervantes, Aristotle, and the Persiles*, 121) and that were based on a misreading of Aristotle's *Poetics* (45–48, 346). In the *Poetics* Aristotle distinguishes between a historical and factual truth (the proper subject of historiography) and an ideal, aesthetic truth (the proper subject of poetry). Thus, even if Cervantes had not had access to the details of Aristotle's ideas on epistemology, he would probably have had knowledge of the concept of a creative mental activity that is independent of the restrictions of sense-data. However, it is likely that Cervantes was aware of the theories of perception of Aristotle and Aquinas that were curriculum staples. Whereas Américo Castro, for example, felt the need to document probable traces and definite evidence of Neoplatonic thought in Cervantes's writings, in Renaissance Spain "la filosofía aristotélica predomina ampliamente sobre la platónica" (["Aristotelian philosophy predominates widely over Platonic philosophy"]: Guillermo Fraile, *Historia de la filosofía española*, 2 vols. [Madrid: Castalia, 1971–1972], 1: 231). Aristotelianism was the official philosophy in sixteenth-century Spain: José Luis Abellán, *Historia crítica del pensamiento español* (Madrid: Espasa Calpe, 1979), 2: 173. It would have been unlikely that Cervantes did not know about such theories, even if his knowledge came more from conversations than from reading. There can be no doubt that he was interested in the subject. Yet his knowledge may well have come from reading as well. There is a reference in the *Quijote* (1. 47) to the *Súmulas* by Gaspar Cardillo de Villapando, an important textbook in Spanish universities. The *Súmulas* is not a discussion of *De anima* but a presentation of Aristotle's theories in logic; however, the same author

Thus, in Platonic and Aristotelian–Thomist epistemology, as for Don Quijote, immediately-given reality-phenomena, empirical reality as such, cannot be the object of actual knowing. Aristotle and Aquinas held such phenomena to be given as meaningless appearances, or phantasms (*phantasmata*), which must be rendered intelligible by the activity of the mind. If one sees Cervantes as having drawn on principles of Platonist, Aristotelian, and Thomist epistemology for the way he conceives details of Don Quijote's actions and ideas in relation to enchantment, Cervantes's specific adaptation of those theories would seem to have taken him well beyond the simple scheme of psychology based on bodily humors in, e.g., Huarte de San Juan's *Examen*

---

wrote a commentary on Aristotle's *De anima* entitled *Apologia Aristotelica adversus eos, qui aiunt animam cum corpore extingui* published in Alcalá in 1560 and in 1569: See Marcial Solana, *Historia de la filosfía española: Epoca del Renacimiento*, 3 vols. (Madrid: Real Academia de Ciencias, 1941), 2: 112–16; Gonzalo Díaz Díaz, *Hombres y documentos de la folosofía española*, 2 vols. (Madrid: CSIC, 1983), 2: 146–47; Abellán, *Historia crítica*, 176–79. Yet the most famous commentator on Aristotle's *De anima* was Pedro Martínez Brea, who published his *In libros tres Aristotelis De anima Commentarii* in Sigüenza in 1575. Let us recall that Castro (*El pensamiento de Cervantes*, 106) believes Cervantes to have had a good command of Latin. Martínez de Brea "señala las diferencias entre el apetito sensitivo, que sólo atiende al tiempo presente, y otro intelectivo que atiende al presente, pasado y futuro" (["points out the differences between the sensory inclination, which notices only the present, and the other, intellective inclination, which notices present, past and future"]; Abellán, *Historia crítica*, 179–80). Even if Cervantes had not read or heard of the epistemological theories attributed directly to works by Aristotle, he was sure to have heard about or read Thomas Aquinas's important elaboration. The sixteenth century was the golden age of Thomism both in Spain and Italy. The principal faculty positions in theology were reserved by universities (even in Alcalá de Henares) for the teaching of Thomist doctrine. As Aubrey Bell observes, at the time "those obstinate questionings of sense and outward things were in the air of Europe" (*Cervantes* [Norman, OK: University of Oklahoma Press, 1947], 118). Cervantes did not use philosophical terminology or explicitly broach the issues discussed in this study. He used the language of fiction. As Américo Castro notes, "Cervantes was not a philosopher, but dramatized in his works, especially in the *Quijote*, one of the central problems that caused unrest in modern thought in the dawn of the formation of the great systems" (*El pensamiento de Cervantes*, 89; my translation). With a perspective different from my own, Robert Felkel has published an interesting article in which he argues that Don Quijote's "madness" is a paradigm of intellection's failure due to deficiencies in sensory perception and the associated processes as they are described in Aristotelian–Thomist theories of perception: "Aristóteles, Santo Tomás y la percepción sensorial en el *Quijote*," *Anuario de Letras* 28 (1990): 181–231.

de ingenios. Cervantes first devised a psychology corresponding to the concept of a knowledge of Forms that is actually antithetical to an empirical factualism and then broadened the scope of intelligibility to draw on ethically-charged poetic myth, thus reaching beyond mere cognition to include the aesthetic and ethical modes of apprehension as well.[17] He then personified sense-impressions as malicious enchanters whose spells or "enchantment" — manifested as a superstitious respect for empirical truth-claims (a full endorsement of epistemological realism) — enslave their victims and make them believe in sensory images, in "phantasms." Don Quijote sallies forth into the world of fiction as the iconoclast of realistically-circumscribed, empirical truth-claims to the categorical "malice" of which eventually he himself heroically succumbs. Of course, whatever "malicious" distortions of reality Don Quijote imagines himself to experience he sees as being presented to him as illusions, so the reader may choose to remain on a literal level and dismiss them as meaningless fantasy. As Don Quijote himself states after wrecking the puppet show of Maese Pedro (actually the fugitive Ginés de Pasamonte in disguise), "Estos encantadores que me persiguen no hacen sino ponerme las figuras *como ellas son* delante de los ojos, y luego me las mudan y truecan en las que ellos quieren" (["These enchanters who pursue me merely place figures *as they are* before my eyes, and then they turn them into what they want them to be"]: 2. 26; my emphasis). In Don Quijote's view, the realities that he has perceived have been transformed into illusions, into elements of the mundane reality that everyone else sees. What can be seen to start out as a humorous probing of "the way in which desire can loosen a person's grasp on reality" and then becomes a contest between an aesthetics based on empirical reality and an aesthetics that is based on illusion and validates the free play of the imagination (Forcione, *Cervantes, Aristotle, and the Persiles*, 341; also 339–48), assumes, for the non-literal-minded reader, the broad, allegorical dimensions of an epic struggle between the right of a disruptive, ideal truth to insist upon the validity of its claims and the right of a factual truth to repudiate those claims once and for all as idle fantasy. That same opposition shifts to the arena of reader response, as the reader is faced with a decision as to how to interpret the novel.

The objects that Don Quijote substitutes for ordinary elements of everyday life are always values that he must struggle for or disvalues that he must struggle against. He

---

[17] For a discussion of the relation between ethical and aesthetic values, of how there is a series of aesthetic qualities that are bound to the ethical conduct of persons and are conditioned by it, see Hartmann, *Ethics*, 2: 403–5.

considers to be in a state of "enchantment" and deceitful appearance that which has a finite utility value that is, relatively speaking, merely "materially intelligible" and has no bearing on moral aspirations. As a proponent of knightly heroism, Don Quijote is primarily concerned with the ethical struggle and character-values. For him empirical facts alone lack "reality" because they lack moral significance, a perspective, as we have seen, that is reminiscent of the Platonic distrust of sensory perceptions and of the Aristotelian–Thomist depreciation of sensory, "material intelligence" as the passive experience of an isolated image that is in itself an unintelligible appearance because of its inability to refer to anything beyond itself. Cervantes's debt for Don Quijote's belief that it is the ideal alone that is real would, I repeat, be to Plato, for whom the forms of things in the physical world subsist non-materially as expressions of a noumenal or intelligible world. Don Quijote "artificially" transforms "material knowledge," expels the iconoclastic phantoms of a literal factuality, and liberates meaning by transforming objects, "remaking reality" in conformity to what he perceives to be the claims and predicative demands of universal moral interests. Hartmann has observed that poets contribute to the historical process of humanization by giving expression to the more positive values through a process of connecting "the aesthetic vision with the seriousness of the ethical struggle" (*Ethics*, 2: 328). Don Quijote embodies the principle of artistic transformation, dematerializing things, suspending their posited reality, conferring upon them a poetically transcendent universality, and making them intelligible — not only cognitively and passively, but with a new ethical impress, as factors in the creation of values. He thus administers finite reality's rebirth as poetic imagery. It is often impossible to know what conscious motives prompted the work of an author who lived centuries ago, but in Don Quijote's peculiar psychology on the subject of enchantment Cervantes may well have intended to encapsulate some of his own views on the nature of artistic creation. If Don Quijote's idea of enchantment is emblematic of some of Cervantes's ideas concerning art, the possible connection of the enchantment motif to the theories discussed would support the view developed by Castro, Forcione, and others that Cervantes regarded poetic art largely as a mode of apprehension, and would suggest that he viewed aesthetics not merely as a science of forms but as a cognitive and epistemological domain as well.

§

One sign that philosophical inquiries into the essential nature of artistic creation are, in our own day, acknowledging the importance of epistemological issues is that some recent theories concerning the cognitive, semantic value of metaphor (the central poetic figure) address points similar to those discussed here. The most paradoxical element in Don Quijote's concept of the way enchantment works is his self-conscious acceptance of the truth-value of perceptions that he himself recognizes as deviating from empirical fact. His attitude seems to be summed up in the words with which he tells Sancho quite candidly that the way he sees Dulcinea is the way he imagines her, whether it is the truth or not:

> Yo imagino que todo lo que digo es así, sin que sobre ni falte nada, así en la belleza como en la principalidad, y no la llega Elena, ni la alcanza Lucrecia, ni otra alguna de las famosas mujeres de las edades pretéritas, griega, bárbara, o latina.
>
> [I imagine that everything I say is true, without anything being added or left out concerning either her beauty or her eminence, and Helen doesn't equal her any more than Lucretia approaches her, nor any other of the famous women of past ages, Greek, barbarian, or Latin].
> (1. 25)

Don Quijote simply denies what is in his factual experience and replaces it with a cherished vision. As a guide to making decisions in everyday life, such a *modus operandi* must be impractical to say the least, as Don Quijote discovers. However, the mental process that Paul Ricoeur considers to lie at the center of the poetic imagination is remarkably similar. Ricoeur's theory incorporates Husserl's principle of the phenomenological suspension of presuppositions about the nature of experience and what is distinctly reminiscent of Coleridge's view that imaginative synthesis is preceded by a stage at which the fixed, definite character of images is dissolved. For Ricoeur imagination begins with the subject's turning his back, as it were, on conventional modes of thought; it is a negative making oneself "absent to the whole of things," for "to imagine is to make oneself absent to the whole of the world."[18] Metaphor, specifically, is "a deviant predication," a "semantic impertinence" ("The Metaphorical Process," 143). Once imagination has succeeded in suspending the direct reference of thought

---

[18] Paul Ricoeur, "The Metaphorical Process," in *On Metaphor*, ed. S. Sacks (Chicago: University of Chicago Press, 1974), 141–59, here 152.

and emotion to the objects of our ordinary discourse and the literal emotions of everyday life (vs. poetic emotions), it performs its next task, that of applying synthetic insight to the projection of new possibilities of redescribing the world. "Image as absence is the negative side of image as fiction," and symbolic systems have the power to remake reality (155, cf. 152, 145).

The question of whether it is possible to alter reality to some degree — or even fundamentally, or if it is possible to create new reality — by altering the way in which it is perceived (the supposition that was so powerfully censured by Marx and Engels in their critique of Feuerbach in *German Ideology* and that underlies the difference between naturalism, or the picaresque, and what Lukács refers to as "realism," which is actually just more romantic than naturalism) — this question is what is ultimately at issue in Cervantes's complex presentation of the way Don Quijote conceives of enchantment. As Mark Johnson notes of Ricoeur's emphasis on the imagination's role in the creation of meaning (imagination's semantic feature),

> The underlying issue is whether "reality" is objectively given, so that, as knowers, we can only stand apart and comment on it, or whether we have a "world" only by virtue of having a language and system of value-laden concepts that make experience possible for us. This, as Ricoeur and many others note, is not a question limited to metaphor — it is a fundamental ontological and epistemological issue. (*Philosophical Perspectives in Metaphor* [Minneapolis: University of Minnesota Press, 1981], 41)

Johnson is aware that the way one judges the value of symbolic images (and their associated emotions) for making truth-claims will depend on the concept one has of truth: is it descriptive of an objective reality that exists in itself and would exist even if there were no minds to be aware of it, or is "truth" the linguistic manifestation of cognitive processes that are experienced as we encounter our world "not passively, but by means of projective acts influenced by our interests, purposes, values, beliefs, and language" (Johnson, *Philosophical Perspectives in Metaphor*, 41)? Clearly the latter alternative, which is the nominalist view — i.e., that our means of formulating truths are mere names or vocal utterances without any corresponding realities — assigns much greater scope and value to the free human will and creative imagination, which explains the prestige that theory enjoyed in Cervantes's day as an element in the philosophy of nominalism. Nominalism differed from Thomism in being voluntaristic in the tradition of Augustinianism. In positing what today seems a distinctly "Fichtean" concept of subjective idealism emerging from the moral will, Cervantes was undoubtedly influenced by the nominalists, whose teachings were very much in vogue in sixteenth-century Spain. In our age a similar desire for freedom from traditional forms of thought probably explains a good deal of the widespread interest in, for example, Derrida's denial that subjective conceptions can define anything that has independent, real existence outside the mind and in the structuralist claim that social and cultural phenomena, like literary works, are semiotic systems whose elementary units are not objective facts but conventional relational elements, arbitrary signs.[19] As Genette has observed, "structuralism is not only a method; it is also what Ernst Cassirer calls a 'general tendency of thought,' or as others would say (more crudely) an ideology. . . ."[20] Whether the ideas upon which structuralism is based stand to prove as fruitful in our day as their prototype did in the post-medieval period has been a subject of much recent controversy.

Cervantes lived in a world that for a time had been cordoned off from the rest of Europe in order to defend, ironically, a religion that advanced the doctrine of free will. Following the Neoplatonist teachings of Augustine, the emphasis on the superiority of the will over the intellect was powerfully reasserted in Europe by the nominalists.

---

[19] In the concluding observations of his book *The Aesthetics of Thomas Aquinas*, trans. H. Bredin (Cambridge, MA: Harvard University Press, 1988), while commenting on connections between scholasticism and structuralism, Umberto Eco notes, "In fact the claim of Scholastic thought is that it does resolve the real into explanatory models — except that these models are believed to be features of reality, not just constructs of the intellect. Still, in medieval disputes about universals, the opposition between nominalism and conceptualism was expressed in terms similar to those used nowadays in Structuralism. It is not altogether clear whether Structuralism would persevere to the end in denying an ontological significance to their epistemological models. At all events, both the Scholastics and the Structuralists engage in inquiries based upon the notion of universals. . . . It is not by chance that one of the most important issues in contemporary Structuralism is the investigation of linguistic universals. It matters little that these are universals of human psychology and are therefore brain structures, not Platonic universals. More important is the final outcome of this debate, namely the reaffirmation of an atemporality in the structures of the mind . . ." (217–18). I am indebted to Leo Cabranes Grant for knowledge of this reference.

[20] Gérard Genette, "Structuralism and Literary Criticism," in *Modern Criticism and Theory*, ed. David Lodge (New York: Longman, 1989), 63–78, here 68.

Nominalism emerged in the fourteenth century as a challenge to the dogmatic authority of philosophical (ontological) realism. It received a new impetus from the influence of Reform piety and entered Spain as a progressive force with the founding of the Universidad de Alcalá de Henares in the early sixteenth century. As it developed, nominalism itself contributed to the forging of dogma, viz., the doctrine of merit.[21] Some critics in our own day would seem to consider the influence of linguistics in contemporary literary criticism to have followed a course that is comparable to the influence of nominalism. Emphasis on the view that truth is a function of language is seen as having fostered the attitude that the subject of language can only be language itself, that what one may consider "truth" is never more than a linguistic formulation and a function of language's inherent formal conventions, what Frederick Jameson has (following Heidegger) termed "the prison-house of language" and Terry Eagleton calls "the poststructuralist dogma that we are prisoners of our own discourse."[22] For his part, Don Quijote, who has an unmistakable tendency to equate truth and language (especially the language of fictional discourse), establishes himself from the outset as an opponent of literal, uninspired truth-claims and drab objectivity. He consciously defies the existence of a self-evident factuality. Cervantes the romanticist author (he is a "realist" as well) can be said to do likewise; however, unlike Cervantes's, Don Quijote's heightened vision is categorical. Even when, after his second sally, he is placed in a cage like a criminal or a heretic (1. 46), he insists that the cage is an illusion, the creation of enchanters. Sancho would seem to have the last word, with his observation that the cage in which Don Quijote is being carried home "tiene más parte de malicia que de encanto" (["has more of malice than of enchantment]": 1. 48). The implication of Sancho's common-sense attitude would seem to be that, whether it is perceived concretely or abstractly and acts physically or psychologically, a cage is illusory only if one can get out of it.

---

[21] On nominalism's entry into Spain in the early sixteenth century through the efforts of Cardinal Francisco Jiménez de Cisneros, see Bataillon, *Erasmo y España*, 10–66. On the importance of nominalism in relation to the theological controversies that developed in Spain in the middle of the sixteenth century, see Creel, *The Religious Poetry of Jorge de Montemayor*, 25–26; also cf. Stephen Menn, "Suárez, Nominalism, and Modes," in *Hispanic Philolosophy in the Age of Discovery*, ed. Kevin White (Washington, DC: Catholic University of America Press, 1997), 226–56.

[22] See Frederick Jameson, *The Prison-House of Language* (Princeton: Princeton University Press, 1972), passim, and Terry Eagleton, *Literary Theory* (Minneapolis: University of Minnesota Press, 1983), 144.

In a way, what Don Quijote claims is obviously ridiculous, but only if one tries to apply to him the standards of conventional modes of thought and refuses to accept the poetic imagination's "semantic impertinence," its deviant withdrawal from the objects of our ordinary discourse, for what it is. Don Quijote is a fictional character who has been aberrantly displaced into the world of historico–empirical actuality and whose very existence is a function of the principle of poetic imagination. He represents both the virtues of poetic heightening and its potential vices. The virtues are evident in the fact that serious readers study Cervantes's novel in the first place. The vice that Don Quijote represents is error itself, i.e., the tendency to take fictional claims literally and read them dogmatically as fact instead of as polysemous symbol. When we laugh at Don Quijote's delusions and, in our literal-mindedness, dismiss his behavior as mere folly, we commit the same error, which is also the error that structuralism and post-structuralism have objected to and, some would claim, sometimes even exemplified, viz., thought's formalistic tendency to carve out its own self-complacent niche in the intellectual environment, grow one-sided, and effect a quasi-mystical retreat from life's complexity in the process.

Any language system tends to lapse into pseudo-objectivity by becoming self-directing and self-certifying through the elaboration and fulfillment of its own characteristic form. It is a typical feature in the work of Cervantes for motifs that are idyllic (in Schiller's sense of the coincidence of the ideal and reality) to suggest another, critical and ironic dimension, and it should not surprise us to find that such is the case in the way he represents the poetic imagination as well. Don Quijote's lengthy disquisitions on the subject of knight-errantry, as he entrenches himself deeper and deeper in his signifying system, are, in addition to his visual fantasies, a noteworthy example. Instead of being the condition for actual knowing, Don Quijote's authorative, encyclopedic frame of reference takes on dimensions and proportions of another, mythological form of organized illusion, a *"phantasma"* the very fiction of which his hallucinatory images of absent phenomena are (to use Ricoeur's terms ironically) the negative side. Don Quijote's compulsive cataloguing of "facts" that he has taken from the romances of chivalry tempts the reader to speculate that the derivation of poetic symbolism does not always entail the process that Aristotle and Aquinas describe as a transfer of the phenomenon into an idea and then, as Goethe held,[23] into a suggestive

---

[23] Johann Wolfgang von Goethe, *Maximen und Reflexionen*, in *Goethes Werke: Festausgabe*, ed. Robert Petsch, 18 vols. (Leipzig: Bibliographischen Instituts, 1926), 14: 214–436, here 391, No. 1113. That passage in English is as follows: "Symbolism transforms an

image, but that it can also start with a metaphysics in the form of images and affects, or quasi-rational presuppositions born more of a suspension of reference to objective reality than of an impartial observation of it, and that it can then transfer those images into the form of a pseudo-non-fictional, rationalistic discourse that is simply a displaced form of fiction. Just as fiction can have an axiological basis, positive thought can have a fictional basis — at least, as A. J. Greimas maintains, in the human and social sciences.[24] It was most likely Freud's sensitivity to the inescapable importance of a conceptual framework with formal characteristics in organizing the immediate sensations of experience that prompted him to describe his own work as "metapsychology."[25]

An additional area, then, that the *Quijote* can be seen to address indirectly and somewhat ironically in association with the enchantment motif and that Cervantes explores further in works such as "El coloquio de los perros" ["The Dogs' Colloquy"] is the issue of the extent to which the literary dialogue, with its conventional claim to being universally edifying, has a didactic value that is necessarily relative to the frame of reference of its (fictional) speakers.[26] Such a theme is, of course, not without broad

---

object of perception into an idea, the idea into an image, and does it in such a way that the idea always remains infinitely operative and unattainable so that even if it is put into words in all languages, it still remains inexpressable." (trans. Linda Stopp, *Maxims and Reflections*, ed. Peter Hutchinson [London: Penguin Books, 1998], 141. Also see Hazard Adams, *Philosophy of the Literary Symbolic* (Tallahassee: University Press of Florida, 1983), 57.

[24] This principle is the basis of Greimas, *Narrative Semiotics and Cognitive Discourses*, trans. P. Perron and F. H. Collins (London: Pinter Publishers, 1990), which analyzes the "resemblances between the more or less abstract organization of discourse that claims to be scientific and the figurative forms of the narrative discourses of literature and myth" (57).

[25] See note 26 below. Also, in regard to Freud, in his letter to Albert Einstein published under the title "Why War?" Freud writes, "It may perhaps seem to you as though our theories are a kind of mythology and, in the present case, not even an agreeable one. But does not every science come in the end to a kind of mythology like this? Cannot the same be said to-day of your own Physics?" (Freud, *The Standard Edition of the Complete Works*, trans. James Strachey [London: Hogarth, 1964], 22: 211).

[26] Northrop Frye discusses the importance of a conceptual framework in science and of symposium and dialogue in Renaissance art: *Anatomy*, 15, 59. See *Le dialogue au temps de la Renaissance*, ed. M. T. Jones-Davies (Paris: Touzot, 1984); Virginia Cox, *The Renaissance Dialogue* (Cambridge: Cambridge University Press, 1992); Luca Bianchi, "From Jacques Lefèvre d'Etaples to Giulio Landi: Uses of the Dialogue in Renaissance Aristotelianism," in *Humanism and Early Modern Philosophy*, ed. Kraye and Stone, 41–58;

implications. We are very likely still discovering the extent to which our world and our relation to it would be unimaginable for us were they not organized in some sort of fictional framework. From this point of view a fundamental trait that fiction and real life could be seen to have in common is that the individuals who populate both can be thought of as metaphors in a vast creative fabric, and largely self-conceived metaphors at that. Thus regarded, poetic imagination assumes the character of a moral adventure, one that demands the exercise of free will and that is also not without risk. As Lessing observed, a heretic is a person who sees with his own eyes.[27]

One reason that the character Don Quijote has such rich metaphorical value is that he can be seen both as exercising a vital free will and as not doing so. Don Quijote rejects one set of conventions (sense-knowledge) on the grounds that it is illusory in order to be able to embrace another set of conventions (chivalric romanticism) with an attitude of naive indifference to the problem of what is or is not illusory. In this sense his situation is comparable to that of the deconstructionist critic, who is unable to dispense with the conventions of the very logocentric language from which he wishes to disassociate himself. Just as a thinker without a language is inconceivable, so is a human being inconceivable without a fantasy world. So observes Francis Bacon:

> Doth any man doubt that, if there were taken out of men's minds vain opinions, flattering hopes, false valuations, imaginations, as one would, and the like, but it would leave the minds of a number of men poor shrunken things, full of melancholy and indisposition, and unpleasing to themselves? One of the Fathers, in great severity, called poesy *vinum daemonum* because it filleth the imagination; and yet it is but with the shadow of a lie. But it is not the lie that passeth through the mind, but the lie that sinketh in and settleth in it, that doth the hurt.[28]

---

and Anne Godard, *Le dialogue à la Renaissance* (Paris: Presses Universitaires de France, 2001).

[27] George Seldes, *The Great Thoughts* (New York: Ballantine, 1885), 243.

[28] The patristic quote containing the expression *"vinum daemonum"* [wine of devils] is from St. Augustine, *The Confessions of St. Augustine*, I. xvi, 26: see *The Essays of Francis Bacon*, ed. Mary Augusta Scott (New York: Charles Scribner's Sons, 1908), 4, n. 1.

Finite Reality's Rebirth as Poetic Imagery 275

The *Quijote* would seem to advance the proposition that healthy fictional presuppositions should be considered sacred. When they are not, the result can be a crisis such as that which is presented in the intercalated narrative "El curioso impertinente" [The Tale of Impertinent Curiosity]. Don Quijote's recurrent self-deceptions concerning the identity and intentions of others cause him to behave violently; hence, they must eventually be dispelled. On the other hand, his idealization of Aldonza Lorenzo causes harm to no one. Sancho — who eventually learns, under Don Quijote's influence, to liberate his own poetic imagination — playfully yet maliciously takes it upon himself iconoclastically to contradict his companion's illusions concerning the being whom Don Quijote describes as "único refugio de mis esperanzas" (["the only refuge of my hopes"]: 2. 29). It is ironic that Sancho's naturalistic description of the Dulcinea to whom he claims to have spoken when she was winnowing wheat in the barnyard is a fictional invention as well. While Sancho's fictionalization of Aldonza Lorenzo may be less fanciful than Don Quijote's, it lacks elevation. So it is that Sancho must make restitution for his act of profanation in the form of three thousand three hundred lashes. It is thus implied that imagining that things can only be as they appear, that sense-impressions are an adequate basis for knowledge, is comparable to a delusion or a fantasy, to being under a "spell." It is thus also implied that the "enchanted," or fictional, aspect of such a one-sided epistemological realism, of the assumption that the only reality attributable to objects of our knowledge is a reality of their own, is that it is at once too naive and too cynical: too naive because it ignores its own partiality and, hence, its own fictional character; too cynical because it disregards the crucial importance of subjective factors for conceiving ways in which reality can be recast and improved.

In Cervantes's novel (for all the pregnant and contradictory implications that one may wish to see in the circumstance) it is the very incarnation of the quixotic vision himself, Don Quijote, who insists that what the general run of people think they see in the world around them is, in fact, a fiction created to mislead them, and yet who admits quite frankly that what *he* claims to be true is what he imagines and wills to be true. One implication of that attitude on Don Quijote's part could be that fiction is a fundamental ingredient in any perception of reality. It could also follow, both logically and from Don Quijote's example, that once one accepts that fact one can aspire to build a reality on the fiction that is most inspired and most elevated. At that point the role of learning is not merely to justify empirical knowledge but to help provide a road to knowledge of a higher kind.

Conclusions

The preceding studies address ways in which works of early modern literature contributed to the process of cultural renovation that was occurring when they were written. If the interpretations of individual works are successful they should have shed light not only on how those works are related to cultural–historical change but also on qualities in those works that give them a typically "Renaissance" flavor. The Renaissance is certainly not the only period of historical transition and cultural change in Western civilization, yet in certain of its features it is different from any other. It is set apart by the fact that it roughly corresponds to the beginning of the modern period. It is also different in the specific ways in which it contrasts with the period that preceded it, the Middle Ages, although today we see that contrast as being less marked than was previously thought. In his study on the modernity of the sixteenth century, Henri Hauser in 1930 listed the following as the distinctly innovative, modern features of the Renaissance: the conception of the world and of science, the emergence of both an individual and a social morality, the feeling of the soul's inner freedoms, the existence of both an internal politics and an international politics, the appearance of capitalism and formation of a proletariat, and the birth of the national economy.[1] Of the foregoing, the feature that is most relevant to the focus used in the present volume is the emergence of individual morality. The new emphasis on values of the individual, the transcendence of a traditional morality based on collective moral principle, was,

---

[1] *La modernité du XVIe Siècle* (1930) (Paris: Armand Colin, 1963), 65.

as has been observed in the foregoing studies, largely a consequence of the new secular moral culture that broke with the dogma of Original Sin by affirming natural human goodness and the value of behavior that is consistent with the law of human nature (Hauser, *Modernité*, 32). It should not surprise us that much of the innovation that occurred in the Renaissance drew little attention to itself and its departure from the past. The process of modernization has met with resistance always and everywhere. One example is the heroic struggle of eighteenth-century encyclopedists against the intellectual and temporal authority of the Church. Without trying to draw comparisons between different periods, suffice it to say that in the Renaissance the emergence of individual freedom and the liberalization of culture constituted a radical change that for the first time conflicted on a large scale with a cultural and economic establishment that had exercised its hegemony for almost a millennium. The established order was represented above all by the aristocratic Church, the largest landowner in Europe. In Spain the Church formed an alliance with monarchic government, and the resistance to change was relentless and powerful. Yet the modernization of culture and eventually of society did take place, in spite of fact that in many ways change was combated. The means Renaissance humanists used to precipitate a "transvaluation of values" were effective largely because they were subtle and inconspicuous. The example of Montemayor's anti-dogmatic, liberatingly ambivalent, "Nicodemist" strategy in his *Diana* is one instance, yet the essence of Montemayor's strategy is present to varying degrees in all the works we have examined. The observation with which Henri Hauser concludes his study is, "And among the great spirits who, mixed together with the imprudent and the bold, transmit to future generations the flame of the Renaissance, how many are wearing masks?" (*Modernité*, 65; my translation).

The Renaissance introduced a vogue for a new ethical ideal, a new ideal moral disposition that is represented in the works we have studied. That ideal is a synthesis of the old and the new. The old quality was the element of life as a source of suffering, the world as a vale of tears. That trait was in keeping with the age-old penitential Christianity, which, incidentally, became strongly accentuated in the course of the sixteenth century, in the more conservative tendencies within the Church. The new quality, the one that gives Renaissance literary culture its unique flavor, is that it combines with the quality just mentioned the element of childlike innocence, purity of heart. In the works we have analyzed in the present volume, that quality is presented both in ways that are obvious and in ways that are not obvious. To give examples of the obvious ways, in Garcilaso's Sonnet 1 the poet-persona speaks of himself as having surrendered "sin arte" [artlessly] to the lady who will cause his destruction; in the

Mexía stanza the persona goes optimistically to his perdition with the ingenuous assumption that his love will exonerate him; in Garcilaso's Sonnet 2 the persona represents himself as crying like a child; in Garcilaso's Canción 1 the persona refers to himself as clinging to the lady like a lost child; in Garcilaso's Sonnet 22 the poet–persona stands saddened and in pain before the lady who, by raising her hand, shattered his youthful illusion of an ideal love; in Garcilaso's Sonnet 38 the persona is again represented as bathed in tears and "rending the air with sighs" because of the distance separating him from the lady upon whose presence he depends as though she were his mother; in Fray Luis de León's Sonnet 2 the poet–persona is again unable to tear himself away from the comforting presence of the lady upon whom he has come to depend the way an infant depends upon its mother; in Fray Luis's "En la Ascensión" the disciples refer to themselves as the babes who suckled at Christ's breasts; in *Lazarillo de Tormes* the protagonist is an eternal child, always foolish and powerless; in Ribeiro's *Menina e Moça* the tearful melancholy of disillusioned youth is the dominant note; in Montemayor's *Diana* the same quality of naive melancholy is combined with a pristine sexual innocence that, paradoxically, is uncontrollably passionate nonetheless; and in *Don Quijote* the protagonist is an elderly man who derives genuine moral strength from the ethos of immature ideals.

It is, I repeat, the combination of the first, outwardly pessimistic quality with the naive innocence of the second quality that gives the works studied here their uniquely "Renaissance" flavor. That combination is more than an external characteristic of style; it contains the secret of how Renaissance literature was subtly and inconspicuously able to effect progressive change under circumstances that were extraordinarily hostile to such change. An attitude of gloomy melancholy toward a life of suffering is the worldly wisdom that can come only from breadth of experience in life. In contrast, the pure-mindedness of the child can only be the result of a lack of experience. Neither of these extremes is desirable, but their combination, their synthesis, is highly desirable: the only way a full knowledge of the world is able to synthesize with purity of heart is if the latter exercises a redemptive power over the former, so that the experienced and worldly-wise person is assuaged and liberated by the naive simplicity of childlike innocence. The orientation that results is that of one whose eyes are opened yet who remains untainted by evil, of one who is aware of the realities of life but not rendered resentful, cynical, or malicious. That synthesis itself is precisely what effects progressive change in the individual and in the world. As Hartmann observes, the trustfulness of the pure mind is a power that has an influence for the good. "Nothing works so powerfully, so convincingly, for good, and so transforms others in their innermost character, as the mere presence of a pure-minded person who pursues the right undisturbed, just as he sees and understands it in his simplicity" (*Ethics*, 2: 214).

In tragic art the greatest advance was accomplished. It was Bakhtin who recognized the opposition between tragedy's "pure and open seriousness, always ready to submit to death and renewal" and what he called "the intolerant, dogmatic seriousness of the Middle Ages."[2] Not all of the works we have examined are predominantly tragic or elegiac. The Mexía stanza is not; *Lazarillo* is more ironic than tragic; and *Don Quijote* is a comic epic. Yet even these works have a tragic dimension, and the others are predominantly elegiac. Perhaps the best way to understand the mysteriously edifying and even triumphant character of tragedy is by seeing it as a synthesis of purity and the fullness of life. In all the works we have examined and in tragedy, the dramatic situation portrayed is set into motion by some violent act that is usually the result of an irrational/mean ("low": i.e., determined ontologically [by the egoism of natural law as the latter is manifested as instinct] vs. axiologically) character trait such as greed, servility, or a tyrannical will to power: often that violent act is evidenced vestigially as the brutal rebuff of a devoted lover. In any case, that circumstance gives the works a fatalistic surface in which there is depicted the ritual "death" of those ideals of healthy human relations that constitute the spiritual "cement" of the community and that are often represented metaphorically as the outward well-being of a tragic hero or heroine. That "death" is then countered by the fact that, in spite of the paralyzing and disorienting effects of the loss of human innocence, a spiritual rebirth is effected in the reader or audience member and the community by the fact that the protagonist's ethos of purity stands as an impressive bulwark against the violence suffered. That exemplary resistance is evidenced and celebrated even if the hero or heroine has incurred guilt (or, in the lyric we have been analyzing, even if the persona's emotional neediness compromises his appearance of a conventionally heroic aloofness, of an "existence for itself"). Macbeth, for example, displays such resistance to the pathological tendencies within himself, even if he does so "involuntarily." How? Purity is incapable of cunning, of understanding and reacting to evil or defending itself against it. If it were able to succeed in doing so, purity would not be lost and the experience of that loss would not be a source of pain. Macbeth's propensity for naive idealism reasserts itself as the agony of remorse that drives him to madness. In the lyric by Garcilaso and Fray Luis

---

[2] *Rabelais and His World* (1965), trans. H. Iswolsky (Bloomington: Indiana University Press, 1984), 121–22.

that we have examined, the personas also suffer: those rebuffed lovers even suffer willingly, for in their single-mindedness in love they continue to love passionately even when their love is not reciprocated. Again, in Hartmann's words, "He who is pure does not actualize; his ethos is not in the pursuit of ends" (*Ethics*, 2: 216). Perhaps the necessary failure to actualize is the most apt way of accounting for both the frustration of the tragic hero/heroine and for our impression of his/her high moral stature, which is rooted in an element of naive innocence. As has already been discussed, Hartmann's reference is to the fact that the value intended can stand in opposition to the morally higher value of the intention and that the attainment of values frequently conflicts with the value of the commitment to their attainment, since the striving for that attainment would lose moral value if the reality aimed at were actualized (*Ethics*, 2: 84–85). A person's estimate of the value of purity, even if that estimate is not conscious, is so much the higher if he or she endures unbearable pain in a struggle against the inevitable and irretrievable loss of that value. In that way, the experience of pain becomes a sign of distinction, an aesthetic value, and the synthesis of knowledge of the world and personal integrity come to constitute a powerful basis for progressive, humanistic culture and for the advancement of a more humane and just social order.

In sum, in early modern literature the worldliness and secularism of Renaissance culture — its emphasis on, for example, the love of the sexes and the ecstasy of the passionate fulfillment of that love, these being regarded as values worth dying for — was counterbalanced by exempla of the moral pre-eminence of purity of heart. The result was a group of extraordinarily fruitful advances that included breakthroughs in various areas simultaneously. Four of those areas were as follows. First, the evocation of the *pain* of disenchantment or remorse, by representing a character's struggle against the loss of naive innocence in a world where such innocence makes one especially vulnerable to suffering, both brought literature into closer contact with life in a world seen as not being guided by Providence and made that literature relatively immune to censorship because its mournful tone seemed consistent with the anthropological pessimism of the dominant, ecclesiastical culture. Second, the new literature's sympathetic attitude towards protagonists and personas drawn from real life complemented the humanistic agenda of affirming the natural nobility of "Man," of advancing the principle of the inherent goodness of human nature (once denounced as "Pelagianism"). The indirect threat that such an ideology represented to the Church is more understandable if one considers the threat to the Church's role in overseeing penitential observances and administering grace and salvation that is represented by the heterodox Catholic Reformist doctrine that Christ's Passion effects remission of all human sins, both personal and original. The humanist assertion that human nature is innately virtuous is a secular equivalent of the Reformist (both Catholic and Protestant) repudiation of the doctrine that works alone have the power to justify. In either case the Church's role as mediator is rendered relatively superfluous. Third, the ideal of individual, subjective moral culture that is represented in the synthesis of spiritual purity and multifaceted fullness of experience in the world represents an important gain for civic culture. Not only are people now able to reconcile independent critical intelligence (speculative rationalism and the new spirit of skepticism, as opposed both to Christian optimism and to the pessimistic dogma of the corruptness of human nature) with a positive, constructive interest in human affairs, but they are also much better equipped to rise above life's brutal blows and disappointments. Fourth, an enormous advance was realized in aesthetics. Not only was it now possible to combine heroism and irony as it had been combined in ancient tragedy, but the idyllic and satirical also played a role in contributing to the emergence of a colorful, complex, and non-didactic vision of life, as tragic art was now extended beyond drama to lyric and to prose fiction. In literary movements subsequent to the Renaissance, the element of disillusionment and pain at loss of purity of heart became more and more emphasized until the memory of the ideal innocence that was being mourned as lost became obscured and that oblivion itself became an esoteric, modernist expression of protest.

Works Cited

A. PRIMARY SOURCES

Adler, Alfred. *The Individual Psychology of Alfred Adler: A Systematic Presentation in Selections from His Writings.* Ed. Heinz L. Ansbacher. New York: Basic, 1956.

———. *The Neurotic Constitution* (1926). Trans. Bernard Glueck and John E. Lind. 2nd English ed. North Stratford, NH: Ayer, 1998.

———. *The Practice and Theory of Individual Psychology.* Trans. P. Radin. New York: Harcourt, 1924.

Alonso, Dámaso. *Obras completas.* 8 vols. Madrid: Gredos, 1972.

Saint Thomas Aquinas. *Summa Theologica.* Trans. Timothy Suttor. In *Complete Works.* 61 vols. New York: McGraw, 1970. Vol. 11.

Aristotle. *De Anima.* Trans. R. D. Hicks. New York: Arno, 1976.

———. *The Ethics of Aristotle: The Nicomachean Ethics.* Trans. J. A. K. Thompson. London: George Allen & Unwin, 1953.

———. *Nicomachean Ethics.* Trans. Terence Irwin. Indianapolis: Hackett, 1985.

Bacon, Francis. *The Essays.* Ed. Mary Augusta Scott. New York: Charles Scribner's Sons, 1908.

Bembo, Pietro. *Gli Asolani* (1505). Trans. Rudolf B. Gottfried. Bloomington: Indiana University Press, 1954.

———. *Prose e rime.* Ed. Carlo Dionisotti. Classici Italiani 26. Torino: Tipografia Torinese, 1960.

Bergson, Henri. *The Two Sources of Morality and Religion* (1932). Trans. R. Ashley Audra and Cloudesley Brererton. Garden City, NY: Doubleday, 1956.

Bernard of Cluny. *De contemptu mundi*. Trans. R. E. Pepin. East Lansing, MI: Colleagues Press, 1991.

Boccaccio, Giovanni. *Thirteen Most Pleasant and Delectable Questions of Love*. Trans. Harry Carter. New York: Clarkson N. Potter, 1974.

Boethius, Anicius Manlius Severinus. *The Consolation of Philosophy*. Trans. I.T. Carbondale, IL: Southern Illinois University Press, 1963.

Cancionero de Estúñiga. Ed. Manuel and Elena Alvar. Zaragoza: Institución Fernando el Católico, 1981.

Castiglione, Baltasar. *El cortesano* (1525). Trans. Juan Boscán (1533). 2nd ed. Buenos Aires: Espasa-Calpe, 1946.

Cervantes Saavedra, Miguel de. *El ingenioso hidalgo don Quijote de la Mancha*. Ed. Martín de Riquer. Barcelona: Editorial Juventud, 1968.

———. *La Galatea*. In *Miguel de Cervantes: Obras Completas*, ed. Ángel Valbuena Prat, 605–767. Madrid: Aguilar, 1967.

———. *La Galatea*. Ed. Francisco López Estrada. Madrid: Cátedra, 1999.

Dilthey, Wilhelm. "Shakespeare y sus contemporáneos." In idem, *Literatura y fantasía* (1954). In *Obras completas de Wilhelm Dilthey*, trans. Emilio Uranga and Carlos Gerhard. 9: 54–102. México: Fondo de Cultura Económica, 1963.

———. "The Great Poetry of the Imagination." In *W. Dilthey: Selected Writings*, trans. H. P. Rickman, 79–84. Cambridge University Press, 1976.

Fairbairn, W. Ronald D. "Observations on the Nature of Hysterical States." *British Journal of Medical Psychology* 27 (1954): 105–25.

———. *Psychoanalytic Studies of the Personality* (1952). London: Routledge & Kegan Paul, 1976.

Ficino, Marsilio. *Commentary on Plato's Symposium on Love*. Trans. Sears Jayne. Dallas: Spring, 1985.

Fray Luis de León. *Poesía completa*. Ed. José Manuel Blecua. Madrid: Gredos, 1990.

———. *Cantar de Cantares de Salomón*. Ed. José Manuel Blecua. Madrid: Gredos, 1944.

———. *Obras completas castellanas*. Ed. P. Félix García. Madrid: Editorial Católica, 1959.

———. *Obras poéticas del maestro Fray Luis de León*. Ed. P. José Llobera. 2 vols. Cuenca: Talleres tipográficos del Seminario, 1931–1932.

———. *Original Poems*. Ed. Edward Sarmiento. Manchester: Manchester University Press, 1968.

———. *Poesías*. Ed. Oreste Macrí. Barcelona: Editorial Crítica, 1982.

———. *Poesías*. Ed. Ángel C. Vega. Madrid: Saeta, 1955.

———. *Poesías completas*. Ed. Cristóbal Cuevas. Madrid: Castalia, 1988, repr. 2000.

Freud, Sigmund. *Collected Papers*. Trans. Joan Riviere (1924). 5 vols. London: Hogarth Press, 1950.

———. "Instincts and their Vicissitudes" (1924). In Standard Edition, 14: 109–40. London: Hogarth Press, 1957.

———. *The Standard Edition of the Complete Psychological Works*. Trans. James Strachey (1953). 24 vols. London: Hogarth, 1964.

———. "Three Contributions to the Theory of Sexuality" (1905). In Standard Edition, 7: 135–243. London: Hogarth, 1957.

Garcilaso de la Vega. *Obras completas con comentario*. Ed. Elias L. Rivers. Columbus, OH: Ohio State University Press, 1974.

———. *Obra poética y textos en prosa*. Ed. Bienvenido Morros. Barcelona: Crítica, 1995.

Goethe, Johann Wolfgang von. *Maxims and Reflections*, ed. Peter Hutchinson. Trans. Linda Stopp. London: Penguin Books, 1998.

———. *Maximen und Reflexionen*. In *Goethes Werke: Festausgabe*, ed. Robert Petsch, 18 vols. Trans. Linda Stopp, Leipzig: Bibliographischen Instituts, 1926. 14: 214–436.

Gorky, Maxim. *Letters*. Trans. V. Dutt. Moscow: Progress, 1966.

———. *On Literature: Selected Articles*. Trans. V. Dober. Moscow: Foreign Languages Publishing House, n.d.

———. *Twenty-Six Men and a Girl and Other Stories*. New York: Avon, 1957.

———. *Untimely Thoughts: Essays on Revolution, Culture and the Bolsheviks, 1917–1918*. Trans. Herman Ermolaev. New York: Eriksson, 1968.

Hartmann, Nicolai. *Ethics* (1926). Trans. Stanton Coit. 3 vols. London: Unwin, 1932.

———. *Ontología* (1934–1954). Trans. José Gaos. 5 vols. 2nd/3rd ed. México: Fondo de Cultura Económica, 1986.

Hegel, G. W. F. *Aesthetics: Lectures on Fine Art*. Trans. T. M. Knox. 2 vols. Oxford: Clarendon, 1975. Vol. 1.

———. *Hegel's Philosophy of Right* (1833). Trans. T. M. Knox. London: Oxford University Press, 1967.

Heine, Heinrich. *The Poetry and Prose of Heinrich Heine*. Ed. Frederic Ewen. New York: Citadel, 1948.

———. *Selected Works*. Trans. Helen M. Mustard. New York: Random House, 1973.

San Juan de la Cruz. *Obras completas*. Ed. Lucinio Ruano de la Iglesia. Madrid: Biblioteca de Autores Cristianos, 1982.

Jung, C. G. *The Collected Works*. Trans. R. F. C. Hull. 20 vols. London: Routledge & Kegan Paul, 1957–1979.

———. *The Integration of the Personality*. Trans. Stanley Dell. London: K. Paul, 1940.

———. *Man and His Symbols*. New York: Doubleday, 1964.

Klein, Melanie. *Love, Hate and Reparation: Two Lectures by Melanie Klein and Joan Riviere*. London: Hogarth Press, 1967.

La vida de Lazarillo de Tormes y de sus fortunas y adversidades. Ed. Joseph V. Ricapito. 14th ed. Madrid: Cátedra, 1985.

León Hebreo. *Diálogos de amor*. Trans. Inca Garcilaso de la Vega. Ed. P. Carmelo Sanz de Santa María, S.I. In *Obras completas de Inca Garcilaso de la Vega*, 1: 3–227. BAE, 132–135. Madrid: Atlas, 1960.

———. *Diálogos de amor* (1535). Trans. Carlos Mazo del Castillo. 2nd ed. Barcelona: PPU, 1993.

Montemayor, Jorge de. *El Cancionero del poeta George de Montemayor*. Ed. Angel González Palencia. Madrid: Sociedad de Bibliófilos, 1932, repr. 1942.

———. *La Diana*. Ed. Juan Montero. Barcelona: Crítica, 1996.

———. *Los seite libros de la Diana*. Ed. Francisco López Estrada. 5th ed. Clásicos Catestellanos 127. Madrid: Espasa-Calpe, 1970.

———. *Segundo cancionero espiritual*. Antwerp: Juan Latio, 1558.

Plato. *The Collected Dialogues*. Ed. Edith Hamilton and Huntington Cairns. New York: Bollingen Foundation, 1961.

Ribeiro, Bernardim. *História de Menina e Moça*. Ed. D. E. Grokenberger. Lisbon: Studium Editora, 1947.

———. *História de Menina e Moça: reprodução facsimilada da edição de Ferara,*

1554. Ed. José V. de Pina Martins. Lisbon: Fundação Calouste Gulbenkian, 2002.

———. *Obras Completas*. Ed. Aquilino Ribeiro and M. Marques Braga. 2 vols. Lisbon: Sa da Costa, 1950.

Sannazaro, Jacopo. *Arcadia and Piscatorial Eclogue*. Trans. Ralph Nash. Detroit: Wayne State University Press, 1966.

Scheler, Max. *Formalism in Ethics and Non-Formal Ethics of Values* (1913–1916). Trans. Manfred S. Frings and Roger L. Funk. Evanston, IL: Northwestern University Press, 1973.

———. "The Meaning of Suffering." Trans. Daniel Liederbach. In *Max Scheler (1874–1928): Centennial Essays*, ed. Manfred Frings, 121–63. The Hague: Nijhof, 1974.

———. *The Nature of Sympathy*. Trans. Peter Heath. London: Routledge, 1954.

———. *Person and Self-Value: Three Essays*. Trans. M. S. Frings and Bernard Noble. Dordrecht: Nijhoff, 1987.

———. *Ressentiment*. Trans. William H. Holdheim. New York: Free Press, 1961.

Schiller, Friedrich von. *Naive and Sentimental Poetry and On the Sublime: Two Essays*. Trans. Julius A. Elias. New York: Ungar, 1966.

Santa Teresa de Jesús. *Obras*. Ed. Silverio de Santa Teresa. Burgos: El Monte Carmelo, 1954.

Tolstoy, Lev. *What is Art?* Trans. Charles Johnston. Philadelphia: Henry Altemus, 1898.

Troeltsch, Ernst. *Protestantism and Progress: A Historical Study of the Relations of Protestantism to the Modern World* (1912). Trans. W. Montgomery. Repr. Boston: Beacon, 1966.

B. SECONDARY WORKS

Abellán, José Luis. *Historia crítica del pensamiento español*. 5 vols. Madrid: Espasa-Calpe, 1979.

Adams, Hazard. *Philosophy of the Literary Symbolic*. Tallahassee: University Press of Florida, 1983.

Aguirre, J. M. "Reflexiones para la construcción de un modelo de la poesía castellana del amor cortés." *Romanische Forschungen* 93 (1981): 55–81.

Alfonsi, Sandra Resnick. *Masculine Submission in the Troubadour Lyric*. New York: P. Lang, 1986.

Alonso Cortés, Narciso. "Sobre Montemayor y 'La Diana'." In *Artículos históricos-literarios*, 127–40. Valladolid: Imprenta Castellana, 1935.

Alpers, Paul. *What is Pastoral?* Chicago: University of Chicago Press, 1996

Aristotelismus und Renaissance, ed. E. Kessler et al. Wiesbaden: Harrassowitz, 1988

Arribas, Julián. Introduction to Jorge de Montemayor, *Los siete libros de la Diana*, 1–22. London: Tamesis, 1996.

Asch, Stuart S. "The Analytic Concepts of Masochism: A Reevaluation." In *Masochism: Current Psychoanalytic Perspectives*, ed. Robert A. Glick et al., 93–115. Hillsdale, NJ: Analytic Press, 1988.

Asensio, Eugenio. "Bernardim Ribeiro a la luz de un manuscrito nuevo: Cultura literaria y problemas textuales." In idem, *Estudios portugueses*, 199–223. Paris: Fundação Calouste Gulbenkian, 1974.

———. "El *Romance* de Bernardim Ribeiro 'Ao longo da ribeira': Texto nuevo e interpretación." In idem, *Estudios portugueses*, 225–42. Paris: Fundação Calouste Gulbenkian, 1974.

———. "Una nueva edición de *Menina e Moça*," In idem, *Estudios portugueses*, 189–97. Paris: Fundação Calouste Gulbenkian, 1974.

Avalle-Arce, Juan Bautista. *La novela pastoril española*. Madrid: Revista de Occidente, 1959.

———. *Nuevos deslindes cervantinos*. Barcelona: Ariel, 1975.

Bain, Alexander. *The Emotions and the Will*. 3rd ed. New York: Appleton, 1976.

Bakhtin, Mikail. *Rabelais and His World* (1965). Trans. Hélène Iswolsky. Bloomington: Indiana University Press, 1984.

Bataillon, Marcel. *Erasmo y el erasmismo*. Barcelona: Editorial Crítica, 1983.

———. *Erasmo y España: Estudios sobre la historia espiritual del siglo XVI* (1937). Trans. Antonio Alatorre. 2nd Spanish ed. México: Fondo de Cultura Económica, 1966.

———. "Humanismo, erasmismo y represión cultural en la España del siglo XVI." In idem, *Erasmo y el erasmismo*, 162–78.

———. Introduction to Erasmus of Rotterdam, *Enquiridion o manual del caballero cristiano*, ed. Dámaso Alonso, 7–84. 2nd ed. Traducciones del siglo XVI. Madrid: Revista de Filología Española, 1971.

Bell, Aubrey F. G. *Cervantes*. Norman, OK: University of Oklahoma Press, 1947.
———. *Luis de León: A Study of the Spanish Renaissance*. Oxford: Clarendon Press, 1925.
Bianchi, Luca. "From Jacques Lefèvre d'Etaples to Giulio Landi: Uses of the Dialogue in Renaissance Aristotelianism." In *Humanism and Early Modern Philosophy*, ed. Kraye and Stone, 41–58. London: Routledge, 2000.
Blüher, Karl Alfred. *Séneca en España: Investigaciones sobre la recepción de Séneca en España desde el siglo xiii hasta el siglo xvii*. Trans. Juan Conde. Biblioteca Románica Hispánica, 2: 329. Madrid: Gredos, 1983.
Boase, Roger. "Imagery of Love, Death, and Fortune in the Poetry of Manuel Ximénez de Urrea (1486–c. 1530)." *Bulletin of Hispanic Studies* 57 (1980): 17–32.
Bolgar, R. R. *The Classical Heritage and Its Beneficiaries*. Cambridge: Cambridge University Press, 1954.
Bonnafoux, Denise. " 'En la Ascensión' de Fray Luis de León." In *Mélanges à la Mémoire d'André Joucla-Ruau*, ed. Chalon Paul et al., 491–500. Aix-en-Provence: Université de Provence, 1978.
Bosco, Umberto. *Francesco Petrarca*. Bari: Editori Laterza, 1961.
Bourke, J. *Will in Western Thought*. New York: Sheed, 1964.
Bousquet, Jacques. *Mannerism: The Painting and Style of the Late Renaissance*. Trans. Simon Watson Taylor. New York: Braziller, 1964.
Bouwsma, William J. "The Liberation of the Self." In idem, *The Waning of the Renaissance 1550–1640*, 20–34. New Haven: Yale University Press, 2000.
Bowlby, John. *Attachment and Loss*. 3 vols. New York: Basic, 1969–1980.
———. *The Making and Breaking of Affectional Bonds* (1979). London: Routledge, 1995.
Boyle, Marjorie O'Rourke. *Petrarch's Genius: Pentimento and Prophecy*. Berkeley: University of California Press, 1991.
Bradley, A. C. "Hegel's Theory of Tragedy." In *Hegel on Tragedy*, ed. Anne and Henry Paolucci, 367–88. New York: Harper & Row, 1962.
Bredvold, Louis I. *The Natural History of Sensibility*. Detroit: Wayne State University Press, 1962.
Brumble, David. *Classical Myths and Legends in the Middle Ages and Renaissance*. Westport, CT: Greenwood Press, 1988.
Brown, Peter. *The Body and Society: Women, and Sexual Renunciation in Early Christianity*. New York: Columbia University Press, 1988.

———. *The Cult of the Saints*. Chicago: University of Chicago Press, 1982.
Brumble, D. *Classical Myths and Legends in the Middle Ages and Renaissance*. Westport, CT: Greenwood Press, 1988.
Bultmann, Rudolf. *The Gospel of John: A Commentary*. Trans. G. R. Beasley-Murray, R. W. N. Hoare, and J. K. Riches. Philadelphia: Westminster, 1971.
Burdach, Konrad. *Riforma, Rinascimento, Umanesimo: Due dissertazioni sui fondamenti della cultura e dell'arte della parola moderna*. Trans. Delio Cantimori. Florence: G. C. Sansoni, 1935.
Camamis, George. *Estudios sobre el cautiverio en el Siglo de Oro*. Madrid: Gredos, 1977.
Carey, Douglas M. "*Lazarillo de Tormes* and the Quest for Authority." *PMLA* 94 (1979): 36–46.
Carreño, Antonio. " 'Las voces de mis duelos' (XIII, 38): El *Libro de Job en tercetos* de Fray Luis de León." In *San Juan de la Cruz and Fray Luis de León: A Commemorative International Symposium*, ed. Mary Malcolm Gaylord and Francisco Márquez Villanueva, 33–53. Newark, DE: Juan de la Cuesta, 1996.
Cascardi, Anthony J. "Instinct and Object: Subjectivity and Speech-Act in Garcilaso de la Vega." *Journal of Interdisciplinary Literary Studies* 6 (1994): 219–43.
Castro, Americo. *El pensamiento de Cervantes*. Madrid: Revista de Filología Española, 1925.
———. Introduction to *La vida de Lazarillo de Tormes y de sus fortunas y adversidades*, ed. Everett W. Hesse and Harry F. Williams, V–XII. Madison, WI: University of Wisconsin Press, 1948.
Chevalier, Jean, and Alain Gheerbrant. *A Dictionary of Symbols* (1969). Trans. John Buchanan-Brown. London: Penguin Books, 1996.
Chevalier, Maxime. *Lectura y lectores en la España de los siglos XVI y XVII*. Madrid: Turner, 1976.
Chorpenning, Joseph F. "Christ the Nursing Mother in Fray Luis de León's 'En la Ascensión'." *Journal of Hispanic Philology* 11 (1987): 199–204.
Cirlot, J. E. *A Dictionary of Symbols*. Trans. Jack Sage. London: Routledge: 1967.
Clark, Mary T. *Augustine, Philosopher of Freedom*. New York: Desclée, 1958.
Coen, Stanley J. "Sadomasochistic Excitement: Character Disorder and Perversion." In *Masochism: Current Psychoanalytic Perspectives*, ed. Glick et al., 43–59.
Colombí-Monguió, Alicia de. Review of A. J. Cruz, *Imitación y transformación:*

El petrarquismo en la poesía de Boscán y Garcilaso de la Vega and Antonio Gargano, *Fonti, Miti, Topoi: Cinque Studi su Garcilaso*. *Kentucky Romance Quarterly* 38 (1991): 95–106

Cooper, Arnold M. "The Narcissistic-Masochistic Character." In *Masochism: Current Psychoanalytic Perspectives*, ed. Glick et al., 117–38.

Coster, Adolphe. "Luis de León." *Revue Hispanique* 53 (1921): 1–468; 54 (1922): 1–346.

Cox, Virginia. *The Renaissance Dialogue*. Cambridge: Cambridge University Press, 1992.

Cranz, F. Edward. *A Bibliography of Aristotle Editions 1501–1600*. Baden-Baden: Koerner, 1984.

Creel, Bryant L. *Don Quijote, Symbol of a Culture in Crisis*. Valencia: Albatros-Hispanófila, 1988.

———. "Ribeiro, Bernardim." In *Encyclopedia of the Renaissance*, ed. P. F. Grendler. 6 vols., 5: 340–41. New York: Scribner, 1999.

———. "Canción I y Soneto II de Garcilaso y el problema del masoquismo en la lírica amatoria renacentista." In *Studia Aurea: Actas del III Congreso de la Asociación Internacional Siglo de Oro (Toulouse, 1993)*, 1: 299–307. Toulouse–Pamplona: GRISO-LEMSO, 1996.

———. "Garcilaso y el mito de la sumisión al amor-hado en la tradición cancioneril." In *Actas del XIII Congreso de la Asociación Internacional de Hispanistas, 1998*, ed. Florencio Sevilla and Carlos Alvar, 309–17. Madrid: Castalia, 2000.

———. *The Religious Poetry of Jorge de Montemayor*. London: Tamesis, 1981.

Cruz, Anne. *Discourses of Poverty: Social Reform and the Picaresque Novel in Early Modern Spain*. Toronto: University of Toronto Press, 1999.

———. *Imitación y transformación: El petrarquismo en la poesía de Boscán y Garcilaso de la Vega*. Amsterdam: John Benjamins, 1988.

———. "Spanish Petrarchism and the Poetics of Appropriation." In *Renaissance Rereadings: Intertext and Context*, ed. Maryanne Cline Horowitz, 80–95. Urbana: University of Illiois Press, 1988.

Culler, Jonathan. *Structuralist Poetics*. Ithaca, NY: Cornell University Press, 1975.

Damasio, Antonio R. *Descartes' Error: Emotion, Reason, and the Human Brain*. New York: Avon, 1994.

Damiani, Bruno M. *"La Diana" of Montemayor as Social and Religious Teaching*. Lexington, KY: University of Kentucky Press, 1983.

Darst, David H. "Garcilaso's Love for Isabel Freyre: The Creation of a Myth." *Journal of Hispanic Philology* 3 (1979): 261–68.

———. *Juan Boscán*. Boston: Twayne, 1978.

Deeken, Alfons. *Process and Permanence in Ethics: Max Scheler's Moral Philosophy*. New York: Paulist Press, 1974.

Delumeau, Jean. *La civilisation de la Renaissance*. Collection Les Grandes Civilisations. Paris: Artaud, 1967.

Denomy, Alexander J. *The Heresy of Courtly Love*. Gloucester, MA: Peter Smith, 1965.

Deyermond, Alan. "The Corrupted Vision: Further Thoughts on *Lazarillo de Tormes*." *Forum for Modern Language Studies* 1 (1965): 246–49.

———. *Historia de la literatura española: La Edad Media* (1971). Trans. Luis Alonso López. 15th ed. Barcelona: Ariel, 1992.

———. *Lazarillo de Tormes: A Critical Guide*. London: Grant & Cutler, 1973.

Le dialogue au temps de la Renaissance, ed. M. T. Jones-Davies. Paris: Touzot, 1984.

Díaz Díaz, Gonzalo. *Hombres y documentos de la filosofía española*. 1980; 2 vols. to date. Madrid: Consejo Superior de Investigaciones Científicas, 1983. Vol. 2.

Diccionario de Autoridades. 3 vols. Madrid: Gredos, 1990.

Djuth, Maryanne. "Liberty" and "Will." In *Augustine Through the Ages: An Encyclopedia*, ed. A. D. Fitzgerald, 495–98, 881–85. Grand Rapids, MI: Eerdmans, 1999.

Domínguez Ortiz, Antonio. "El Renacimiento español." In *El Renacimiento*, ed. Domínguez Ortiz et al., 5–27. Madrid: Ministerio de Cultura, 1978.

Dubrow, Heather. "Lyric Forms." In *Cambridge Companion to English Literature 1500–1600*, ed. Kinney, 178–99.

Dunn, Peter N. "*Lazarillo de Tormes*: The Case of the Purloined Letter." *Revista de Estudios Hispánicos* 22 (1988): 1–14.

Durán, Manuel. *Luis de León*. New York: Twayne, 1971.

———, and Miguel Atlee. *Fray Luis de León: Poesía*. Madrid: Cátedra, 1985.

Durkheim, Emile. *The Division of Labor in Society* (1893). Trans. W. D. Halls. New York: Free Press, 1984.

———. *Emile Durkheim on Morality and Society: Selected Writings*. Ed. Robert N. Bellah. Chicago: University of Chicago Press, 1973.

Eagleton, Terry. *Literary Theory: An Introduction*. Minneapolis: University of Minnesota Press, 1983.

Eco, Umberto. *The Aesthetics of Thomas Aquinas*. Trans. Hugh Bredin. Cambridge, MA: Harvard University Press, 1988.

Egido, Aurora. "Contar en *La Diana*." In *Formas del breve relato*, ed. Y.-R. Fonquerne, 137–55. Madrid: Casa de Velázquez, 1986.

Eidelberg, Ludwig, ed. *Encyclopedia of Psychoanalysis*. New York: Free Press, 1968.

Eisenberg, Daniel. *A Study of Don Quijote*. Newark, DE: Juan de la Cuesta, 1987.

Elliott, J. H. "The Decline of Spain." In *Crisis in Europe, 1560–1660*, ed. Trevor Henry Aston, 167–93. New York: Basic, 1965.

El Saffar, Ruth. *Beyond Fiction: The Recovery of the Feminine in the Novels of Cervantes*. Berkeley: University of California Press, 1984.

Engammare, Max. *Le Cantique des Cantiques à la Renaissance*. Geneva: Droz, 1993.

Erasmus, Desiderius. *Querela Pacis*. In *Opera Omnia Disiderii Erasmi Roterdami*, ed. O. Herding, 4.2. Amsterdam: North-Holland, 1977.

Felkel, Robert W. "Aristóteles, Santo Tomás y la percepción sensorial en el *Quijote*." *Anuario de Letras* 28 (1990): 181–231.

Ferguson, Wallace K. *The Renaissance in Historical Thought: Five Centuries of Interpretation*. New York: Houghton, 1948.

Figueroa, Diego J. "La 'Oda a la Ascensión' de Fray Luis." *Religión y cultura* 10 (1965): 211–28.

Fiore, Robert L. *Lazarillo de Tormes*. Boston: Twayne, 1984.

Forcione, Alban K. *Cervantes, Aristotle, and the Persiles*. Princeton, NJ: Princeton University Press, 1970.

Fosalba, Eugenia. *La Diana en Europa: ediciones, traducciones e influencias*. Barcelona: Universitat Autònoma de Barcelona, 1994.

Fraile, Guillermo. *Historia de la filosofía española*. 2 vols. Madrid: Castalia, 1971–1972. Vol. 1.

Frenk Alatorre, Margit. *Estudios sobre la lírica antigua*. Madrid: Castalia, 1978.

———, ed. *Lírica española de tipo popular*. 1966. Madrid: Cátedra, 1989.

Fromm, Erich. *Escape from Freedom* (1941). New York: Holt, 1964.

Frye, Northrop. *The Secular Scripture: A Study of the Structure of Romance*. Cambridge, MA: Harvard University Press, 1976.

———. *Anatomy of Criticism: Four Essays*. Princeton: Princeton University Press, 1957.

———. *Fables of Identity: Studies in Poetic Mythology*. New York: Harcourt, 1963.

———. *Myth and Metaphor: Selected Essays 1974–1988*. Charlottesville, VA: University Press of Virginia, 1990.

Gallego Morell, Antonio. *Garcilaso de la Vega y sus comentaristas*. Granada: Universidad de Granada, 1966.

García de la Concha, Víctor. *Nueva lectura del "Lazarillo": el deleite de la perspectiva*. Literatura y Sociedad 28. Madrid: Castalia, 1981.

Gargano, Antonio. *Fonti, miti, topoi: Cinque saggi su Garcilaso*. Naples: Liguori, 1988.

Genette, Gérard. "Structuralism and Literary Criticism." In *Modern Criticism and Theory*, ed. David Lodge, 63–78. New York: Longman, 1989.

Gerrig, Richard J. *Experiencing Narrative Worlds*. New Haven: Yale University Press, 1993.

Gibbs, Raymond W. J. *The Poetics of Mins: Figurative Thought, Language, and Understanding*. New York: Cambridge University Press, 1994.

Gicovate, Bernard. *Garcilaso de la Vega*. Boston: Twayne, 1975.

Gillette, Marie. "Foolish Fancies? Maybe Not. Symptoms of Melancholy in *La Diana*." *Romance Notes* 39 (1998): 95–102.

Gilman, S. "The Death of Lazarillo de Tormes." *PMLA* 81 (1966): 149–66.

Godard, Anne. *Le dialogue à la Renaissance*. Paris: Presses Universitaires de France, 2001.

Gombrich, E. H. *Aby Warburg*. 2nd ed. Oxford: Phaidon, 1986.

Goodwyn, Frank. "New Light on the Historical Setting of Garcilaso's Poetry." *Hispanic Review* 46 (1978): 1–22.

Graff, Gerald. "Determinacy/Indeterminacy." In *Critical Terms for Literary Study*, ed. Frank Lentricchia et al., 163–76. Chicago: University of Chicago Press, 1990.

Green, Otis H. *Spain and the Western Tradition*. 4 vols. Madison, WI: University of Wisconsin Press, 1964.

Greimas, Algirdas Julien. *Narrative Semiotics and Cognitive Discourses*. Trans. Paul Perron and Frank H. Collins. London: Pinter Publishers, 1990.

Grotstein, James S. *Splitting and Projective Identification*. New York: Jason Aronson, 1981.

Guillén, Claudio, "La disposición temporal del *Lazarillo de Tormes*." *Hispanic Review* 25 (1957): 264–79.

Guntrip, Harry. *Personality, Structure, and Human Interaction: The Developing Synthesis of Psycho-dynamic Theory* (1961). New York: International Universities Press, 1977.

Gutherie, W. C. *Orpheus and Greek Religion*. New York: Norton, 1966.

Hagen, Oskar. *Patterns and Principles of Spanish Art*. Madison, WI: University of Wisconsin Press, 1948.

Hamilton, N. Gregory. *Self and Others: Object Relations Theory in Practice*. Northvale, NJ: Aronson, 1988.

Hamlyn, D. W. *Sensation and Perception: A History of the Philosophy of Perception*. 1961. London: Routledge & Kegan Paul, 1963.

Harnack, Adolph von. *History of Dogma*. Trans. Neil Buchanan. 7 vols. New York: Russel, 1958.

Hatzfeld, Helmut. "Literary Mannerism and Baroque in Spain and France." *Comparative Literature Studies* 7 (1970): 419–36.

Hauser, Arnold. *Mannerism: The Crisis of the Renaissance and the Origin of Modern Art*. Trans. Arnold Hauser and Eric Mosbacher. 2 vols. London: Routledge, 1965.

———. *The Social History of Art*. Trans. Stanley Godman. 4 vols. New York: Vintage Books, 1957.

Hauser, Henri. *La modernité du XVIe siècle* (1930). Paris: Armand Colin, 1963.

Heiple, Daniel L. *Garcilaso de la Vega and the Italian Renaissance*. University Park, PA: Pennsylvania State University Press, 1994.

Hinshelwood, R. D. *A Dictionary of Kleinian Thought*. London: Free Association Books, 1989.

Holland, Norman N. *The Brain of Robert Frost*. New York: Routledge, 1988.

Horney, Karen. *Our Inner Conflicts: A Constructive Theory of Neurosis*. New York: Norton, 1945.

Huizinga, Johan. *The Waning of the Middle Ages: A Study of the forms of Life, Thought and Art in France and The Netherlands in the Fourteenth and Fifteenth Centuries* (1924). London: Arnold, 1955.

———. *The Autumn of the Middle Ages* (1924). Trans. R. J. Payton and U. Mammitzsch. Chicago: University of Chicago Press, 1996.

Humanism and Early Modern Philosophy, ed. Jill Kraye and M. W. Stone. London: Routledge, 2000.

Hutchinson, Steven. *Cervantine Journeys*. Madison, WI: University of Wisconsin Press, 1992.

Ihrie, Maureen. *Skepticism in Cervantes*. London: Tamesis, 1982.

Jaén, Didier. "La ambigüedad moral del *Lazarillo de Tormes*." *PMLA* 83 (1968): 130–34.

Jameson, Frederick. *The Prison-House of Language: A Critical Account of Structuralism and Russian Formalism*. Princeton: Princeton University Press, 1972.

Jerrold, Maude F. *Francesco Petrarca: Poet and Humanist*. Port Washington, NY: Kennikat Press, 1970.

Johnson, C. B. "Montemayor's *Diana*: A Novel Pastoral." *Bulletin of Hispanic Studies* 48 (1971): 25–35.

Johnson, Mark. *The Body in the Mind: The Bodily Basis of Meaning, Imagination, and Reason*. Chicago: University of Chicago Press, 1987.

———, ed. *Philosophical Perspectives on Metaphor*. Minneapolis: University of Minnesota Press, 1981.

Jones, R. O. *The Golden Age: Prose and Poetry*. London: Ernest Benn, 1971.

Kamen, Henry. *European Society 1500–1700*. London: Hutchinson, 1984.

Kelley, Joan. "Did Women Have a Renaissance?" In eadem, *Women, History, and Theory*, 12–50. Chicago: University of Chicago Press, 1984.

Kenniston, Hayward. *Garcilaso de la Vega: A Critical Study of His Life and Works*. New York: Hispanic Society of America, 1921.

Kettle, Arnold. *An Introduction to the English Novel*. 2 vols. New York: Harper & Row, 1960.

King, Margaret L. and Sarah Covington. "Women." In *Encyclopedia of the Renaissance*, ed. P. F. Grendler, 6 vols., 6: 317–28. New York: Scribner, 1999.

Kirschner, Suzanne R. *The Religious and Romantic Origins of Psychoanalysis: Individuation and Integration in Post-Freudian Theory*. New York: Cambridge University Press, 1996.

Klibansky, Raymond, Erwin Panofsky, and Fritz Saxl. *Saturn and Melancholy: Studies in the History of Natural Philosophy, Religion, and Art, by Raymond Klibansky, Erwin Panofsky, and Fritz Saxl*. New York: Basic, 1964.

Kristeller, Paul Oskar. "Florentine Platonism and Its Relations with Humanism and Scholasticism." *Church History* 8 (1939): 201–11.

———. *The Philosophy of Marsilio Ficino*. Trans. Virginia Conant. Gloucester, MA: Peter Smith, 1964.

———. *Renaissance Thought: The Classic, Scholastic, and Humanist Strains* (1955). New York: Harper & Row, 1961.

———. *Studies in Renaissance Thought and Letters*. Roma: Edizioni di Storia e Letteratura, 1956.

Lakoff, George, and Mark Johnson. *Metaphors We Live By*. Chicago: University of Chicago Press, 1980.

Lapesa, Rafael. *Garcilaso: Estudios completos*. Madrid: ISTMO, 1985.

———. *Poetas y prosistas de ayer y hoy*. Madrid: Gredos, 1977.

Lázaro Carreter, F. "Los sonetos de Fray Luis de León." In *Mélanges à la mémoire de Jean Sarrailh*, 2 vols., 2: 29–40. Paris: Centre de Recherche de l'Institut d'Etudes Hispaniques, 1966.

Lazareth, William H. "ELCA Lutherans and Luther on Heterosexual Marriage." *Lutheran Quarterly* 3 (1984): 235–68.

Levin, Leslie. *Metaphors of Conversion in Seventeenth-Century Spanish Drama*. London: Tamesis, 1999.

Lewis, C. S. *The Allegory of Love: A Study in Medieval Tradition*. Oxford: Oxford University Press, 1939.

———. *The Discarded Image*. Cambridge: Cambridge University Press, 1964.

———, and E. M. W. Tillyard. *The Personal Heresy: A Controversy by E. M. W. Tillyard and C. S. Lewis*. London: Oxford University Press, 1939.

Lida de Malkiel, María Rosa. *Juan de Mena, poeta del prerrenacimeinto español*. Ed. Yakov Malkiel. México: El Colegio de México, 1984.

Lipari, Angelo. *The Dolce Stil Novo According to Lorenzo de' Medici: A Study of his Poetic "Principio" as an Interpretation of the Italian Literature of the Pre-Renaissance Period, Based on his "Comento."* New Haven: Yale University Press, 1936.

López Estrada, Francisco. "La epístola de Jorge de Montemayor a Diego Ramírez Pagán (Una interpretación del desprecio por el cortesano en la *Diana*)." In *Estudios dedicados a D. Ramón Menéndez Pidal*, 7 vols., 6: 387–406. Madrid: Consejo Superior de Investigaciones Científicos, 1956.

———. *Libros de pastores en la literatura española*. Biblioteca Románica Hispánica 2: 213. Madrid: Gredos, 1974.

Lucka, Emil. *The Evolution of Love*. Trans. Ellie Schleussner. London: George Allen & Unwin, 1922.

Luhmann, Niklas. *Love as Passion: The Codification of Intimacy*. Trans. Jeremy Gaines and Doris L. Jones. Cambridge: Polity, 1986.

Lukács, Georg. *Realism in Our Time: Literature and the Class Struggle.* Trans. John and Necke Mande. World Perspectives 33. New York: Harper & Row, 1964.

Ly, Nadine. "Garcilaso: Une autre trajectoire poétique." *Bulletin hispanique* 83 (1981): 263–329.

Macpherson, Ian. "Secret Language in the *Cancioneros*: Some Courtly Codes." *Bulletin of Hispanic Studies* 62 (1985): 51–63.

Maçedo, Helder. *Do significado oculto da "Menina a Moça."* Lisbon: Moraes Editores, 1977.

Mancing, Howard. *The Chivalric World of "Don Quijote": Style, Structure, and Narrative Technique.* Columbia, MO: University of Missouri Press, 1982.

———. "The Deceptiveness of *Lazarillo de Tormes*." *PMLA* 90 (1975): 426–32.

Manero Sorolla, María Pilar. "La configuración imaginística de la dama en la lírica española del Renacimiento: La tradición petrarquística." *Boletín de la Biblioteca Menéndez Pelayo* 68 (1992): 5–71.

Marañón, Gregorio. "Sobre la novela picaresca." In idem, *Obras completas*, ed. Alfredo Juderías, 1: 1019–27. Madrid: Espasa-Calpe, 1966.

Maravall, José Antonio. *Poder, honor y élites en el siglo XVII.* Madrid: Siglo XXI, 1979.

———. *La literatura picaresca desde la historia social (siglos XVI y XVII).* Madrid: Taurus, 1986.

Márquez Villanueva, Francisco. "La locura emblemática en la segunda parte del *Quijote*." In *Cervantes and the Renaissance*, ed. Michael D. McGaha, 87–112. Easton, PA: Juan de la Cuesta, 1980.

———. "La actitud espiritual del *Lazarillo de Tormes*." In idem, *Espiritualidad y literatura en el siglo XVI*, 67–137. Madrid: Alfaguara, 1969.

Martin, Alfred Wilhelm Otto von. *Sociology of the Renaissance.* New York: Harper & Row, 1933.

Menéndez Pelayo, Marcelino. *Orígenes de la novela* (1905). Nueva Biblioteca de Autores Españoles. 4 vols. Repr. Madrid: Bailly-Baillière, 1925.

Menéndez Pidal, Ramón. *De Cervantes y Lope de Vega.* Buenos Aires: Espasa-Calpe, 1948.

Mirollo, James V. *Mannerism and Renaissance Poetry: Concept, Mode, Inner Design.* New Haven: Yale University Press, 1984.

———. "The Mannered and the Mannerist in Late Renaissance Literature." In *The*

Meaning of Mannerism, ed. Franklin W. Robinson et al., 7–24. Hanover, NH: University Press of New England, 1972.

Mujica, Barbara. *Iberian Pastoral Characters*. Washington, DC: Scripta Humanistica, 1986.

Navarrete, Ignacio, *Orphans of Petrarch: Poetry and Theory in the Spanish Renaissance*. Berkeley: University of California Press, 1994.

Navarro González, Alberto. "La locura quijotesca." *Anales cervantinos* 1 (1951): 273–94.

Nieto, José C. *Juan de Valdés and the Origins of the Spanish and Italian Reformation*. Geneva: Droz, 1970.

Nilsson, Ingela, *Erotic Pathos, Rhetorical Pleasure: Narrative Technique and Mimesis in Eumathios Makrembolites' Hysmine and Hysminias*. Uppsala: Uppsala University Library, 2001.

Nygren, Anders. *Agape and Eros*. Trans. Phillip S. Watson. London: S.P.C.K., 1953.

O'Callaghan, Michelle. "Pastoral." In *Companion to English Renaissance Literature and Culture*, ed. Hattaway, 307–16.

O'Malley, John W. *Trent and All That*. Cambridge, MA: Harvard University Press, 2000.

Ortega y Gasset, José. *Meditations on Quixote*. Trans. Evelyn Rugg and Diego Marín. New York: Norton, 1961.

———. "La picardía original de la novela picaresca." In idem, *Obras completas*, 6th ed., 2: 121–25. Madrid: Revista de Occidente, 1957–1962.

Panken, Shirley. *The Joy of Suffering: Psychoanalytic Theory and Therapy of Masochism*. New York: Aronson, 1973.

Parker, Alexander A. *Literature and the Delinquent: The Picaresque Novel in Spain and Europe 1599–1753*. Edinburgh: Edinburgh University Press, 1967.

Peers, E. Allison. *A History of the Romantic Movement in Spain* (1940). 2 vols. Repr. New York: Hafner, 1964.

Perry, T. A. "Ideal Love and Human Reality in Montemayor's *Diana*." *PMLA* 84 (1969): 227–34.

Pfänder, Alexander. *Phenomenology of Willing and Motivation and other Phenomenologica*. Trans. Herbert Spielberg. Evanston, IL: Northwestern University Press, 1967.

Pinker, Steven. *The Blank Slate: The Modern Denial of Human Nature*. New York: Viking Press, 2002.

Predmore, Richard L. "La función del encantamiento en el mundo del *Quijote.*" *Anales cervantinos* 5 (1955–1956): 63–78.
Prieto, Antonio. *Garcilaso de la Vega.* Madrid: S.G.E.L., 1975.
Reid, Louis Arnaud. *A Study in Aesthetics.* New York: Macmillan, 1954.
Reiss, Edmund. *Boethius.* Boston: Twayne, 1982.
Renaissance Readings of the Corpus Aristotelicum, ed. M. Pade. Copenhagen: Museum Tusculanum, 2001.
Rennert, Hugo A. *The Spanish Pastoral Romances.* 2nd ed. Philadelphia: University of Pennsylvania, 1912.
Renouvier, Charles. *Essais de Critique Générale.* Paris: Armand Colin, 1919.
Rhodes, Elizabeth. *The Unrecognized Precursors of Montemayor's "Diana."* Columbia, MO: University of Missouri Press, 1992.
———. "Skirting the Men: Gender Roles in Sixteenth-Century Pastoral Books." *Journal of Hispanic Philology* 11 (1987 [1988]): 131–49.
Ribot, Th. *The Psychology of the Emotions.* London: Walter Scott, 1906.
Ricapito, Joseph V. Introduction to *Lazarillo de Tormes,* 11–85. Madrid: Cátedra, 1985.
———. *Bibliografía razonada y anotada de las obras maestras de la picaresca española.* Madrid: Castalia, 1980.
Rico, Francisco. *La novela picaresca y el punto de vista* (1970). Barcelona: Seix Barral, 1973.
Ricoeur, Paul. *Freedom and Nature* (1950). Trans. Erazim V. Kohák. Evanston, IL: Northwestern University Press, 1966.
———. "The Metaphorical Process as Cognition, Imagination, and Feeling." In *On Metaphor,* ed. Sheldon Sacks, 141–59. Chicago: University of Chicago Press, 1979.
Riley, E. C. *Don Quijote.* London: Unwin, 1986.
Rivers, Elias L. *Garcilaso de la Vega, Poems: A Critical Guide.* London: Grant and Cutler, 1980.
———. "Garcilaso de la Vega and the Italian Renaissance: Texts and Contexts / Review Article." *Calíope* 2 (1996): 100–8.
———. *Poesía lírica del Siglo de Oro.* Madrid: Cátedra, 1988.
Rosenblatt, Louise M. *The Reader, the Text, the Poem: The Transactional Theory of the Literary Work.* Carbondale, IL: Southern Illinois University Pres, 1978.
Ruiz Pérez, P. "Sobre los sonetos de Fray Luis de León." *Edad de Oro* 11 (1992): 149–60.

Sabat de Rivers, Georgina. "La moral que Lázaro nos propone." *Modern Language Notes* 95 (1980): 233–51.
Salgado Júnior, António. *A "Menina e Moça" e o romance sentimental no renascimento.* Aveiro: Gráfica Aveirense, 1940.
Sánchez Gázquez, Joaquín J. "Juan Ginés de Sepúlveda, un hispano a la altura del siglo XVI: Lutero y Erasmo." In *Acta Conventus Neo-Latini Abulensis,* ed. Schnur, 575–83.
Schiesari, Juliana. "Mo(u)rning and Melancholia: Tasso and the Dawn of Psychoanalysis." *Quaderni d'Italianistica* 11 (1990): 13–27.
Schmitt, Charles B. *Aristotle and the Renaissance.* Cambridge, MA: Harvard University Press, 1983.
Seldes, George. *The Great Thoughts.* New York: Ballantine, 1885.
Selke de Sánchez, Angela. *El Santo Oficio de la Inquisición.* Madrid: Guadarrama, 1968.
Sena, Jorge de. *Estudos de literatura portuguesa.* Lisbon: Edições 70, 1981.
———. "Maneirismo e Barroco na poesia portuguesa dos séculos XVI e XVII." *Luso-Brazilian Review* 2 (1965): 29–53.
Senabre, Ricardo. *Tres estudios sobre Fray Luis de León.* Salamanca: Universidad de Salamanca, 1978.
———. "La oda de Fray Luis a la Ascensión." In idem, *Estudios sobre Fray Luis de León,* 69–88. Salamanca: Universidad de Salamanca.
Sewall, Richard B. *The Vision of Tragedy.* New Haven: Yale University Press, 1959.
Shipley, George A. "The Critic as Witness for the Prosecution: Making the Case against Lázaro de Tormes." *PMLA* 97 (1982): 225–53.
———. "The Critic as Witness for the Prosecution: Resting the Case against Lázaro de Tormes." In *Creation and Re-Creation: Experiments in Literary Form in Early Modern Spain: Studies in Honor of Stephen Gilman,* ed. R. E. Surtz, 105–24. Newark, DE: Juan de la Cuesta, 1983.
———. "Lazarillo de Tormes was Not a Hardworking, Clean-Living Water Carrier." In *Hispanic Studies in Honor of Alan D. Deyermond: A North American Tribute,* ed. J. S. Miletich, 247–55. Madison, WI: Hispanic Seminary of Medieval Studies, 1986.
———. "Lázaro and the Cathedral Chaplain: A Conspirational Reading of *Lazarillo de Tormes,* Tratado VI." *Symposium* 37 (1983): 216–41.
Sito Alba, Manuel. "¿Un tiento de Garcilaso en poetas portuguesas? (Notas a la

lectura de la Égloga III)." *Boletín de la Real Academia Española* 56 (1976): 439–50.

Smillie, William Mark. "Phantasia: In Defense of Thomas Aquinas' Account of Imagination." Ph.D. diss., University of Notre Dame, 1992.

Snell, Ana María. "Tres ejemplos del arte del soneto en Garcilaso." *Modern Language Notes* 88 (1973): 175–89.

Solana, Marcial. *Historia de la filosofía española: Época del Renacimiento (siglo XVI)*. 3 vols. Madrid: Real Academia de Ciencias Exactas, Físicas y Naturales, 1941.

Solé-Leris, Amadeu. *The Spanish Pastoral Novel*. Boston: Twayne, 1980.

Sombart, Werner. *The Quintessence of Capitalism: A Study of the History and Psychology of the Modern Business Man*. Trans. M. Epstein. London: Unwin, 1915.

Sorabji, Richard. *Necessity, Cause, and Blame: Perspectives on Aristotle's Theory*. Ithaca, NY: Cornell University Press, 1980.

Soufas, Teresa Scott. *Melancholy and the Secular Mind in Spanish Golden Age Literature*. Columbia, MO: University of Missouri Press, 1990.

Spengler, Oswald. *The Decline of the West: Perspectives of World History* (1922). Trans. Charles Francis Atkinson. 2 vols. New York: Knopf, 1926–1928.

Spitzer, Leo. *Estilo y estructura en la literatura española*. Barcelona: Editorial Crítica, 1980.

Steiner, George. *The Death of Tragedy*. New York: Knopf, 1968.

Stone, Lawrence. "The Rise of the Nuclear Family in Early Modern England: The Patriarchal Stage." In *The Family in History*, ed. Charles E. Rosenberg, 13–57. Philadelphia: University of Pennsylvania Press, 1975.

Sullivan, Henry W. "Don Quixote de la Mancha: Analyzable or Unanalyzable?" *Cervantes* 17 (1998): 4–20.

Sypher, Wylie. *Four Stages of Renaissance Style. Tranformations in Art and Literature: 1400–1700*. Garden City, NY: Doubleday, 1955.

Thesaurus of Epigrams, ed. Edmund Fuller. New York: Crown, 1943.

Thompson, Colin P. " 'En la Ascensión': Artistic Tradition and Poetic Imagination in Luis de León." In *Medieval and Renaissance Studies on Spain and Portugal in Honour of P. E. Russell*, ed. F. W. Hodcroft et al., 109–20. Oxford: Society for the Study of Medieval Languages and Literature, 1981.

———. *The Strife of Tongues: Fray Luis de León and the Golden Age of Spain*. Cambridge: Cambridge University Press, 1988.

Tillyard, E. M. W., and C. S. Lewis. *The Personal Heresy: A Controversy by E. M. W. Tillyard and C. S. Lewis*. London: Oxford University Press, 1939.

Tillier, Jane Yvonne. "Passion Poetry in the *Cancioneros*." *Bulletin of Hispanic Studies* 62 (1985): 65–78.

Torner, Eduardo M. *Lírica hispánica: relaciones entre lo popular y lo culto*. Madrid: Castalia, 1966.

Tylus, Jane. "Pastoral on the Continent." In *Encyclopedia of the Renaissance*, ed. P. F. Grendler, 6 vols., 4: 413–17. New York: Scribner, 1999.

Urban, Wilbur Marshall. *Language and Reality: The Philosophy of Language and the Principles of Symbolism* (1939). London: Unwin, 1951.

Valency, Maurice. *In Praise of Love: An Introduction to the Love-Poetry of the Renaissance*. New York: Octagon Books, 1975.

Van Beysterveldt, Anthony. *La poesía amatoria de siglo XV y el teatro profano de Juan del Encina*. Madrid: Ínsula, 1972.

Vaquero Serrano, María del Carmen. *Garcilaso: Aportes para una nueva biografía. Los Ribadeneira y Lorenzo de Figueroa*. Toledo: Oretania, 1999.

———. *Garcilaso: Poeta del amor, caballero de la guerra*. Madrid: Espasa-Calpe, 2002.

Vossler, Karl. *Fray Luis de León*. Trans. Carlos Clavería. Buenos Aires: Espasa-Calpe, 1946.

———. *Introducción a la literatura española del Siglo de Oro*. Madrid: Cruz y Raya, 1934.

Waley, Pamela. "Garcilaso's Isabel, and Elena: The Growth of a Legend." *Bulletin of Hispanic Studies* 56 (1979): 11–15.

———. "Lazarillo's Cast of Thousands, or the Ethics of Poverty." *Modern Language Review* 83 (1988): 591–601.

Walser, E. "Les publications de la Bibliothèque Warburg." *Révue de Littérature Comparée* 7 (1927): 352–58.

Warburg, Aby. *The Renewal of Pagan Antiquity*. Trans. David Britt. Los Angeles: Getty Research Institute, 1999.

Wardropper, B. W. "The *Diana* of Montemayor: Revaluation and Interpretation." *Studies in Philology* 48 (1951): 126–44.

———. "The Implications of Hypocrisy in the *Lazarillo de Tormes*." In *Studies in Honor of Everett W. Hesse*, ed. W. C. McCrary and José A. Madrigal, 179–86. Lincoln, NE: Society of Spanish and Spanish-American Studies, 1981.

———, ed. *Spanish Poetry of the Golden Age*. New York: Irvington, 1971.

———. "El trastorno de la moral en el *Lazarillo*." *Nueva Revista de Filología Hispánica* 15 (1961): 441–47.
Weinsheimer, Joel C. *Gadamer's Hermeneutics: A Reading of "Truth and Method."* New Haven: Yale University Press, 1985.
Wellek, René, and Austin Warren. *Theory of Literature* (1942). 3rd ed. New York: Harcourt, 1977.
Werkmeister, W.H. *Nicolai Hartmann's New Ontology*. Tallahassee: Florida State University Press, 1990.
Westphal, Merold. *History and Truth in Hegel's Phenomenology*. Atlantic Highlands, NJ: Humanities Press, 1979.
Whinnom, Keith. *La poesía amatoria en la época de los Reyes Católicos*. Durham: University of Durham Press, 1981.
———. Introduction to Diego de San Pedro, *Cárcel de amor*, 7–66. Madrid: Castalia, 1971.
———. *Medieval and Renaissance Spanish Literature: Selected Essays*. Ed. Alan Deyermond, W. F. Hunter, and Joseph T. Snow. Exeter: University of Exeter Press, 1994.
Whittlesey, E. S. *Symbols and Legends in Western Art: A Museum Guide*. New York: Scribner's Sons, 1972.
Williams, Charles. *Outlines of a Romantic Theology*. Ed. Alice Mary Hadfield. Grand Rapids, MI: William B. Eerdmans, 1990.
Williams, Raymond. *Modern Tragedy*. Stanford, CA: Stanford University Press, 1966.
Williamson, Edwin. *The Half-way House of Fiction: "Don Quijote" and Arthurian Romance*. Oxford: Oxford University Press, 1984.
Williamson, George. *A Reader's Guide to the Metaphysical Poets* (1968). 2nd ed. Repr. London: Thames and Hudson, 1974.
Willis, Raymond S. "Lazarillo and the Pardoner: The Artistic Necessity of the Fifth *Tractado*." *Hispanic Review* 27 (1959): 267–79.
Wimsatt, William K. *The Verbal Icon*. Lexington, KY: University of Kentucky Press, 1954.
Wind, Edgar. *Pagan Mysteries in the Renaissance*. New Haven: Yale University Press, 1958.
Winters, Yvor. *In Defense of Reason. Primitivism and Decadence: A Study of American Experimental Poetry*. New York: Swallow, 1947.

Woods, M. J. "Pitfalls for the Moralizer in *Lazarillo de Tormes.*" *Modern Language Review* 74 (1979): 590–98.

Woodward, L. J. "Author-Reader relationship in the *Lazarillo del [sic] Tormes. Forum for Modern Language Studies* 1 (1965): 43–53.

Zimic, Stanislav. *Apuntes sobre la estructura paródica y satírica del "Lazarillo de Tormes."* Madrid: Iberoamericana, 2000.

Index of Names

Peninsular writers of belles lettres who are the subjects of chapters are listed in the Index of Subjects.

Abellán, J. L., 264 n.16
Abrams, M. H., 165 n.21
Adams, H., 273 n.23
Adler, A., 172
   on courage, 87
   on dreams, 60
   on love lyric and artistic depictions of masochism, 64
   on masochism, 64, 85–86, 89, 91 n.58
   psychology, 192 n.21
   subjection and adaptation of will, 24–25
   submission of persona to tyrannical lady, 85
   on unhappiness caused by love, 19 n.16

Aguirre, J. M.
   and Christian optimism, 11
   interpretation of love, 7–9, 10
   interpretation of the rhetorical element in *cancionero* lyric, 24
   and love's compatibility with free will, 12
   on the meaning of passion, 24
   perspective and "love by destiny" motif, xiii
   religious elements of language, 23
Alcina, J. F., 197 n.3
Alemán, M.
   Guzmán de Alfarache, 179, 183
Alfonsi, S. R., 88 n.55
Alighieri, D. *See* Dante
Alonso, D., 160

Index of Names 307

Alonso Cortés, N., 239 n.35
Alpers, P., 212 n.22, 222 n.6
Apuleius, 212
Saint Thomas Aquinas, 50, 257 n.7, 264, 265 n.16, 270 n.19
   transfer of phenomenon into an idea, 272
Aristotle, 185, 185 n.10, 202, 203, 209–10, 256, 257, 258, 259
   and assignment of guilt, 187–88
   concept of voluntary action, 39–40, 48 n.22
   De anima, 263–64, 265 n.16
   difference between sexual appetite and erotic passion, 231
   ethics applied to *Lazarillo de Tormes*, xvii, 193
   Eudemian Ethics, 185
   and excusing factors in assignment of guilt, 185, 187–88, 188 n.16
   and involuntary action, 185
   on nature of love, 41 n.17, 237–38
   "non-culpable ignorance" in Garcilaso's poetry, 36
   Poetics, 264 n.16
   transfer of phenomenon into an idea, 272
   on virtuous action, 40
Arribas, J., 221 n.3
Artz, F., 62
Asch, S., 71
Asensio, E., 196 n.1
Atlee, M., 156–57

Saint Augustine, 40 n.15, 50, 202, 203, 256, 274 n.28
   superiority of will over intellect, 270
   on true freedom, 236 n.27
Avalle-Arce, J. B., 227 n.16
   on *Diana* [Montemayor], 223
   on enchantment motif in *Don Quijote*, 254 n.4

Barbezieux, R. de, 208
Bacon, F., 274
Bain, A., 236, 241 n.42
Bakhtin, M.
   significance of the Renaissance, xxiii
   on tragedy, 280
Barthes, R., 165 n.21
Bataillon, M., 199 n.8, 203 n.14, 217 n.31, 224 n.11, 225, 240 n.37, 243 n.48, 244 n.51, 271 n.21
Beardsley, M. C., 32 n.4
Bell, A., 162, 165 n.20, 265 n.16
   biographical study of Fray Luis de Léon, 155–56
   compares Fray Luis to Savonarola, 156
Bembo, P., 231, 264 n.16
   Gli Asolani, 230, 248
Bergler, E., 69
Bergson, H., 246 n.56
Saint Bernard, 161, 163, 172 n.25
   commentary on the *Song of Songs*, 173 n.28

Sermo in Ascensione Domini, 161 n.15
Bernard of Cluny, 204 n.15
Bernstein, I., 70
Berquin, L. de, 225
Bianchi, L., 273 n.26
Bieber, I., 69
Blecua, J. M., 159 n.9, 161, 173 n.28
Blüher, K. A., 236 n.27
Blumstein, A., 70
Boase, R.
   interpretation of "prison of love," 16 n.14
   and love's compatibility with free will, 11–12, 25
   perspective and "love by destiny" motif, xiii
Boccaccio, G., 209–10, 249
   Elegia di madonna Fiametta, 209
   extract from *Filocolo*, 209
Boethius, 235–26 n.27
   The Consolation of Philosophy, 235 n.27
Bolgar, R. R., 185 n.10, 212 n.24, 235 n.27, 257
Bonnafoux, D., 173 n.29
Booth, W., 109 n.10
Boscán, J., 41 n.17, 105 n.7, 202, 202 n.13
   translation of 1553, 228
Bosco, U., 54 n.2
Bourke, J., 51 n.26
Bousquet, J., 62–63, 140 n.21, 142 n.24
Bouwsma, W., xxiii n.2, 22 n.20

Bowlby, J., 151–52
Boyle, M. O'Rourke, 54 n.2
Bradley, A. C., 79 n.42
Bredvold, L. I., 219 n.33
Brenner, C., 67, 70
Brown, P., 10 n.9, 40 n.15
Brumble, D., 38 n.12, 72 n.33, 213 n.25, 237 n.31
Bultmann, R., 174 n.30
Burdach, K., xxiii

Cabranes Grant, L., 270 n.19
Cadalso, J., 226 n.14
Calvin, J., 49, 113, 226 n.14
Camamis, G., 71
Camões, L. de, 72
   adapts Psalm 137 to pastoral literature, 200
Cardillo de Villapando, G.
   Apologia Aristotelica adversus eos, qui aiunt animam cum corpore extingui, 265 n.16
   Súmulas, 264–65 n.16
Carey, D., 180 n.5
Carreño, A., 172 n.27
Carreter, F. L., 145 n.27, 187
Cartagena, A. de, 236 n.27
Cartagena, P. de, 4
Cascardi, A., 38 n.13
Cassirer, E., 270
Castiglione, B. de, 100, 228, 231, 264 n.16
   El cortesano, 228, 230 n.18
   Il Corteggiano, 100, 228, 231
      influence of on Garcilaso, 100

Castillo, D. del, 4–5
Castro, A., 179 n.4, 256, 265 n.16, 267
  on Cervantes's command of Latin, 265 n.16
  enchantment motif in *Don Quijote*, 254 n.4
  on *Lazarillo de Tormes*, 183–85
  Neoplatonist influences on Cervantes, 264 n.16
  and Neoplatonist theory of perception, 262–63
  on the picaresque novel, 178
Chekhov, A., xii, 196
Chevalier, J., 92 n.59
Chevalier, M., 185
Chorpenning, J. F., 173 n.28
Churton, E., 160
Cirlot, J. E., 18 n.15, 35 n.9
Clark, M. T., 235 n.27
Coen, J., 60
Coen, S., 71
Coleridge, S., 268
Colombí-Monguió, A. de
  on Sonnet 22 [Garcilaso], 103, 105
Cooper, A.
  on masochism, 65 n.24, 70
Córdoba, S. de, 82
Cortegana, L. de, 212 n.24
Coster, A., 145 n.27, 165 n.19
Covington, S., 240 n.36
Cox, V., 273 n.26
Cranz, F. E., 185 n.10
Creel, B. L., 28 n.1, 72 n.30, 76 n.36, 83 n.49, 139 n.18, 200 nn.9, 10, 217 n.31, 224 n.11, 225 n.13, 238 n.34, 240 nn.38, 39, 241 nn.41, 43, 243, 271 n.21
Cruz, A., 56 n.7, 62 n.16, 103 n.5
  distinction between Aristotelian and Platonic love, 41 n.17
  on imitation of model texts, 105 n.7
  on the picaresque novel, 187
Culler, J., 164

Damasio, A., xxiv, 76 n.37
  consciousness and metaphor, xv, 76 n.37
  on emotions and reason, 138 n.17
Damiani, B., 222–23
Daniells, R., 62
Dante
  Divina Commedia, 53
Dardanio. *See* Ramírez Pagán, D.
Darst, D., 40 n.17, 54
Deeken, A., 47 n.20
  on the value of the morally noble, 10 n.9
Delumeau, J., 239 n.36
Denomy, A.
  on "heresy" of courtly love, 40, 83 n.48
Derrida, J., 270
Deyermond, A., 34
  on character of *cancionero*, 2
  on interpreting narrative, 109 n.10
  on *Lazarillo de Tormes*, 180 n.5, 181 n.6, 186 n.13, 191 n.21

Díaz Díaz, G., 265 n.16
Dickens, C., 187
Dilthey, W.
    on masochism, 78
    on personal destiny, 92
Djuth, M., 235 n.27
Domínguez Ortiz, A., 21 n.18
Donne, J., 141, 222
Doren, A., 237 n.31
Dubrow, H., 212 n.22, 222 n.6
Dunbar, H. F., xxv
Dunn, P., 179 n.4
Duns Scotus, 50
Durán, M.
    biographical study of Fray Luis de Léon, 156
    and "En la Ascensión" [Fray Luis de Léon], 156–57
D'Urfé, H., 214
    L'Astrée, 214
Durkheim, E., 242 n.44, 246 n.56
Durrell, L., 236 n.28

Eagleton, T., 271
Eco, U.
    on similarities between nominalism and structuralism, 270 n.19
Eidelberg, L.
    on masochism, 65, 69–70
Einstein, A., 76 n.37, 273 n.25
Eisenberg, D., 255 n.4, 261 n.14
El Brocense. *See* Sánchez de las Brozas, F.
Elliott, J., 206

El Saffar, R., 254 n.4
Empson, W., 164
Encina, J. del, 4
Engammare, M., 173 n.28
Engels, F. *See* Marx, K.
Erasmus, D., 199, 200 n.8, 242, 243 n.48, 264 n.16
    Complaint of Peace, 242
    Enchiridion, 243 n.48
    pacifist viewpoint of adopted by Ribeiro, 199–200
Estrada, L., 222

Fairbairn, R., 144
    on *Diana* [Montemayor], 150
    and "En la Ascensión" [Fray Luis de Léon], 173
    and the interpretation of imagery, xv–xvi
    and *Lazarillo de Tormes*, 188
    Protestant elements in, 150
    psychological theories of, compared to Jung, 135, 149–50
    quest for love theory as motivation, 62
    on Sonnet 2 [Fray Luis de Léon], 146–48, 149–50, 153
    on Sonnet 38 [Garcilaso], 128–29, 131–33, 135, 138
Felkel, R. W., 258 n.9, 265 n.16
Fenichel, O., 80
    submission of persona to tyrannical lady, 68, 69
Ferenczi, S., 67
Ferguson, W. K., 86 n.52

Feuerbach, L., 269
Fichte, J., 270
Ficino, M., 50, 52, 257 n.7
    characterizes humanity as universal love, 235 n.24
    theory of love, 172, 228 n.17, 231, 232, 241, 246–47
Fielding, H., 183
Figueroa, D. J.
    and "En la Ascensión" [Fray Luis de Léon], 161, 162–63, 165
Fiore, R. L., 175 n.1
Fischer, N., 67–68
Fish, S., xxv
Fitzmaurice-Kelly, J., 160
Fonseca, A. de, 55
Forcione, A. K., 261 n.14, 264 n.16, 266, 267
Fosalba, E., 221 n.3
Foucault, M., 165 n.21
Freire, I., 55
Frenk, M., 23
Freud, S., 76 n.37, 130 n.11, 224, 273, 273 n.25
    and aggressive instinct, 243
    on group morale, applied to "En la Ascensión" [Fray Luis de Léon], 173
    and love-melancholy, 243–44
    on masochism, 65, 70, 77 n.38, 89, 243–44
    submission of persona to tyrannical lady, 68
    super-ego, 150
Frings, M. S., 237 n.32

Fromm, E., 126 n.6
Frye, N., 83 n.48, 197 n.5, 198 n.7, 273 n.26
    and "allegorization" of literature, 60–61
    on forced conceits in poems of paradox, 59–60
    on the metaphor of life as a journey, 36 n.9
    on role of poetry, 46
    and "secular scripture," xii
    on thematic criticism, 60, 61
    on tragic suffering, 21 n.18, 140 n.20
Fuentes, A., 212 n.24

Gadamer, H.-G., 260
Gallego Morell, A., 122
García, F., 145 n.27, 161, 165 n.19
García de la Concha, V., 179 n.4
Gargano, A., 56 n.7
    association of Garcilaso with Petrarch, 111
    motif of captivating hand, 110, 111
    on Sonnet 22 [Garcilaso], 96–98, 103, 104–5, 106–7, 108
Genette, G., 270
Gerrig, R., 186
Gheerbrant, A., 92 n.59
Gibbs, R., xxiv–xxv, 76 n.37
Gicovate, B., 61
Gillette, M., 244 n.50
Gilman, S., 190
Gil Polo, G., 40 n.17
Godard, A., 274 n.26

Goethe, J. W. von, 272–73
Gombrich, E. H., 130 n.12
Góngora, L. de, 72–73
Goodwyn, F., 54, 61
Gorky, M.
    on heroism, 139
    and *Lazarillo de Tormes*, 179, 183, 193, 194
    meaning of metaphor, xii
    on the picaresque novel, 179, 182
    on self-preservation in the Renaissance, 92–93
Graff, G., 55–56
Grajal (Jew supported by Fray Luis de León), 155
Green, O., 34
    on character of *cancionero*, 2
    on *Diana* [Montemayor], 227
Greimas, A. J., 273, 273 n.24
Grotstein, J. S., 130 n.12
Guillén, C., 180 n.5
Guntrip, H., 62 n.17, 88, 91, 132, 188
Gutherie, W. C., 213 n.26

Hagen, O., 51
Haller, A., 87
Hamilton, N. G., 130 n.12
Hamlyn, D. W., 257 n.7, 259
Harnack, A. von, 250 n.65
Hartmann, H., 82
Hartmann, N., 61 n.13
    "aporia of free necessity" applied to love, 43, 44
    on characteristic trait of the nobility, 20 n.17
    characterizes personal love, 245 n.53
    and Christianity, 238
    contribution of poets to humanization, 267
    on courage, 13
    on the discernment of values, 138
    Ethics, xxi, 38, 40, 42, 44, 45, 46, 87, 109 n.9, 112 n.12, 139, 171, 239, 266 n.17
    on free will, 48 n.22, 112 n.13
    and *Lazarillo de Tormes*, 191
    on morality, 143, 153
    phenomenological theory of, xxi–xxii, 128
    on the Platonic Eros, 10 n.9
    significance of pure mind, 279–80, 281
    on suffering, 84–85
    on values and moral freedom, 47, 48 n.22, 49
    on well-being, 234 n.23
Hatzfeld, H., 141 n.22
Hauser, A., 62, 217
    on individuality, 86 n.52
    on manneristic style, 65, 140
    on pastoral literature, 211
    significance of the Renaissance, xxiii–xxiv
    on tragic suffering, 21 n.18, 140 n.21
Hauser, H., 217, 277–78
Hegel, G.
    character of love, 66, 78, 83 n.48
    characterization of tragic hero, 79

Index of Names

on negativization of the sensuous and finite, 235 n.25
on self-identification, 66, 92
on self-sacrifice, 84
"supreme contingency," 249 n.63
Heidegger, M., 271
Heine, H., 83 n.49, 117–18, 210
Heiple, D., 55 n.4
    biographical approach to reading Garcilaso, 57–59, 60, 62
    on Sonnet 22 [Garcilaso], 96–98, 100–1, 103, 112
    on Sonnet 38 [Garcilaso], 122–23, 125, 134–35
    on Spanish Petrarchism, 34
Herrera, F. de, 97 n.1
    on Sonnet 22 [Garcilaso], 107–8
    on Sonnet 38 [Garcilaso], 122, 125–26, 134
Hinshelwood, R. D., 90 n.56, 132, 142
Holland, N., 127
Horney, K., 68, 80, 131 n.14, 141
Huizinga, J., 86 n.52
Husserl, E., 263, 268
Hutchinson, S., 35 n.9

Ignatius of Loyola, 83, 243
Ihrie, M., 255 n.4

Jaén, D., 180 n.5
Jameson, F., 271
Jerrold, M. F., 54 n.2
Jiménez de Cisneros, F., 271 n.21
Johnson, C. B., 220 n.1
Johnson, M., 223 n.9
    on the image schema of "paths," 36 n.9
    on imagination, 269
    meaning of metaphor, xxiv–xxv, 76 n.37
Jones, R. O., 227 n.16
Junemann, G.
    and "En la Ascensión" [Fray Luis de León], 162, 165
Jung, C. G., 128, 132 n.15, 144
    and interpretation of imagery, xv–xvi, 197 n.4
    and *Lazarillo de Tormes*, 188, 192
    on Sonnet 2 [Fray Luis's de León], 148–50, 153
    on Sonnet 38 [Garcilaso], 134, 135–38, 142–43
Juvenal, 87

Kelley, J., 239 n.36
Kenniston, H., xiv
    biographical approach to reading Garcilaso, 55, 56
    and love's incompatibility with free will, 29
Kernberg, O., 68
Kettle, A., 187
Kierkegaard, S., 141
King, M. L., 240 n.36
Kirschner, S. R., 76 n.37
Klein, M., 75 n.35
    on masochism, 88
    on "primary confusion" of the ego, 142
Klibansky, R., 142 n.24

Krafft-Ebing, R.
  on sexual bondage, 73
  submission of persona to tyrannical lady, 68, 70
Kristeller, P. O., 51 n.26, 172 n.26, 228 n.17, 231, 232, 235 n.24, 247, 257 n.7

Lakoff, G., xxiv–xxv, 76 n.37
Lapesa, R., 34, 41 n.17, 54 n.3
  biographical approach to reading Garcilaso, 55, 56, 61, 62
  discovery of the individual in love lyric, 143
  on Garcilaso's early poetry, xiv, 9, 51
  importance of *La trayectoria poética de Garcilaso*, 1
  interpretation of fateful love, 7
  interpretation of the rhetorical element in *cancionero* lyric, 24
  on "love by destiny" motif, xiii, 2–3, 27–28
  and love's incompatibility with free will, 12, 29, 31–33, 35, 37, 38–39, 40, 43, 46, 48, 52
  love that dominates will, 41 n.17
  on Sonnet 1 [Garcilaso], 35–38
  theories applied
    autobiographical character of Garcilaso's poetry, 55–56
    conformity to fate in Sonnet 1, 37
  love as fate in *cancionero* poetry and Garcilaso, 33, 37, 46
  love by destiny, 33, 41 n.17
  will to self-destruction as cloak for surrender to fate, 33, 39
Lazareth, W. H., 250 n.56
León, F. de, 250
Levin, L., xii
Lewis, C. S., 88 n.54, 198 n.6
  on danger as a result of a lady's modesty, 101–2
  meaning of "allegory," xii n.1
  opposition to "personal heresy" concept, 32 n.4
Lewis, H. B., 71
Lida de Malkiel, M. R., 11
  perspective and "love by destiny" motif, xiii
Lipari, A., 53 n.1
Llobera, J.
  and "En la Ascensión" [Fray Luis de Léon], 157, 161, 165, 171
López-Estrada, F., 221, 223 n.7, 258 n.9
Lucka, E., 242–43, 243 n.46
Luhmann, N.
  on the meaning of passion, 12–13, 23–24
  perspective and "love by destiny" motif, xiii
Lukács, G., 249 n.62
Luther, M., 200 n.8, 250
Ly, N., 61

Index of Names

MacCoull, L. S. B., 145 n.27, 152 n.28, 160 n.9, 189 n.17
Maçedo, H., 195 n.1, 213
Machado, A., 143
Macpherson, I.
    levels of meaning in *cancionero* poetry, 9
    perspective and "love by destiny" motif, xiii
    on sensual desire, 12
Macrí, O.
    and "En la Ascensión" [Fray Luis de Léon], 161, 162–63, 164, 165
Makrembolites, 229 n.17
Mancing, H., 179 n.4, 255 n.4
Manero Sorolla, M. P., 131 n.13
Marañón, G., 178, 179 n.4
Maravall, J. A., 69 n.28, 187, 240 n.38, 245 n.54
March, A.
    Cant 121.6 compared to Garcilaso's Sonnet 38, 119
    and *Diana* [Montemayor], 249
    influence on Garcilaso, 1–2, 126
Márquez Villanueva, F., 180 n.5, 256 n.5
Martin, A. W. O. von, 240 n.38
Martínez, F. de la Rosa, 161
Martínez Brea, P.
    In libros tres Aristotelis De anima Commentarii, 265 n.16
Martínez López, E., 55
Marx, K. (and F. Engels)
    German Ideology, 269

Maupassant, G. de
    Bel Ami, 183
Medici, L. de', 53–54, 53 n.1
Mena, J. de, 11
    Las Trezientas, 202 n.12
Menéndez Pelayo, M.
    on *Diana* [Montemayor], 222, 223, 229 n.17, 236, 242
Menéndez Pidal, R., 240
Meneses, J., 201, 202–3, 205–5
Menn, S., 271 n.21
Merino, A., 160
Mikkeli, H., 257 n.8
Milton, J.
    Il Penseroso, 240
Mirollo, J. W., 63 n.18, 140 n.21, 141 n.22, 142 n.24
Molina, T. de
    La fingida Arcadia, 241 n.43
Montero, J., 221 n.3
Moreno Báez, E., 41 n.17, 258 n.9
Morros, B.
    on Sonnet 38 [Garcilaso], 121–22, 123, 125, 134–135
Mujica, B., 223 n.7

Navarrete, I., 56 n.7, 62
Navarro González, A., 254 n.4
Nicodemus, 226 n.14
Nieto, J., 225
Nietzsche, F., 101, 235 n.25
Nilsson, I., 299 n.17

O'Callaghan, M., 212 n.22, 222 n.6
Ockham, W. of, 50

Olinick, S., 71
O'Malley, J. W., 218 n.32
Ortega y Gasset, J.
    on *Don Quijote*, 254 n.4
    on the picaresque novel, 178, 179
Ortiz, Fray Francisco, 113 n.14

Panken, S., 67–72, 77 n.38, 80
Parker, A., 175 n.1
Pascal, B., 247
Saint Paul, 238
Peers, E. A., 142 n.24, 226 n.14
Perry T. A., 220 n.1
Petrarch. F., 32, 103, 111, 222, 249
    Canzoniere/Rime, 171
    Canzone 23 compared to Garcilaso, 111
    and *Diana* [Montemayor], 249
    influence on fifteenth-century Castilian lyric, 32–33
    influence on Garcilaso, 2, 27–28, 96, 103, 105, 111, 126, 141, 249
    metaphor of love, 58
    motif of the "lady," 54
    Rime, 171
    Sonnet 15 compared to Garcilaso's Sonnet 38, 119
Pevsner, N., 62
Pfänder, A., 48
Pidal, P. J., 7
Pinker, S., 193 n.22, 225
Plato, 50, 257, 258, 259, 267
    Meno, 258
    Socrates' prayer in *Phaedrus*, 99

Symposium, 170, 241
Predmore, R., 254 nn.3, 4, 255
Prieto, A., 61

Quevedo, F. de
    El Buscón, 179, 183

Ramírez Pagán, D., 201–2, 203–4
Reich, A., 71, 72, 80, 89
Reich, W., 63, 68
Reid, L. A., 237 n.33
Reik, T., 68–69
Reiss, E., 235 n.27
Rennert, H., 223
Renouvier, C., 49
Rhodes, E., 223–24, 224 n.11, 225, 250 n.66
Ribot, Th., 231, 243
Ricapito, J., 180 n.5, 183
Rico, F., 180 n.5
Ricoeur, P., 6 n.34, 272
    on imagination, 268, 269
    meaning of metaphor, xxiv, 60, 260
Riley, E. C., 253, 254
Rivers, E.
    on love lyric and artistic depictions of sadism, 63–64
    on masochism, 85
    on Sonnet 1 [Garcilaso], 36 n.10
    on Sonnet 22 [Garcilaso], 96–98, 100–1, 102, 103, 106–7, 112
    on Sonnet 38 [Garcilaso], 121, 122–23, 125, 134–35
Rojas, F. de
    La Celestina, 221

Index of Names 317

Rosenblatt, L. M., 181 n.7
Rousseau, J., 87
Rowland, D., 62
Rudel, J., 211
Ruiz, J. (Arcipreste de Hita), 72–73
Ruiz Pérez, P., 145 n.27

Sabat de Rivers, G., 180 n.5
Salgado Júnior, A., 196 n.1
Salinas, P., 183
Salzman, L., 80
Sánchez, A. Selke de, 113 n.14
Sánchez de las Brozas, F. (El Brocense), 97 n.1, 99, 123
    interpretation of Garcilaso's Sonnet 22, 108
Sánchez Gázquez, J. J., 199 n.8, 203 n.14
San Juan, H. de, 258 n.9
    Examen de ingenios para las ciencias, 258 n.9, 266
San Juan de la Cruz, 65, 72, 88
    analogies of love in poetry, 24
    "Llama de amor viva," 80–81
Sannazaro, J.
    Arcadia, 197, 200, 204–5
San Pedro, D. de, xiii, 16, 22, 216, 249
    Cárcel de amor, 22
    "prison/bonds of love/loving" motif, xiii
Sarmiento, E., 158 n.8, 160
Savonarola, G., 113
    commentary on the psalm "Miserere Mei Deus," 171
    compared to Fray Luis de Léon, 156

Scève, M., 141
Scheler, M., 109 n.9, 231, 243 n.47, 247 nn.58–60
    and behavior of the lady, 113 n.16, 114–15, 262 n.15
    and Christianity, 238
    concept of intentional feelings, 47 n.20
    definition of love, 170
    on discernment of values, 138
    distinction between "bodily shame" and "psychic shame," 112 n.12
    on fateful love, 49–50, 122 n.4
    and hero's purity of will, 11 n.10, 22
    and "immanent tragedy of sexual love," 113 n.15
    on individual within the social unit, 194
    on "martyr" and "hero" characters, 10 n.9
    on moral freedom, 48 n.22
    observations on love's role in death, 74
    on passionate willing, 122 n.4
    phenomenological theory of, xxi, 128
    on positive values, 245 n.55
    on protective function of sexual modesty, 101
    on self-identification, 66
    theory of tragic, guiltless guilt, xiii
    on tragic suffering, 21 n.18
    views life as a tendency toward power, 235 n.25

and well-being, 234
  on will and actions, 50
Schiesari, J., 141 n.22
Schiller, F., 87, 272
Schmitt, C. B., 256 n.6
Scotus, D., 50
Seldes, G., 274 n.27
Selke de Sánchez, Á., 113 n.14
Sena, J. de, 206, 246 n.57
Senabre, R., 160 n.9
  and "En la Ascensión" [Fray Luis de Léon], 161, 162–63
Seneca, 236 n.27
Sepúlveda, J. G. de, 200 n.8
Shakespeare, W., xxi, 29, 78 n.40
  Hamlet (character), 207
  Macbeth (character), 280
  A Midsummer Night's Dream, 222
  Twelfth Night, 222
  Two Gentlemen of Verona, 222
Shipley, G. A., 176 n.2, 179 n.4
Sidney, P., 221–22
Sito Alba, M., 54
Smillie, W. M., 259 n.10
Smollett, T., 183
Snell, A.
  on Sonnet 22 [Garcilaso], 97–98, 99, 100, 103, 107
Socrates, 99
Solana, M., 265 n.16
Solé-Leris, A., 34, 223 n.9
  on character of *cancionero*, 2
  on *Diana* [Montemayor], 230
  and love's compatibility with free will, 29
  on melancholy, 227

Sombart, W., 246 n.56
Sorabji, R., 36 n.11, 40 n.14, 48 n.22, 139, 185, 188
Soria
  character's pain alleviated by sexual clemency, 8
  fateful love lament, 20–21
  interpretation of poem by, 6–7, 9, 16
  love as irresistible fate of "imprisonment," 7
  A. Van Beysterveldt on "voluntary captivity," 16–17
Soufas, T. S., 34 n.8
Spengler, O., 244 n.52
Spitzer, L.
  and enchantment motif in *Don Quijote*, 254 n.4
  and "perspectivism" in Cervantes, 263
Statius
  Thebaid, 160 n.9
Steiner, G., 21 n.18
Stone, L., 68, 69 n.28
Suárez, F., 271 n.21
Sullivan, H., 127
Swift, J., 87
Sypher, W., 62, 140 n.21

Tamayo de Vargas, T. de, 97 n.1
  interpretation of Garcilaso's Sonnet 22, 108
Tasso, T., 141
Santa Teresa de Jesús, 65, 72, 88
  "Vivo sin vivir en mí," 81–82
Thompson, C. P., 173 n.28

Index of Names

and "En la Ascensión" [Fray Luis
 de Léon], 157, 161, 162–63,
 164, 165 n.20, 171
Tillier, J.
 on concept of passion, 13, 24
 interpretation of the "prison of
 love," 15
Tillyard, E. M. W., 32 n.4
Titian, 117
Tolstoy, L., 127, 165 n.21
Torner, E., 18
Troeltsch, E., 237 n.31
Turgenev, I., 196
Tylus, J., 212 n.22, 222 n.6

Urban, W.
 meaning of metaphor, xii–xiii,
 xxv, 60–61
Urrea, X. de, 11

Valdés, J. de, 225
Valency, M., 208
 on "heresy" of courtly love, 83
 n.48
 on Renaissance Neoplatonism,
 211
Van Beysterveldt, A.
 on depictions of lover as victim, 6
 interpretation of love, 7–9
 interpretation of the rhetorical element in *cancionero* lyric, 24
 and love's compatibility with free
 will, 12
 on the meaning of passion, 24
 and moralistic asceticism, 11

perspective and "love by destiny"
 motif, xiii
religious elements of language, 23
and "voluntary captivity," 16–17
Vaquero Serrano, M. del Carmen, 126
 n.5
Vargas Llosa, M., xx
Vega, A. C., 145 n.27, 160, 165
Vega, L. de, 40 n.17
Vossler, K.
 and "En la Ascensión" [Fray Luis
 de Léon], 161, 162
 on Fray Luis de Léon, 156
 on the style of Garcilaso's heroic
 characters, 111

Waley, P., 54, 180 n.5, 189
Walser, E., 237 n.31
Warburg, A., 130 n.12, 142 n.24, 164
Wardropper, B., 180 n.5, 226, 220 n.1
 and *Lazarillo de Tormes*, 184 n.9,
 191 n.21
Warren, A., xxii, 79 n.41, 88 n.54, 89
Weinsheimer, J. C., 260
Wellek, R., xxii, 79 n.41, 88 n.54, 89
Werkmeister, W. H., 43 n.18, 76 n.37,
 109 n.9
Westphal, M., 66 n.25, 78 n.39, 92
Whinnom, K.
 interpretation of love, 8–9, 41
 n.17, 59 n.9
 interpretation of "prison of love,"
 16 n.14
 on meaning of the association of
 love, 59 n.9

perspective and "love by destiny" motif, xiii
on sensual desire, 11, 12
Whittlesey, E. S., 214 n.28
Wilde, O., 234 n.23
Williams, C., 10 n.8, 53 n.1
Williamson, E., 255 n.4
Williamson, G., 222 n.4
Willis, R., 180 n.5, 191 n.21

Wimsatt, W. K.
concept of "intentional fallacy," 32 n.4
poem as "verbal icon," 46
Wind, E., 212 n.23, 213 n.25
Winters, Y., 248 n.61
Woods, M. J., 177 n.3, 180 n.5
Woodward, L. J., 179 n.4

Zimic, S., 176 n.2, 189 n.17

Subject Index

Authors of secondary works and of primary sources that are neither the subjects of chapters nor discussed in detail are listed in the Index of Names. The names of literary characters and mythological figures appear here in capital letters.

abandonment
    disciples mistake Christ's ascension for, 161
    feeling of expressed in "En la Ascensión" [Fray Luis de Léon], 157–58, 161, 164

ABINDARRÁEZ, 241

"above"
    and "below" in "En la Ascensión" [Fray Luis de Léon], 172
    represented critically, 151

"absolute contingency"
    paradox of, and supernatural *"agua mágica"* (magic philtre) in *Diana* [Montemayor], 248–49

abstraction
    as process of interpreting sense impressions, 264

abyss
    as lady's forgetfulness, 137
    as mother archetype, 137
    of regression, 137
    of the unconscious mind, 137

ACTAEON, 72 n.33

Actaeon archetype
    poet as, 72

acts
    values of, 49

actual person
    autonomy of, 47

act-value
    poem as, 111
adaptation
    and resilient detachment, 93
aesthetic
    Renaissance, of stubborn dejection, as Romantic prototype, 248
aesthetic appeal
    of emotional intensity, 152
aesthetic objects
    implicitly affirming character of, 184
aesthetic values
    derivation of, 263
    and mature, exemplary strength of character, 151
    and moral value of noble pain, 281
    as object values, 111
    and pastoral, 202–7
    related to ethical values, 266 n.17
    in Renaissance, 77, 200, 207–12
aesthetics
    advances in, and idyll, 282
    advances in, and non-didactic vision of life, 282
    advances in, and satire, 282
    advances in, through combining heroism and irony, 282
    advances in, and tragic art, extending to lyric and prose fiction, 282
    as cognitive and epistemological domain, 263
    as contest between ideal truth and factual truth, 262, 263
    as science of forms, 267
aggression, 65, 68
    absence of in *Lazarillo de Tormes*, 188–89
    against self, 131
    instinct of, tied to sexual instinct, in Freudian doctrine 244
    masochistic, 68
    neutralization of, 90
    of persona, in Sonnet 2 [Fray Luis de León], 147
    persona's, turned inward toward the ego, 140
    redefinition of, and sublimation, 90
    repressed, 68
    and sadistic poetic fantasies 68
    as self-affliction, 148
    sublimation of, and self-abnegation, 82
    toward lady, concealed by harmless ineptness, generosity, and suffering, 68
aggression of lady
    deliberately provoked, 68
    provocation of, source of masochistic guilt, 68
aggressive heroism, xviii
aggressive mastery
    metaphorical, as mystical triumph of its "victim," 81
agua mágica (magic philtre in *Diana* [Montemayor]), 150

Subject Index 323

ALANIO, 228–29
ALBANIO, 3 n.3
Albigensians
    Church's crusade against, 83 n.49, 239
ALDONZA LORENZO, 261, 275
alienation
    of loved one as defensive strategy, 69
    Renaissance mannerism rooted in, 65
allegorization, 56, 60, 125
allegory, xii, 53, 54
ALONSO QUIJANO, 86–87, 251, 252
Alumbrados, 206, 206 n.19, 207 n.19, 224 n.11
Amadís de Gaula, 214, 221
AMADÍS DE GAULA, 3 n.3, 189
amatory lyric
    anticipates ethics of values, 153
    as precursor of psychodynamics, 153
ambiguity, 96
    haunting, popular and *cancionero* lyric share tone of, 17
    moral, in *Lazarillo de Tormes* 177
    and reader's experience of anxiety, 130
ambivalence
    during process of individuation, 126, 126 n.6
    of persona, in Sonnet 2 [Fray Luis de León], 146
    in Sonnet 38 [Garcilaso], 126
    toward lady, 131–33

AMOR, 212
anagogic meaning, 61
ANDROMEDA, 216
angry wind
    metaphor of, 173
anguish
    in "En la Ascensión" [Fray Luis de León], 157, 161, 162, 163, 164, 170, 171, 172 n.27, 173
    in Garcilaso, 124, 168
    as pre-condition for integration of personality, 138
    in Sonnet 2 [Fray Luis de León], 145
anima
    ambivalent character of, as mother–imago, 135
    persona's projection of, in Sonnet 2 [Fray Luis de León], 148
animals
    domesticated *vs.* beasts of prey, 198
anthropocentrism, 236
anti-libidinal ego
    and aggression, 140
    in R. Fairbairn's theories, 149
    lady as, 140
    as metaphor, 140
    and persecution of libidinal ego, 140
    of persona, in Sonnet 2 [Fray Luis de León], 146, 148, 149
anxiety
    characteristic of early modern period, 63
    morbid, xv, 129

obsessional, 129
phobic, 129, 146
phobic, of being shut in, 147
separation, of apostles in "En la Ascensión" [Fray Luis de Léon], 172–73
AONIA, 213, 214–15
Apologia Aristotelica adversus eos, qui aiunt animam cum corpore extingui [G. Cardillo de Villapando], 265 n.16
appetite, 52
appetitive, 265 n.16
sensitive, 265 n.16
AQUELISA, 213
Arcadia [Sannazaro]
pastoral setting of, 198, 200, 205
reflects divisions at the royal court, 204–5
tension between setting and characters, 197
textual excerpts from, 205
Arcadia, 198, 205, 207
archetypal meaning, 61
aristocratic values, 234
and *Diana* [Montemayor], 234
Aristotelian concept of
moral accountability, xvii
voluntary action, 39, 40
Aristotelianism, 257–59, 265
influence of, in Renaissance, 256–57, 257 n.7
ARMINA, 214, 217
ARSENIO, 230
ARSILEO, 230

art, 64–65
as mode of apprehension, 267
Arthurian tradition, 214
ascent
and high peak as mid-point of integrated personality, 138
ascetic depreciation of love of sexes, 7
asceticism, 80
and *Diana* [Montemayor], 242–44
healthy, of "the great style," 244–45, 244 n.52
positive, lay alternative to official, monastic type, 244
asceticism, negative
alternative to, of cult of chaste ecstasy in love, 242, 243
related to love of war, 242–43
vs. positive, 242–45
asceto-monasticism, xviii, 226
L'Astrée [H. d'Urfé], 214
attachment theory [J. Bowlby], 151
Augustinianism, 207 n.19, 270
authoritarianism, xviii, 69
of early modern period, related to submission to tyrannical lady, 69
monarchic, and reinforcement of violence and ethic of honor, 240
author's biography
reflected in literature, 217
auto-eroticism
and masochism, 65
autonomy
gained through pain, 247

human, xvi, xviii, 237
human, in *Diana* [Montemayor], 245
moral, 126, 248
moral, as devotion in lovesickness, 248
of the person, 112
of vital feeling, 237 n.30
super-sensuous moral, affirmed in *Diana* [Montemayor], 245
AVALOR, 196, 197, 199, 210–11, 213–14, 215, 218, 219
axiological determination, 113
 vs. ontological determination, 113
axiology, xii, xxi

bad object(s)
 internalized, return of caused by anxiety, 173–74
Baroque, 206 n.18
BEATRICE, 53 n.1
beauty
 corporeal, 230
 feminine, and feminine virtues exalted in *Diana* [Montemayor], 239
 feminine ideal of, in *Diana* [Montemayor], 228
 human, 229 n.17
 as ideality, 248
 individual human, celebrated in *Diana* [Montemayor], 243
 internal *vs.* external, 97
 match of outer and inner, in Sonnet 22 [Garcilaso], 98–100, 113
 modesty as a quality of, 115
 personified as lady in Sonnet 22 [Garcilaso], 104
 personified as modesty in Sonnet 22 [Garcilaso], 102, 104
 spiritual, contemplation of, 230
BELISA, 230
BIMARDER, 197, 199, 213–14
biographical fallacy, xiv, 32, 54, 55, 56, 61, 62, 87, 88, 89, 93, 127
 and clinical view of masochism, 64
 as principle not inconsistent with consideration of author's experiences, 89
 vs. language's being inseparable from human beings who use it, 127
 vs. moderate adherence to New Criticism, 126–27
 vs. attention to historical criticism, 127
birth
 of individuality, 142
 pain of in "En la Ascensión" [Fray Luis de Léon], 173
Blas, Gil. *See* Gil Blas
bliss (central happiness). *See also* Gaiety
 concealed by surface of suffering in *Diana* [Montemayor], 247
 as condition for loving truly, 247
bodily shame, 112, 112 n.12
body
 contempt of, 243
 bondage/captivity, and release from, xiv–xv, 71, 73, 74, 90–93, 92

of frustration, release from, 92
in love–anguish, 92
of persona, in lady's oblivion as, 92
as prelude to joy, 92
sexual, 73
and Sonnet 2 [Garcilaso], 90–93
Bonnie and Clyde, 185
Book of Sorrowful Longing. See *Livro das Saudades*
BOVARY, EMMA. See EMMA BOVARY
El Buscón [Quevedo], 179, 183
Byzantine structure
in *Diana* [Montemayor], 226, 229 n.17

Cabalism, 195 n.1
callous indifference of beloved
as representing tyrannical contempt for sentimental culture, 246
cancionero, xiii, 1, 3, 12, 16, 21, 25, 33, 41 n.17, 51
Cancionero de Estúñiga, 4–5
cancionero love lyric, 6, 8, 10. See also love lyric; Petrarchism; elegiac love lyric
dialectical thematic complexity of, 8
idealism in, 8
cancionero lyric, 9, 17
elevated tone of, 9
formal refinement of, 9
genuine emotion of, 9
hyperbolic rhetoric of, 9
levels of meaning in, 9
theme of love in, 23
word play in, 9
Cárcel de amor [Diego de San Pedro]
influence of, 22
castration
emotional, and paralysis, in Sonnet 38 [Garcilaso], 141
casual determination
defense against *vs.* coexisting with, 112
Catholic reformism, 243
Catholic Reformists, 207 n.19
causal order, 112 n.13
CÉLADON, 214
CELIA, 229, 230
censorship
immunity to provided by mournful tone, 281
Cervantes, Miguel de, xix, 252
coexistence of Platonist and Aristotelian influences in writings of, 257 n.7
concept of "feigned Arcadia," 241
concept of *phantasma*, 259, 263, 264, 265, 272
and contemporary Spain, 270–71
and *Don Quijote*, 75, 117, 253. See also *Don Quijote*
"El coloquio de los perros", 273
La Galatea, 258
and *Lazarillo de Tormes*, 180, 187, 189
motif of the "lady," 54–55
and picaresque novel, 182

Subject Index

and Platonist and Aristotelian theories, 256–57, 265, 267
and principle of artistic transformation, 267
and Sonnet 22 [Garcilaso], 117
successor of Montemayor, 251
chain of love, 16
chains of love/loving, motif of
meanings of, 18–21
metaphorical implications of, 22
rhetorical value of, 22
chaste innocence
as ideal of ingenuous character, 233
chastity, xviii
broader implications of in *Diana* [Montemayor], 242
vs. negative asceticism, 242
chivalric romance, 196
chivalrous idealism, 198
chivalry, heroic
rejected by Ribeiro in favor of romantic, 197
Christ, xvi
as ambivalent object, xvi
ascending, parallels imperious lady, 171
as nursing mother, 172–73, 172–73 n.28
and "blessed daring," 167, 170
passion of, as effecting remission of all human sins, 281–82
reproached in "En la Ascensión" [Fray Luis de León], 156–57, 160, 164, 167
as super-ego who binds together the disciples, 173
transmutation of, xvi
Christian elements of language, 23
veil implicitly heterodox celebration of love of sexes in love lyric, 23
Christian optimism, 11
Christian salvation
and romantic love, fulfillment of desiring self in, 83, 83 n.48
Christianity, xiii, 11, 73, 198, 234
and the appeal to lady's compassion, 73
as disinterested, 238
ecclesiastical, 239
emphasis on value of passion different from stoicism, 239
evangelical, 239
as incompatible with eudaemonism, 238
as other-worldly eudaemonism, 238
Church
counterreformist, 203
resistance to modernization by authority of, 278
role as mediator challenged, 282
CIRCE, 137
civic culture
gains of in Renaissance, 282
classicism, Renaissance, xxiii, 217, 226. See also humanism, and Greco-Roman classicism
Diana's estrangement from stability of, 227

and humanism, 100
and *kalokagathia*, 118
and quality of the genuine, 165
cognition, human
    metaphoric nature of, 76 n.37
El coloquio de los perros [Cervantes], 273
comedy, 198 n.7
conceptismo, 51
concepts
    as memory images, 259
concupiscence
    and love, 41 n.17
conflict
    between progressive and regressive urges, 133
    obsessional. *See* obsessional conflict
    phobic. *See* phobic conflict
consciousness, xxv, 48, 49
    neural basis of, xxv
consent
    as act that completes willing, 34 n.6
The Consolation of Philosophy [Boethius], 235 n.27
contemporary readings of literature, xxi, 60
context, xxiv
    all meaning depends upon, xxiv
    and interpretation of figurative language, xxiv
Il Corteggiano [B. de Castiglione], 100, 228, 231
El cortesano [B. de Castiglione], 228, 230 n.18

courage
    in love, 75
    and neurosis, 87
    to act, as fortitude in suffering, 153
courtly love, xvi, xxiii, 2 n.3, 3, 6, 7, 10, 12, 33, 41 n.17, 80, 88, 207–12, 250
    as heresy, 7
    heresy of, 40
    and Inquisition, 83 n.49
    as metaphor, xvi
    in Spain, 7
    traditional allegorical motifs in, 101
    vehicle of progressive change, xxiii
courtly love literature
    conventional motifs of, 211
    love as an irresistible power, 212
    traditions of, 207–8, 209
courtly romanticism
    Renaissance revival of related to Christian–humanist irenicism, 240
coyness, 106
creativity, poetic, 259
"criteria of adequacy" of an interpretation to a text, 181, 181 n.7
critical approach, xix
    based on theories of C. G. Jung and R. Fairbairn compared, 149–50
    and conservatism, xix
    "contemporary readings," xxi
    emphasis on the romantic, xix

is a function of critic's imagination, xix
Marxist, xix
philosophical, 128
psychoanalytic, 127, 128
reader-response, xxiv
and use of data from author's biography, 155
critical authority, xix
limitations of, xix, xx
critical interpretation
and "criteria of adequacy," 181, 181 n.7
metaphorical, xxii. See also metaphorical interpretation of literature
principal challenge of, xxiv
and text as ultimate basis of interpretation, 127
through recording changes literature effects in readers, xxv
critical method
ground rules for interpretation, 109
interpretive convention of crediting facts as provided by poet or narrator, 109–10 n.10
criticism, literary
contemporary formalistic post-structuralist, comparable to nominalism, 271
historically oriented, 127
psychoanalytic, 127
cultural renovation, 10. See also Early modern period, cultural renovation in
culture
liberalization of, 278
CUPID, 98, 117. See also EROS
curialism
conceives life as conformity to temporal authority, 241–42
traditionalistic, as empirical monism, 241
"El curioso impertinente" [Cervantes], 275
cynicism
in *Lazarillo de Tormes*, 177

DARINTO, 258 n.9
Daunger, allegorical motif
as quality of enmity in the lady, 101
death, 37, 42, 54, 59
of Arsileo in *Diana* [Montemayor], 230
of Celia in *Diana* [Montemayor], 229
and destruction, instinct of, 244
of hope, 106, 113
leading to rebirth, 92
and loss of libido, 148
metaphorical, in *Diana* [Montemayor], 225, 250
pain of in "En la Ascensión" [Fray Luis de Léon], 173
as persona's threat of self-punishment, 75
and purgation of weakness, 92
as regressive descent, 137
rescue by, 74

for sake of passion, 42
and sexual climax, 73
in Sonnet 2 [Fray Luis de León], 147
and transition to life, 92
of unloved lover, 241
violent, 75
decision
conscious, not require explicit deliberation, 48
deconstruction, 274
degradation, of *Lazarillo de Tormes*
extending to self-degradation, in *Lazarillo de Tormes*, 194
as parody of complacent respectability, 194
dejados, 224 n.11
dependence, infantile
abandonment of, 147
in R. Fairbairn, compared to C. G. Jung, 149
feelings of absolute, 147
of persona on lady, 91
regressive, 91
in Sonnet 2 [Fray Luis de León], 145, 146, 148
surrender of, 133
symbolized by road, in Sonnet 38 [Garcilaso], 135
transition from infantile to mature, 143
transitional stage between, and mature dependence, 129
and the undifferentiated ego, 129
and vulnerability to feelings of rejection, 131

dependence, mature
in R. Fairbairn, compared to C. G. Jung's theories, 149
transition to, 129, 147
dependence, theories based on, and J. Bowlby's attachment theory, 151
depreciation
nagging, motivated by resentment, 174
depression, 59
from trauma of loss, 173
deprivation
of loving, 142
descent
as death followed by rebirth, 137
desire, sensual
frustration of, 236
symbols of, 137
despair
feeling of expressed in "En la Ascensión" [Fray Luis de Léon], 158, 163, 171, 174
devoted lover, in *Diana* [Montemayor] paralleled by Christian faithful, 245
Devotio moderna, 249
devotion in love, 198
exemplary, 199, 229
ideal, 241
rhapsodic, 248
Diana [Montemayor], xviii, 72, 72 n.31, 220–51
and ambivalent effects of "*agua mágica*," 241
apparent conservatism of, xviii
appeal in its day, 221–23

Subject Index

axiological dimension of, 234
"*Canto de Orfeo*," 239–40
and Christian and Catholic doctrine, 245
and Christianity, 236–39
contrasts with violence of romances of chivalry, 240
as departing from warrior ethos and heroic quest, 242
enormous appeal to women of the day, 239
ethic of, as countering rigid ecclesiastical morality, 245
ethos of, 234
framing narrative of, 221, 241
heretical implications of, 249–50
humanistic character of, xviii
incompatible with bellicose or defensive indignation, 240–41, 242
innovative character of, xviii
Inquisitoral censorship of, 83 n.49, 250–51
interpolated narratives of, 221, 224 n.11
lack of natural beauty in, 197
love in, devoid of masochism, 244
lovers devotion in, as counterpart of justification by faith, 250
meaning of, for initiated readers of the day, 236
meaning of pseudo-bucolic setting for readers of the day, 236
modern views of, 222–25
naive innocence of passionate love, xviii

neopaganism in, 222
Neoplatonic dualism of, *vs.* curialist empirical monism, 241–42, 242 n.44
originality of, 227
pastoral motif, 200
popularity of, 221–22
as reaction against new sociopolitical rigidity, 246
and Renaissance literature of sentimental love, 207
and secular antecedents, 249–50
as secular complement of Christian spirituality, 245
success of, xviii
survey of plot motifs, 228
unevoked bucolic setting in mirrors unfulfillment of characters, 197, 200
DIANA (in Montemayor's *Diana*), 204, 214, 233, 241
DIANA (goddess), 72 n.33
Diana archetype
   lady as, 72
Dianoia, 61
DINA, 208–9
DIONYSUS, 146 n.27, 213, 214
disenchantment, pain of, 281
disinterestedness in love, 80
disposition
   carries responsibility, 48
Divina Commedia [Dante], 53
Divine sovereignty, implied by ascension
   as obstacle to love between mankind and God, in "En la As-

censión" [Fray Luis de Léon], 95
dogmatism
　authoritarian, 262
Dolce stil nuovo, 53
DON FELIS, 229, 240
DON LUIS, 117
Don Quijote, 75, 78, 87, 93, 117, 139 n.19, 189, 218, 221, 249 n.64, 252–71
　barber's basin as helmet motif, 253, 259–60
　central element of childlike innocence in, 279
　character's heightened vision, 271
　criticism on, 253–54
　delusions of, 272
　Don Luis' song to Doña Clara, 117
　enchantment motif, 253–54, 254–55 n.4, 259, 266–67, 268, 273
　Ortega y Gasset on, 254 n.4
　perspectivism in, 189
　as representing errors of formalistic intellectualism and oversimplification, 272
　E. C. Riley on, 253, 254
　as satire of militarism, 241
　theme of enchantment, xviii–xix
　theme of "feigned Arcadia," 241 n.43
　themes of unfounded suspicion and mutual distrust, 117
DON QUIJOTE, xviii, xix, 54, 75, 93, 189, 252–53, 254, 255, 256, 259, 260–61, 262, 263, 265, 266, 267, 268, 269, 271, 272, 274, 275
　as embodiment of artistic transformation, 267
　equates truth and language, 271
　as fictional projection Platonist and Aristotelian theories of perception, 259
　immune to discouragement and despair, 189
　as incarnating the Platonist concept of mind, 259
　and Maese Pedro, 93
　as neurotic, 86–87
DONA [DO TEMPO ANTIGO], xviii, 196, 197, 198, 199, 208, 213, 214, 215, 216
DOÑA CLARA, 117
dreams, 60, 83 n.48
dualism
　vs. monism in *Diana* [Montemayor], 241–42
DULCINEA DEL TOBOSO, 54, 93, 253, 260, 268, 275
　symbolic meaning of, 93

early modern period
　artistic intuition in, 128
　characterized by anxiety, 62–63
　complexity of, xxii
　conflict in, xxii
　and crisis, xxii
　cultural renovation in, 10
　society in, xxiii. *See also* Early modern society
early modern society, xxii–xxiv

oppressive character of, xxiii
eclecticism, 23
    and Nicodemism, of *Diana* [Montemayor], 226 n.14
eclogues
    conventional form of, 195
    by Garcilaso, 197, 200
    by Ribeiro, 195
ego
    anti-libidinal. *See* anti-libidinal ego
    central (moral), 148–49
    libidinal. *See* libidinal ego
    loss of, 75, 130
    negation of, 92
    and object relations, 128
    overcoming disintegration of, 149
    of persona, splits in, in Sonnet 2 [Fray Luis de León], 146
    and psychopathology, 129
    self-sabotage of, 140
    splitting of, 129
    and split with ego-ideal, 130
    undifferentiated, of persona, 129, 148
ego-ideal, 130, 132
Elegia di madonna Fiametta [Boccaccio], 209
elegiac love lyric, 10, 45, 77, 82, 111, 249. *See also cancionero* love lyric; love lyric; Petrarchism
    and depictions of sadistic cruelty, 63
    satirical dimensions of, 77–78
elegiac pastoral romance, 196
El laberinto de Fortuna [Juan de Mena]. *See Las Trezientas*

EMMA BOVARY, 236
emotion
    displayed by an orphaned humanity, 161, 163, 164, 168, 172–73
    Fray Luis de León's display of, 156
    lustful transference of, 68
    sincerity of in "En la Ascensión" [Fray Luis de León], 162
    of vexation at Christ's departure, 157
emotional bonds. *See* attachment theory
empirical reality, 263
empiricism
    theory of knowledge, 257 n.7
enchantment
    A. Castro on, 256, 262–63, 267
    and chivalric romances, 255
    of Don Quijote, farsical treatment of, 256
    as Don Quijote's obsession, 253–54
    as fiction, 275
    as metaphor, xix
    motif in *Don Quijote*, 253–54, 254–55 n.4, 259, 265–67, 268, 269, 271, 273
    motif in *Don Quijote*, critical interpretations of, 254–56, 254–5 n.4
    Ortega y Gasset on, 254 n.4
    as personification of sense impressions, 266
    R. Predmore on, 255–56
encyclopedists, 278

ends
- will directed by, 112. *See also* finalistic determination

"En la Ascensión" [Fray Luis de Léon], 95
- and ambivalence toward loved one, 173
- association with iconographic tradition, 164
- attitude of dissent in, 156
- authenticity of challenged, 160–61, 162, 163
- broader significance of, 174
- Christ as super-ego who binds together the disciples, 173
- Christ reproached in, 156–57, 160, 167
- compared with "Noche serena," 164
- and concept of love, 170
- contrasts heaven and earth, 159
- contrasted with book of Job, 161, 163
- M. Durán and M. Atlee on, 156–57
- earlier version of poem, 159–160, 159 n.9
- as expressing viewpoint of Christ's disciples, 157
- and feelings of abandonment, 157–58, 161, 162
- and feelings of desolation, 158
- and foreboding of violence and confusion, 158–59
- influenced by Old Testament/book of Job, 161, 163, 166
- interpretations of based on poet's biography, 156, 164–65, 172
- interpreted metaphorically, 157, 172
- ontological gulf between humankind and sovereign God, 95
- and Platonic concept of love, 170–71
- poem depicts process of loss of morale, 173–74
- as representing humanity as a whole, 157
- similarity to Garcilaso's poetry, 167–68, 170, 174
- sincerity of emotions in, 162
- textual excerpts of, 157 (stanza one), 158 (stanzas two and three), 159 (stanzas four and five)
- C. P. Thompson on, 162–63, 171
- tone of anguished protest in, 161
- underlying sense of bitterness, 166, 167
- K. Vossler on, 156, 162
- writing influenced by imprisonment, 164–65
- written from viewpoint of Christ's disciples, 157, 164, 171

Enlightenment (period), 214

epic
- revenge is central theme of, 240

epiphany
- moment of in *Diana* [Montemayor], 239

epistemological realism. *See* realism, epistemological

Subject Index

epistemology
    Aristotelian, 264 n.16
    Aristotelian–Thomist, in *Don Quijote*, 259, 263, 264 n.16, 265, 267
    of Plato and Aristotle, 257 n.7
    Platonic, 265
    realism, xix
Erasmians, 207 n.19
Erasmism
    and irenicism of *Diana* [Montemayor], 240
    and Nicodemism, 226
Eros
    Freud on, 244
    Greek conception of, 41 n.17
    and incontinence, 41 n.17
    and life-affirmation, 245
    Platonic, 45
    M. Scheler on, 66
EROS (CUPID), 41 n.17, 137, 212, 244, 245
erotic feeling
    ambivalence of, in *Diana* [Montemayor], 226
erotic innuendo, 8
erotic passion. *See also* sexual love
    Aristotle on, 231
Eroticism, 8. *See also* sensuality
    veiled, 8
essence of material things
    as object of intellectual knowledge, 263
ethics, sentimental, 218
Eudaemonism, practical
    as incompatible with Christian optimism, 238

renunciation of in *Diana* [Montemayor], 234
Eudemian Ethics [Aristotle], 185
EURYDICE, 137
evangelism, 200
Examen de ingenios para las ciencias [Huarte de San Juan], 258 n.9, 266
exciting, frustrating object
    attacked by anti-libidinal ego, 132
    in R. Fairbairn's theories, 149
    lady as, in Sonnet 2 [Fray Luis de León], 146, 148
"excusing factors" in assignment of guilt (in Aristotle), 185, 187–88, 188 n.16
eyes
    motif of, 108, 110
    personification of, 25
    and seeing, 25
    two, symbol of unity, 149

fact, empirical, 253, 255
factualism, empirical, 266
fallibility
    A. Castro on Cervantes' depiction of, 254 n.4
fanaticism
    cold, opposed by *Menina e Moça*, 218
    pernicious, 219
fantasies
    of Don Quijote, 253, 254 n.4, 255
    visual, of Don Quijote, 272
fantasy
    as delusion, 275

of hatred on part of rejecting loved one, 75
and human being, 253
as human necessity, 274
and lady, 88
as means of fomenting aggression, 68
of mystic, 88
of release from tyranny of unfulfillment, 72
of repudiation of dependent self, 92
sadistic, in poetry, 68

fatalism
as blind necessity, 39
and fortune, and Renaissance Christian–Platonism, 38 n.12
as incomprehensible fixed order, 39
as irresistible force in Garcilaso, 39
of offending communal command, 42
passionate love in Garcilaso not referred to as, 39
as passionate willing, 38, 39, 49
sexual love as, 225
submission to, as metaphor, 52

fate, 16, 50, 52
arising from without, *vs.* from within, 250
attitude of surrender to, 15, 28, 37. See also fateful passion; love by destiny; love, as surrender to adverse fate, R. Lapesa's theory of; necessity, fateful; Original Sin; medieval fatalism
and St. Augustine on true freedom, 235 n.27
Boethian concept of, 235 n.27
of love, 229–30
noble, of renouncing sensuous being, 235
stoic concept of, 235 n.27

fateful love 7, 17, 29, 51. *See also* fatalism, as passionate willing; love by destiny; will, dominated by love, according to R. Lapesa
as based on value preference, 49
as form of consciousness, 49
as passionate willing, 43, 49
as value of the individual, 49

fateful passion, motif of, xiii, 3, 9, 28, 74. *See also* fate, attitude of surrender to; love by destiny
as aesthetic and moral value, 40
as erotic innuendo, xiii
in Garcilaso, meaning of, 40
interpreted rhetorically and metaphorically, 3
as metaphor, 31
rhetorically motivated, xiii

father figure, in *Lazarillo de Tormes*, 188
as symbol, 188

fear, 126
servile, and oppressive penitential asceticism, 243

feelings
of anxiety and dependence, 142–43

contracted, 241, 241 n.43
  of impotence, 151
  of love and esteem, 142–43
  of persecutory anxiety, 151
"feigned Arcadia," 241
  theme in Cervantes and Tirso de Molina, 241
FELICIA, 150, 237, 241, 249
FELISMENA, 229–30, 240
fertility
  as devotion in love in *Menina e Moça*, 198
  and pastoral, 205
  vs. sterility, in *Menina e Moça*, 198
FIAMMETTA, 209–10
fiction
  and cognition of the world, 274
  an element of positive thought, 273, 273 n.24, 273 n.25
  as fundamental in any conception of reality, 275
  as language, 265 n.16
  as requiring elevation, 275
  as sacred, 275
  as similar to science, 273, 273 n.24
  criteria for assessing narrator's truthfulness, 186 n.13
  real-world impact of, 186
La fingida Arcadia. *See* feigned Arcadia
FILEMÓN, 236
Filocolo, 209
finalistic determination, 112 n.13. *See also* ends, will directed by
fleeing
  from bad object, 134
  from individuation to the object, 135
  from the object to individuation, 135
  to the object, *vs.* from the object, 135
  and phobic anxiety, 133
  vs. departure, 134
forms
  Platoic, 258
  theory of, 266
Franciscanism, 249
Fray Luis de León, xv
  analysis of author's life, 155
  attention to inner conflicts, xvi
  as biblical scholar, 161
  characterized as courageous, 156
  commentary of the book of Job, 166
  compared to Savonarola, 156, 171
  "En la Ascensión" [Fray Luis de Léon], xvi, 72, 72 n.32, 95, 151, 279
  Exposición del Libro de Job, 166–67
  imprisonment, 155–56, 165
  "Noche serena," 72, 164
  Nombres de Cristo, 166
  seen as writing in the tradition of St. Bernard, 161, 163
  Sonnet 2, xv, 119, 144–53, 173, 279
  Sonnet 2 compared to Sonnet 38 [Garcilaso], 150–51
  suffering innocence in lyric of, 280–81

supporter of Grajal during Inquisition, 155
freedom
　advanced through fashion for love–melancholy, 246
　ambivalent, of "cured" Sireno in *Diana* [Montemayor], 241
　as absolute determination by self and from within, in *Diana* [Montemayor], 247–48
　contrary to determination from without, 46
　delirium of, in *Diana* [Montemayor], 226
　from the transitory, in Neoplatonism, 242
　as independent of a consciousness of it, 48
　individual, 278
　inner, Erasmian ideal of, 243
　the lover's voluntary forfeiture of, as the ultimate free act, 246–67
　moral, individualistic ethic of, 245
　"negative," 17
　"positive," 17
　of subjectivity, 247
　of thought and will, 93
　of the will, 112 n.13
freedom, moral
　ambivalent nature of, 126 n.6
　and decision, 45
free necessity, 43, 44
　as comparable to fateful love, 43
　and will, 43, 44
free will, 112 n.13

displays of, as cloak for surrender to fate, according to R. Lapesa, 33, 39
　doctrine of, 270
　of tragic hero, 79
fullness of life, 36

gaiety, 45. *See also* joy, pagan; Hellenism
　in *Diana* [Montemayor], 227
　masked by suffering in love, 235
　voluntaristic, concealed by aura of fatalism, 45
GALEONE, 209
Garcilaso de la Vega
　attention to inner conflict, xvi
　Canción 1, 3, 28, 51, 63, 73, 74, 93, 171, 279
　Canción 2, 9, 28, 51, 168
　Canción 4, 9, 28, 29, 51, 171
　compared to Petrarch, 111
　Eclogue 2, 171
　familiar with Castiglione's *Il Corteggiano*, 100
　influenced by Renaissance classicism, 100
　intuitive perceptions of, 128
　lyric of, as antecedent of *Diana* [Montemayor], 249
　and lyric with satirical aspects compatible with sublimity, 87
　metaphorical reading of, 89–93
　and passionate willing as irresistible force, 124
　poetic tradition cultivated by, 157
　and satirical aspects of portrait of

self-effacing persona, 87
as secular humanist, 117
Sonnet 1, xiv, 3, 9, 28, 29, 30, 35–38, 51, 119, 122, 123, 278
Sonnet 2, xiv, xvi, 57–60, 73, 74, 90–92, 93, 174, 279
Sonnet 3, 57
Sonnet 4, 66
Sonnet 6, 9, 28, 39, 51, 119
Sonnet 9, 57, 168
excerpt of, 168
Sonnet 10, 168
Sonnet 11, 28
Sonnet 12, 28
Sonnet 17, 119
Sonnet 22, xv, 28, 95–118, 279
Sonnet 23, 105
Sonnet 25, 39
Sonnet 26, 28, 51, 169
excerpt of, 169–70
Sonnet 29, 28
Sonnet 37, 168–69
excerpt of, 168–69
Sonnet 38, xv, xvi, 28, 51, 119–44, 150–51, 173, 279
Sonnet 38 compared to Sonnet 2 [Fray Luis de León], 150–51
stylistic maturity, 28
suffering innocence in lyric of, 280–81
K. Vossler recognizes heroic character of style, 111
genuine, the
as quality of classicism, 165
German Ideology [K. Marx and F. Engels], 269

GIL BLAS, 183
GINÉS DE PASAMONTE, 93, 266
Gli Asolani [P. Bembo], 230, 248
gloom, surly, 219
gnostic dualism, 195 n.1
Golden Age
Spain's, 22
Vergilian, 207
Golden Ass/Metamorphoses [Apuleius], 212
good object(s)
unmet need for, 132
goodness
as loving disposition, xi
natural human, 278
GRISÓSTOMO, 218
guilt, xvii, 22
as condition for moral freedom, 44, 45
consequences of, accepted for sake of passion, in Garcilaso and Mexía, 42
as consistent with influence of environment (in Aristotle), 193
deliverance from, in religion, 45
and disaster as consequences of guilt, 153
"guilty," 22
in *Lazarillo de Tormes*, xvii
mitigated by "excusing factors," xvii
moral issue of freedom and, 46
as presupposing the possibility of acting differently, 46
social ground of, 191
tragic, or "guiltless," 22

will to, 45
will to, implicit secularism of, 45
Guzmán de Alfarache, 179, 183

HAMLET, 207
hand motif
    as metaphor/symbol, 98, 116 n.18
heart
    associated with nobility of central feeling, 25
HELEN, 201–2, 268
Hellenism, 117. *See also* joy, pagan; gaiety
    frenzied, in *Diana* [Montemayor], 226
helpless despair, persona's
    aesthetic appeal and axiological basis of, 139
helplessness
    of persona, in Sonnet 38 [Garcilaso], 141
    traumatic, 68
heresy, 200, 274
heroic romance, 209
heroism
    and indignation, 240
    in *Lazarillo de Tormes*, 189
    and mastery of erotic instincts, 11
    violent, opposed by *Diana* [Montemayor], 240–41, 242
heterodoxy
    of *Diana* [Montemayor], 226 n.14
heterodoxy of spirit, 83 n.49, 207
high peak, motif of, 121, 122, 123, 124, 125, 128, 132, 133, 134
    ascent to, 134
    as metaphor for high moral attainment/virtue, 134
    as object of progressive movement, 138
    reaching, as realization of ego-ideal, 138
    as world of light, 137
High Renaissance, 65, 74, 200, 226
    and erosion of individual freedom, 246
historiography
    the subject of, 264 n.16
homosexual
    desire, 229 n.17
    love, 229 n.17
hope
    of one as individual, and moral autonomy, 143
human goodness, natural
    affirmed in *Diana* [Montemayor], 245
human innocence, affirmed in *Diana* [Montemayor], 245
human nature
    in *Don Quijote*, 253
human physical nature, xviii
    implicitly exonerated in *Diana* [Montemayor], 245
humanism
    born of striving for general renewal, xxiii
    Christian, and secularization of piety, 242
    and Christian moral idealism, xxiii
    doctrine of inherent human goodness, *vs.* power of Church, 281

and Greco–Roman classicism, xxiii
heterodoxy of, 10
Italian, 223
and pagan skepticism, xxiii
Renaissance, xiii, xiv, xv, 21
Renaissance, and influence of Aristotle and Plato, 256
and scholasticism in Renaissance, 257 n.7
secular, 117
secular equivalent of Reformist opposition to emphasis on doctrine of merit, 282
secular, *vs.* Christian heteronomy, 237, 238, 239
secularizing, and shift away from theocentric morality, 236
Humanists, Renaissance
persecuted, 203
subjected to malevolence, 204
hunger, as symbol, 188
Hysmine and Hysminias [Makrembolites], 229 n.17
and *Diana* [Montemayor], 229

ideal being, 261
ideal essence of personality, 113, 114
ideal ethos of personality, 109, 112
ideal, the
surrender to dominating power of, 82
idealism, xix
aesthetic, xix
moral, xix
Neoplatonist, 242
seen as manipulation, 76

stubborn, in *Diana* [Montemayor], 241
subjective, 256
vs. factualism, 266
ideality
as authority in *Diana* [Montemayor], 242
ideas
having existence separate from object, 258
reality/intelligibility of, 258
identification, xvi
feminine, 71
infantile, 126, 127, 133
infantile, and struggle to abandon illusory emotional security, 151
and infantile dependence, xvi, 129
and love, 74
of lady with mother, in Sonnet 2 [Fray Luis de León], 148
of persona's ego with lady as ambivalent object, 140
secondary, 91
as substitute for attainment of desired object, 91
identity
adult, 146
differentiated, 149
identity diffusion, 67
illuminism, 195 n.1
illusion
in *Don Quijote*, 252–53, 255, 265
imagery
metaphorical, 89
poetic, 272

prison, 11. *See also* prison/bonds of love/loving
war, 11
imagination
   in critical approach, xx
   in *Don Quijote*, 252–53
   poetic, 268
   role of in creating meaning, 269
   role of in creating metaphor, 260, 268–69
   and social evolution, xxiv
In Cold Blood, 185
indignation
   as defense of unloved lover, absent in *Diana* [Montemayor], 241
   gratuitous, and *Don Quijote*, 241
individual moral culture, the new
   as advancing critical intelligence, 282
   as advancing social activism, 282
   ideal of, represented by synthesis of purity and experience, 282
   as strengthening the ability to suffer in life's struggles, 282
individual person
   conceived of in *Diana* [Montemayor], as uncorrupted by Original Sin, 243
   modern concept of, as bearer of the moral good, 237
   value of, affirmed, 42
   values of, and *religio amoris*, 45
   values of the, covertly celebrated, 24
individuality/individualism, xxiii, 7, 21, 31, 139, 143, 218
   attainment of, and overcoming regressive tendency, 136
   birth of, 135, 144
   courageous, 25
   and differentiation, 133
   in Garcilaso and Mexía, 31
   as individual consciousness, 136
   of masochist, 85
   modern, 140
   noble rebellion of, 21
   as reaction against Christian heteronomy, 237
   as reaction against ecclesiastical conception of life in *Diana* [Montemayor], 237
   of *religio amoris*, 45
   religious, 249
   in Renaissance, 85–86 n.52
   transition to, 140
   triumph of, in Renaissance culture, 249
   vs. the undifferentiated state, 129, 133
individuation, xvi, 9, 10, 126 n.6, 147, 149
   as balance of power between conscious and unconscious, 142
   and differentiation, 129, 133
   fear of, in Sonnet 38 [Garcilaso], 141
   C. G. Jung's point of view, 135
   in male, and integration of thought and feeling, 135–36, 137–38, 142
   and ordeal, 136
   and self-conquest, 135

in Sonnet 2 [Fray Luis de León], 147, 149
struggle to achieve, depicted in Fray Luis de León's Sonnet 2, 153
symbolized by road, 135
as transition between infantile and mature dependence, 119
ingenuousness
languishing, of *Diana* [Montemayor], 242
In libros tres Aristotelis De anima Commentarii [P. Martínez Brea], 265 n.16
innocence, 236 n.28
childlike, 278
ideal of, obscured since Renaissance, 292
naive, 279
oblivion of as esoteric modernist expression of protest, 282
super-sensuous, in *Diana* [Montemayor], 242
Inquisition, 206 n.19
and Fray Luis de Léon, 155–56
Portuguese, and censorship of *Diana* [Montemayor], 83 n.49
insignificance, perverse feelings of
vs. magnificence of partner, 68
instincts
egoism of, 75
integration, of unconscious into consciousness, 149. *See also* individuation, in male, and integration of thought and feeling

intelligible reality, xix
intention of the ideal, moral value in, 153
intentional fallacy, 32 n.4, 55. *See also* personal heresy
intertextual influences and problems in criticism, 105, 111
introjection, 75
irenicism
compared to modern pacifism, 240
and *Diana* [Montemayor], 240, 240 n.37, 242
and Erasmism, 240
irony
of *Lazarillo de Tormes*, 183–84
and metaphorical inversion, 79
satiric, in *Lazarillo de Tormes*, 177
in Sonnet 38 [Garcilaso], 127
isolation
of humanists, 203, 206
of noble sentiment in *Menina e Moça*, 198–99, 200

JANO, 208–9
JANUS, 143
JARIFA, 241
Jesuits
penitential asceticism of, compared to Erasmism, 243
JOB (biblical character), 161, 163–64, 166, 172 n.27
journey, metaphor of
life as, 35 n.9
and paths, 36 n.9
thinking as, 35 n.9

Jungian psychology
  compared to R. Fairbairn, 135, 149–50
  and myth, 150
  "Renaissance" and humanistic characteristics of, 150

kalokagathia, 100
knight errantry, 272
KNIGHT OF MIRRORS, 252, 253

lady
  aggression of, 66
  aloofness of, and persona's despair, 130, 130 n.11
  as ambivalent, 140
  ambivalent identity of, 116
  as anima–imago, 137
  as anti-libidinal ego, 140
  as bad internal object, 75, 131–33
  as bearer of high values, 35
  as captor in Sonnet 2 [Garcilaso], 90
  as cruel tormentor, 66, 72, 74
  cruel, as personified projection of poet's own aggression, 66
  cruelty of, and persona's frustration, 75
  cruelty of, and persona's self-reproach, 75
  cruelty of, represented metaphorically, 74
  as despot, 31, 35
  as Diana archetype, 72
  as dominant and aloof in Sonnet 38 [Garcilaso], 151
  elusive, 117
  as exciting object, 146
  as fantasized internal object, 88
  in Garcilaso's poetry, 171
  as good object, 131–33
  as heavenly bride, 138
  as image of persona's anti-libidinal ego, 91
  influence of, as function of persona's attitude, 137
  internal nature of, 102
  introjection of, 67
  in Jungian interpretation of Sonnet 2 [Fray Luis], 149
  as mother, 138
  as object of libidinal ego, 146
  as object of quest for love, 62
  as object of sensuous pleasure, 98
  as persona's regressive tendency, 148
  persona's idealization of, while incorporating her in unconscious as bad object, 132
  as personification of persona's morbid subjectivity, 59
  as powerful sovereign, 69–71
  pride of, 102
  and projection of libido, 135
  as prospective ideal being, 93
  as protective mother, 91
  and quality of *Daunger*, 102
  as reality *vs.* fiction, 53–55
  regarded ambivalently, 131
  rejecting, as exciting object, 131
  rejecting indifference of, 128
  as rejecting object, 91, 129, 146

remote, 140
as remote value, 152
representing ontological determination, 113
role and symbolic meaning of, 91
sheltering warmth of, 131–33
as sinister fantasy, 75
in Sonnet 2 [Fray Luis de León], 145
in Sonnet 38 [Garcilaso], 122, 123, 124
as source of danger or of power, 137
as sovereign, 74
snub by, 109
as spiritual person, 97, 98, 99
as split object, 131–33
as symbol for cyclical order of nature, 118
as the ideal in general, 62
as the future, 93
as threatening, in Sonnet 2 [Fray Luis de León], 151
tyrannical, 67–93
tyranny of, interpreted, 88
vain, 68
LAMENTOR, 217
language
as confining, 271
logocentric, 274
pseudo-objective tendencies of, 272
La Celestina [F. de Rojas], 221
La Galatea [Cervantes], 258
Las Trezientas [Juan de Mena], 202 n.12

Lazarillo de Tormes, xvi, xvii, 175–95, 221
absence of aggression in, 188
absence of kindness in, 186
absence of love in, 187
anonymous authorship, 180, 185
"Aristotelian," deterministic interpretation of, 181–82, 192–93
degradation in, extending to self-degradation, 194
division in critical views of, xvii
as entertainment, 185
compared to film treatments of picaresque, 185–86
compatibility of Aristotelian and Platonist interpretations of, 193
conflicting interpretations of, 178–93
as entertaining with baseness, 180, 181, 182
exploitation of, 194
M. Gorky on, 179, 183, 193, 194
heroism in 189
humor in, 186
influence on Cervantes, 180, 187, 189
influence on *Don Quijote*, 189
innovative character of, 180
and ironic inversion of ideality, 182, 184–85
"jocose epidermis" of, 187
as morally equivocal, 181
nobility of character in, 189
original appeal to readers, 185–86, 185 n.11

pessimistic tone of counteracted, 186
"Platonist," less tolerant interpretation of, 181–82, 192–93
as a precursor of picaresque genre, 175 n.1
problem of classifying, xvii
protagonist of, as eternal child, 279
as purging bad conscience of readers, 180–81
and question as to author's intentions, 181
reader's response to as conditioned ideologically, 181
realism of, 180, 183
as satiric exposé, 177
world of, solidarity lacking in, 194
LAZARILLO DE TORMES, xvii, 175–95
affliction of, 176
ambiguous child–adult identity of, 190
as courageous, 189–90
as cynic, 177
degradation of, 184, 190
as degraded by poverty, 185, 190
deprived of love, 187
as devoid of malice, 188
emotional deprivation of, 188
as eternal child, 191–92 n.21
as example of natural human goodness, 188
as exploiter, 177
guilt of, society's share in, 191
as ignorant, 177
immaturity of, 190
as inspiring pity, 180, 181
ironic triumph of, 191
as lacking moral autonomy and power of an adult, 191, 191–92 n.21
as manipulator, 176, 178
moral disfranchisement of, 190
as never loved, 192
as panderer, 177
as psychologically deprived, 191
reader's amusement at degradation of, 184
resilience of, 189
as rogue, 177
"social rebirth" of, 189
and society, as both negligent of self, 192
as victim, 177, 180
LÁZARO, xvii, 176–77, 181, 182, 183–84, 185, 186 n.13, 188–89, 191–92, 193, 194
association with Lazarus (biblical character), 190
learning
empirical, *vs.* creatively elevating, 275
León Hebreo, 257 n.7
comparison of "carnal" and "spiritual" passion, 231
Diálogos de amor, 50
and *Diana* [Montemayor], 237–38
on love and reason, 232
on love's compatibility with free will, 50
lesbianism, 229 n.17
libidinal ego
in R. Fairbairn's theories, 149

internal masochistic hindrance of, 141
and needs, 140
persona as, 140
of persona, in Sonnet 2 [Fray Luis de León], 145, 148
regressive, 130
role in emotional process, 153
suppression of, 130
libidinization of suffering, masochistic, 70–71, 73
ecstatic, 73, 80–84
as relief from submissive feelings of shame, 71
and subject–sovereign relationship, 70–71
libido
aggressive, as source of intense anxiety, 91
aggressive, subordination of, 73
and aggressive impulses, 65
and agoraphobic ego repression, 91
and asceticism, 244–45
Freud's view of, 244
fulfillment of, in Christianity and romantic love, 83
independent initiative of, in C. G. Jung, 150
intensity of, challenge of recovering, 153
intensity of, sufficient, 153
liberation of, in C. G. Jung, 150
loss of, 34, 59
loss of, and death, 148
lost, 150
and love's goal of good object relationships, 128
needs of, 145
of persona, in Sonnet 2 [Fray Luis de León], 147
positive strivings of, 244
progressive, doubtful triumph of in Sonnet 38, 138, 149
progressive, rebirth of, 137
regressive, and infantile detachment, 135
rescue of, from desire through salvation, 83
search of, as quest–romance, 83, 83 n.48
strengthening of, 150
suppression of, in R. Fairbairn, 150
untamable, 217
Libro de buen amor [Juan Ruiz], 72–73
literal interpretation, 17, 32
literature
expressive view of, 165, 165 n.21
philosophy's debt to, 128
psychology's debt to, 128
and social change, xxiv
traditional conventions of, 79
Livro das Saudades, xvii, 72, 196, 219. See also *Menina e Moça*
"Llama de amor viva" [San Juan de la Cruz], 80–81
Los siete libros de la Diana. See Diana
love, xiv, 3. *See also* love-idealism; love of the sexes; love of the remote
act of, as the highest good, 236
adult, 225

ambivalent, 19
as anguish and helplessness, 8
"Aristotelian" and "Platonic," 40–41 n.17
Aristotle on, 41 n.17, 237–38
based on esteem, 227, 230. *See also* love, born of reason
being deprived of, 142
belongs to death, 74
born of the eyes, 229
born of the mind, 229
born of reason, in *Diana* [Montemayor], 228, 230
born of reason but not governed by it in *Diana* [Montemayor], 232
broad concept of in Plato's *Symposium*, 170
chaste ecstasy in, vs. negative asceticism, 242, 243, 244–45
Christian–evangelical, presented in secular terms in *Diana* [Montemayor], 236
as Christian paradox, 8
compatible with reason and freewill, 11, 12, 31
compulsion in, 11
as compulsive concupiscence, 7
concept of that is illustrated in *Diana* [Montemayor], 231
consciousness of affinity as reason for, 172
as consistent with uncontrollable passion in *Diana* [Montemayor], 228
and courage, 78

as courage, xiv
creative value of, 170
and death, 216
for delight, 209
devotion in, 37, 79, 198
devotion in, as fertility, 198
as disinterested, in *Diana* [Montemayor], 237
as dynamic act of discovering value preferences, 47
elevated character or, 78
ennobling innocence of, 23
eternal frustration of, as "noblesse oblige," 248
as evil, 41 n.17
exclusive, noble character of, 115
as faith, 199
as fate, xiv
"fated," 227
M. Ficino sees conciousness of affinity as reason for, 172
as fulfillment of the will, 45
as fundamental fact of human nature, 128
as good, 41 n.17
Hegel on, 66
as heroic, 7
homosexual, 229 n.17
hopes of, reborn, in Sonnet 22 [Garcilaso], 95
ideal of in *Diana* [Montemayor], 239
of ideal ethos of individual personality of the beloved, 109
as ideal of moral value-being in *Diana* [Montemayor], 233

of ideal oughtness, 116 n.16
idealism of surrender in, 19
identical with goodness in *Diana* [Montemayor], 234
ignited by sensual desire, 227
insane ("amor loco"), 227, 228
as inspired form of militance, 209
irrational, 41 n.17
as irresistible power, 32, 209
irrevocable, 241
jeopardy of, as projection of poet's unfulfillment, 74
justification for, 128
lesbian, 229 n.17
as martyrdom of an élite, 248
as medieval and fatalistic, in *Diana* [Montemayor], 227
as moral greatness, 10
as movement toward realization of higher values, 95
as mutual subjection and adaptation of will, 24
of nearest, 152–53
of nearest and remotest as values of similar grade, 153
need for, 63, 73, 75
noble, 20
not contrary to will, 44
not genuinely accepted, 142
as object of quest, identifiable with the lady, 62
obstacles to, 15
obstructed by defensive modesty, in Sonnet 22 [Garcilaso], 95
as its own object in *Diana* [Montemayor], 242

as occasion for suffering or death, 34
passionate, as intense willing, 43
personal, way viewed in classical culture, 38
as personification of poet's obstinance, 74
Platonic, in *Diana* [Montemayor], 228, 228–29 n.17
as possessing will of its own, 43
potentially degrading effects of, 142
preferential character of, 31
as presupposing spiritual personhood, 193
and reason, 41 n.17
of remotest, 152–53
reproaches of, as persona's self-reproach, 75
romantic elements of, 8
as ruled by appetite, 227
M. Scheler on Platonic concept of, 170
scholastic conception of, 41 n.17
as seemingly hostile and negative, in *Diana* [Montemayor], 227
as seemingly irrational force contrary to the will in *Diana* [Montemayor], 227
of sexes as subjection of rational will, 7
sentimental, 207
sexual, as self-identification with another, 66
as source of central joy, 19
as source of suffering, 41 n.17

subjection to, as metaphor, 50
as surrender to adverse fate, 3, 31, 37, 42
as surrender to fate, R. Lapesa's theory of, 6, 29, 31, 33, 37
tragic, 51
unfulfillable nature of interpreted, 38 n.13
unfulfillable need for, 90
unhappy, as passionate willing, 44, 52
unrequited, 43, 198
for utility, 209
value of, 128
value of, celebrated as pseudo-erotic suffering in *Diana* [Montemayor], 236
vs. mere sensual desire, 40, 228
vs. preoccupation with the self, 38 n.13, 45
"virtuous," 209
of war, 242
as willed submission, 31
love–anguish, xiii, 3, 9, 36, 92, 127, 225
bondage in, 92
thinly masking central bliss, 9, 23
tragic–heroic, 9
view that Montemayor's emphasis on it is retrograde, 230–31
love by destiny, xiii, 2, 3, 4, 27, 28, 41 n.17. *See also* fateful love; will, subjugated by love; love, attitude of surrender to
love–idealism, xviii, 54, 87
misguided, 87

love lyric, 11, 21, 23. *See also* cancionero love lyric; elegiac love lyric; Petrarchism
religious language in, 23
love lyricism
early modern, 21 n.18
emphasis on individual willing, 21 n.18
emphasis on subjectivity, 21 n.18
secular, religious adaptations of, 82
love–melancholy
accompanied by central feelings of happiness in *Diana* [Montemayor], 234
devoid of masochism in *Diana* [Montemayor], 244
and *Diana* [Montemayor], 243–44
in *Diana* [Montemayor], as defiant triumph over tyrannical contempt for sentimental culture, 246
fashion for as force of a new freedom, 246
as outward designation of central bliss *Diana* [Montemayor], 243
love of the remote, 45
love of the sexes
as courageous striving, 38
and enthusiasm for human beauty in *Diana* [Montemayor], 229 n.17
exoneration of, in *Diana* [Montemayor], 228 n.17
and marriage, 250
not primarily sensual, 24

only analogous to Christian love,
    24
  secular affirmation of in *Diana*
    [Montemayor], 224 n.11
love passion
  immutable, in *Diana* [Montemayor], 241
  as independent of ethical quality
    of love's origin, 227
  masochistic fulfillment of, 80
  as metaphor, 10
lover
  actual presence of, 171
  as martyr. *See* Martyrdom of lover
  prospective, aspired to by lover in
    Garcilaso's poetry and in "En
    la Ascensión" [Fray Luis de
    Léon], 171
  self-conscious image of, 14
  as tragic hero, 10
lovesickness, 227
  detachment of lover's will to love
    from incapacitation effects of,
    in *Diana* [Montemayor], 234
LUCRETIA, 268
Luscitano. *See* Montemayor, J. de
Lutheranism, 207 n.19
  and Nicodemism, 226
Lutherans, 207 n.19
lyric, Renaissance
  contribution to creation of individuality, 144
lyrical, the
  as a quality in literature, 145

MACBETH, 280

madness
  of the brave, 139
  of Don Quijote, 256, 265 n.16
  of Don Quijote as metaphor for
    error of formalistic intellectualism, 272
MAESE PEDRO, 93, 266
"man" (humankind), motif, of, 118
  the teleological entity, 118
mannerism, 65, 116, 141 n.22, 142,
    206 n.18, 207, 216–17
  of Arcadian wilderness in *Diana*
    [Montemayor], 236
  and compatibility of heroic and satiric dimensions, 151–52
  in *Diana* [Montemayor], 226
  and emergence of individuality,
    140
  and motifs, 256
  and play on readers' expectations
    in *Diana* [Montemayor], 228
    n.17
  and Romanticism, 142 n.24
  of Sonnet 22 [Garcilaso], 116
Marianism, 41 n.17
martial prowess
  a curse, in *Diana*'s Felismena
    [Montemayor], 240
martyrdom
  of lover, 8, 10, 10 n.9
  to love passion, as mark of an
    elite, 248
masochism
  and *Diana* [Montemayor], 244–45
  of negative asceticism compared to
    sadism, 243

as sadism towards the self, *vs.* true sadism, in Freudian doctrine, 244
masochist, 77–78
    as masochistic, 77 n.38
    as victim, 77 n.38
masochistic character formation, xiv, 63
    aggressive meaning of, 66
    and avoidance of threat of feeling worthless, 86
    basic phenomenon of, in Garcilaso's poetry, 89
    and biographical fallacy, xiv
    broader implications of, 64
    complexity of, 66
    L. Eidelberg on, 65
    and fantasy of self-destruction and incorporation, 70
    feminine, 71, 72
    feminine, and ecstatic self-degradation, 80
    Freud on, 65
    incompatible with self-sacrifice, 84
    interpreted metaphorically, xiv, 90
    to justify feelings of neglect, 73
    and literature, 92
    as means of restoring wounded narcissism, 69
    as metaphor, 6, 75
    metaphorical elaboration of, 94
    morbid, of persona, as metaphor for courageous passion, 79
    as mortification of self, 80
    and narcissistic mortification to alleviate phobic apprehension of punishment, 69–70
    as normal, 80, 85
    and pseudo-masochism, 85
    seen clinically, and biographical fallacy, 64
    and self-hatred, as displaced sadistic ambivalence, 70
    and self-loathing, 75
    submissive meaning of, 66
    and suffering, as condition for pleasure, 65
masochistic fantasy
    and allegorical interpretation, 64
    and poetry's depiction of cruel lady, 66
matter
    sense-knowledge recognizes only, 263
meaning
    liberation of, 267
meaning, literary, 46
    hypothetical nature of, 46
medieval fatalism, 3, 25, 28, 33, 38
    camouflaged as free-will, according to R. Lapesa, 39
    and Original Sin, 40
medieval traditionalism, xiii, xiv, xv, xxiii
melancholia, 34, 59
melancholy, 34 n.8, 141 n.23, 219, 224 n.11
    as "chastity," 225
    as depreciation of human sexuality, 225
    in *Diana* [Montemayor], 227
    pathos of, in early modern period, 142 n.25

Subject Index

and pre-Romantic mannerism, 142 n.24
tearful, of disillusioned youth in *Menina e Moça*, 279
tone of in Ribeiro's writing, 197
tortured, in *Menina e Moça*, 197
true, *vs.* sign of central bliss, 243
unrequited fertility assumes form of, 198
memory, 259, 261
MENINA, 196, 198, 208, 212, 213, 215, 216
Menina e Moça, xvii, 72, 72 n.31, 195–219, 279
abrupt end of indicated by prologue, 196–97, 216, 217
Arthurian motif in, 214
E. Asensio on, 195 n.1, 225
blending of genres and motifs, 197, 200, 216
censored by Portuguese Inquisition, 217–18
censorship of, xvii
central theme, 198
classification of form of, 196, 200
compared to fiction by Turgenyev and Chekhov, 196
compared to novels by Diego de San Pedro and Montemayor, 216
concept of love in, 208, 210
and culture of sentiment, xviii
dominant note of, 279
elliptical plot of, 196, 216
hostility of world to social sentiment, 198, 212
inward strife of characters in, 197
H. Maçedo on, 195 n.1
mannerism of, xviii
masterpiece by Ribeiro, 195
melancholy tone, 197, 198
mysteries of, 195
opposition of fertility and sterility as central theme, 198, 212, 314
original title of, 196
Orphic–agricultural religion in, 198
pastoral motifs, 207
portrays nature as a chaotic sphere, 197–98
and Reform struggle, xviii
revolutionary spirit of, 218
significance of, xvii–xviii
tension between setting and characters, 197, 216
similar to Sannazaro's *Arcadia*, 197
similar to Garcilaso's eclogues, 197
textual excerpts from, 199, 215–16, 219
times and significance of, xvii
tone of tortured melancholy, 197
tragic atmosphere of, 197
water–stone symbolism in, 215
work as an extended metaphor, 195 n.1
Metamorphoses/Golden Ass [Apuleius], 212
metaphor, xii–xiii, xiv, xvi, 60, 124, 254 n.4

barber's basin as helmet, 253, 259–60
boulder as sterility, 212
clichéd, 59
communicative and social functions of, xxv
"deviant" character of, 259–60
in *Don Quijote*, xix, 253
enchantment for epistemological realism, xix
experientialist view of, xxv
first stanza of *Canción* 1 [Garcilaso] as, 74
flute as phallic symbol, 213–14
horse as lust or as freedom, 213
implications of, xxv
as insight symbol, xxv
and interpretive community, xxv
love as a cruel tyrant, 210
Menina e Moça [Ribeiro] as extended, 195 n.1
nightingale as freedom, 212
poem as, xvi
power of, to create a reality, xxiv
power of, to shape values, xxiv
readers changed by, xxv
rhetorical subtlety of, 88
robed monk as wolf in sheep's clothing, 204
rock swept by water as forsaken lover, 215
royal court as sea of divisions, 201, 203, 204
as semantic impertinence, 268
and symbol, xii–xiii
value of according to recent theories, 268–69, 274
water as fertility, 212
water–stone, 215
windmills as giants, 253
wolves as diabolical messengers, 213
metaphorical death, in *Diana* [Montemayor], 225
metaphorical interpretation of literature, xxii
metaphorical inversion, ironic, 79, 85
metaphysic
Platonist, 259
metaphysical problems
no proof for solutions to, xx
Mexía, Hernán, xiv, 3, 280
on freedom and guilt, 44, 45
inspired nature of passion, 35
love as unrelieved suffering in poetry, 3
love determined by free will, 32, 38, 50
passion driven by nobility of character, 41–43
passion resulting from despotic power, 30–31
poem in *Cancionero general*, 30–31, 32–33, 35, 38, 41–42, 44–45, 50, 279
Middle Ages, 210, 214, 277
mid-point
of futility and anguish, 138
of integrated personality, 138
mind
Aristotelian view of, 259
Platonist view of, 259

as reality, 263
MINERVA, 201–2
"modern man"
   Montemayor's shepherd as image of, from Renaissance point of view, 248
modernism, 217
   expresses protest esoterically as oblivion of innocence, 282
modernity, 51, 94
modesty, xv, 73, 95, 114. *See also* Shame
   appeal of, in Sonnet 22 [Garcilaso], 115
   conventional reflex of, 113
   defensive, 101
   excessive, 117
   feminine, 114
   precipitous, 101
   as a quality of beauty, 115
   requirement of a response of, 112
   severe, harsh, 101
   as spur to love, 95
   and tension between love and sex drive, 115
"*Monachatus non est pietas*," 244
MONTANO, 228
Montemayor, Jorge de, xviii, 3, 40 n.17, 200–6, 220, 221
   adapts Psalm 137 to pastoral literature, 200
   as Catholic reformist, 225
   Cancionero espiritual, 224 n.11
   Diana, xviii, 3, 29, 40, 72, 72 n.31, 197, 200, 214, 216, 220–51, 220 n.1. *See also Diana*
   as humanist, 225
   letter to Diego Ramírez Pagán, 201–2, 203–4
   letter to Jorge Meneses, 201, 202–3, 205–6
   preference for pastoral life, 203
   religious poetry, 200 n.9, 217 n.31, 224 n.11, 225, 238, 240
   religious poetry and *Diana*, elements in common, 243
   religious writings, 224 n.11
   resident at the Spanish court, 200–1
   Segundo cancionero espiritual, 171–72, 224 n.11
Montemor, George/Jorge de. *See* Montemayor, Jorge de
moral apathy and *Lazarillo de Tormes*, 183, 185
moral culture, the new, individual. *See* individual moral culture, the new
moral disfranchisement
   in *Lazarillo de Tormes*, xvii
   of Lazarillo de Tormes, 190–91, 191 n.20
   vs. moral death, 190
moral law
   mechanical conformity to, incompatible with freedom, 44
morale of group
   cause for loss of, 173
morality
   emergence of individual *vs.* collective in Renaissance, 277
morbid anxiety, 59, 132, 133, 141, 142

and ego's compulsive need to cathect with bad object, 132
Garcilaso's interest in, 141
and power of bad object, 132
mortification of self
moral value of, 80
mother figure
clinging, 148
identification with, xvi
in C. J. Jung's theories, 149
lost, in *Lazarillo de Tormes*, 188
nourishing, 188
as object of the regressive libido, 137
regression to, 136
as regressive tendency, xvi
as subject's regressive tendency, 137
as symbol, 188
threatening, 148
motifs
barber's basin as helmet, 253, 259–60
and Cervantes' writing, 272
enchantment, 253–54, 259, 269, 273
and manneristic literature, 256
movement
alternatives of progressive and regressive, in Sonnet 38 [Garcilaso], 133–35
mystic
desires of, 88
mystical union
as surrender, 82
mysticism

Christian, optmistic nature of, 224 n.11
as megalomania or as morally aspiring self-fulfillment, 89
myth
an element of science, 273, 273 n.24, 273 n.25
heroic and romantic character of, 150
poetic, 266
poetic, *vs.* historico–empirical reality, 253
and science, 273, 273 n.25
mythopoeic rendition of reality, 259

NARBINEL. *See* BIMARDER
narcissism
injured, 71
reparation of injured, 72
narcissistic mortification, 69–70
Natural Born Killers, 185
nature
beauty of evoked by Ribeiro, 197
as divinely sanctioned order, 197
physical order of, 112
necessity
fateful, external, *vs.* internal, felt, and voluntary, 39
as incompatible with moral value, 134
Neoplatonism, 82, 117, 211, 213, 241–42, 245, 256, 262, 270, 257 n.7
and *Diana* [Montemayor], 223
in *Don Quijote*, 259, 263
dualistic, 242

idealistic ethos of, 242
New Critics, 126
Nicodemism, 225–26, 226 n.14
   in *Diana* [Montemayor], 225, 249, 278
   generalized as strategy in Renaissance literature, 278
   as presursor of realism, 229 n.17
   strategic character of, 226 n.14
Nicomachean Ethics [Aristotle], 187–88, 188 n.16
NISE, 144, 145, 148, 149
   great power exercised by, 153
   significance of the name, 145–46 n.27
nobility of character
   in *Lazarillo de Tormes*, 189
nobility, moral
   and willing sacrifice of personal well-being, 234
   as vital value, 235
"Noche serena" [Fray Luis de León], 72, 164
Nombres de Cristo [Fray Luis de León], 166
nominalism, 269–71
   contributions to forging orthodox doctrine of merit, 271
   in influence in Renaissance Spain, 271, 271 n.21
   and subjectivism, 76 n.37, 270, 270 n.19, 271
   vs. conceptualism, 270
non-culpable ignorance, Aristotle's theory of, 36

object(s)
   accepting, 131–33
   bad, 132
   defined, 128–29
   differentiated, 134
   exciting, frustrating. *See* exciting, frustrating object
   good. *See* good object(s)
   incorporated, 147
   loss of, and ego-loss, 130
   needed, 148, 149
   original, 149
   rejecting, 131–33
   split, internal, 135
object relationship(s)
   good, and the need to be treated as a person, 128
   satisfactory, importance of establishing early in life, 188
object values, 111
obscurity
   as element of style in Renaissance, 207
   masked as candor in courtly love, 207
obsession
   anguished, 140
obsessional anxiety. *See* anxiety, obsessional
obsessional conflict, 133
Occamism, 257 n.7
ODYSSEUS, 137
Oliver Twist, 187
ontological determination
   represented by lady, in Sonnet 22 [Garcilaso], 113, 114, 115

represented by persona, in Sonnet 22 [Garcilaso], 113, 114
vs. axiological determination, 113
Opico, 205
optimism, Christian
    as incompatible with eudaemonism, 238
ordeal
    of final moral decisions, 136
Original Sin, xviii, 18, 23, 40, 117, 250
    and *Diana* [Montemayor], 225, 243, 245
    doctrine of, related to R. Lapesa's concept of love as fate in Garcilaso and *cancionero* lyric, 40, 40 n.15
    dogma of, 278
ORLANDO, 209
ORPHEUS, 137, 240
Orphic
    legend, 213
    religion, 198
oscillation
    as aesthetic value in Renaissance, 140
Orthodoxy
    external, of *Diana* [Montemayor], 226 n.14
ought, 45
    and morality's double face, 143
ought of personality, 45, 143
Ought-to-Be, 42, 43, 47, 139
Ought-to-Do, 42

PABLOS THE "BUSCÓN," 183–84
pagan skepticism, xxiii

pagan traditions in Renaissance, 21
pain. *See* suffering; passion; passionate love of the sexes
    as comparable to death and to birth, 173
    of death from exposure, as metaphor for love–anguish, 74
    as determined by unredeemed state of subject, 248
    enhances value of purity, 281
    figured as cruel lady, 74
    incongruous degree of, in Sonnet 2 [Fray Luis de León], 147
    of love, suffered happily in *Diana* [Montemayor], 234
    noble, as an accompaniment of life's progress, 247
    self-inflicted, 67–68
    sign of distinction, 281
passion, 7, 8, 37
    the changing meaning of the word, 12–13, 23–24
    of Christ, as effecting remission of all human sins, 281–82
    depth of, 229
    exquisitely ambiguous conception of in *Diana* [Montemayor], 231–33
    masochism as metaphor for, 79
    restrained by reason, 7
    and strong modesty, 115
    uncontrollable, 229
passionate love of the sexes, xviii, 10, 3
    celebration of, beneath surface of, in *Diana* [Montemayor], 225

as consistent with naive innocence, 225
masochism as metaphor for, 79
naive innocence of, xviii
a noble value, 10
opposed to reason, 31
as Original Sin, 40
passionate surrender
  as rhetorical mask of individual freedom, 23
passionate willing
  in Garcilaso, 124
passions
  negation of, *vs.* discipline of, 243
pastoral, 200–7
  as fashion at court, 222, 223
  fashion for in Renaissance, 200
  and fertility, 205
pastoral literature, 195, 197, 198, 200, 220–21
  A. Hauser on, 211
  of Iberian Renaissance, 220
  prototypes for, 200
  Spanish, 220
  trends in, 197, 200
  typical endings of, 216–17
  vehicle for romantic sentiment, 211
pastoral spirituality, 221, 221 n.2
pathetic satire, 87
pathos, 93
perception, theory of
  Neoplatonist, 262
PERSEPHONE, 213, 240
person
  actual, 113
  ideal, 113
  spiritual, as unity of acts, 110
persona (in Jungian psychology)
  male, 136
  a man's one-sided identification with, 138
  vs. feelings, 138
persona (speaker)
  as fictional character subject to metaphorical interpretation, 32
  identified with author, 32
  as image of his own libidinal ego, 91
personal heresy, 32 n.4. *See also* intentional fallacy
personality (individual human identity), xvi, 114, 143, 232, 249. *See also* individuality
  actual, empirical, 114
  claims of as a value, xvi
  demands of as non-contingent ideals, 249
  development of, in Jung's view, 135–36
  ethos of, 47
  and greatness valued in Renaissance, 153
  its legitimate claim to self-fulfillment, 22
  not absolute determinant of actual person, 47
perspectivism, 189, 254 n.4. *See also* truth, relativistic conception of
pessimism, 224 n.11, 228, 239

anthropological, guise of in Renaissance literature, 281
outward, 279
Petrarchism, 2, 10, 27, 41 n.17, 54, 222, 223, 230, 249. *See also* cancionero love lyric; elegiac love lyric; love lyric
phantasmata (phantasms/sense impressions). *See also* sense impressions
  as delusions, 263
  as meaningless appearances, 265
  as organized illusion analogous to fiction, 272
Phariseeism, 199
phenomonological ethics of values, 128
phenomenology, xxi
Philosophia Christi [Erasmus]
  pacificist viewpoint of adopted by Ribeiro, 199
philosophical approach to literature
  justification for, 128
phobic anxiety. *See* anxiety, phobic
phobic conflict, 133
  in Sonnet 2 [Fray Luis de León], 145
picaresque novel, 175
  as corrosive and negative, 178
  as ethically equivocal, 185
  as immoral and pessimistic, 178
  and ironic inversion of ideality, 182, 184–85
  main objection to, 183
  and "negative idealism," 178
  source of its disorienting effect, 184

pícaro [rogue/knave], 175–76, 183–84
piety, reform, 271
Platonism, xix, 257–59, 257 n.7, 258, 261, 265, 267
poet
  as Actaeon archetype, 72
  as benign and loving, 90
  jeopardy of, as analogue of persona's frustration, 75
  as submissive subject of powerful lady–sovereign, 69–71
poetic imagery. *See* imagery, poetic
poetry
  the subject of, 264 n.16
popular lyric, xiii, 3, 17
power
  of bad object, as function of persona's need, 132
  despotic, of lady, 31
  of physical beauty, 98
  overwhelming, of lady's opinion of persona, in Sonnet 38 [Garcilaso], 141
powerlessness, feelings of, 126
pride, moral
  in passion, 42, 43
prison/bondage imagery
  ambiguous, 25
  in lyric complexly ambiguous, 25
  and phobic anxiety, 147
prison/bonds of love/loving, motif of, xiii, 15, 16, 18. *See also* imagery, prison
progressive urge, of persona, in Sonnet 2 [Fray Luis de León], 148
projection, 107, 115

projective identification
    to disown and forgive the bad in oneself, 71
    in Sonnet 2 [Garcilaso], 90
Protestantism, 117, 217
prudishness, 106
Psalm 137 ("Super flumina Babylonis")
    poetic adaptations of, 71, 200
    as prototype for Renaissance pastoral literature, 200
PSYCHE, 212
psychic shame, 112, 112 n.12
psychoanalysis, xxi–xxii. *See also* psychodynamic theory
    aim of, as opposed to tragic art, 76
    and cognitive reliability, 76 n.37
    limitations and value of, when applied to idealistic lyric, 76–85
    Renaissance precursors of, 141
    and truth, 76 n.37
    value of, to interpret lyric, 76–77, 76 n.37, 77–78 n.38
psychoanalytic approach to literature, 89
psychodynamics
    and amatory lyric, 126
psychology, xxi
psychopathology, 129
purity, xi–xi
    commemorated, xii
    as counterbalance to secularism, 281
    "death" of, xi
    of mind/heart, power of, 279
    reborn, xii

QUIJANO, ALONSO. *See* ALONSO QUIJANO

rationalism, xxiii, xxiv
    and artistic style, xxiv
    and capitalism, xxiv
    early modern, xxiii
    Heideggerian concept of, 76 n.37
    Neoplatonist speculative, 256
    and social system, xxiv
reader response
    arena of, 266
real necessity/ontoloical necessity, 43, 44
    comparable to "fate," 43
realism, 185, 216, 221
    epistemological, 254 n.4, 266, 275
    and naturalism, 269
reality
    and Aristotelianism, 258–59
    Don Quijote's conception of, as that which has moral significance, 267
    empirical. *See* empirical reality
    and modern critics, 268
    and Platonism, 258–59
    of objects, as pre-given and finite, 275
    of objects as subject to heightening, 275
    and understanding of the world, 252
    world subjected to sinister forces, 253
reason, 7, 8
    dominated by passion, 7

rebirth
    of finite reality as poetic imagery, 267
    into adulthood, 92
    ironic social, in *Lazarillo de Tormes*, 190
reckless courage
    tone of, 35
recogidos, 224 n.11
Reformation, 271
reformism
    Catholic, doctrines of as threat to Church control, 281
    spirit of, 117
reformists
    persecution of, 206 n.19
reform piety, 271
regression, 91, 128, 133, 143
    abandonment of, 142
    to dominating mother, 136
    in face of resistance, 136
    and fantasy of dreamer, 134
    and feelings of dependence, 133
    as retreat from quest, 136
    in Sonnet 2 [Fray Luis de León], 148
relativism, 263
religio amoris, 45, 21 n.18, 83 n.49, 94
    secular equivalent of religion of grace, 21 n.18
    as secular inversion of traditional religiosity, 45
    and values of the individual, 45
religion
    moral command of, incompatible with freedom, 45
    vision of Orphic–agricultural, according to Ribeiro, 198
Renaissance, xx, xxi, xxii–xxiv, 28, 51, 65, 77, 78–79 n.40, 85–86 n.52, 143, 200, 207. *See also* early modern period
    aesthetic values in, 77
    alienation in, 65
    as covertly innovative, 278
    crisis of, 90
    culture of, 249
    and emergence of individual morality, 277
    and emphasis on human will, 51
    "flavor" of literary works, 279
    M. Gorky on, 92
    issue of distinguishing, from Middle Ages, 85–86 n.52
    meaning of term, xxiv
    modern features of, 277
    as period of crisis, 65
    perspective, 25
    and rationalism, xxiv
    romantic concept of, 28
    sentimental love in, 207
    and situation of humanist–intellectual poets, 89–93
    and social dynamism, xxiv
    temperament of, *vs.* rigorously ascetic traditionalism, 245–46
repression, cultural, 203 n.14
rescue. *See also* salvation
    from anxieties of reality, as fulfillment, 83 n.48
    of personality, from collision with reality, 85

Subject Index

rescue fantasies, xv, 71, 80
    and death, 74
    and flattery, 74
    and poetic imagery, 71
    and reparation of injured narcissism, 71
    and theme of longing for deliverance, 71
resurrection of the flesh
    Christian doctrine of, complemented by erotic life-affirmation in *Diana* [Montemayor], 245
revenge
    sadomasochistic, 243
rhetoric
    as a dimension of psychodynamics, 73
    of praise, 7
    of seduction, problem of, 74
rhetorical intent, 17, 45
    of eliciting pity, 17
rhetorical manipulation by protagonist–narrator of *Lazarillo de Tormes*, 176
Ribeiro, Bernardim, xviii, 195, 196, 197, 200, 200 n.10, 206, 208–9, 213
    cultivation of the eclogue, 195, 200, 215
    Eclogue I, 215
    Eclogue IV, 208–9
    introduces pastoral in Portugal, 195
    Menina e Moça, 72, 195–219, 279
    writers of eclogues, 195

riddle, in poetry, 60
road, motif of, 121–22, 123, 133, 134, 143
    confining narrowness of, 133
    narrow, 133
    symbol for individuation and self-conquest, 135
    symbol for infantile dependence, 135
role reversal, male–female, 59, 91
    in Sonnet 2 [Garcilaso], 91
roman courtois, 209
romance
    chivalric, 255, 263, 272, 274
    pastoral, 256
romance epic, 209
romances of chivalry, 221, 223, 254, 255, 263, 272
romantic hero, 217
romantic love
    positive strivings of, as vehicle for postulating new ethos in Renaissance, 246
    term defined, 246
    viewed as presupposing asceticism, 24
romantic virtues
    opposed by heroic in *Menina e Moça*, 198
romanticism, xix, 217
    antecedents of, in Spanish Renaissance, 142 n.24
    categorical, of Don Quijote, 271
    of Cervantes, 271
    Cervantine, xix
    chivalric, 274

courtly, feminine character of revived, 239
Renaisssance, precursors of, 142, 142 n.24
and Ribeiro, 197
sacrifice
love as, 49, 74
of personal well-being, as condition of moral value-being, 235
of self, as incompatible with self-gratification, 84
of self, not a means to self-gratification, 84
sadism
artistic depictions of, in sixteenth century, 63
of beloved captor, 74
directed at self, 73
malevolent, of lady, as metaphor for irresistible femininity, 79–80
and masochism, in *Canción* 1 [Garcilaso], 64
as related to the historical epoch of an author, 64
true, *vs.* masochistic (sadism towards the self), 244
of war, compared to masochism of negative asceticism, 243
sadomasochism
eroticized, 71
metaphorical significance of, 66
salvation. *See also* rescue
analogous to attainment of the loved object, 250

as fulfillment of libido, 83
SANCHO PANZA, 54, 93, 251, 253, 255, 260–61, 268, 271, 275
SANSÓN CARRASCO, 252, 253
satire, xv
implied, in *Lazarillo de Tormes*, 176
in *Lazarillo de Tormes*, 177
pathetic, xv
scholasticism, 256
and humanism in Renaissance, 257 n.7
self-degradation
ecstatic abandonment to, 68
self-determination through values, 113
self-humiliation
vs. punishment for self-aggrandizement, 68
self-sabotage
persona's, as pretender to lady's favor, 141
SELVAGIA, 228–29, 230, 241
sense data, 258
restrictions of, 264 n.16
sense impressions, xix, 263. *See also* *phantasmata*
as basis for knowedge, 275
ethical opposition to, 257–58
sense knowledge
vs. intellectual knowledge, 263
sense perception, 257 n.7, 265 n.16
as experience of unintelligible appearance, 267
senses
fallibility of, 254 n.4
sensibility
ideals of, 214

Subject Index 365

    man of, 219
sensual desire (sexual appetite)
    Aristotle on, 231
    equated with sexual love, 231
    love as conditioned by, 233
    mitigation of, 230
    as natural appetite free from moral reproach, 231
sensual nature
    as consistent with spiritual pursuits in *Diana* [Montemayor], 232
sensuality, xiii, xv, 8, 11, 12. *See also* eroticism
    emphasized through defensive modesty, xv
    unabashed, metaphorically compatible with central vitality in *Diana* [Montemayor], 236
sensuousness
    vs. voluptuousness in *Diana* [Montemayor], 229
sentimental love
    literature of, 207
sentimental romance, 196
separation, from an incorporated object, 147
severe morality
    fallacy of, 113
sexual desire
    Aristotle on, 231
    Montemayor's view of, 231
sexual drive
    as adverse fate, 40
    generic character of, 115
sexual innocence
    in *Diana* [Montemayor], 228 n.17

sexual instinct
    crude, 112
    Freud on, and *Diana* [Montemayor], 244, 245
sexual love. *See also* erotic passion
    equivocal representation of in *Diana* [Montemayor], 232
    Montemayor's modern conception of, 231
    not identical with aggressive sexual instinct, in Freudian doctrine, 244
    as self-identification with another, 66
    as subject of new literature exalting claims of personality, 249
shame, 112, 112 n.12, 114. *See also* modesty
    bodily *vs.* psychic, 112, 112 n.12
SIRENO, 150, 228–29, 230, 240, 241
skepticism, 217
smallness, feelings of
    release defeatist tendencies, 174
solidarity
    absent in the world of *Lazarillo de Tormes*, 194
    lacking in the mass, 194
Sonnet 22 [Garcilaso]
    allegorical meaning of, 113, 117, 118
    beauty, personified as the lady, 104
    compared to Sonnet 23, 104
    consistent with tradition of courtly love literature, 101
    A. Cruz on, 105 n.7

current general interpretation of, 96–97
defensive modesty as obstacle to love, 95, 101
details of language, 98–103, 116 n.18
earlier interpretations of, 96–98, 99, 100–1, 102, 112, 116
El Brocense on, 97 n.1, 99, 108
elevated character of, 115
fallacy of severe morality, 113
general subject of, 96–97, 109–10, 114, 117, 118
importance of the lady's hand, 98, 107–8, 110, 111
influenced by Socrates, 99
interpretation by A. de Colombí-Monguió, 103, 105
interpretation by A. Gargano, 96–98, 103, 104–5, 106–7, 108, 110, 111
interpretation by D. Heiple, 96–98, 100–1, 103, 112
interpretation by E. Rivers, 96–98, 100–1, 102, 103, 106–7, 112
interpretation by A. M. Snell, 97, 98, 99, 100, 103, 107
lady shields herself with her hand, 97, 102–3, 104, 106, 107
lady to provide evidence of her sensitive humanity, 100
lady's eyes not mentioned, 110
lady's modesty as central issue of, 104, 114
lady's preoccupation with the sensual, 107
lady's presumption of sensuousness, 113
C. S. Lewis on quality of danger, 101–2
love that becomes grief, 95
matching of lady's actual with her ideal essence, 112
matching of lady's outer and inner beauty, 98–100, 113
opposition between spirituality and sexual instinct, 112
persona recognizes lady's beauty, 98–99
persona wonders about lady's spiritual beauty, 99–100
and persona's despair, 95, 101
and persona's disillusionment, 101
persona's speech, 111
and Petrarch's lyrics, 96, 103, 105, 111
possible influence on Cervantes, 117
presents persona's point of view, 109, 111, 114
previous reading by Herrera, 97 n.1, 107–8
previous readings by Tamayo, 97 n.1, 108
and Renaissance classicism, 100
M. Scheler on sexual modesty, 101, 114–15
text and translation of, 96
theme of the elusive lady, 118
as token of the capacity to love, 114
and tradition of rhetoric of praise, 114

Subject Index

tribute to the power of beauty, 114–15
SOPHIA, 237
spiritual person, 112
spiritual pursuits
    as consistent with sensual nature in *Diana* [Montemayor], 232
spirituality
    Christian, and physical self-abnegation, 80
spirituality, secular, 83, 94
    heterodoxy of, 83
stagnation and change, crossroads between, 143
sterility
    of present age, and *Menina e Moça*, 219
stoicism, 238, 239
strife and injustice of world
    as evidence of mankind's regressive avoidance of rebirth, 174
structuralism, xix,
    as ideology comparable to nominalism, 270, 270 n.19
    reaffirms atemporality in structures of mind, 270, n.19
    as similar to nominalism, according to U. Eco, 270 n.19
subjection to love
    as metaphor, 50
subjection to tyranny
    in early modern society, obliquely condemned by elegiac love literature, 246
subjectivism
    emotionalistic, in *Diana* [Montemayor], 226
    unbounded, of Montemayor's characters in *Diana* [Montemayor], 249
subjectivity, individual
    as fictional virtual reality, 127
    morbid, 142
    obsessed and phobic, examined in Garcilaso's poetry, 141
submission
    masochistic, 59
    and rescue of personality, from colliding with reality, 85
submission of persona to tyrannical lady, 67–93
    and A. Adler, 85
    and E. Bergler, 69
    and I. Bernstein, 70
    and I. Bieber, 69
    and A. Blumstein, 70
    and C. Brenner, 67
    and A. Cooper, 70
    and L. Eidelberg, 70
    and O. Fenichel, 68, 69
    and S. Ferenczi, 67
    and N. Fischer, 68
    and S. Freud, 68
    and K. Horney, 68
    and O. Kernberg, 68
    and R. Krafft-Ebing, 68
    and C. S. Lewis, 71
    and W. Reich, 63, 68
    and T. Reik, 69
    and socio–historical context, 90
    in Sonnet 2 [Garcilaso], 90–93
    and L. Stone, 68

as sublimation of temporal desire, in both romantic love and Christianity, 82, 83, 83 n.48, 83 n.49
suffering, xiv, 34, 46, 73, 84, 127. *See also* melancholy; anguish
   as cloak for Renaissance pagan joy, xiv, xviii
   of disciples in "En la Ascensión" [Fray Luis de Léon], 157–59, 161, 162, 163–4
   for a higher value, in *Diana* [Montemayor], *vs.* powerlessness, 247
   innocent, 73
   libidinization of, 70–71
   in love, cult of, 235
   in love, grateful surrender to, 248
   in love, as involuntary *vs.* voluntary, 34
   in love, Renaissance vogue for, 233
   in love, unrelieved, 219
   necessary, *vs.* masochism, 85
   in religious lyric, 88
   as a value, 84
   voluptuous intensity of, 73
   willingness to accept, 44, 45
Sufism, 195 n.1
Súmulas [G. Cardillo de Villapando], 264–65 n.16
super-ego, 150
   appeal of, as challenged by traumatic anxiety in wartime, 173
   authority of, and morale of a group as per Freud, 173
   Christ as, shaken by his absence, 173–74
   collapsing authority of, and deterioration of sense of duty, 174
   equivalent of in R. Fairbairn, *vs.* C. G. Jung, 150
"Super flumina Babylonis." *See* Psalm 137
SYLVANO, 228–29, 230, 234, 241
symbol
   as metaphor, xii–xiii
symbolic images
   value of for making truth-claims, 269
symbolism
   derivation of, 272–73, 272–72 n.23
   poetic, 272–73, 272–72 n.23
   power of to remake meaning, 269

Temple of Diana, 227
temporal being, 81
temporal order
   conformity to, in traditionalistic curialism, 241
temporal process, the
   coexistence of will with, 112
   determination by, 112–13
TERESA PANZA, 93
text
   coherence of, as ultimate basis of interpretation, 127
theocracy, 203
theory of perception. *See* perception, theory of
THESEUS, 137

Thomism, 265 n.16, 270
thought and feeling
    coordination of, 135–38, 138 n.17
THYL EULENSPIEGEL, 183
Titans, 213
tragedy, xiii, xv, 22, 113 n.14, 117, 198 n.7
    as always ready to submit to death and renewal, 280
    edifying effects of, 280
    hero's confined sphere of choice in, 22
    immanent, of sexual love, 113 n.14, 117
    pure and open seriousness of, 280
    M. Scheler's theory of, xiii
    as synthesis of purity and fulness of life, 280
    triumphant character of, 280
tragic art, 9, 34, 51, 93, 224 n.11
    contribution to individuation, 9
    as quasi-religious spiritual exercise, 93
    and self-determined hero, 78
tragic hero/heroine
    actions exhonerated, 22
    "falls into guilt," 22
    free will of, 79
    moral stature of, rooted in failure to actualize, 281
    not determined from without, 78–80
    not a victim of circumstances, 78
    retains purity, 22
    revival in Renaissance, 153
tragic–heroic willing, sentiment of, 13.
    See also tragic heroism
    absent in popular lyric, 13
    individualism of, 13
    and martial values, 13
    Renaissance and courtly character of, 13
tragic heroism, 21. *See also* tragic–heroic willing, sentiment of
tragic suffering, 21 n.18
    N. Frye on, 21 n.18
    A. Hauser on, 21 n.18
    not an effect of moral guilt, 21 n.18
    M. Scheler on, 21 n.18
    G. Steiner on, 21 n.18
transubstantiation, 245
transvaluation of values. *See* values, transvaluation of in Renaissance
troubled sea, metaphor of, 173
truth
    and Don Quijote, 260–61
    factual, 264 n.16
    historical, 264 n.16
    as mere linguistic formulation, 271
    objectively descriptive, *vs.* linguistic manifestation of cognitive processes, 269
    relativistic conception of, 254 n.4. *See also* Perspectivism
Two Gentlemen of Verona, 222

unconscious, feminine
    of persona, 135
unequal relationship, 146
unfulfillment in love
    fate of, as sign of distinction, 233

sadness of, in *Diana* [Montemayor], 233

value(s), xiv, xxi, xxii. *See also* value theory; ethics of values
  as mere ideal forms without actual power, 47
  attainment of, *vs.* of commitment to their attainment, 281
  autonomy of, xxi
  effectiveness of, dependent upon human will, 47
  intended, *vs.* of intention
  of the individual, xiv
  of the individual as compatible with self-sacrifice, 49, 74
  of the individual as higher than collective values, 49
  transvaluation of in Renaissance, 278
value feelings, 116 n.18
value theory, xiv
VENUS, 117
verbal icon
  poem as, 46
villancico, 15, 17, 18, 23
  pathos alonside lightness of tone in, 23
virtue (moral value)
  of character is a consequence of fine upbringing, 188 n.16
  incompatible with determinism, 139
  represented by high peak, 134
vital feeling
  autonomy of, 237 n.30

"Vivo sin vivir en mí" [Santa Teresa de Jesús], 81–82
volition, 42, 44

wandering, as symbol, 188
war
  renunciation of, for love in *Menina e Moça*, 199
  sadomasochistic voluptuousness of, *vs. Diana* [Montemayor], 242
well-being
  and the noble, 234 n.23
  of tragic hero, not incompatible with his/her exemplary resistance to violence, 280
  as value, 234
weltschmertz, romantic
  anticipated by lovesick shepherds of *Diana* [Montemayor], 248
WERTHER, 236
will, xiv, 1, 48
  bad, 45
  good, 45
  increasingly seen in Renaissance as autonomous, 22 n.20
  as libidinal ego, 153
  of love, 43, 45
  love's, *vs.* forced, 218
  morbid tenacity as commitment of, 34
  as passion, xiv, 35
  subjugated by love, R. Lapesa's theory of, 2, 6, 29, 33, 34
  to suffer, 44, 84
  as the will of love, 35

will to live, 52
will to power
   vs. humanistic secularization of piety, 242
will to self-destruction, 35, 46
   as cloak for surrender to fate, according to R. Lapesa, 39
   as charged with intent, according to A. Pfänder, 48, 48 n.22
   decision of, as involving preference, 39
   dominated by love, according to R. Lapesa, 41 n.17
   in Mexía, 38
   rhetorical meaning of, 39
   in Sonnet 1, 37
   superiority over intellect as per nominalists, 270
willfulness
   unrestricted by dependence on the external, in *Diana* [Montemayor], 247–48
women
   eulogized in *Diana* [Montemayor], 239, 239 n.35
   renewed appreciation of and devotion to in Renaissance, 239
works, doctrine of salvation through
   implicitly denigrated in *Menina e Moça*, 217
world
   as projection of mind, 258
worthiness to be loved, 113 n.16

Young Girl. See Menina e Moça
YSMENIA, 228–29

ZEUS, 213